To Be Young and Gifted

edited by

Pnina S. Klein and Abraham J. Tannenbaum

ABLEX PUBLISHING CORPORATION
NORWOOD, NEW JERSEY

Cover photo by Yuval Klein.
Cover design by Deb Hoeffner.

Printed in the United States of America.

Library of Congress Cataloging-in-Publication Data

To be young and gifted / edited by Pnina Klein and Abraham J. Tannenbaum.
    p. cm.
    Includes bibliographical references and indexes.
    ISBN 0-89391-839-3.—ISBN 0-89391-956-X (pbk.)
    1. Gifted children. I. Klein, Pnina S. II. Tannenbaum, Abraham J.
    BF723.G5T6 1992
    155.45'5—dc20   92-19814
                                                   CIP

Ablex Publishing Corporation
355 Chestnut Street
Norwood, New Jersey 07648

Contents

Preface

The title of this book is neutral in sentiment. It could have started with "Ah" (a grin), to denote pleasure , or "Oh" (a groan) to suggest displeasure, in being young and gifted. We omitted the value judgment simply because the age group targeted here usually doesn't feel one way or the other about it. Only later, beginning with the middle elementary through the high school years, do some precocious children start to wonder whether their giftedness is a blessing or a burden. When this happens, it is often due to parental and peer (and sometimes even teacher) pressure on the gifted to conform socially, academically, or artistically, thus forcing them to make a choice between the pursuit of excellence or of popularity. Children who face such a dilemma do so at a time of life when more and more others become significant to them, significant enough to make mediocrity a condition of worth. However, during the years between the onset of speech and the primary grades at school, there is hardly any awareness, much less self-consciousness, about being precocious, especially when caretakers are careful not to call attention to it.

True, there exist some popular caricatures of underage dandies who are prodded by parents to strut their talents publicly, as if they were some kinds of precious freaks. According to this scenario, these pampered and showcased little cartoon creatures are supposed to grow up haunted by their celebrity status at a tender age. But mercifully, such cases are rare, except perhaps among prodigies, who are themselves a rare breed. Most precocious children in their first half-decade of life want to perform as best they can, and their parents are just as eager to help them along. Aside from parent and young child, nobody else seems interested. Teachers and influential peers are not yet on the scene, and developmental psychologists appear to have other priorities. Therefore, little is known about these children, thus far.

Why, indeed, should a behavioral scientist devote any efforts to clarifying the nature of giftedness in children so young? Is there any advantage in getting to them before they are well into their school years? Can't we wait until they are older and more amenable to investigation? Or, to be even blunter, who needs a book on being young and gifted? The simplest answer is that we should know more about precocity in young children because it's there—something like the reason for climbing Mt. Everest. But there are more cogent reasons. One relates to the understanding of normative development, which is impossible without taking into account extreme deviations from the norm. Along with central tendencies in human ability, there is the equally important matter of human diversity, not only in the variety of existing aptitudes, but also in the range of power that a random population can generate in any one aptitude. This applies to humans at *all* age levels, including young children.

Especially important are the understandings needed to nurture budding or potential giftedness. Among Lewis Terman's major contributions through his longitudinal studies of high-IQ children is that giftedness does not spring to life spontaneously and unaccountably in adulthood, as if it were born whole, without antecedent traces. Instead, there is a long period of incubation which can be detected in many cases as far back in life as the elementary school years. This idea of a link between early promise and eventual fulfillment has direct meaning for caretakers and educators in the sense that it underscores the importance of nurturance. Challenging precocious children to the limits of their abilities is supposed to help incubate talent, and every bit of help is welcome, inasmuch as the stakes are so high. If Terman is right in calling attention to the importance of beginning signs of giftedness, then school age may not be the earliest time to tease out high potential and to initiate the nurturing process. As the research reported in this book suggests, there is good reason to hypothesize that precocity is indeed recognizable and amenable to productive stimulation much sooner in life than many educators seem to suspect.

The dearth of professional literature on gifted young children was brought to our attention dramatically a few years ago by a reviewer who was highly critical of a new book of readings on the subject. After giving it poor ratings, he offered, as something of a consolation, the "comforting" thought that there simply isn't enough serious work in the field to assemble into a book-length document. In other words, you can't expect the editor who put the book together to find quality material that doesn't exist.

We took the reviewer's lamentation as a challenge not only to find authors who have produced solid new insights, but to encourage more research attention to the young gifted child as a result of the auspicious beginnings by these authors. Our efforts were not intended as acts of posturing bravado or brashness, as if to show that we could venture into territory that too many scholars fear to tread. Instead, we looked for researchers who are already there and whose work is solid enough to attract others to join them. The search took us to widely spaced places in the world, including Australia, Canada, Israel, Norway, and coast to coast in the United States, a "journey" that we believe was truly worthwhile. Not only do the chapters provide a kind of worldwide prospectus, they also show how the gifted at a tender age can become an international concern. And rightly so, because so much insight into the development of precocity can be gained by looking more closely than ever at these children virtually from the time they are born, as this book attempts to do.

No brief sketch of the book's chapters can encapsulate their content. The best we can do is touch on the topics to give an idea of the collection's overall coverage and organization. There are altogether five sections which contain reports prepared expressly for this volume. They admittedly do not reflect the full range of topics addressed in the literature, but whatever is dealt with here is enough to suggest the need for much more work in the field and the promise of meaningful payoffs if such investments of effort were made.

The first section, "Prologues and Caveats," begins with Tannenbaum's introductory chapter which is really an account of the state of the art. He feels that it is too early to draw definitive conclusions from reported research, but the outcomes are exciting enough to warrant replication and further study. Also, his description of young prodigies raises some intriguing questions concerning popular beliefs about the nature of giftedness and how to identify it in children.

Following the Tannenbaum piece, there is a chapter on creative giftedness by Sternberg and Lubart. Although it does not deal directly with young children, the reader can derive a better understanding of how complex the creative process is and that it is naive to claim, as many educators do, that children are highly creative, by virtue of their spontaneity and free spirit, until they reach the middle elementary school years, when education becomes more controlling and ritualized. Creativity requires far more than freedom from outer controls, as Sternberg and Lubart make abundantly clear.

Another kind of caveat is offered by Hundeide, from an anthropological perspective which emphasizes the functional meaning of cognitive enrichment and how these understandings are culture bound. Among a variety of important messages to caretakers of the gifted in western society is the notion that, in other parts of the world, parents offer praise of *special*, not *expected*, behaviors.

In the second section "Early Development of Giftedness," Horowitz opens with a consideration of developmental theories and how they affect the identification of high potential at a young age. Current thinking favors nonlinearity in human development, which implies that diagnosticians should be modest about the predictive validity of their assessments, especially when the child is not yet of school age. Gross's detailed account of three extremely high-IQ children provides a glimpse into the early development of individuals in a population that is often neglected, especially at a very young age. One of the many vivid outcomes of her study is that so much diversity exists among these children. We hope that it encourages more behavioral scientists to differentiate between the gifted and gifted, not just the gifted and nongifted.

Part III begins with a chapter by Nancy and the late Halbert Robinson on the qualities of standardized tests and their qualifications for use in assessing superior potential in young children, even infants. The Robinsons also stress how difficult it is to obtain reliable and valid measurements of children before they are of school age. For this age group, they counsel the use of a wide-ranging variety of tests, along with relevant "collateral information." Jackson follows with a detailed report on young children who learn to read before they are old enough to enter school. Parents and teachers have often wondered if such an accomplishment is a harbinger of superior language achievement at school. According to Jackson's own research data, along with other studies which she cites, early reading skills are not sure-fire signs of giftedness, much to the surprise of educators who often promote such an assumption. Kanevsky closes the section with a report of her own research on young high-IQ children matched in mental age with older, normal-IQ subjects. In this chapter she focuses primarily on *how*, rather than just *how well*, they perform, in order to provide some insight into the unique *processes* of problem solving, not just the extraordinary *powers* demonstrated by precocious children. The results are eye-openers.

Part IV deals with the effects of enriching the environments of gifted young children. Thus far, experimentation with these early stimuli has yielded highly encouraging results. Klein developed systematic mediated learning experiences for parents to administer to their offspring in the first years of life. She originally tested her methods with socially disadvantaged families whose children needed intensive readiness experiences to help them enter school with real hopes for success. Because of the positive outcomes of this research, she has expanded her program to service the potential of precocious young children as well. Her approach to the mediating process and how it has fared thus far are described in some detail in her chapter. Moss follows with further evidence of the promising effects of mothers' mediation (she calls it "scaffolding") of their 3- and 4-year-olds' cognitive development. Unlike Klein, she worked exclusively with mothers of high-IQ subjects, and the results were similarly impressive. From the Klein and Moss studies, conducted independently of each other, it is easy to see why caretaker–child interaction is a fertile area for research aimed at cultivating the potentialities of young children at all ability levels, including the upper extremes.

The book closes with its fifth section on the young gifted child's growth as a socialized being. Rothman deals with moral development, a topic that is unaccountably missing in the literature on gifted children of all ages. The absence of exploratory or experimental studies is especially puzzling in light of the fact that parents and teachers often testify to signs of giftedness in this domain. They refer to children whose sense of honesty, sensitivity to the feelings of others, and pro-social attitudes and behaviors seem to be clearly advanced. By elaborating on relevant literature, Rothman takes an important step toward filling the void, especially as it pertains to moral giftedness. The Ari and Rich chapter on grouping patterns and instructional strategies anticipates life at school when young gifted children reach the age of formal classroom experiences. Once they grow to that age, the school will have to deal with the problems of maximizing their achievement and integrating them with peers who function at different ability levels and come from various socio-cultural groups. Ari and Rich elaborate on the complexity of these issues before proceeding to offer guidelines for dealing with them.

In closing, we wish to acknowledge with unqualified gratitude the contributions of the book's authors whose chapters we have just introduced only briefly. In response to our call for papers, they produced a collection which may never have seen the light of day if not for the poor review of a similar book published a few years ago. We are deliberately witholding names of the authors, editor, and reviewer of that volume, because it would only rake up a painful experience for all of them. But they did inspire our desire to have another go at understanding the gifted young child. For this we thank them, sincerely.

Pnina S. Klein
Abraham J. Tannenbaum
June 1992

part I

Prologues and Caveats

chapter 1

Early Signs of Giftedness: Research and Commentary

Abraham J. Tannenbaum

Teachers College
Columbia University
New York, NY

By far the largest scale, longest running longitudinal investigations of gifted children are the *Genetic Studies of Genius*, conducted by Lewis Terman and associates.[1] A popular myth claims that the sample population was identified strictly on the basis of high IQ. But the truth is that candidates could qualify for IQ testing only if they were the youngest in their classes or nominated by teachers as the brightest among their agemates. If the children had been identified by IQ exclusively, they would have numbered at least 4,500 instead of the 1,500 or so who became subjects of the study (Hughes & Converse, 1962). The teachers' tendency to recommend only *proven* achievers ruled out two out of every three pupils with IQs of

---

[1] The multivolume *Genetic Studies of Genius* reports research conducted by Lewis M. Terman and his associates (Terman & Oden, 1925, 1947, 1959; Cox, 1926; Burks, Jensen, & Terman, 1930). Terman helped prepare the 1959 volume but died more than 2 years before its publication. Several additional follow-up studies have been prepared by Melita Oden (1968), Pauline S. Sears and Ann Barbee (1977), Robert R. Sears (1977), and Pauline S. Sears (1979).

140 and above and as many as four out of every five children with IQs of 135 and above, on grounds that their school records were not impressive enough. Those who did qualify, therefore, had already demonstrated their precocity in class, albeit necessarily in the three Rs and the like, but not necessarily in the arts and the like.

Among the many outcomes of Terman's research is that rapid cognitive development during childhood is fairly likely to eventuate in superior achievement in the worlds of higher level education and careers. This link between early promise and its eventual fulfillment has added force to the argument that nurturing the potential of able students in the first dozen years of schooling promises to yield rich dividends for society when the children grow into their adult years of productivity.

But what of the years *before* schooling? Can high potential be discerned so early in life with any degree of reliability or validity, and nurtured with any hope of future payoff? The Terman data offer no answers, since they were gathered on older children who had already reached the upper elementary grades, where their identification as gifted could be helped by school records, an impossibility among children under school age. Perhaps because preschoolers have never yet figured in this kind of longitudinal study, there is less apparent urgency to invest special efforts in investigating and nurturing giftedness among them, or to test whether such efforts can be effective at all in the long run. It may also explain why research on the earliest possible signs of excellence in children is relatively sparse.

CHILD PRODIGIES

In order to appreciate how high the human mind can reach in the first years of life, it is instructive to consider the amazing mental feats of child prodigies. So striking is their display of brilliance that they occasionally fall victim to exploitation, overprotection, and even abuse. Sometimes they are pushed to exhibit their talents before adoring audiences who subject them to constant overweening flattery. Some also feel the excessive pressure of their "stage mothers" (and/or fathers) to achieve acclaim and fame as quickly and resoundingly as possible. No less familiar is the image of young prodigies deprived of normal childhoods of play and friends in favor of organizing their lives exclusively around study and practice, lest their extraordinary skills begin to atrophy. So, whereas talent in the young is indeed a blessing, the more awesome the talent, the more mixed the blessing can become.

Child prodigies appear in fewer varieties of ability than do brilliant adults or even school-age students. Most reveal their magic in mathematics, music, chess, or language mastery, although a few can also be found in the fine arts, but not in scientific invention or social leadership. Within their talent domains they represent some of the best possible evidence that brainpower alone at a tender age is a good, but not a foolproof, harbinger of brilliance in adulthood. For if tested and demonstrated proficiency in the first years of life were the *only* forerunners of eventual success, regardless of factors associated with personality, milieu, and just plain luck, what better proof of proficiency could there be than early prodigious behavior? The child prodigy already has a *proven* record of achievement, not just the promise of a great future in some undefined field of excellence, based on such remote indicators as IQ and other aptitude measures.

Yet there are many instances of early brilliance fizzling out by the end of the prodigies' adolescent years, as for example, in Bamberger's (1986) studies of young violinists. She explains this "midlife crisis" as the prodigy's undergoing "serious cognitive reorganization" and facing simultaneous demands from audiences for more mature instrumental interpretations. Too often, these wonder children fail to measure up as they grow into a new stage of life because "there can be neither return to imitation and the unreflective, spontaneous 'intuitions' of childhood, nor a simple 'fix-up' " (p. 411). When the mismatch between internal development and external expectations are uncorrectable, the prodigy remains just a "has-been," or a "might-have-become," thus demonstrating that early genius *by itself* is no guarantee that distinction in the mature years is sure to follow.

After his detailed study of six young geniuses—two whizzes in chess; one each in music, math, and creative writing; and a young polymath labeled "omnibus prodigy"—Feldman (1986) reports follow-up information that "only one of the six prodigies . . . has gone more or less in a straight line from where he started to where he is now" (p. 235). Why the turnaway? Possibly because of the absence of experiential and situational circumstances which Feldman deems necessary to facilitate the flowering of genius. But the retreat is not always into oblivion. Some prodigies simply change direction and make their marks in other fields. For example, Merrill Kenneth Wolf graduated from Yale College in 1945, when he was only 14 years old. He majored in music at Yale and continued studying music for 7 years after graduation. But he gave up plans of becoming a professional in that field when he entered medical school and most recently served as a professor of neuroanatomy at the University of Massachusetts Medical School. Again, much as we may expect the young genius to follow a straight line toward success in his or her domain of excellence, it is possible that the line will bend in an unforeseeable direction or even fail to reach high enough to any advanced-level achievement.

Some Prodigies and Their Feats[2]

It would be naive to "homogenize" prodigies, as if they were all alike in their early personal traits and histories. They *do* have their own individualities, except for the fact that they all seem to have been born with talents fully formed, not just nascent aptitudes requiring prolonged training or stimulation. Indeed, "nurturists" in the perennial nature/nurture controversy would find it hard to explain prodigious accomplishments among children who haven't been alive long enough to be enriched by their environments. "Naturists" are no less stymied in solving the mystery, because other child prodigies are so rarely found in a prodigy's family tree.

How incredibly diverse and mentally advanced young geniuses are can best be illustrated by a few biographical sketches. For example, Whipple (1924) cites the early extraordinary accomplishments of prodigies in previous centuries. One of them, Karl Witte, born in Austria in 1800, had already learned to read German, French, Italian, Latin, and Greek by the age of 9, and matriculated shortly afterwards at the University of Leipsig, where he was awarded the Ph.D. "with distinction" before he had reached his 14th birthday. Two years later, he earned the Doctor of Laws degree and was then appointed to faculty at the University of Berlin. When he was 23 years old, he issued an essay, "On Misunderstanding Dante," which has been regarded as one of the most prized 19th-century contributions to literary criticism.

Whipple (1924) also summarizes the tragically short life story of Christian Heineken, a German who was born in 1721 and who died in his fifth year. But what an incredible amount of learning was crammed into such a brief lifetime! When he was only 10 months old, his parents were stunned by his precocity of observation and speech and promptly appointed a tutor for him. Whereupon he was taught Biblical stories, which he had to memorize, then verses on

---

[2] Child prodigies who are no longer alive or have reached adulthood are mentioned by name; however, those who were still in their childhood at the time this book was published are referred to only by letter names, and the sources of information about them are not mentioned, in order to protect their privacy.

the creation of our planet, followed by studies of the history of the world, arithmetical fundamentals, and the names of bones and muscles. One tutor reported that, when he was 4 years of age, Christian could recite 1,500 Latin proverbs and numerous anecdotes in French. He could read printed and written German, and answer many questions in history. He became famous throughout Europe for his erudition, but by age 4 years, 4 months, he was dead. There is, of course, no way of knowing how much scholarship he could have contributed to the world of ideas if he had lived to a ripe old age.

Among the better known child prodigies in the early part of the 20th century, when intelligence testing came into vogue, were those identified by Hollingworth (1942) on the basis of IQ 180 and above. Montour (1976) recorded the achievement history of three children in the Hollingworth sample, one of whom, labeled "E," was born in 1908 and had an IQ of 187 when tested at the age of 8. Although he did not speak until about age 2, he could read by age 3, and during his years in elementary school, he studied geometry, algebra, and some Latin, Greek, German, Spanish, Portuguese, Hebrew, and Anglo-Saxon. Admitted to Columbia University at age 12, he graduated at 14 and earned his doctorate 8 years later. At the same time, he received several degrees in theology and eventually became a minister of the Episcopal Church. From 1972 until retirement, he was Dean of Chapel at Jesus College, Cambridge.

Another of the Hollingworth IQ 180+ children described by Montour, child "L," also passed the admissions examination to a university (Harvard) at age 12, also read English fluently at age 3, and also studied foreign languages in his elementary school years. But unlike "E," he never completed a doctorate after engaging in graduate studies at Oxford. But he did enter medicine and served in the Army Medical Corps in World War II before taking over his father's medical practice. The only other academic interest he retained was that of witchcraft, on which he lectured from time to time.

In commenting on the Hollingworth subjects discussed by Montour, Radford (1990) notes, "It is rather obvious that in each case, the later years, while very far from representing failure, do not equal the exceptional performance of childhood and youth" (p. 53).

Among the prodigies who are still in their childhood years, "A" could read a restaurant menu from the time he was barely out of his toddler stage, and by age 2 he was assembling 1,000-piece jigsaw puzzles successfully. At age 10, he was enrolled in the Johns Hopkins Weekend Center for Talented Youth as a student in advanced math and in Latin. Since he is now just a young adolescent, only time can tell how far early precocity will carry him in his later education and career.

At age 3, "B" 's talents developed with astonishing speed. In that one year, he began composing music, started to study piano formally with his mother, and performed brilliantly on the 12,000-pipe organ in New York's Riverside Church. At age 6, he could play Bach's intricate "Fifteen Inventions" from memory on the piano, an instrument which he had already mastered so well that the famous Juilliard School of Music in New York admitted him as one of the youngest piano students in its history. Aside from his musical genius, he demonstrated the ability to absorb sixth- and seventh-grade math before reaching his seventh birthday, by which time he had already taught himself to read and write Russian and English. He is currently in the primary elementary grades and actively engaged in sports and other games with friends, as befits most children his age, without any perceptible sacrifice of advancement in his art.

Finally, there is "C," who has not yet reached his twelfth birthday but already shows promise of becoming a virtuoso violinist. As is often the case among musical prodigies, his special talents range beyond just mastery of a musical instrument. At the tender age of only 22 months, he was already studying Hebrew in his native America, and by age 4 he could read and write nine languages. So much for the popular prejudice that young geniuses *necessarily* specialize in a single skill area, but perform without distinction in all other domains of talent.

Reviewing the examples presented thus far, it appears that little, if anything, has changed in the *kinds* of genius displayed by prodigies over three centuries of record keeping. Yehudi Menuhin was a 20th-century prodigy on the violin, but so was Mozart in the 18th-century, although until about 100 years before Mozart's birth there must have existed countless would-have-been young virtuoso violinists who lived and died in obscurity simply because that instrument had not yet been developed during their lifetimes. Similarly, today's children of preschool age can already be spotted for their potential as future dance soloists in classical Russian ballet, which would have been impossible until the late 19th century when that dance form evolved. So while it may appear that young genius bursts forth spontaneously and fully developed, as if "out of Zeus' head," the truth is not quite so simple. For, as Feldman (1986) points out, history has to be ready for the specific talent to emerge. The era of violinists can begin only after the historic appearance of the violin, and there can be no classical Russian ballet dancer until the historic debut of the classical Russian ballet as a celebrated dance form. Older domains of achievement, however, allow for a longer history of prodigious behavior. Hence, it is not surprising to find young geniuses in languages and mathematics dating back to ancient times, when these areas of knowledge already existed, although the numbers of prodigies probably increase as subspecializations in a discipline multiply in the course of time.

Some Prodigies and Their Failures

Obviously, child prodigies do not necessarily sustain their genius and go on to achieve renown in adulthood. Brilliance fades in many of them as they grow older, and they eventually become indistinguishable in the crowd. The extent of their descent is astounding when one considers the heights they had reached so quickly after birth. A familiar example is the failure of young musical instrumentalists whose technique in performance is awesome, but who never mature into performing artists lionized by critics and concert audiences.

The flash-in-the-pan phenomenon occurs not only in music but in other domains of excellence as well. However, Bamberger's (1986) hypothesis as to why it is so prevalent among musical prodigies may not apply elsewhere as, for example, in creative writing. Consider the case of Daisy Ashford, a British literary prodigy born in 1881, who produced a comic masterpiece when she was only 4 years old. Her famous novel, *The Young Visitors*, sold hundreds of thousands of copies and is still in print, even though it was written when she was only 9 years old. Yet, despite the fact that she lived to age 90, she stopped writing in early adolescence. It is not easy to imagine why a 9-year-old with enough skills, tastes, insights, sensitivities, and sensibilities to write a novel that is praised by literati to this day simply stopped producing any literary fare over nearly eight of her last decades of life.

Undoubtedly, the best known, and possibly most tragic case, of aborted young genius is William James Sidis (Whipple, 1924; Montour, 1977). Born in 1898 to a respected medical psychologist who named him after the famous Harvard philosopher-psychologist and who used tyrannical "hot-house" methods to teach his son as much and as quickly as possible at home, William began his studies before the age of 2. He learned to read and to spell by age 3 and could use the typewriter before his fourth birthday. By age 5, he could read Russian, French, and German, and when he entered first grade at 6, he was able to complete the first 7 years of schooling in half a year. He then spent 2 years studying at home, where he was tutored in algebra, geometry, trigonometry, and differential and integral calculus, before entering high school, which he finished in only 3 months. Before he was 8 years old, he passed the entrance examination at the Massachusetts Institute of Technology and the anatomy examination at Harvard Medical School. But Harvard considered him too young to enter college when he applied at age 9, thus forcing him to wait until he was 11 years old before receiving permission to enroll as a special student majoring mainly in mathematics and science. Within a year of his admission he was already lecturing on higher mathematics, and he succeeded in graduating *summa cum laude* at age 15. From that time on until his death in 1944, he experienced failure as a college instructor, sought anonymity in a series of low-paying clerical jobs, and eventually descended into obscurity. Like Daisy Ashford, William James Sidis was the personification of "early ripe, early rot," an old popular adage turned canard because it applies to so few cases.

In an attempt to explain the Sidis tragedy, Montour (1977) draws a sharp contrast between Sidis's early upbringing and that of Norbert Wiener, his contemporary and also a celebrated child prodigy who went on to become the creator of cybernetics and to enjoy a brilliant scholarly career. The elder Sidis, Boris, a martinet-scholar, had a fierce disdain for primary school education and taught his son at home where the environment for learning could only be described as "white hot" in its intensity. When his son was ready for college, Boris would accept nothing lesser in prestige than Harvard University. Soon after his graduation at age 16, William started his decline by participating in a radical protest march, which was far less tolerated then than now, and subsequently failed in his brief attempt at college teaching before settling for a series of modest clerical jobs which hardly taxed his mental abilities and gave him the anonymity he craved. Disappointed at his son's inability to live up to expectations, Boris disowned him.

Norbert Wiener's father, Leo, on the other hand, while making strong demands on young Norbert, was far more supportive of his son's development and seemingly far less an authoritarian figure within his family. Instead of relying heavily on tutorials at home, Leo sent his son to public school for an early education. Later, he enrolled him in Tufts University instead of insisting on Harvard as the only institution qualified to nurture Norbert's extraordinary abilities. Most of all, Leo was a loyal father who defended his son against criticism instead of holding him to the highest standards of success as a condition of his love and encouragement.

Nobody can say for sure that the contrast in father–son relationships made the differences between William James Sidis's failure and Norbert Wiener's triumph in their adult years. There are probably many more clues to be found in the structure of their abilities, temperaments, and the gamut of their social relationships. In fact, the childhood years may not have been the critical ones in both cases. For Norbert Wiener also suffered from a difficult adolescence, and it is only around age 30 that he began to fulfill his promise, possibly due to his wife's display of confidence in him. Sidis, on the other hand, could not form a stable relationship with a woman who might have given him the sense of security that he needed.

Not all child prodigies who underwent pressureful childhoods ended up as failures. John Stuart Mill was also force-fed an early education by an impatient and demanding father, but that did not prevent him from becoming one of the most prominent 19th-century British philosophers. Nor did it seem to depress his IQ, estimated by Cox (1926) as the highest among 282 eminent historical figures whose biographical histories enabled her to determine how well they would have performed on modern tests of intelligence. When Mill was 3 years old, he had learned enough Greek from his father to study the works of various Greek prose authors, including Herodotus and Xenophon. At age 8, he began studying Latin and tutoring his younger sister, and by the time he was 12, he had progressed through elementary geometry and algebra, as well as a huge body of literature and history. But despite his career as a brilliant thinker and writer, he suffered a terrible emotional crisis when he was only 20. Despairingly, he began to wonder whether his lifelong devotion to intellectual esoterica was worth all that effort. This self-doubt and suspicion that spending so much time on his own realm of ideas crowded out too many opportunities for encountering other (possibly more) important and exciting pursuits seemed to haunt him for the remainder of his life. It therefore appears that the fulfillment of a prodigy's early potential is no guarantee of emotional contentment or even stability in later years.

Conversely, severe developmental handicap does not necessarily inhibit a prodigy's accomplishments. Child "D," for example, was diagnosed at age 2 as autistic and suffers from that disorder even today in his early adolescence. Soon after his autism was discovered, he listened to his older brother play Christmas carols on the piano and, without any encouragement, went to the piano and tentatively picked out the same notes. By age 11, he had already composed reams of music, some of it for 14 instruments simultaneously, and could play some of the most complicated pieces by great composers. By then he was studying with a renowned music teacher who found that, in a matter of months, he could master a whole realm of music. Blessed with an extraordinary memory, he only has to hear a musical piece once before he can play it perfectly. After hearing Beethoven's Fifth Symphony in concert, he returned home and transcribed the entire score for piano. Afterwards, he added several pages of his own variations. But after showing that he can play the "Moonlight Sonata" without even seeing the keyboard, he has been seen to jump off his piano stool and, with arms flailing, chase his father around the room while bellowing almost unintelligible words in a strange, guttural voice.

"D" 's teacher claims to have taught many child prodigies but believes that he is the first real genius among them. Few people in the world have his astounding repertoire of millions of memorized sounds, and if he can be taught to extract some of them and re-form their sequences, he may become a great composer. He also has absolute pitch, which means he can listen to 10 different sounds played at once and identify each one. More important, he also possesses an expressive capacity and ability to render melodic phrases tenderly in ways that reveal a sensitive, passionate yearning for musical meaning. He may spend the rest of his life creating and performing great music while suffering the affliction of ritualized, compulsive physical behavior, an inability to relate to people in a meaningful way, and virtually no use of conventional language. Perhaps his music making will eventually make his life bearable as he suffers from the scourges of autism. Time will tell.

Lessons To Be Learned from Child Prodigies

Probably the most striking feature in prodigious behavior is that it starts so early in life. It appears almost as a freakish deviation from the norm, a mutation which seems to deny conventional wisdom that differences between individuals are in degree, not in kind, and that we are all brothers and sisters under the normal distribution of ability, any ability. But whether prodigies are distinctive in degree or kind from other young mortals, it is noteworthy that they specialize so early in life. Some excel in music, others in mathematics, still others in languages, and so forth, thus raising doubts that children are generalists who sample subject matter domains cafeteria-style before beginning to dig deeply into one or two, no earlier than in their adolescent years.

Out of conviction that extraordinary mental growth in children proceeds only along a narrow range of abilities, Feldman (1980) cites case studies of child prodigies to challenge some basic Piagetian developmental theories. According to Feldman, Piaget believed that, *universally*, children's cognitive growth progresses in sequential stages which are not only predictable but also encompass *all* thinking capacities of every child at each stage of development. If, then, a young prodigy performs at the level of a gifted adult in a specific field, he or she should be advanced in other domains as well. But when Bensusan (1976) administered four cognitive-developmental measures to two 8-year-old chess masters and to a 10-year-old musician-composer, the results showed that, despite their excelling in chess and music, respectively, these child prodigies performed age appropriately in logic, role taking, spatial reasoning, and moral judgment. Such findings led Feldman to conclude that the Piagetian universals simply do not apply to highly gifted children.

However, Radford (1990) seems to question Feldman's reasoning on grounds that it is circular and not quite supported by its underlying evidence. According to Radford, Feldman starts out by defining prodigies as those with extremely specialized gifts, but he excludes those with extremely high tested general intelligence. He then selects a sample of child prodigies, most of whom conform to his prior definition, and after studying them, concludes that it is in the *nature* of child prodigies to be specialized, thus completing the circularity of his logic. Furthermore, Radford argues that "it is clear from his own accounts that even his selected six prodigies are not in fact restricted to one specialized talent" (p. 58). But regardless of whether Feldman's or Radford's interpretations are valid, what *accounts* for such astounding achievement in children who have not yet reached school age remains a deep mystery.

What *does* come through clearly from studies of child prodigies is that the frequency of unfulfilled promise among them shows how limited the early signs of precocity can be in forecasting future success. Psychologists often criticize the IQ and other measures of ability as far from perfect predictors of achievement and devote enormous energies to improve on these instruments or devise alternatives to them. Yet these tests do not measure real accomplishments; they only reflect a potential for it, *by inference*, from problem-solving behavior that is only distantly related to any domain-specific mastery or creativity. Prodigious behavior, on the other hand, is the best possible measure of early mental power, because it is *openly masterful now* rather than a *remote symptom of promise for the future*.

Still, despite early signs of genius in a particular area of productivity or performance, some children who are blessed with it find that their blessing is short-lived. Why? Unquestionably because it is impossible to anticipate children's growing differences in lifestyle, life experience, and the lucky (or unlucky) breaks which influence their development so powerfully. If child prodigies can sometimes turn out to be failures as adults, how much more so can we expect occasional failure among preschoolers designated "merely" as developmentally accelerated by any device for discerning otherwise hidden mental strength.

DEVELOPMENT AND MEASUREMENT
OF EARLY GIFTEDNESS

Compared to other age groups, young children have rarely been subjects of investigation for signs of giftedness. Feldman (1980) would probably argue that Piaget's theory concerning the universality of developmental stages does not apply to the one-in-a-hundred rapid young learners any more than it applies to the one-in-ten-million young geniuses. Like prodigies, rapid learners seem to show uneven patterns of growth as evidenced by the finding that preschoolers identified as gifted on the basis of cognitive measures score only slightly better than average on tests of gross and fine motor skills (Roedell, Jackson, & Robinson, 1980; Kitano & Kirby, 1986).

Children with high tested intelligence also appear to develop heterogeneously. For example, in Terman's study sample averaging IQ 151, only half of the children learned to read before reaching school age, and as Nancy Jackson points out in this volume, learning to read early is no foolproof precursor of extraordinary achievement in the school years and beyond. However, at the extremely high IQ levels (i.e., 180 and above), rapid intellectual development seems to occur on a broad front. As Hollingworth (1942) points out, her small sample of elementary school children with IQs of 180 and above already showed significant advancement in speaking vocabulary and sentence production before their fourth birthdays. They also had early histories of precocity in conceptual skills such as discriminating and labeling colors, drawing, identifying shapes, and solving puzzles.

References to high-IQ children inevitably raise questions concerning the relationship of giftedness to superior tested intelligence. Despite widespread efforts to discredit the IQ as a measure of human potential (cf. Guilford, 1967; Gould, 1981; Sternberg, 1985), two realities have to be faced: first, published research on precocious children still overwhelmingly equates giftedness with high IQ. Second, efforts to detect signs of precocity in the first 2 or 3 years of children's lives deal mainly with measures administered to normative populations and how these test scores correlate with follow-up IQs obtained on these same children when they are old enough to be assessed validly and reliably on a Stanford-Binet-type instrument. This latter fact is of particular importance to any discussion of hidden potential among infants and toddlers. For inasmuch as IQ scores explain no more than 25% to 50% of the variance in scholastic achievement, and the earliest assessments of any kind explain no more than 10% to 50% of the variance in IQ, any attempt to connect children's beginning signs of cognition with eventual school performance must remain suspect. Yet there is no way to avoid reviewing evidence on the earliest correlates of IQ since these are virtually the only kinds of data presented in the research literature on symptoms of precocity among infants and toddlers.

Acceleration Through Developmental Stages

There has been little effort to examine how precocious children progress through Piaget's sensorimotor, preoperations, concrete operations, and formal operations stages. From the few studies recorded thus far, it would seem that the results are more consistent for later stages than for earlier ones. Some research reports low correlations between progress through early stages and scores on IQ and language mastery tests (Smolak, 1982; Moore, Nelson-Piercy, Abel, & Frye, 1984). On the other hand, Kaufman (1968, 1971) obtained correlations of more than .6 between a Piaget-type test and both the Lorge-Thorndike and Gesell tests administered to a group of kindergarten children. These positive results are substantiated by the findings of Zigler and Trickett (1978), who report correlations between the two types of tests hovering around .7. In a follow-up study of Kaufman's kindergarten sample, it was found that both the Piaget and Lorge-Thorndike instruments had similar correlations of better than .6 with first-grade achievement.

The evidence pertaining to concrete and formal operational stages seems to be clearer. Keating (1975), for example, reports a study of preadolescents (fifth and seventh graders), with each age group divided into subsamples of bright and average pupils, based on scores obtained on Raven's Standard Progressive Matrices. When Piagetian tasks were administered to the four groups, results showed that the brighter children outperformed their average peers on the formal operational tasks. Similarly, Carter and Ormrod (1982) found a close association between high IQ and the early attainment of formal operations.

A reasonable explanation for the more consistent findings in the later stages than in the earlier ones is offered by Pendarvis, Howley, and Howley (1990), who point out that formal operations relate directly to mathematical and language concepts, which are not unlike those tested by IQ measures and which precocious children acquire quickly and efficiently. On the other hand, children who are still at the sensorimotor and preoperations stages are not yet ready to engage in the kinds of problem solving that are incorporated in IQ. Pendarvis, et al. (1990) also note how difficult it is to assess progress *through* a single stage on account of the lack of calibrated, quantifiable growth steps within stages. What compounds the difficulty in drawing inferences about concept development from empirical research based on Piaget's theories is the lack of research "to determine whether or not progress in cognitive development is measurably continuous. It is possible that cognitive development occurs so covertly that qualitatively different stages emerge quite suddenly" (p. 231). Apparently, Tuddenham's (1971) pessimism is as justified today as it was two decades ago, when he commented that "the evidence thus far obtained has about extinguished whatever hope we might have had that we could place each child on a single developmental continuum equivalent to mental age, and from his score predict his performance on content of whatever kind" (p. 75).

Although the early developmental histories of cognitively gifted children have not yet produced a clear stage theory that is generalizable for these populations, more promising insights may be emerging with respect to the flowering of artistic talent. DeAngelis (1990) reports on a panel discussion of *Wunderkinder* (wonder children) in art, conducted at the 1990 National Convention of the American Psychological Association. At that symposium, developmental and clinical psychologist Claire Golomb of the University of Massachusetts at Boston analyzed a sample collection of drawings produced over the years by an Israeli boy named Eytan, then 18. The chronological sequence of Eytan's works, according to Golomb, seems to support Arnheim's (1972) theory that both children and adult artists undergo distinct stages of development in graphics, including their understanding of perspective. In other words, maturation in drawing involves a search for increasingly more satisfying solutions to graphic problems, as well as an organized mental activity that proceeds along a stage-like path.

Eytan's earliest drawings at age 2 are *topographical*, or frontal-view figures, not unlike those of most children that age. Soon afterwards, however, he started using what Arnheim calls *orthographic projection*, in which objects are presented in the frontal parallel plane, perpendicular to the viewer's sight, similar to what is shown in a two-dimensional side view of a car. From 2 years, 3 months on, he departed from the kinds of art expected of less talented children at comparable ages of development. At that time, he attempted to portray more than canonical forms by adding sides or faces to that side view. By age 3, more complex kinds of orthographic juxtapositions emerged. Eytan also began at this age to use both divergent and isometric projections. In a divergent perspective, a side view of a car also incorporates aspects of the grill, bumper, and roof, all of which are seen together with the side. Isometric projection, on the other hand, involves a more naturalistic view of the object. Finally, at age 3 years, 8 months, Eytan began to visualize his subjects in convergent perspective, considered by some artists and critics as the highest level of perspectival understanding. In convergent perspective, the lines of the drawing, if extended outward, would all meet at a single point.

If the case of Eytan can be generalized to other young artists, it would seem that developmental stages in drawing are in some ways the same and in other ways different for young artists and nonartists. The sameness consists of a fairly predictable succession of visions of the world as depicted in their drawings, except that the gifted progress through the stages more rapidly. But the contrast in *rates* of development is one of degree rather than kind, and therefore quantifiable. What cannot be quantified, however, involves the quality, idiom, inspiration, creativity, and depth of insight which distinguishes the Eytan's from the amateurs, even in their preschool years. It is admittedly awkward to think of qualitative aspects of giftedness as marching through developmental stages in some kind of orderly fashion. But attempts should be made to monitor them to determine whether age-stage theories apply to the gifted, or whether each gifted child marches to the beat of a different drummer through the early years of mental growth. Such a line of research may help clear up some of the many mysteries surrounding the first sequences of gifted behavior in young children, not only in the arts but in all domains of productivity and performance.

Early Predictors of Giftedness

It has been known for a long time that thinking skills are manifest as early as infancy. Kagan (1976) cites studies to show that 4-month-old infants attend longer to wavelengths corresponding to red and blue than to other colors, and that 13-week-olds study concentric patterns longer than nonconcentric ones. These are only small samples of a huge array of indications that infants are alert, receptive, and discriminating in response to external stimuli. But are any of these signs of alertness forerunners of gifted behavior?

As noted earlier, the research that purportedly addresses the question deals mostly with early correlates of later IQ scores in normative populations. It is again important to emphasize the fact that IQ in itself is far from a totally valid sign of any kind of giftedness, no matter how *giftedness* is defined. We are therefore left with a literature on infant behavior that reports imperfect predictors of an imperfect predictor of precocity in childhood and beyond. The problem is compounded by the focus on normative populations in these studies, since broad-range sampling often produces correlations that don't apply to the upper extreme of the continuum. Note, for example, a Scottish study quoted by Knobloch and Pasamanick (1963) in which developmental evaluations of 6-month-olds correlated .54 with Stanford-Binet IQs obtained 5 years later. However, as Knobloch and Pasamanick point out, "the poorest correlations were obtained for those eighteen children who scored between 125 and 140 on the five-year examination" (p. 80). The authors report a similar-type study in which measures taken at age 40 weeks and 3 years show correlations of .46 for 48 White children and .63 for 56 Black children, all of whom had 3-year IQs lower than 120. By way of contrast, the 17 Whites and 8 Blacks with IQs above 120 had correlations of .09 and − .35, respectively.

Doubts about the relationship of infant measures and subsequent high tested intelligence are reinforced in a study by Willerman and Fiedler (1977). Out of a total sample of 114 4-year-olds, a 100 children with Stanford-Binet IQs of 140 and above had been tested on the research version of the Bayley Scales of Mental and Motor Development administered when they were 8 months old. These scores were then correlated with performance on the WISC and Wide Range Achievement Tests (WRAT) by 95 of the children at age 7. Results show that the Bayley Mental and Motor Tests did not correlate with Stanford-Binet IQs at age 4 or with WISC IQ and WRAT measures administered 3 years later. These outcomes cannot be attributed to the restricted range in IQ, because when the sample group was compared with a normative cohort on the Bayley Scales, no differences were found. Nor did such variables as birth weight and birth order differentiate between the IQ 140 and above and the IQ 139 and below subsamples. The Willerman-Fiedler results tend to confirm those reported by Bayley (1955) on the Berkeley Growth Study designed to observe the development of tested intelligence over a 25-year period. Bayley's target group had a mean IQ of 117 on the Wechsler-Bellevue at age 16 and a mean IQ of 129 on the Stanford-Binet at age 17. The independent variables tested during infancy included sensory functioning in reaction to stimuli, motor coordination, memory, and recognition of differences. None of these early behaviors could predict IQ scores when the children were 16 and 17 years old.

After factor analyzing Bayley's data, Hofstaetter (1954) discovered that sensory-motor alertness predominantly accounts for tested mental functioning up to the age of twenty months. From 20 to 40 months, the dominant source of test variance is *persistence*. From age 20 months on, the factor of sensory-motor alertness contributes almost nothing to the variance, but beginning in about the 48th month of life, most of the variance is accounted for by the factor of manipulation of symbols. In the second decade of life, this factor accounts for nearly all the variance.

The radical change in functioning that seems to occur sometime around age 4 may explain Bloom's (1964) findings on relationships between a person's infancy- and childhood-IQ scores. He reports that, in the Berkeley study as well as in others of its kind, measures of mental functioning were administered to children every year after birth until age 17, and the last score in the series was correlated with each of the previous 16. Results show that scores obtained in the first years of life correlate negligibly with the score at age 17; afterwards, the coefficients climb abruptly to about .7, and then to beyond .8 before leveling off (see Figure 1.1).

Impressive as Bloom's coefficients are in confirming the stability of IQ, it should be kept in mind that the consensus he depicts is based solely on correlational studies. Specifically, his summary shows how well each 17-year-old's IQ rating, *relative to that of other 17-year-olds*, can be predicted by mental tests administered to these individuals at earlier times in their lives. In other words, the *rank order* of scores remains fairly much the same from 7 to 17. But what about the scores accumulated over the years for one person— do they remain reasonably unchanged at each annual testing? Apparently not, judging from any number of investigations. For example, in a study of 252 unselected children from an urban community, Honzik, MacFarlane, and Allen (1948) found that, from ages 6 to 16, nearly 60% of the group showed IQ changes of 15 points or more, although the shift of average IQ for the total sample never exceeded five points.

A somewhat similar investigation was conducted on younger children, some tested at age 2, others at age 3, and retested 2 years later

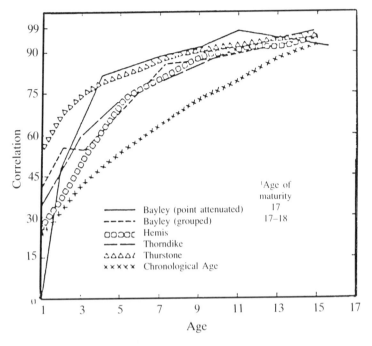

Figure 1.1.   Correlations between intelligence at each age and intelligence at maturity¹ contrasted to select growth curves for intelligence (Bloom, 1964, p. 64; reprinted with permission of author).

on the Stanford-Binet Short Form (Jackson, 1978). Here, too, the results appeared quite changeable from the first administration to the second. The group totaling 65 children with IQs averaging 131 at ages 2 or 3 showed a *mean* change of only 4.8 points (to IQ 136), but the standard deviation of difference scores was 18.5. Nineteen registered gains, and five recorded losses, of more than 16 points over the 2-year period. Furthermore, the directions of change were related to initial IQ levels. Children who tested below the sample median of 130 at the first administration were more likely to show gains than losses on retesting (24 versus 8), whereas those with initial IQs at or above the median were more likely to sustain losses than gains (24 versus 9). Jackson concludes: "This pattern suggests that children's scores were indeed regressing on retest, but to a population mean close to the sample mean rather than to the mean of 100 for the standardization population of the Stanford-Binet" (p. 6). This should come as a surprise to psychologists who assume that the farther a test score deviates from a population average, the more likely it is that subsequent scores on tests which correlate with the first measure will drift toward that average.

Considering what seems to be a contradiction between correlational and test-retest data on the stability of IQ, is there a possibility that they can be made compatible? The answer is that they are not inconsistent at all; they merely yield different kinds of insights. Correlational studies reveal that, if person A scores higher than person B at the first testing, he or she is more likely to score higher on the subsequent test, even though the scores of A and B may change from one testing period to the next. Test-retest investigations, on the other hand, show how changeable an individual's IQ scores are from time to time, even on the same (kind of) instrument. Among children who are not yet of school age, there is neither kind of stability in IQ scores.

Figure 1.1 is sometimes interpreted as evidence that a child's cognitive abilities are more malleable in the first 3 or 4 years of life than in the school years and beyond. Such reasoning would justify showing preference for early compensatory education programs, like Head Start, in order to help socially disadvantaged children accelerate their cognitive development at an age when it is allegedly easiest for them to do so. However, an equally logical argument is that the apparent unconnectedness between levels of infant and childhood performance is basically an artifact of the two ability measures. One is necessarily loaded with sensorimotor-type content, which is the only kind possible for assessing mental levels in infancy. The other kind of test is heavily saturated with cognitive abstractions, many of them transacted verbally. If the two instruments could somehow measure the same skills and yet maintain the same face validity and reliability, the relationship between them would perhaps be much stronger. But performance measures of any kind are necessarily influenced by the subject's environment and repertoires of behavior, both of which change radically from infancy to childhood.

Hopefully, a direct assessment of human potential through monitoring brainwave activity will someday bring us closer to the ultimate test of cognitive stability within individuals. Until that day comes, a prospect which does not seem promising at the moment, it will remain necessary to evaluate children by performance and to infer their mental capacities from it. The scores yielded by such measures are necessarily "contaminated" by all kinds of personal and situational influences which are unique to every individual. Furthermore, human capacity is not fixed like some remote terrain to be discovered and mapped. It is instead an open system, dynamic and modifiable, which means that even a direct measure would only be of a static, snapshot nature (Feuerstein, 1979).

A look at the kinds of characteristics of giftedness observed in infants and in preschoolers reveals clearly how they change from one

Table 1.1.   Indicators of Giftedness in Infants and Preschoolers

Lewis (1975)	Lewis and Brooks-Gunn (1981)	Guilford et al. (1981)	Fagan and McGrath (1981)	B. White (1985)	Lewis and Michalson (1985)	Freeman (1985)	Indicator	Group
✓			✓		✓		Attention	INFANTS
	✓				✓		Memory	INFANTS
					✓		Curiosity	INFANTS
					✓		Pleasure in learning	INFANTS
					✓		Motivation	INFANTS
						✓	Curiosity	PRESCHOOLERS
						✓	Concentration	PRESCHOOLERS
		✓			✓	✓	Memory	PRESCHOOLERS
						✓	Sense of humor	PRESCHOOLERS
				✓	✓	✓	Advanced language development	PRESCHOOLERS
		✓			✓		High frequency of questions	PRESCHOOLERS
				✓			Sensitivity to discrepancies	PRESCHOOLERS
				✓			Anticipation of future events	PRESCHOOLERS
				✓			Abstract thinking	PRESCHOOLERS
				✓			Perspective taking	PRESCHOOLERS
				✓			Original thinking	PRESCHOOLERS
				✓			Complex planning and execution	PRESCHOOLERS
				✓			Effective use of resources	PRESCHOOLERS
				✓			Concentration, information capacity	PRESCHOOLERS
					✓		Self-concept	PRESCHOOLERS
					✓		Socioemotional adjustment	PRESCHOOLERS
					✓		Motivation	PRESCHOOLERS
					✓		Persistence	PRESCHOOLERS
					✓		Task orientation	PRESCHOOLERS
					✓		Social knowledge	PRESCHOOLERS
				✓	✓		Interact with older children/adults	PRESCHOOLERS
				✓			Ability to express affection/annoyance	PRESCHOOLERS
				✓			Ability to express pride in accomplishments	PRESCHOOLERS
				✓			Ability to role-play and make-believe	PRESCHOOLERS
				✓			Ability to follow and lead comfortably	PRESCHOOLERS
				✓			Capacity and desire to compete	PRESCHOOLERS

developmental level to the next, as depicted in Table 1.1 by Lewis and Louis (1991, p. 367).

The contrast between infants and preschoolers is obvious and striking. As expected, the infants don't have the language mastery, higher level thinking skills, work habits, or social skills that can be found and measured in preschoolers. Inasmuch as IQ-type tests are heavily loaded with conceptual and language aptitudes, it is much easier to apply these kinds of measures to preschoolers than to infants. In fact, assessments of attention and memory in children under age two and one-half seem to be better clues to subsequent intellectual functioning than are scores on conventional IQ tests (Fagan & McGrath, 1981). These doubts about the predictive validity of ability measures appear to have been confirmed by results of a detailed longitudinal study on the prediction of IQ and language skills from various performance and psychosocial background factors, conducted by Bee et al. (1982) on a sample of 193 young children. Among the outcomes was the finding that scores on the Brazelton Neonatal Behavioral Assessment Scale, a measure of reflexive and psychomotor abilities in children under 24 months of age, were poor predictors of IQs obtained when the sample was 4 years old.

Considering the recent arousal of interest in the phenomena of *habituation* and *novelty preference* in infants as signs of precocity which can be recognized before age 2, it is worthwhile to take note of the evidence and of what these phenomena are specifically. Such insights may well constitute a kind of breakthrough in dipping successfully below any previously known period in a child's life when valid predictors of later giftedness seem to reveal themselves. Storfer (1990), Fisher (1990), and Lewis and Brooks-Gunn (1981) report studies to show that habituation behavior as early as age 2 months explains anywhere from 10% to 25% of the variance in tests of intelligence and/or language development administered between 3 and 8 years of age. Storfer (1990) also summarizes evidence showing that novelty preference scores on infants ages 6 and 7 months correlated anywhere from .37 to .57 with WISC-R vocabulary subtests and Peabody Picture Vocabulary Tests (PPVT) administered at 3 and 7 years of age. Nobody knows why these particular infant behaviors are so revealing, but the findings have been so consistent that they cannot be spurious or accidental.

Habituation, or decrement of attention, is usually assessed by the rate or amount of time an infant spends in looking at an object. Greater decrements, quicker decays, or relatively lesser amounts of cumulative looking time are generally interpreted as being more efficient styles of information processing. Response to novelty, or novelty preference, refers to recovery of attention and is measured by the excess amount of time that infants spend looking at novel, compared with familiar, stimuli. Obviously, neither of these infant behaviors per se involves reasoning skill, certainly not of the verbal-abstract kind assessed by IQ. Nor do they reflect gifted behavior of any sort, no matter how much meaning one tries to read into them. They are not driven by any theory of intelligence, just as IQ does not pretend to be; like IQ, they are simply practical devices that forecast particular competencies without explaining the connection between predictor and predicted. As long as one can be sure that, for example, IQ correlates with foreign language learning consistently at a .4+ level (Pimsleur, Mosberg, & Morrison, 1962), who cares whether the IQ test contains foreign language or offers hints as to what it takes to master foreign language? Similarly, if there is good reason to recognize *any* sign of precocity earlier than ever in a child's life, who cares how much face validity these symptoms have?

Indeed, it may be sensible to initiate measurement as early as possible in the hope that it can figure meaningfully in research on enriching mental development even among newly borns. Fisher (1990) refers to a series of longitudinal studies in progress by Catherine Tamis-LeMonda of New York University and by Marc Bernstein of the National Institutes of Child Health and Human Development, which suggest that babies who receive considerable stimulation from their mothers measure higher in cognitive abilities later. For example, 2-month-olds encouraged by their mothers to pay attention to the environment were more likely to explore objects and to vocalize, when not distressed, at age 5 months. It was also found that, even when the effects of the stimulation were factored out, habituation explained some of the variance in ability. Moreover, when combined, habituation and stimulation explained more of the variance than each separately.

Still, it is prudent to reserve judgment on the validity of infant measures until more data are analyzed for different populations with varied birth histories under contrasting experimental conditions. Even if the impressive evidence presented thus far eventually becomes indisputable, a question will remain as to whether these tests can predict subsequent giftedness as impressively as they correlate with IQ.

**Effects of Caretaker—Child Interaction
on Precocious Development**

Existing evidence seems to show that, before age 2, the frequency of *caretaker-initiated* linguistic teaching experiences is a strong predictor of preschool IQ. Afterwards, much depends on *interactive* language-mastery experiences, as well as those that are spatially and multisensorially oriented (Storfer, 1990). The chapters by Pnina

Klein and by Ellen Moss in this volume demonstrate the impact of mothers stimulating their young children's language mastery, reasoning and problem-solving skills, and spatial, perceptual, fine-motor, and expressive/artistic aptitudes. These reports are consistent with Carew's (1980) studies showing that as much as 55% of the variance in IQ at age 3 could be accounted for by earlier intellectual experiences *unilaterally* provided by other people. Thus, before age 2, the child simply looked and listened attentively as visual and auditory stimuli paraded by. The key influence was from language activity structured by an adult or initiated jointly by the adult and the child. On the other hand, no correlation was found between 3-year IQ and the incidence of intellectual experiences between 12 and 21 months of age when these were generated by the child during solitary play. But after age 2, the child could not benefit much from unilateral stimulation by the caretaker. Language experiences had to be interactive in order to produce meaningful results.

Not only do investments in enriching infants' and toddlers' cognitive skills affect IQs in normative preschool populations; they are also associated with the early histories of gifted adults as well as high-IQ and prodigious school-age children. In his study of 23 of the highest IQ subjects in Terman's population, Fowler (1983) discovered that the skill areas in which the children excelled most were linked to those stimulated most from early infancy to age 5. Others benefiting from intensive tutoring in the earliest years of life include such immortals as Francis Galton, Frank Lloyd Wright, Wolfgang Amadeus Mozart, and Yehudi Menuhin. In the aforementioned studies, much more is known about the *contents* of caretaker–child interaction than about the *dynamics*. Carew's (1980) research on some aspects of the nature of early stimulation is encouraging, so much so that it suggests the need to broaden the monitoring of ways in which mothers enrich their offspring's growth. Perhaps the insights already gained from the Ellen Moss and the Pnina Klein investigations, as reported in later chapters, provide a basis for longitudinal research on the consequences of various specific *strategies* used in teaching infants, toddlers, and preschoolers, which eventuate in gifted behavior, regardless of the *skills* being taught.

From existing evidence on caretaker influences, it should not be inferred that only some kind of instruction promotes cognitive growth. Mixed with the stimulation of learning is loving care, an important ingredient of parent–child interaction for most young children. Clarke-Stewart (1973) interviewed 36 mothers on the degree of acceptance and social stimulation they provided their children, ages 9 to 18 months. Results showed that the infant's cognitive, language, and social development related significantly to maternal care. Verbal stimulation from the mother had an especially strong effect on the offspring's ability to comprehend and express language. Also, a close relationship was noted between the complexity of infants' play and the amount of time the mothers spent playing with them and acting as mediators of the physical environment. Noteworthy, too, is the observation that the reciprocal mother–child influence on social interaction became evident in the course of the experiment. The more the child looked at the mother, approached and vocalized to her, or shared objects with her, the more affectionate and attached the mother became. This maternal responsiveness to social signals from infants probably enhances their later intellectual and social performance.

The Clark-Stewart findings seem to have been generally confirmed in a population of gifted adults, judging from Sloane's (1985) study of home influences of children who grew up to excel individually as Olympic swimmers, world-class tennis players, concert pianists, sculptors, research mathematicians, and research neurologists. These subjects were interviewed in their mid-30s and asked to recall the nature and extent of parental encouragement to fulfill their early promise. Generally, the respondents described a nurturing, challenging home environment. Parents wanted them to be involved in learning activities as often as possible, to do their best, to make productive use of time, and to measure up to high standards of performance. Homework was checked regularly at home, and children quickly learned the family's code that work had to be finished before play could be started. Little time was allowed for idling, as parents arranged for a steady stream of constructive activities for their children. In the early years of the children's talent development, parents introduced them to their respective talent fields. Often, older siblings or relatives, as well as parents, taught the children informal lessons in these disciplines, but at a later stage of development, special instructors were brought in to raise the challenges to new heights. Later still, the parents' own direct roles in the children's lessons and practice disappeared entirely as the outside tutors took complete charge. These tutors were carefully selected to provide often costly services at advanced levels.

A cautionary note: it would be simplistic to assume that behind *every* great person there is a loving, culturally rich family background. True, evidence shows that renowned historical figures usually enjoyed a supportive upbringing. For example, McCurdy (1959) examined the childhood home life of 27 geniuses selected from Cox's (1926) list and found that 20 of them received a considerable amount of affection and intellectual stimulation from their parents, whereas only 3 suffered comparative neglect or abuse. On the other hand, in their study of over 300 famous men and women, Goertzel, Goertzel, and Goertzel (1978) cite case after case of great people whose childhoods were agonizing and who came from troubled homes where the mothers were either "smothering" or domineering, and the fathers were failure-prone. In these households, the offspring strove for excellence possibly as a sign of protest against parental overindulgence or oppression. Therefore, whatever seems *logically* essential in childrearing practices for the nurturance of giftedness sometimes fails to be confirmed *empirically*.

The inconsistency of the picture suggests that perhaps there are no generalizations, except that much depends on the special chemistry between person and parent. For one child, a particular nurturance at home may inspire creative work; for another child, the same parental influence may have an adverse affect, or none at all. This would imply a need to determine what kinds of home environments and childhood individualities constitute the best matches in fostering extraordinary potential in children.

All in all, giftedness develops through an array of uniquely exquisite efforts by a caretaker who cares for the child's special qualities and who takes wise steps to accelerate their ripening. Whereas most precocious young children require lovingkindness and skillfully supportive stimulation in order to encourage peak performance, a few react most productively to strict parenting and pressure to progress. Nobody knows what kinds of personality respond best to what kinds of upbringing. But one fact is self-evident: The relationship between nature and nurture is interdependent. Children with superior inner resources can fulfill their promise only if the nurturance they receive is "tailor-made" to meet their special needs; but without the requisite inner resources in a child, no amount (or type) of nurturance can make the difference between mediocrity and excellence.

FINAL THOUGHTS

Despite a fast-growing stockpile of research on giftedness in children—the September 1990 issue of the *Journal of Educational Psychology* devotes a large section to the subject, possibly for the first time in this publication's long history—little attention has been directed to the gifted among infants, toddlers, and preschoolers. What emerges more clearly than anything else from the limited *existing* evidence is knowledge about what constitutes an optimal environment for learning in the first years of life. There is less information on how to assess high potential in early childhood.

Lagging farthest behind are clues to what constitutes giftedness, especially in preverbal stages of development. But enough is known from the relatively few recorded studies to suggest that precocity may already exist in children almost as soon as they are born, and that they probably can specialize in particular skill domains even before they are of age to enter the first grade. Only longitudinal research would make it possible to determine the staying power of early signs of excellence, provided that the caretaking practices could also be enriched and monitored systematically.

From what is known thus far about the importance of cognitive stimulation in the first stages of life, it is reasonable to hypothesize that optimal benefits can be gained if it varies according to children's individual strengths. This makes sense, not only for prodigies, whose specializations are obvious and who receive support and training to hone their unique skills; it probably applies also to children whose high potentialities are less obvious and who excel, for example, in moral and social domains, which are usually not represented by prodigious feats. These talents have already been sighted in the few attempts made so far to search for them. Golda Rothman's chapter in this volume reveals the existence of exceptional moral sensitivity even among preschoolers. An investigation by Abroms and Gollin (1980) of high social intelligence among preschoolers shows that prosocial behavior is measurable in children as young as age 34 months. Furthermore, IQ at the upper extreme of the normal range seems to be associated with different types and intensities of social activity. For example, Wright (1990) observed that, among 3-, 4-, and 5-year-olds with mean IQs of 148, subjects in the upper ranges (i.e., median IQ of 160 +) engaged in dramatic play for 70% of the free-play period, as compared to only 53% by a subsample in the lower ranges (i.e., median IQ of 137). Of course, replications and elaborations of such studies have to be conducted before iron-clad inferences can be drawn.

In conclusion, giftedness in young children is a treasure waiting to be fully uncovered. The probes made thus far promise an abundance of riches, if more efforts are invested in this enterprise. One can only hope that past probers will usher in future uncoverers, because the prizes which still lie hidden may well prove to be priceless.

REFERENCES

Abroms, K. I., & Gollin, J. B. (1980). Developmental study of gifted preschool children and measures of psychosocial giftedness. *Exceptional Children, 46,* 334–343.

Arnheim, R. (1972). *Toward a psychology of art: Collected essays.* Berkeley, CA: University of California Press.

Bamberger, J. (1986). Cognitive issues in the development of musically gifted children. In R. J. Sternberg & J. E. Davidson (Eds.), *Conceptions of giftedness* (pp. 338–413). Cambridge, UK: Cambridge University Press.

Bayley, N. (1955). On the growth of intelligence. *American Psychologist, 10,* 805–818.

Bee, H. L., Barnard, K. E., Eyres, S. J., Gray, C. A., Hammond, M. A., Spietz, A. L., Snyder, C., & Clark, B. (1982). Prediction of IQ and language skill from perinatal status, child performance, family characteristics and mother-infant interaction. *Child Development, 53,* 1134–1156.

Bensusan, R. (1976). *Early prodigious achievement: A study of cognitive development.* Unpublished master's thesis, Tufts University, Medford, MA.

Bloom, B. (1964). *Stability and change in human characteristics.* New York: John Wiley.

Burks, B. S., Jensen, D. W., & Terman, L. M. (1930). *The promise of youth. Follow-up studies of a thousand gifted children.* Palo Alto, CA: Stanford University Press.

Carew, J. V. (1980). Experience and the development of intelligence in young children at home and in day care. *Monographs of the Society for Research in Child Development, 45* (Nos. 6–7), 1–89.

Carter, K., & Ormrod, J. (1982). Acquisition of formal operations by intellectually gifted children. *Gifted Child Quarterly, 26*(3), 110–115.

Clarke-Stewart, K. A. (1973). Interactions between mothers and their young children. *Monographs of the Society for Research in Child Development, 38,* 1–109.

Cox, C. M. (1926). *The early mental traits of three hundred geniuses.* Palo Alto, CA: Stanford University Press.

De Angelis, T. (1990, November). Gifted children artists may yield development clues. *Monitor,* p. 30.

Fagan, J. F., & Mc Grath, S. K. (1981). Infant recognition memory and later intelligence. *Intelligence, 5* (2), 121–130.

Feldman, D. H. (1980). *Beyond universals in cognitive development.* Norwood, NJ: Ablex Publishing Corp.

Feldman, D. H. (1986). *Nature's gambit.* New York: Basic Books.

Feuerstein, R. (1979). *The dynamic assessment of retarded performers.* Baltimore, MD: University Park Press.

Fisher, K. (1990, April). Interaction with infants is linked to later abilities. *Monitor,* p. 10.

Fowler, W. (1983). *Potentials of childhood* (2 vols.). Lexington, MA: Lexington Books.

Freeman, J. (Ed.). (1985). *The psychology of gifted children: Perspectives on development and education.* New York: Wiley.

Goertzel, M. G., Goertzel, V., & Goertzel, T. G. (1978). *300 eminent personalities.* San Francisco: Jossey-Bass Publishers.

Gould, S. J. (1981). *The mismeasure of man.* New York: Norton.

Guilford, A. M., Scheuerle, J., & Shonburn, S. (1981). Aspects of language development in the gifted. *Gifted Child Quarterly, 25,* 159–163.

Guilford, J. P. (1967). *The nature of human intelligence.* New York: McGraw-Hill.

Hofstaetter, P. R. (1954). The changing composition of "intelligence": A study of t technique. *Journal of Genetic Psychology, 85,* 159–164.

Hollingworth, L. S. (1942). *Children above 180 IQ.* New York: World Book.

Honzick, M. P., Mac Farlane, J., & Allen, L. (1948). The stability of mental test performance between two and eighteen years. *Journal of Experimental Education, 4,* 309–324.

Hughes, H. H., & Converse, H. D. (1962). Characteristics of the gifted: A case for a sequel to Terman's study. *Exceptional Children, 29,* 179–183.

Jackson, N. E. (1978, August). *Identification and description of intellectual precocity in young children.* Paper presented at the annual convention of the American Psychological Association, Toronto.

Kagan, J. (1976). Emergent themes in human development. *American Scientist, 64,* 186–196.

Kaufman, A. S. (1968). *A child's IQ: How it relates to a child's performance on the perceptions of a conservation of mass experiment* [Mimeo]. New York: Teachers College, Columbia University.

Kaufman, A. S. (1971). Piaget and Gesell: A psychometric analysis of tests built from their tasks. *Child Development, 42,* 1341–1360.

Keating, D. P. (1975). Precocious cognitive development at the level of formal operations. *Child Development, 45,* 276–280.

Kitano, M., & Kirby, D. (1986). *Gifted education: A comprehensive view.* Boston: Little, Brown.

Knobloch, H., & Pasamanick, B. (1963). Predicting intellectual potential in infancy. *American Journal of Diseases of Children, 106,* 43–51.

Lewis, M. (1975). The development of attention and perception in the infant and young child. In W. M. Cruickshank & D. P. Hallahan (Eds.), *Perception and learning disabilities in children* (Vol. 2, pp. 137–162). New York: The Syracuse University Press.

Lewis, M., & Brooks-Gunn, J. (1981). Visual attention at three months as a predictor of cognitive functioning at two years of age. *Intelligence, 5*(2), 131–140.

Lewis, M., & Louis, B. (1991). Young gifted children. In N. Colangelo & G. A. Davis (Eds.), *Handbook of gifted education* (pp. 365–381). Boston: Allyn & Bacon.

Lewis, M., & Michalson, L. (1985). The gifted infant. In J. Freeman (Ed.), *The psychology of gifted children* (pp. 35–57). New York: John Wiley.

Mc Curdy, H. C. (1959). The childhood patterns of genius. *Smithsonian report for 1958.* Washington, DC: The Smithsonian Institution.

Montour, K. (1976). Three precocious boys: What happened to them? *Gifted Child Quarterly, 20,* 173–179.

Montour, K. (1977). William James Sidis, the broken twig. *American Psychologist, 32,* 265–279.

Moore, C., Nelson-Piercy, C., Abel, M., & Frye, D. (1984). Precocious conservation in context: The solution of quantity tasks by nonquantitative strategies. *Journal of Experimental Child Psychology, 38,* 1–6.

Oden, M. H. (1968). The fulfillment of promise: 40-year follow-up of the Terman gifted group. *Genetic Psychology Monographs, 77,* 3–93.

Pendarvis, E. D., Howley, A. A., & Howley, C. B. (1990). *The abilities of gifted children.* Englewood Cliffs, NJ: Prentice-Hall.

Pimsleur, P., Mosberg, L., & Morrison, A. V. (1962). Student factors in foreign language learning: A review of the literature. *Modern Language Journal, 46,* 160–170.

Radford, J. (1990). *Child prodigies and exceptional early achievers.* New York: The Free Press.

Roedell, W. C., Jackson, N. E., & Robinson, H. B. (1980). *Gifted young children.* New York: Teachers College Press.

Sears, P. S. (1979). The Terman studies of genius, 1922–1972. In A. H. Passow (Ed.), *The gifted and the talented: Their education and development* (The 78th Yearbook of the National Society for the Study of Education, pp. 75–96). Chicago: University of Chicago Press.

Sears, P. S., & Barbee, A. H. (1977). Career and life satisfaction among Terman's gifted women. In J. S. Stanley, W. C. George, & C. H. Solano (Eds.), *The gifted and the creative: A fifty-year perspective* (pp. 28–65). Baltimore: Johns Hopkins University Press.

Sears, R. R. (1977). Sources of life satisfactions of the Terman gifted men. *American Psychologist, 32,* 119–128.

Sloane, K. D. (1985). Home influences on talent development. In B. S. Bloom (Ed.), *Developing talent in young people* (pp. 439–476). New York: Ballantine.

Smolak, L. (1982). Cognitive precursors of receptive vs. expressive language. *Journal of Child Language, 9,* 13–22.

Sternberg, R. (1985). *Beyond IQ: A triarchic theory of human intelligence.* Cambridge, UK: Cambridge University Press.

Storfer, M. D. (1990). *Intelligence and giftedness.* San Francisco: Jossey-Bass.

Terman, L. M., & Oden, M. H. (1925). *Mental and physical traits of a thousand gifted children.* Palo Alto, CA: Stanford University Press.

Terman, L. M., & Oden, M. H. (1947). *The gifted child grows up.* Palo Alto, CA: Stanford University Press.

Terman, L. M., & Oden, M. H. (1959). *The gifted group at midlife.* Palo Alto, CA: Stanford University Press.

Tuddenham, R. D. (1971). Theoretical regularities and individual idiosyncrasies. In D. R. Green, M. P. Ford, & G. B. Flamer (Eds.), *Measurement and Piaget* (Chap. 4). New York: McGraw-Hill.

Whipple, G. M. (1924). Historical and introductory. In G. M. Whipple (Ed.), *The education of gifted children* (Twenty-third Yearbook of the National Society for the Study of Education, pp. 1–24). Bloomington, IL: Public School Publishing Co.

White, B. (1985). Competence and giftedness. In J. Freeman (Ed.), *The psychology of gifted children* (pp. 59–73). New York: John Wiley.

Willerman, L., & Fiedler, M. F. (1977). Intellectually precocious preschool children: Early development and later intellectual accomplishments. *The Journal of Genetic Psychology, 131*, 13–20.

Wright, L. (1990). The social and nonsocial behaviors of precocious preschoolers during free play. *Roeper Review, 12*, 268–274.

Zigler, E., & Trickett, P. K. (1978). IQ, social consequence, and evaluation of early childhood intervention programs. *American Psychologist, 33*, 789–796.

chapter 2

Creative Giftedness in Children

Robert J. Sternberg
Todd I. Lubart*

*Department of Psychology
Yale University
New Haven, CT*

It was time to select children for the gifted program in the Maplevale Elementary School. Jack Dumfrey, the gifted coordinator, sighed and took out his tape measure, as he had every year for the past 20 years. He lined up the children at each grade level, measured their height, and then chose for the gifted program the children who scored in the top 5% of their grade in terms of height. Another year's selection process was thus completed.

No one reading this story is likely to believe it. Of course, it is apocryphal. But a main thesis of this chapter is that the primary basis we now use for selection of children for gifted programs— conventional intelligence tests—are not a whole lot more valid than the tape measure for identifying gifted children. And in terms of test-retest reliability, of course, they are worse.

Use of height as a measure to assess giftedness is not a wholly

* Preparation of this chapter was supported by a grant from the McDonnell Foundation. Requests for reprints should be addressed to Robert J. Sternberg, Department of Psychology, Yale University, Box 11A Yale Station, New Haven, CT 06520.

invalid procedure. The Terman study of the gifted found that gifted children do tend to be a bit taller, on the average, than are nongifted children (Terman & Oden, 1959). And the conventional wisdom is that people who are taller are more likely to be promoted up the ranks in the organizational ladder in later life, giving height a bit of predictive value for practical as well as academic success. Yet people are likely to be reluctant to use height as a predictor of gifted performance, because its predictive value is presumably too weak.

This reluctance leads us to question why people would be a whole lot happier using IQ. If IQ predicts only 4% of the variance in measures of occupational success (Wigdor & Garner, 1982), or even if it predicts two or three times that variance, can we feel confident making decisions on the basis of such data? And we need to remember that the small percentage of variance accounted for is at a group level. Much weaker prediction can be expected at the level of the individual.

It is important to distinguish between reproductive giftedness of the kind sometimes seen in children and productive or more creative giftedness. A child may play the piano or violin with excellent technical proficiency, but such proficiency is not tantamount to creativity. Some child prodigies excel through rote repetition rather than creative contribution. Perhaps it is for this reason that Torrance (1984) has stressed the importance of assessing creativity in identifying gifted youngsters.

Recognizing the weakness of identification models based wholly on intelligence, a number of investigators have suggested considering creativity as well as intelligence (as conventionally defined) in assessing giftedness (see, e.g., Feldhusen, 1986; Renzulli, 1986; and other chapters in Sternberg & Davidson, 1986). But those who have suggested that creativity be used in identifying the gifted have often been no more specific in specifying just what creativity is than have users of the intelligence criterion in specifying what intelligence is.

Using creativity as a criterion for identifying gifted children makes good sense. If we consider later, adult contributions to the world that lead individuals to be labeled as gifted, they are more likely to be creative contributions than contributions of sheer intelligence. Indeed, it is easy to think of almost countless individuals in a variety of fields who have left their mark on the world because of their creativity, but how many can one think of whose mark has depended on their sheer intelligence of the kind measured on IQ tests? The high-IQ people without high creativity seem as adults to blend into the woodwork, at least with respect to making lasting contributions. The high-creatives are much less likely to disappear.

We believe there are two reasons why creativity has received much less attention than intelligence in the identification of the gifted. First, intelligence is easier to measure than creativity. But many theorists of intelligence now believe that the intelligence we measure through conventional tests is just a small portion of what intelligence is all about (e.g., Feuerstein, 1979; Gardner, 1983; Sternberg, 1985; Vygotsky, 1978), just as the creativity measured by conventional creativity tests is probably only a small part of what creativity is all about (Amabile, 1983; see also essays in Sternberg, 1988). In recent work on intelligence, we have sought to suggest how conceptions of intelligence might be broadened so as better to identify giftedness broadly (e.g., Sternberg, 1986). In this chapter, we seek to suggest a conception of creativity that is broader than typical conceptions and that may help us better identify the creatively gifted. By broadening our conceptions of constructs relevant for giftedness, we have a chance of going beyond narrowly valid measures—including height—in the identification of the gifted.

Our conception of giftedness differs from many conventional ones in three key ways. First, we go beyond the cognitive in including both personality and motivational aspects of the psyche as integral parts of giftedness. Second, we go beyond the individual in suggesting that a major determinant of whether a child is labeled gifted does not depend on the child at all, but rather upon the environment in which the child develops and is evaluated. Giftedness lies in part in the environment, not in the person. And it lies especially in the interaction of person with environment. Third, our model is neither a strictly additive one nor a multiple-threshold one: Rather, it is an interactive one. A strictly additive model is one in which scores on a set of measures are added up (perhaps in weighted fashion), and if their sum is high enough, a person is labeled as gifted. A multiple-threshold model is one in which an individual must score above a certain level on each of a set of measures to be designated as gifted. An example of a multiple-threshold model is Renzulli's (1986), in which above-average ability, high motivation, and high creativity are all necessary for identification. In our model, the variables interact complexly, making it difficult to predict at an individual level whether a particular combination of the six facets of the model will generate gifted performance. Yet higher values on more facets are likely to be associated with greater probabilities of gifted performance.

The six facets of our model are aspects of intellectual processes, knowledge, intellectual style, personality, motivation, and context. We will describe each of these facets in turn.

INTELLECTUAL PROCESSES

When one of us was in Israel recently, he was eating dinner with three college professors at an outdoor restaurant in Jaffa. As the group was eating, a scruffy, dirty beggar started walking toward the dining table. Three of the professors began inching their hands toward their pockets. Perhaps they didn't want to be ripped off, or perhaps they were getting some change ready to give to the beggar. The fourth individual got up from the table, ostensibly to go to the men's room but actually to avoid a confrontation with the beggar. The beggar proved to be more clever than the college professors. With all four pairs of hands removed from the table, and one individual on the way to the men's room, the beggar had no trouble scooping the food off the absent individual's plate and returning to his haven across the street, where he proceeded to consume his newly acquired meal.

Problem Definition and Redefinition

Creatively gifted individuals are able to see problems in ways that others do not see those problems. The beggar taught us that lesson. We defined the situation of his approach in a conventional way: He didn't. Indeed, his plan depended on our traditional definition of the age-old problem of what to do when beggars approach. He needed our hands out of the way when he went to scoop up the food off the plate.

The ability of an individual to redefine problems in novel but ingenious ways is frequently manifested in the production of creative individuals. In psychology, for example, the "greats" such as Sigmund Freud, Jean Piaget, B. F. Skinner, and Herbert Simon have in common their reconceptualization of problems in ways that led them each to create a new paradigm that others then followed. In the case of Freud it was psychoanalysis; for Piaget it was genetic epistemology; for Skinner, radical behaviorism; and for Simon, information processing. Frank Lloyd Wright has written that his creative contributions to architecture started forming when, as a child, he played with blocks. None of these individuals was solely responsible for any of these paradigms. As Isaac Newton observed, we render our creative contributions by standing on the shoulders of giants. But each individual took an important set of ideas and empirical findings and showed how they could be interpreted in a way that defied the conventional one. They didn't so much solve problems as redefine them. Of course, the importance of problem redefinition isn't limited to psychology. Great artists such as Picasso, writers such as Hugo, politicians such as Jefferson, and musicians such as Mozart have in common that they redefined a field on their own terms, and were followed by others.

We concur with Arlin (1990) and Getzels and Csikszentmihalyi (1976) in believing that problem finding is an ability qualitatively different from problem solving. Perhaps oddly, one of the greatest problem finders of all, Herbert Simon, does not believe that the two abilities differ in kind (Langley, Simon, Bradshaw, & Zytkow, 1986).

Insight

Creatively gifted people tend to be far more insightful than the typical individual. Our account of insight draws on the theory of Davidson and Sternberg (Davidson, 1986; Sternberg & Davidson, 1982). According to this theory, insights are of three basic kinds.

Insights of selective encoding. A selective-encoding insight involves the noticing of potentially relevant information for the understanding or solution of a problem from amidst a stream of information. It involves separating the wheat from the chaff in a series of observations. The data analyst with a pound of computer output has an opportunity to exercise selective encoding: Most of the information in the output is probably irrelevant to the computer user's purposes in doing the data analysis.

We also use selective encoding in having insights about people. For example, in one of our experiments, we studied social intelligence abilities (Sternberg & Smith, 1985). Subjects were shown pictures of heterosexual couples, half of which depicted couples in a genuine close relationship, and the other half of which depicted subjects who did not know each other who were asked to pose as though they were in a romantic relationship. The subjects' task was to ascertain which couples were real, and which were false. Subjects needed to figure out the body-language cues that would distinguish the real from the fake couples, such as body lean, eye gaze, degree of apparent relaxation, and the like.

A number of creative discoveries by gifted scientists were critically dependent on insights of selective encoding. Penicillin was discovered when Sir Alexander Fleming noticed that a mold in a spoiled petri dish had killed the bacteria in the dish. Archimedes figured out how to determine the volume of an irregular object by noticing that bath water was displaced by a certain amount when he entered the bath. Selective encoding insights apply as well in a field as different from science as art. Rembrandt is known for his extraordinary observation of light, and Rubens for his extraordinary noticing of the sensuality of the bodies of the women he painted.

Insights of selective combination. A second kind of insight is an insight of selective combination. Extraordinary selective combiners are able to put together facts or ideas among which other people do not see a connection. For example, an insightful doctor needs to be able to figure out how to fit together a pattern of symptoms into a diagnosis. An insightful lawyer needs to figure out how to combine a set of facts so as to build a coherent case that supports her client. Charles Darwin's formulation of the theory of evolution emerged in part because Darwin was able to put together pieces of information he observed during his journey to the Galapagos Islands. Selective-combination ability is especially essential in mathematics. Often, the number of possible postulates and theorems upon which to base the proof of a new theorem is fairly limited. What is difficult is figuring out how to string the postulates and theorems together, as in a proof in plane geometry.

Insights of selective comparison. The third kind of insight is an insight of selective comparison. Extraordinary selective comparers are able to relate new information to old information in ways other people don't see: They are unusually good analogizers. For example, the atom as discovered by Niels Bohr was based on a model of a miniature universe. In psychology, we have proceeded through a series of models of the mind—hydraulic system, telephone system, and most recently, computer system. None of these models is perfect. Indeed, analogies are imprecise by their very nature. The idea is to facilitate understanding, not to obtain complete understanding, through a model analogue. A psychotherapist uses selective comparison when he or she has an insight about a patient that depends on his or her seeing an analogy to a patient whom he or she has treated before. A detective has a selective-comparison insight when he or she recognizes how the clues at the scene of a particular crime are reminiscent of those at another crime he or she has solved in the past. In the mystery literature, Sherlock Holmes was the master selective comparer, seeing relations between new and past information that would have eluded almost anyone else.

To summarize, creatively gifted people excel in problem redefinition, selective encoding, selective combination, and selective comparison. In Sternberg's (1985) triarchic theory of human intelligence, the redefinition of problems is a metacomponent, or executive process used in planning for problem solving. The selective operations are all knowledge-acquisition components, or ways of gleaning new information. The metacomponents and the knowledge-acquisition components operate interactively. In other words, the metacomponents, including problem definition and redefinition, control the knowledge-acquisition components, which in turn provide feedback to the metacomponents. The selective operations are not always applied in insightful ways. What renders their use insightful is the recognition of information that is veridical (given the present state of knowledge) and that others would not see.

KNOWLEDGE

A second element of creative giftedness is knowledge. There is now an enormous literature suggesting that experts in a field differ from novices largely in their knowing much more about the field than do the novices (see Chi, Glaser, & Farr, 1988; Lesgold, 1988). Chi and Koeske (1983) found that child experts in memory for dinosaurs drew on extensive knowledge bases about these animals. In order to be genuinely creative in a field, you need to know a lot about the field, if only because, without such knowledge, it is difficult and sometimes impossible to be on the cutting edge of the field: The ignorant risk rediscovering the wheel.

Although knowledge may be necessary for expertise, it is far from sufficient for expertise, and especially for creative expertise. One could know a lot about a field, but not know how to use that information. Or one could know a lot about a field, but not be able to extend what is known in that field. In our opinion, the role of knowledge in expertise has been overstated, because world-renowned experts are not just people who have a lot of knowledge about a field, but rather are people who have made creative contributions to their field. And they may not even be the people who have read the most about it. B. F. Skinner (cited in Greissman, 1988) has described himself as not very well read in psychology, believing that reading too much can interfere with one's having original ideas. Others in psychology have commented that, among scholars, there are the readers and there are the producers, and that it is difficult to be among both.

The suggestion among these individuals is that knowledge can be a double-edged sword. On the one hand, it is necessary to go beyond where a given field is. On the other hand, it can interfere with one's ability to see things in new ways and to have new ideas. The cost of knowledge may be reduced flexibility (Sternberg & Frensch, 1989; Sternberg & Lubart, 1991).

Frensch and Sternberg (1989) actually studied this hypothesis as it applies to expert and novice bridge players. Experts and novices were given bridge-related tasks that were either true to the game of bridge or else induced surface-structural or deep-structural manipulations of the game. The surface-structural manipulations were minor, involving merely a one-to-one relation between the standard task and the new one. They merely changed the names of the suits (clubs, diamonds, hearts, and spades to neologisms) or the order in which the suits were ranked. The deep-structural change was more complex and affected the essential structure of the game. In bridge, it is customary in each round of play for the player who wins the trick (puts down the highest card) to lead off the subsequent trick. This rule of the game provides a basis for bridge-playing strategy. In the deep structurally changed condition, the player putting down the lowest ranked card led bidding in the subsequent round. In other words, the procedure was essentially the opposite of that of the normal bridge game. As expected, they found that experts were substantially more affected by the deep-structural change than were novices, whereas they were not more affected by the surface-structural change. In other words, experts seem to lose flexibility primarily as a result of fundamental changes in the structure of what they are doing. Experts, it appears, need to find in their careers ways of counteracting the effects of entrenchment. It is important to note that, in the Frensch-Sternberg study, the experts recovered after some time. In other words, although they were initially more hurt than the novices by the deep-structural change, they were eventually able to deal effectively with it, once they reintegrated their deep-structural representation of the game.

We believe that in most areas of creative endeavor, the creatively gifted are contrarian: They work against the conventional wisdom and knowledge base. To some extent, this view may be self-evident, as creativity requires novelty of contribution, which by definition is not what other people are contributing. Yet we have noted what we believe to be an interesting paradox. Virtually every scientist we know, especially in our own field of psychology, accepts Kuhn's (1970) theory of the structure of scientific revolutions. In other words, they believe that the truly great contributors to any given field are those who set rather than those who follow existing paradigms. Yet it is the rare scientist who is not threatened by the purveyor of a new paradigm, and, most of the time, we go out of our way to defend our own preferred paradigm against interlopers. There are few scientists who take to heart Popper's (1959) admonition that we should seek to refute rather than to confirm our scientific theories. Whether or not they wish to admit it, refutation of their theories is the last thing most scientists want.

The role of knowledge and contrarianism in creative performance can be clearly illustrated in the field of stock-market investing. In general, those who do the best are, to greater or lesser degree, contrarian—they go against the prevailing trends in the market. But in order to go against the market, they have to know where the market is. The reason that contrarians often do better in investing is that, if everyone else is buying a stock and you buy it too, then the price of the stock has already been bid up by the fact that everyone else is buying it. The way to make money is to buy the stock that other people are not buying, when it's low, and then to sell it when others have followed you and bid the price up to being high. In all domains of creative work, one is not likely to be perceived as highly creative if one is following the pack. Instead, one needs to lead it.

INTELLECTUAL STYLES

An intellectual style is a propensity for using one's abilities in a certain way. It is not the ability itself. Thus, the ability to redefine a problem is a matter of cognitive processing, but the desire to redefine a problem is a matter of intellectual style.

Sternberg (1988) has presented a theory of intellectual styles based upon a notion of mental self-government. The basic idea is that people use their intellectual processes by governing themselves. The principles by which people govern their thinking are analogous to the principles by which governments govern collectivities. Indeed, it is argued that governmental forms may be a reflection of alternative forms of mental self-government.

One aspect of government is its function. Historically, we tend to think of governments as serving three different functions—the legislative, the executive, and the judicial. The legislative function is concerned with the formulation of laws, the executive with the implementation of laws, and the judicial with the evaluation of laws and how well they are followed. Sternberg (1988) argues that these three functions also need to be served at a mental level.

The legislative function involves creation, formulation, and planning of ideas, strategies, products, and the like. A person with a legislative style enjoys doing activities requiring these functions. Such individuals tend to gravitate naturally toward such activities. They like to create their own rules, they enjoy doing things their own way, and they prefer problems that are not prestructured or prefabricated. They like activities that involve constructive planning, such as, perhaps, writing original papers, designing projects, creating new business or educational systems, and designing software.

The executive function involves carrying out the plans formulated by the legislative function. Individuals with an executive style tend to be implementers. They like to follow rules, and to figure out which already existing ways they should do things; they prefer problems that are prestructured or prefabricated, and they prefer to work within a given structure. People with an executive style are likely to enjoy crossword puzzles, solving algebra-word problems, or solving other kinds of problems in which the structure is already given. They are likely to choose occupations in which they follow the lead of others.

The judicial function involves activities of judging. People with a judicial style like to evaluate rules and procedures, to judge existing structures, to analyze people, and often like activities such as writing critiques, giving opinions, and evaluating programs. It is usually easy to spot people with a judicial style because they feel so free to give their opinions on things, often without much regard to their knowledge about the things they are judging.

We would argue that creatively gifted people are likely to prefer a legislative style. Of course, no one follows exclusively one style or another, and to some extent, the style that a person exhibits will be situational. But we are suggesting that creatively gifted people will seek out situations that enable them to use their preferred legislative style. Some people may seek out such situations only within a narrow range of endeavors, perhaps those in which they have exhibited their most creative behavior in the past. Others may be broader in the range of legislative situations they seek out. But without a legislative style, a person will not find himself or herself in situations where creativity is even possible.

It is important to realize that a legislative style does not guarantee excellent creative information processing, and vice versa. In other words, someone may like to create, but not have the cognitive abilities that render his or her creations novel or important; at the same time, someone else may have such abilities, but not enjoy creating. Some third person may have both the abilities and the style, but not have sufficient knowledge about a domain in order to advance it. Our point, quite simply, is that creativity often represents a confluence of the elements of the model. Without at least some measure of each element, it is difficult to be creative. Compensation for lack of elements is probably possible, but only if at least some minimal amount of each of the elements exists.

Another distinction in the theory of intellectual styles is between global and local modes of processing, corresponding to different levels of government such as the federal and the local. Significant creative giftedness requires at least some desire to process information at a global level. Without such a desire, the individual is likely to lose the forest for the trees. It is easy to get lost in detail, but detail can distract one from large issues. At the same time, dealing only with large issues can leave one lost in the clouds. Thus, some grounding is necessary in order to keep one's grander ideas in touch with reality.

Although we believe that the creatively gifted will prefer legislative and global styles, we do not believe that these are styles that are particularly encouraged in schooling, including most programs for the gifted. To the contrary, in most schooling, the teacher specifies what the student is to do, and the student is expected to do it. The student with an executive style is thereby rewarded, whereas the student with a legislative style is not. Moreover, the level of most assignments certainly tends more to the local than to the global. Gifted programs that stress acceleration (see, e.g., Stanley & Benbow, 1986) are no different from regular school curricula, except for being faster paced. Thus, they too benefit the executive local thinker more than the legislative global one. Enrichment programs vary, although those using models such as the Renzulli (1977) triad model encourage more legislative and global expression of style. In this model, the third leg of the triad allows students to design and implement their own projects, with only minimal supervision by a teacher of the gifted. But our experience is that classes for the gifted often tend to be glorified versions of regular curricula rather than fundamentally different curricula that prepare students for creative endeavor. It is no surprise to us, therefore, that students in accelerated programs such as Stanley's do not, in fact, tend to become creative mathematicians or scientists. Their knowledge may be accelerated beyond that of typical students in mathematics or science, but they are being socialized by a curricular process that requires thinking of quite a different sort from that found in math or science.

Particularly disturbing to us is the fact that, not only schools, but the standardized tests used in schools also, favor the executive and local styles almost exclusively. Students receive prestructured problems, and must answer them in a way that corresponds to the structure that the test constructor imposes. The questions, of course, tend to deal with local rather than global levels of processing. Thus, schooling and standardized testing are mutually reinforcing, probably identifying the same people as gifted, but not necessarily those people who would most benefit from instruction for the gifted, and who will stand to make the greatest contributions to society later on. If each assessment is biased in roughly the same way, then the assessments will be mutually reinforcing, and what is interpreted as convergent validity for the same conclusion may be convergent validity for the same wrong conclusion. It is not that we are "against" executive or local or any other styles. Rather, we believe these styles are already highly rewarded, to the exclusion of other styles that, in the long run, may result in greater creativity.

PERSONALITY

There have been various studies of the personalities of creatively gifted individuals (see Barron & Harrington, 1981), and a constellation of personality attributes are often correlated with creative accomplishments. We believe that, in order for creative giftedness to manifest itself, certain aspects of personality play every bit as important a role as aspects of cognitive functioning.

One personality attribute that is consensually agreed upon as important to creative giftedness is tolerance of ambiguity. In many creative enterprises, there is a time during which one is groping for the correct, or at least a highly creative, solution to a problem. But the solution does not always come right away. More often than not, it is elusive, with the result that some "incubation period" is needed in order for the ideas to work themselves out fully (Kaplan & Davidson, 1988). But this period of incubation is likely to be one of emotional discomfort. The thinker worries that perhaps the idea will never come, or that it will not be the correct idea, or that even if it does come it will be too late. As a result, the individual is likely to pressure herself to close on the problem—to generate a solution so that the problem is made a thing of the past. But often the solution that comes early is a satisficing rather than an optimal one (Simon, 1957): It may be good enough to satisfy the constraints of a problem, but no better than that. Thus, in order to produce one's best work, it is necessary to tolerate ambiguity. For the child in school, tolerating ambiguity means not accepting his or her first impulse as necessarily the one to follow. The first idea for a drawing or a book report or a science project or whatever may not be the best idea, and the child needs to learn to wait to make sure that the idea that is pursued is the best of which the child is capable at the time.

A second relevant personality attribute is at least moderate risk taking, which McClelland (1955) links to high achievement motivation. In order to do creative work, an individual must be willing to take risks, if only because creativity by its very nature requires going against an established grain. But children are not always willing to take risks. In fact, Phillips (1984) has found that gifted children, and especially girls, are often likely to be risk-averse. And the research of Dweck and Elliott (1983) suggests that children who have an "entity" conception of intelligence—who believe that intelligence is a stable trait with which one is born and that is manifest through performance—are likely to be risk-averse because they believe that poor performance, even during learning, will be interpreted as failure. Indeed, the educational system today places so much emphasis on good grades that it is scarcely surprising that children become risk-averse, unwilling to take the chance of a low grade appearing on their transcript. Unfortunately, their risk aversion in this case may be sensible, because of the ways grades are used to make decisions. Thus, our institutionalized systems of reward and punishment may discourage children from trying out new things, including ones in which they would discover themselves to be talented.

A third relevant personality attribute is willingness to surmount obstacles. Creative people will almost always encounter obstacles to the display of their creativity. Such obstacles come with the turf when one is challenging existing viewpoints. But it is often hard to be thick-skinned in the face of criticism, particularly for a child who is criticized by a parent or a teacher. Is it any wonder that schools can be so effective at undermining creativity? They are at least as likely to set up roadblocks to the display of creativity as they are to encourage it. And standardized tests, of course, are the same way. There one gets no chance to argue for one's preferred answer or mode of responding. If an answer is incongruent with the test constructor's, one simply loses credit. Biographies of creative individuals virtually always show them to have confronted stumbling blocks in their careers, sometimes blocks that at the time seemed impossible. But the individual who is determined to be creative eventually find ways around these stumbling blocks, although not necessarily right away.

A fourth relevant personality attribute is a willingness to grow. Adults and even children occasionally get rewarded for a creative idea—often only after they have gone to great lengths to get recognition for this idea. Once an idea is rewarded, a natural process of inertia seems to set in. Why take the risk of losing what status one has gained through that idea? Why risk the next idea being a bad idea? Indeed, by regression effects alone, the chances are good that the next idea will not be quite as good as the first really good one. So it is easy to become complacent, and to stabilize or even stagnate in a single position. Perhaps this is why so many people's "creative" careers consist of just a single creative idea. But children and adults who value creativity for its own sake, and not just for the extrinsic rewards it brings, will not be satisfied with one creative idea, but rather will want to have others as well. They will therefore have to be willing to grow, in some cases admitting their old ideas are incomplete or even wrong.

Finally, creative people need some degree of self-esteem. They have to believe in themselves and at least to some extent in their ideas. This belief does not require that they think their ideas are correct or immutable. Rather, they have to believe the ideas are worthy of expression and an attentive audience. In the face of criticism, sometimes there is little but self-esteem to get one through.

To summarize, we suggest that there are personality prerequisites to the manifestation of creativity. Someone may have all the cognitive prerequisites of creativity and yet almost never manifest creative performance, because he or she is unwilling to take risks, lacks self-esteem, or whatever. Personality is as integral to creative giftedness as is any cognitive attribute. Unfortunately, it is rarely measured, even when creativity is measured through testing (e.g., by the Torrance, 1966, tests). But we are not so concerned with whether there are formal measures of these attributes as we are concerned that the attributes conducive to creativity are nurtured in individuals. We believe that these attributes are largely the result of the reinforcement system in the environment. Hence, those involved in education need to be concerned that they create an environment where a child can take risks without punishment, can reflect on whether an initial idea is the best of which he or she is capable, and so on. Personality traits are not immutable: Rather, we can shape the environment to favor various traits. We should be shaping the environment to favor personality traits conducive to, not antithetical to, creativity.

MOTIVATION

Like Renzulli (1986), Feldhusen (1986), and others, we believe motivation to be an essential element of creative giftedness. We believe that four kinds of motivation lie behind the outstanding achievements of gifted individuals.

First is intrinsic motivation. Intrinsic motivation involves the pursuit of something for its own sake and for the sake of the enjoyment it gives to the pursuer, rather than for the sake of external rewards. Amabile (1983) has found that intrinsic motivation is common in creative individuals. Indeed, it is difficult to make a really great contribution to any realm of endeavor if one does not genuinely enjoy what one is doing. Oddly enough, society seems not to recognize this fact. Extrinsic rewards of many kinds are common, and their use risks undermining intrinsic motivation. The very designation of a child as "gifted," and the placement of the child in a gifted program, is an example of an extrinsic motivator. These days, parents and their children are so concerned about placement in a gifted program that they may easily lose sight of why it is that the program might be worthwhile in the first place. The placement, rather than the performance, can become paramount in people's minds. And children not so placed can come to think of themselves as wash-outs, or at least as "nongifted." There is a danger, of course, that the prophecy will become self-fulfilling.

A second kind of motivation that we believe is an underpinning to creative giftedness is effectance motivation (White, 1959), or the desire to achieve competence. This kind of motivation need not be generalized. To the contrary, it may be in just a single field of endeavor. This fact, of course, presents a problem for so-called tests of motivation: The high level of motivation found in the gifted may only be with respect to a limited domain. Without a desire to be very good, or even the best, it is difficult to attain the kind of success in one's endeavors that is likely to lead one to be labeled as "gifted."

A third kind of motivation is achievement motivation (McClelland, Atkinson, Clark, & Lowell, 1953). Whereas competence motivation refers to one's desire to be good at something, achievement motivation refers to one's doing something about it—achieving in the domain in which one has striven for competence.

Finally, gifted children are motivated to seek out novelty (Berg & Sternberg, 1985). They are not satisfied with the way things are, or with boredom. They don't wait for novel stimuli to come to them: They actively seek out such stimuli. They are shapers of the environment (Sternberg, 1985), and in shaping the environment, they often create their own novelties.

In sum, we argue that creative giftedness has a conative as well as a cognitive and an affective aspect. There are probably many children who will be labeled as *gifted* without the motivational backing, because of the way identification today is done. One need not be highly motivated to achieve high test scores, or even fairly good grades in school. But the academically successful children of today are not necessarily the creatively gifted adults of tomorrow. Unless they are motivated in the ways we have discussed above, their last outstanding performance may be their test scores or their grades in school.

ENVIRONMENTAL CONTEXT

Giftedness is not solely a property of a person: It is in part an interaction between a person and his or her environment. The very person who would show up as gifted in one environment might appear quite ordinary in another environment. Thus, in order fully to understand creative giftedness, one needs to understand environmental effects. We believe that the environment is relevant to giftedness in three ways.

First is the issue of whether the environment stimulates creativity. In some of the classrooms we have observed, one can almost feel sparks flying. Ideas are batted around, and one idea leads to another. Unfortunately, such classrooms seem to be the exception rather than the rule. Most classrooms, including classrooms for the gifted, involve a didactic presentation of dry and fairly isolated facts, the importance of which is never made clear to the students. The result is that students come to think of education as the accumulation of facts, most of which will eventually be forgotten in any case. The idea then becomes that the gifted learn the facts faster, or remember them better.

A second important aspect of the environment is in the reward system for creative ideas. Creativity can be encouraged, but, as often as not, it is discouraged, because teachers find it disrupts the plan they have for their class period. Even we, in teaching, find it difficult to reward creative insights when they get us away from a plan we may have had in mind—despite our knowing that rewarding creativity is one of the best ways of generating more of it.

Finally, the environment is important in what it evaluates as creative. The same idea that may be perceived as creative in one environment may be perceived as dull in a different environment. As a result, it is essential that gifted individuals, to the extent possible, select environments that reward the particular kind of giftedness that they display. For example, a creatively gifted child will not necessarily shine in a gifted class that emphasizes acceleration. Nor is he or she likely to excel in a class that essentially is a glorified version of a regular classroom with brighter students in it.

In sum, we need to provide environments that help stimulate

creative ideas, that encourage such ideas when they are presented, and that reward a broad range of creative behavior. Such environments are often difficult to create, because they are so different from what we now have in most classrooms. But without such environments, we will continue to produce children who may be smart, but who are not particularly creative. Moreover, we will continue to select students on the basis of skills among which creativity does not play a part. We believe the future contributions to humankind are most likely to be made by the creatively gifted, and hence we believe society should do what it can to foster this aspect of giftedness.

REFERENCES

Amabile, T. M. (1983). *The social psychology of creativity.* New York: Springer-Verlag.

Arlin, P. K. (1990). Wisdom: The art of problem finding. In R. J. Sternberg (Ed.), *Wisdom: Its nature, origins, and development* (pp. 230–243). New York: Cambridge University Press.

Barron, F., & Harrington, D. (1981). Creativity, intelligence, and personality. In M. R. Rosenzweig & L. W. Porter (Eds.), *Annual review of psychology* (Vol. 32, pp. 439–476). Palo Alto, CA: Annual Reviews.

Berg, C. A., & Sternberg, R. J. (1985). Response to novelty: Continuity versus discontinuity in the developmental course of intelligence. In H. Reese (Ed.), *Advances in child development and behavior* (Vol. 19, pp. 2–47). New York: Academic Press.

Chi, M. T. H., Glaser, R., & Farr, M. (1988). *The nature of expertise.* Hillsdale, NJ: Erlbaum.

Chi, M. T. H., & Koeske, R. D. (1983). Network representations of a child's dinosaur knowledge. *Developmental Psychology, 19,* 29–39.

Davidson, J. E. (1986). The role of insight in giftedness. In R. J. Sternberg & J. E. Davidson (Eds.), *Conceptions of giftedness* (pp. 201–222). New York: Cambridge University Press.

Dweck, C. S., & Elliott, E. S. (1983). Achievement motivation. In P. H. Mussen (Series Ed.) & E. Mavis Hetherington (Vol. Ed.), *Handbook of child psychology* (Vol. 4, 4th ed., pp. 643–691). New York: Wiley.

Feldhusen, J. F. (1986). A conception of giftedness. In R. J. Sternberg & J. E. Davidson (Eds.), *Conceptions of giftedness* (pp. 112–127). New York: Cambridge University Press.

Feuerstein, R. (1979). *The dynamic assessment of retarded performers: The learning potential assessment device, theory, instruments, and techniques.* Baltimore, MD: University Park Press.

Frensch, P. A., & Sternberg, R. J. (1989). Expertise and intelligent thinking: When is it worse to know better? In R. J. Sternberg (Ed.), *Ad vances in the psychology of human intelligence* (Vol. 5, pp. 157–188). Hillsdale, NJ: Erlbaum.

Gardner, H. (1983). *Frames of mind: The theory of multiple intelligences.* New York: Basic Books.

Getzels, J., & Csikszentmihalyi, M. (1976). *The creative vision: A longitudinal study of problem-finding in art.* New York: Wiley-Interscience.

Greissman, B. E. (1988). *The achievement factors.* New York: Dodd, Mead, & Company.

Kaplan, C. A., & Davidson, J. E. (1988). *Incubation effects in problem solving.* Manuscript submitted for publication.

Kuhn, T. (1970). *The structure of scientific revolutions* (2nd ed.). Chicago: University of Chicago Press.

Langley, P., Simon, H. A., Bradshaw, G. L., & Zytkow, J. (1986). *Scientific discovery: Computational explorations of the creative processes.* Cambridge, MA: MIT Press.

Lesgold, A. (1988). Problem solving. In R. J. Sternberg & E. E. Smith (Eds.), *The psychology of human thought* (pp. 188–213). New York: Cambridge University Press.

McClelland, D. C. (1955). Some social consequences of achievement motivation. In M. R. Jones (Ed.), *Nebraska Symposium on Motivation: 1955.* Lincoln: University of Nebraska Press.

McClelland, D. C., Atkinson, J. W., Clark, R. W., & Lowell, E. L. (1953). *The achievement motive.* New York: Appleton-Century-Crofts.

Phillips, D. A. (1984). The illusion of incompetence among academically competent children. *Child Development, 55,* 2000–2016.

Popper, K. R. (1959). *The logic of scientific discovery.* London: Hutchinson.

Renzulli, J. S. (1977). *The enrichment triad model: A guide for developing defensible programs for the gifted and talented.* Mansfield Center, CT: Creative Learning Press.

Renzulli, J. S. (1986). The three ring conception of giftedness: A developmental model for creative productivity. In R. J. Sternberg & J. E. Davidson (Eds.), *Conceptions of giftedness* (pp. 53–92). New York: Cambridge University Press.

Simon, H. A. (1957). *Administrative behavior* (2nd ed.). Totowa, NJ: Littlefield, Adams.

Stanley, J. C., & Benbow, C. P. (1986). Youths who reason exceptionally well mathematically. In R. J. Sternberg & J. E. Davidson (Eds.), *Conceptions of giftedness* (pp. 361–387). New York: Cambridge University Press.

Sternberg, R. J. (1985). *Beyond IQ: A triarchic theory of human intelligence.* New York: Cambridge University Press.

Sternberg, R. J. (1986). A triarchic theory of intellectual giftedness. In R. J. Sternberg & J. E. Davidson (Eds.), *Conceptions of giftedness* (pp. 223–243). New York: Cambridge University Press.

Sternberg, R. J. (1988). Mental self-government: A theory of intellectual styles and their development. *Human Development, 31,* 197–224.

Sternberg, R. J., & Davidson, J. E. (1982). The mind of the puzzler. *Psychology Today, 16,* 37–44.

Sternberg, R. J., & Davidson, J. E. (Eds.). (1986). *Conceptions of giftedness.* New York: Cambridge University Press.

Sternberg, R. J., & Frensch, P. A. (1989). A balance-level theory of intelligent thinking. *Zeitschrift fur Padagogische Psychologie* [German *Journal of Educational Psychology*], *3,* 79–96.

Sternberg, R. J., & Lubart, T. I. (1991). An investment theory of creativity and its development. *Human Development, 34,* 1–31.

Sternberg, R. J., & Smith, C. (1985). Social intelligence and decoding skills in nonverbal communication. *Social Cognition, 2,* 168–192.

Terman, L. M., & Oden, M. H. (1959). *Genetic studies of genius. Vol. 4: The gifted group at midlife.* Palo Alto, CA: Stanford University Press.

Torrance, E. P. (1966). *Tests of creative thinking.* Lexington, MA: Personnel Press.

Torrance, E. P. (1984). Sounds and images productions of elementary school pupils as predictors of the creative achievements of young adults. *Creative Child and Adult Quarterly, 7,* 8–14.

Vygotsky, L. S. (1978). *Mind in society: The development of higher psychological processes.* Cambridge, MA: Harvard University Press.

White, R. (1959). Motivation reconsidered: The concept of competence. *Psychological Review, 66,* 297–323.

Wigdor, A. K., & Garner, W. R. (Eds.). (1982). *Ability testing: Uses, consequences, and controversies.* Washington, DC: National Academy Press.

chapter 3

Cultural Constraints on Cognitive Enrichment

Karsten Hundeide

University of Bergen
Bergen, Norway

Through efforts at developing and implementing Western-based programs of early enrichment and intervention[1], I have been forced to reconsider certain general issues related to intervention in indigenous child-rearing practices. These issues will be dealt with in this chapter.

---

[1] For the last five years, I have been involved in developing a program of early intervention which should be flexible and adaptable enough to be applicable in a variety of cultural settings. I ended up with Pnina Klein's MISC program which is different from most other programs in the field in the sense that it focuses on promoting certain "mediational" aspects of the caregiver–child interaction which we assume are universal conditions for optimal development (Bronfenbrenner, 1979; Feuerstein, 1980; Klein, 1988). This means that we are working inside the existing patterns of interaction between caregiver and child, the indigenous child-rearing practice. It is therefore more like a *method of sensitizing or raising the caregiver's consciousness for the reciprocal and mediational qualities in the interaction between caregiver and child* that we believe are important for the child's development. In this respect, the program is different (although not in conflict) from most other programs which usually tend to focus on activities and toys adjusted to the child's developmental stage (Klein & Hundeide, 1989).

THE MEANING OF PARENTAL ACTIONS
TOWARDS THE CHILD

The general point of this section is that it is not possible to assess the meaning and the effect of isolated actions towards children without taking into account the tacit background of established cultural practices and contracts of interaction between caregiver and child. In other words, *what is communicated between a caregiver and a child through actions or words can only be understood against the background of what is habitually taken for granted in the relationship between the two* (Rommetveit, 1974). For example, punishment by spanking is not necessarily interpreted by the child as rejection and hostility, quite on the contrary; it may be taken as a sign of concern and inclusion into the local moral order that applies within an authoritarian family or community context.

This point was illustrated rather dramatically in research by Dornbush and his co-workers (Dornbush et al., 1987). Within Western societies, *authoritative* parental styles have for some time been known to have superior developmental effects compared with *permissive* and *authoritarian* styles (Baumrind, 1971). These findings were accepted as universally valid, until Dornbush published his studies on academic careers of students of different ethnic origins. He showed that authoritative parenting styles had the expected positive effects on white students, while it had negative effects on Asian students and no effect on black students. In other words, *the "same" socializing practice seemed to have different meaning and effects on different ethnic groups.* When Chinese-American students were asked what they thought about their parents' authoritarian parenting style, they replied, with a smile: "That is how we know our parents love us" (Bronfenbrenner, 1989). What was taken by Western students as a sign of hostility and rejection was seen as an indication of acceptance and concern by their Asian colleagues.

In order to interpret these unexpected findings, I employ the term "contract," as it is used within communicative psychology to describe the tacit agreements which regulate the form, content, and meaning of interaction taking place within a relationship (Blakar, 1984; Hundeide, 1989; Rommetveit, 1974). In a caregiver–child relationship, there is always a "tacit contract" specifying the form, content, and meaning of the relationship between the two, and such contracts may vary between different cultures.

As a consequence, the meaning communicated to a child by the caregiver's actions depends upon the nature of this interactive contract. Thus, the same external action (e.g., correcting the child in an authoritarian manner) may communicate different meanings and have different effects depending upon the nature of the contract. At the same time, different actions may produce similar effects.

In the case of a relationship between caregiver and child based on an authoritarian contract, where both respect and loyalty are taken for granted it may be quite inappropriate to intervene into such a subtle contractual relationship by suggesting, for example, that more praise should be given. Most probably such a suggestion would be discordant with the style of a contractual relationship founded on unilateral respect. Moreover, it is quite possible that "praise" is already being given, but in a manner that is much more subtle than what we are used to, by an approving look, a smile, or simply by the fact that the child is allowed to progress further and try new and more difficult tasks within the same field. *It is the meaning that the child reads into the caregiver's reactions, or lack of reactions, that counts,* and this is part of a subtle expression and contractual relationship between the two, being partly cultural and partly ideosyncratic.

Furthermore, if we encourage a traditional mother to "mediate competence" to a child by giving praise for actions that both child and mother take for granted as obvious duties of the child, it is quite likely that the act of praising may lose its meaning and effect. That is to say, for praise to have any meaning, it has to be given when tasks which are considered special are performed. If praise is given to tasks already accepted as obvious duties, such as washing dishes, it may in fact communicate the opposite message: that a domestic chore is special, rather than an obvious duty, and that it should not at all be taken for granted. Maybe this explains LeVine's puzzle about the effectiveness of taking duties for granted by not giving praise (see below and also Lepper, Greene, & Nisbett, 1973).

In more general terms, we may say that in order to be able to intervene in a predictable way into the relationship between caregiver and child, we need to know about the cultural meaning system implicitly expressed in such contractual relationships and interactive practices at different age levels within that particular culture (Smedslund, 1984).

WHAT IS METACOMMUNICATED DURING AN EDUCATIONAL INTERVENTION?

In addition to the specific meanings "read into" caregivers' actions (e.g., praising or punishing), on another level there is also a metacommunication taking place during the interaction. In the case of

an educational intervention aiming at raising the caregivers' awareness of certain qualities which, ideally, should be present in the
interaction between caregiver and child (Klein & Feuerstein, 1985),
most participants will also relate to certain "metaquestions" such as
the following:

> Why am I here? What is the objective of this episode? What kind of
> "scene" is this? What is my role? What kind of knowledge is this? To
> which domain does it belong? Why have I been elected? How will this
> influence my relationship to others who are not included? (Hundeide,
> 1989)

The questions may vary, but they are generally a result of *the need to
create an interpretive framework which makes sense of the interactive event in accordance with the participant's own background.*
In everyday interaction such "metaframes" tend to be taken for
granted, and consequently, we easily ignore the interpretive metaproblems of the participants when we intervene into a cultural
context not sharing our assumptions for didactic interactions.

These interpretive metaproblems were clearly demonstrated when
an early intervention program (MISC Program, see Klein, 1985) was
implemented among illiterate mothers in poor rural and urban areas in Java. The mothers were taught the basics of mediational
interaction with their children by paraprofessional resource persons
in the local community. Through their reports and through interviews with the mothers, it was possible to get an impression of the
mothers' conception of the messages and the intervention which
had taken place (Braaten, 1989). First of all, it appeared that the
content of the program tended to be categorized as belonging to the
"modern" domain of activities and contents. This is a clearly prestigious category separating the progressive and modern from the
old-fashioned and traditional. Secondly, the participants characterized themselves as "children of x-university," another prestigious
marker of inclusion into a society of people with far higher social
status than they could ever hope to achieve. Thirdly, the content of
the program and the way it was communicated was interpreted by
some of the women as conveying esoteric knowledge for selected
initiates—in line with Javanese mystical tradition.

All these markers, linked to participation in the program, showed
the need to clarify what was happening by creating an interpretive
framework in line with their own cultural background. At the same
time, this framing also gave them a feeling of prestige and social
status, which again created a strong commitment to and enthusi-

asm for the program: *not only did they learn something about mediational interaction in relation to their children, but more important, they were admitted into a prestigious society of initiates, sharing "modern" and esoteric knowledge of child rearing, which gave them a new status and a new perception of themselves in relation to their own community.*

It is quite possible that the most important effect of this program was connected with the indirect effect of *identifying with those who, in their view,* typically represent this type of knowledge.

This point is very important and may explain some other side effects of educational interventions, such as the quite astonishing side effects of acquiring literacy in a largely illiterate society. According to recent studies, female literacy is "the single most important factor in reducing child deaths" (Vittachi, 1989). Furthermore, it also seems to have side effects on family planning, improved nutrition, general health, and a more active orientation toward life. Why then should becoming literate have these additional effects? *Above and beyond simply learning to read, these women seemed to learn something about empowerment: The new identity generally associated with "being literate" is also associated with a conception that life can be improved through a more active and controlled lifestyle. This is "metaknowledge" of paramount significance for their lives. To these women literacy was the key to a new and more self-asserting identity.*

However, acquiring a new competence may also be associated with an identity which represents a threat and an obstacle to learning. According to Goodnow (1990), Australian aboriginal children, when learning English, progress well up to a certain point; it then seems as if they regress and start unlearning their previous language skills. Closer analysis showed that to these children, as well as to their parents, becoming competent in English symbolized "becoming white"—*by becoming fluent English speakers they are transgressing the border into "enemy identity," and this is counteracted by unlearning their previous language skills. In other words, learning was in this case subordinated to the maintenance of an ethnic identity, and when this was threatened, learning had to be sacrificed.*

The so-called "creole effect" among black English speakers seems to be of a similar nature, a marker of ethnic identity in an otherwise fluent black English speaker. Also, general learning problems among ethnic minorities can be interpreted as either symptoms of problems in understanding the "ground rules of interaction" (Mercer & Edwards, 1981), or the new skills may be interpreted as transgression into enemy identity; their newly acquired skills are conceived of as threatening their established ethnic identity and lifestyle (Labov, 1972).

Some immigrants to Norway seem to have language acquistion problems of a similar nature, but in this case it is not only their identity that is being threatened, rather, the threat is one of not being able to "go home." It seems that for some of these immigrants, learning Norwegian symbolizes "giving up going home," resigning the fight to go back to their native country; as a consequence they resist learning Norwegian.

In more general terms, learning or educational intervention always forms part of a "cultural package" (see Berger, Berger, & Kellner, 1973) with metamessages referring to identity, social status, domain of knowledge, style of interaction, and so on. In order to understand the effect and significance of any educational intervention, one has to take these metaaspects into account. It is quite likely that what is metacommunicated may, in fact, have an even stronger impact; precisely because of its tacit nature, it cannot be counteracted. This is, of course, particularly important when operating in a non-Western culture.

THE PROBLEM OF INFLUENCING DEEP-ROOTED CULTURAL CHILD-REARING PRACTICES AND INSTITUTIONALIZED CURRICULA OF DEVELOPMENT THAT MAY BE INCONGRUENT WITH WESTERN CONCEPTIONS AND PRACTICES

As implied in the previous paragraphs, child rearing is not only an individual skill or competence, it is part of a collective, cultural expressive pattern that has its historical roots and functional basis in a way of life that is reflective of both the system of maintenance, social distribution of work within that ecology, and the cultural image of ideal human qualities within that society (Barry, Child, & Bacon 1959; Whiting & Whiting, 1975).

Behind the individual mother there is the more or less tacit *cultural curriculum or agenda of child development* that is sometimes institutionalized in initiation ceremonies to the various stages of development. Such ceremonies signal and inform parents (and children) as to which qualities and competences can be expected from the child at any stage of development (Geertz, 1959). The child's development has to fit into these culturally constructed tracks of development, irrespective of "talent."

Hence, from the point of view of cultural developmental psychology, human development is not merely an individual epigenetic process, but also a cultural and collective one. Both the tracks of development, the way "persons" are constructed within a culture, and not least the "naive theories" of how children should be socialized in order to become such "persons" or "ideal children" are part of wider cultural and historical processes, beyond the particular parent–child dyad (Goodnow, 1984; Schweder & Bourne, 1985; Vygotsky, 1978).

An example from my own research in a slum area in Jakarta may illustrate this point. I interviewed 25 families on their conceptions of child rearing and their image of the ideal child. When asked the question "What in your opinion is the most important thing that parents should remember when they bring up their children?" they all pointed to the importance of promoting certain moral qualities in the children, such as obedience, loyalty, respecting and helping their parents, good behavior, and so on—all clearly moral values. In fact, traditional families are more concerned with morals than with the acceleration of cognitive development (Kagan & Madsen, 1971).

When the same questions were asked of middle-class mothers in Oslo, Norway, the replies were quite different. Rather than indicating certain desirable moral qualities, the individuality of the child was emphasized, together with the importance of an open, reciprocal relationship and the need for the mother to adjust her child rearing to the signals and the nature of the child. The only moral quality to be mentioned was independence. There was no mention of obedience or good behavior (Hundeide, 1988). Such replies are typical and they have been replicated by many researchers within cross-cultural developmental psychology (LeVine & White, 1985; Werner, 1980).

According to some anthropologists, this is more than a casual finding. It seems to reflect two different ways of life with their ensuing different strategies or institutions for survival and social organization; that is, the traditional agrarian society on the one hand, and the modernistic urban society on the other (Inkles & Smith, 1974; LeVine & White, 1985).

This point is exemplified in a comparative study of the value of children (Fawcett, 1983). When asked about the advantages of having children in an interview, the economic value of children in rural agrarian societies was strongly confirmed. In rural areas in the Philippines, 70 percent of the parents gave economic reasons, while only 3 percent gave such reasons in urban Tokyo or in the United States.

In the traditional agrarian society with domestic food production and filial loyalty between family members and the clan, child rearing tends to be stricter and more authoritarian. There is little time for individual involvement with each child, and, in fact, much of the child rearing is done by older siblings. The child is taken for granted as a member of the family team, serving economical functions from an early age—obedience is an important quality in this context. (See LeVine, 1988 on the Gusi tribe in Kenya, and Ochs & Schiefflin, 1985, on the Kaluli tribe living in the tropical forest of Papua New Guinea.)[2]

The urban industralized society, with its emphasis on individual achievement, independence, and competitive coping skills especially regarded in education as the key to upward mobility, presents a clear contrast to this. Here, child rearing tends to be more permissive and interactive—accepting the child as a partner to play with, to explore with, and to mediate to. This corresponds to the development of an obedient and loyal child versus an independent, inquisitive child.

The Use of Praise

Another interesting difference between traditional and modernistic child rearing is the use of praise as a means of reinforcement of children's appropriate behavior. LeVine (1977) found that parents in African and other non-Western cultures seldom use praise, *rather, appropriate behavior is expected and taken for granted.* Par-

---

[2] Still, the form the reciprocity may take can vary, as LeVine pointed out in the study of the Gusi tribe in Kenya. The mother seldom interacted with the infant face-to-face, never looked at it, and never talked to it, but she would respond at once to crying and there was a lot of holding and body contact. In this community the average number of children per family was 10, and it is quite possible that the mother needed to detach herself from getting too emotionally involved with each child in order to cope with her total situation.

A similar defensive detachment reaction is also reported by Scheper-Hughes (1985). She found that under conditions of extreme poverty and high child mortality, mothers tend to neglect passive and nondemanding babies, even though these "character traits" are usual signs of chronic malnutrition. The women in the shanty towns explained that some of the babies lacked a strong will to live, and they felt that "it is best if the weak and disabled die as infant . . . without a prolonged and wasted struggle." So it seems that early bonding carries different meanings to poor mothers in shanty towns and to middle-class mothers. (From P. K. Block's book, *Rethinking Psychological Anthropology.* New York: Freeman and Company, 1988.)

ents respond only when this expectation is violated. In other words, they punish bad behavior, but do not reward good deeds. LeVine is so impressed by how well these procedures seem to work that "one begins to wonder if our own use of praise as a reinforcer is entirely superfluous."

According to LeVine, Western child rearing by "reinforcement-through-praise" does not seem to increase the likelihood of appropriate behavior from the child; rather, it increases the likelihood of *attention-seeking behavior*, which can be said to be found most typically among urban Western children. Maybe this is another aspect of self-centered individualism?

Most programs of cognitive enrichment seem to be based on, or at least congruent with, this individualistic and achievement-oriented conception of the child associated with Western school systems and an urban-industrial way of life (Berger, Berger, & Kellner, 1973; Berry & Annis, 1974; Werner, 1979). By the same token, they are incongruent with the traditional conception of the obedient, loyal child still dominant in most Third World countries. In fact, in many agrarian societies, competition and individualistic display of excellence is discouraged and avoided, as it is considered disloyal and out of place. Loyalty to family and group is considered more important than personal achievement (LeVine & White, 1986; Werner, 1979).

Assuming that we decide to implement a program of early intervention or cognitive enrichment in a traditional community, what would be the impact?

What would be the effect of trying to impose programs fostering independence of mind, an inquiring attitude, and individual achievement orientation in a society dominated by traditional conceptions of unilateral respect and obedience?

Is it possible to be both obedient and loyal, and at the same time cognitively independent, achievement-oriented, inquiring, and analytic? Or is an obedient, loyal orientation more akin to what Witkin describes as a "field dependent," nonanalytic, and global orientation (Witkin & Berry, 1975)?

It is quite possible that we can succeed in changing some of the traditional child-rearing practices, which do not seem to be productive according to a Western conception of development, on a short-term basis. However, the question remains whether we are able to *sustain* these practices in cases where they are out of touch with traditional practices, with the conceptions of the ideal child, the support of the family, the values of society, and the contingencies or functions that sustain such practices.

HOW RELEVANT IS THE CONCEPTION OF INTELLIGENCE IMPLICIT IN OUR PROGRAMS OF COGNITIVE ENRICHMENT TO THE PROBLEMS AND CHALLENGES THAT DISADVANTAGED CHILDREN IN THE THIRD WORLD FACE IN THEIR EVERYDAY LIFE?

In many traditional societies, the Western separation between morality and intelligence does not exist; to be intelligent also includes being moral (LeVine & White, 1986). While it is quite normal in the West to be considered highly intelligent, and at the same time deeply immoral, this is sometimes described as "cleverness" in traditional societies and has clearly negative connotations.

Within traditional societies, to be intelligent means to act in accordance with the moral code of the community. This is also very much in keeping with the agrarian code of maintaining social security through good social relationships. In other words, to be moral in the conventional sense also has an adaptive significance within that society. Those in the community most respected for their moral behavior are also credited with being the wisest and most intelligent (LeVine & White, 1986).

In line with this moral definition of intelligence, there is also a stronger emphasis on social, as opposed to technological, aspects of intelligence in traditional agrarian communities. In a comparative study between the Ivory Coast and Switzerland, where participants were requested to give their spontaneous definitions of intelligence, a much stronger emphasis on social and collective aspects was found in the African sample. In their concept of n'glouele, they included qualities such as willingness to do chores for the family, respect for the elders, and wisdom. In the Swiss population, technological aspects dominated, including qualities like speed of attention and observation, speed of learning, and school intelligence (Schurmans, Dasen, & Vouilloz, 1989).

Another line of research relevant to the question of different conceptions of intelligence is related to what Margaret Donaldson (1977) describes as a "decontexualized" conception of intelligence; where it is seen as an "operative structure" that can carry out deductive operations on problems completely detached from everyday life[3]. When intelligence is being defined in this logical-deductive

---

[3] I would interpret "decontexualized" to mean: contexualized for the narrow Western academic audience and discourses, that researchers take for granted.

way, it is very much out of tune with the spirit of traditional peoples without Western schooling. For them, problems are part of everyday reality, and problem solving means efficient ways for solving everyday problems, evaluated by practical standards from everyday life (Cole & Scribner, 1975; Levy-Strauss, 1978).

Michael Cole (Cole & Scribner, 1975) gives many examples of this from his studies in Liberia. In one of the sorting tasks he presented to the villagers, the correct solution was to produce an abstract, superordinate classification. However, when the villagers were asked "How would a wise man do it?" they invariably came up with functional solutions. (Axe and wood belong together because they are part of the same action of cutting wood.) After having tried various ways, he finally decided to ask "How would a fool do it?" Then the superordinate solution was produced! Conceptions of wisdom and stupidity do not always coincide.

One of the problems which children from traditional communities face when confronted with Western schooling is that of understanding the "framing" or "definition of the problem" and the tacit cultural contracts of interaction applying to typical test situations. They tend to use a practical everyday frame of reference, producing solutions that are considered as failures, because the deductive logical frame of reference, which is the key to relevant definitions of school problems, is not naturally within their conceptual repertoire. They can, however, easily learn it (Greenfield, 1966; Mercer & Edwards, 1981; see also above). Our question is this: How relevant is our conception of deductive-analytic intelligence to the pragmatic challenges of their everyday life at the subsistence level?

I would like in this connection to mention some examples from the slum children I was involved with in Jakarta. Most of them were illiterate, either orphans or abandoned. They survived through begging, shoe-shining, or by helping to carry packages in the supermarket. These children were socially very sensitive and skilled, even manipulative, in their relationship to customers. They had great imitative and role-playing skills and were more than willing to put on an act, appearing as a beggar with a compassionate appeal. Similarly, they were knowledgeable with regard to social hierarchies of power and kinship in their society. They need to know who their friends and their enemies are, who is in power in which domain, and how to appeal to them in order to be accepted. In their world, this is basic survival knowledge, but it is also a social skill.

What these children seemed to be lacking were skills needed for being able to plan ahead for the future, goal directedness, and deductive-analytic reasoning, but the question is whether such knowledge would have been of much use for them within their present existence.

They seemed to live in the present—from moment to moment without planning for the future. Although their spatial skills seemed to be normal, both their imaginative capacity, their world views, and verbal knowledge of their surroundings seemed limited. This was in clear contrast to their practical manipulative and social control of their environment, which was highly developed.

When these children were asked questions like "Who decides whether a road is going to be built here in Simpruk?" quite a few of them answered "God." In fact, God was the key solution to most causal questions of a general nature, whether they were about causes for rain and sunshine or causes for poverty and wealth.

In many ways these children are similar to Feuerstein's description of culturally deprived children, but, taking into account the conditions under which they lived and the alternatives that were available to them, it is not so obvious that reflectivity, planning, and future orientation would be particularly useful for them. These children live in a unique cognitive "world" and they seem to have developed those aspects of intelligence relevant for social survival within this world. I suppose this is the nature of intelligent adaptation.

If we were going to intervene with an enrichment program à la Feuerstein (1980), I suppose we ought to try *and create conditions in their way of life so that the newly acquired cognitive skills could be of use in relation to their future lives.* If we do not change their life conditions, I am afraid cognitive alienation would be the outcome—they would acquire mental tools for which there was no constructive use. In other words, *a program of cognitive enrichment corresponds to a social reality where the skills that are acquired in the program should have a functional meaning.* This is an important consideration in connection with cognitive enrichment.

DEVELOPMENT IS CLOSELY CONNECTED WITH THE SOCIAL DISTRIBUTION OF IDENTITIES AND LIFE CAREERS, AND RELEVANT EDUCATIONAL INTERVENTION HAS TO TAKE REALISTIC LIFE CAREERS INTO ACCOUNT

If we look at cognitive enrichment intervention from a more long-term and pragmatic perspective, I suppose our aim must be to change destinies. We would like children to get out of the cycle of poverty, failure, or drug addiction. Seen from this pragmatic perspective, our problem is not necessarily how to make children more intelligent and knowledgeable per se, or according to Western standards, but rather, to help them to find the "openings" that are available in their own socioecology, and to create suitable conditions that would enable the children to pass through these openings. Which possible life careers can be projected into the future from the position where the child is now? Which skills are required to qualify for the better options? What kind of person can he or she become, what kind of job could he or she possibly get, and which qualifications will be needed for that job?

From a sociological point of view, there are tracks of development or life careers (Berger & Luckman, 1967; Kohli, 1989) varying from one society to another. We have to map out these paths of development within each community and identify those that may be suitable and congruent with a person's "opportunity situation" (Barth, 1966) in order to produce a sociopsychologically relevant program for the person in question.

As an example, in the slum mentioned above, there was a pattern of life careers where there were certain critical choice points with decisive implications for later possibilities. If a boy at the age of seven started to work as a shoe-shine boy, with his own personal enterprise, he was already more or less outside the established society. For this reason he usually ended up inside the slum as a garbage worker, a bicycle-taxi peddler, or as a beggar, as there were no developmental lines or openings into the established society.

If, on the other hand, he chose to become a "market boy," carrying packages for ladies shopping in the supermarket, he became "peripherally involved as a participant in a community of practice" (Lave, 1989). This qualified him informally to take other more demanding jobs until he sometimes ended up with a small business of his own inside the established society. The same applied to those who went to school and learned basic numeracy and literacy, which opened up possibilities for employment outside the slum.

In other words, there are different tracks of development inside the slum world; some of these tracks continue inside the slum, others lead outside. When we intervene, we have to face these social realities and adjust our interventions by *helping the child to acquire the critical qualities or skills necessary to be admitted into more optimal life careers inside this person's world of possibilities.* This is like "bridging the gap" between a life of disadvantage and a more acceptable life, according to the person's own standards.

The basic error of most educational intervention programs lies in the (Cartesian) tendency to see knowledge and skills as com-

pletely unrelated to the way of life within a society. However, as has been pointed out, knowledge and skills are intrinsically and congruently linked to cultural conceptions of the person or the child, to identities, life styles, and life careers which are adapted to the ways of life within a society (Hundeide, 1985).

This misconception may easily lead to attempts to combine intrinsically incongruent, inconsistent, and irrelevant elements. If this is done, the skills learned may create confusion and dependency, or at worst, alienation and mental disturbance (Berger, 1976).

It is important to get away from such a narrow, decontextualized, and "acultural" view of psychological functions, and to start to see such functions in a wider cultural, socioecological, and interactive context.

With regard to intervention, one implication of this viewpoint would be to identify sociocultural life careers or socioecological pathways of development and the conditions that are necessary to get access into the society in question. Giftedness then would be defined as closeness to the life career.

If we do this, the procedures with regard to intervention may become quite different from those hitherto accepted; instead of starting with a fixed collection of mental operations à la Piaget, we might rather start by trying to identify the typical patterns of adaptive skills and behaviors relevant for a child's life within a particular community, and subsequently trying to see how these patterns are socially structured into (presentational) social identities directly linked to socioecological life careers which provide the psychologically possible options for children's future development. In other words, we are mapping children's socioecological space of possible development within a community—the plausible trajectories of development from the position where children may be.

When this is clear we may need *to prepare, train, and provide the conditions necessary for optimal life careers in accordance with their position inside their space of "socioecological pathways"* (Bronfenbrenner, 1989); this is what intervention should be about.

As already mentioned, it is quite possible that this may involve training of children in certain presentational skills critical for social acceptance and access for certain life careers[4]. In other words, it may

---

[4] An intervention program called "Bridging the Gap," developed in Australia, seems to be working along similar lines. They help disadvantaged teenagers into optimal life careers within their world of possibilities, by giving them appropriate training so that they can present themselves with certain critical qualities and skills that are essential for acceptance and for keeping a job.

not be the long-term effects of educational intervention (i.e., preschool) as such that are important for the child's development, but rather the effects of being admitted into a positive and self-sustaining socioecological developmental process by means of the "criterial access skills" which have been provided by the intervention.

CONCLUSION: INTERVENTION WITH "COGNITIVE RESPECT"

According to the perspective presented here, the aim of educational intervention or cognitive enrichment beyond infancy must be to improve children's future lives within their existing social reality, along the lines approved by their community at large, not intervention for its own sake in order to develop some skills that may be out of tune with their lives and needs. For this reason it is important that there is an assessment of the cultural construction of identities and life careers within their social ecology, to find out how patterns of skills and knowledge constitute part of these social constructions that direct children's lives—beyond themselves.

By operating in this way, based on an understanding of children's social realities and opportunity structures related to possible life careers, we are no longer outsiders imposing cognitively alien elements into their situation, but we are at least *trying* to operate as insiders helping to promote the options that seem most acceptable, realistic, and plausible from their own position or point of view (see Pantin, 1983, for further elaboration of this point in practical aid work for disadvantaged children). In order to operate as "insiders," it is not enough only to know the indigenous curriculum of development and the construction of persons and identities within that culture, we also need to know how our "interventions" are interpreted by those who participate: the paraprofessionals and the caregivers.

However basic and universal our educational messages may be, we will always be relating to human beings who try to make sense of our interventions (or even "facilitations") in line with their own cultural meaning system. This implies that there will always be a cultural translation and, as pointed out above, we should not be surprised if our objectives and messages are comprehended as something quite different from what was originally assumed. Possibly, the effects of the program will be more in line with these unintended meanings attributed to the program rather than with our original educational intentions.

This does not mean, however, that educational interventions should not take place. Peter Berger puts it like this:

> On the level of meaning, every "inhabitant" of a world has an immediate access to it which is superior to that of any "noninhabitant." Thus the peasant knows his world far better than any outsider even can. Now, this does not mean that that the outsider may not have information and perspectives bearing on the peasant's world which are not in the peasant's possession. What is involved in this kind of transmission is the "exportation" of the cognitive content from one world to another. What *may* be involved, moreover, is that eventually one world swallows up the other. Empirically this will mean that the "inhabitants" of one world impose their particular modes of perception, evaluation, and action on those who previously had organized their relationship to reality differently.

He goes on to postulate "*the equality of all empirically available worlds of consciousness*" by stating that "human beings have produced an immense variety of ways in which they have sought to relate to reality, to give order to experience and to live meaningful lives. There is neither a philosophical nor a scientific method by which this variety can be arranged in a hierarchy from lower to higher" (Berger, 1976, p. 128). He finally concludes with a point of view that he describes as "*cognitive respect*"—respecting the different cognitive worlds, "taking with utmost seriousness the way others define reality."

With regard to educational intervention this implies not only freedom to participate and operate within preset options, but freedom to participate in the setting of priorities in line with the way they see reality. Maybe *we* can learn something about human values by proceeding in this way.

REFERENCES

Barry, H., Child, I., & Bacon, M. (1959). Relation of child training to subsistence economy. *American Anthropologist, 61*.

Barth, F. (1966). Anthropological models and social reality. *Proceedings of the Royal Anthropological Society* (Vol. 165). London.

Baumrind, D. (1971). Current patterns of parental authority. *Developmental Psychology Monograph, 4*, 1–103.

Berger, P. (1976). *Pyramids of sacrifice*. Anchor Book Edition.

Berger, P., Berger, B., & Kellner, H. (1973). *The homeless mind*. New York: Penguin Books.

Berger, P., & Luckman, T. (1967). *The social construction of reality*. New York: Penguin Books.

Berry, J. W., & Annis, R. C. (1974). Ecology, culture and psychological differentiation. *International Journal of Psychology, 9.*

Blakar, R. (1974). *Communication: A social perspective on clinical issues.* Universitetsforlaget.

Block, P.K. (1988). *Rethinking Psychological Anthropology.* New York: Freeman and Company.

Bronfenbrenner, U. (1989, June). *The ecology of cognitive development: Research models and fugitive findings.* Paper presented at Annual Symposium of the Jean Piaget Society, Philadelphia.

Braaten, E. (1989). Preliminary report from the Bandung-project. University of Bergen, Norway.

Cole, M., & Scribner, S. (1974). *Culture and thought.* New York: Wiley.

Donaldson, M. (1977). *Children's minds.* Fontana Books.

Dornbush, S. M., Ritter, P. L., Leiderman, P. H., Roberts, D. F., & Fraleigh, M. J. (1987). The relation of parenting style to adolescent school performance. *Child Development, 58,* 1244-1257.

Fawcett, J. T. (1983). Perception of the value of children: Satisfactions and costs. In R. A. Bulatao & R. D. Lee (Eds.), *Determinants of fertility in developing countries* (Vol. I). Washington, DC: National Academy Press.

Feuerstein, R. (1980). *Instrumental enrichment.* Baltimore, MD: University Park Press.

Feuerstein, R., & Klein, P. (1985). Environmental variables and cognitive development. In S. Harel & N. Abastaslow (Eds.), *The-at-risk infant.* P. H. Brookes.

Geertz, H. (1959). The vocabulary of emotion: A study of Javanese socialization processes. *Psychiatry, 22.*

Goodnow, J. (1984). Parents' ideas about parenting and development: A review of issues and recent work. In M. E. Lamb, A. L. Brown, & B. Rogoff (Eds.), *Advances in developmental psychology* (Vol. 3). Hillsdale, NJ: Erlbaum.

Greenfield, P. (1966). Chapter in J. Bruner (Ed.), *The Course of cognitive development.* New York: Wiley.

Hundeide, K. (1985). *An indigenous approach to early education.* UNICEF Colombo.

Hundeide, K. (1989). *Barns livsverden. En fortolkende tilnærming til studiet av barn* (The child's lifeworld. An interpretive approach to the study of children). Oslo: Cappelen.

Inkles, A., & Smith, D. H. (1974). *Becoming modern: Individual changes in six developing countries.* Cambridge, MA: Harvard University Press.

Kagan, J., & Madsen, M. (1971). Cooperation and competition of Mexican, Mexican-American and Anglo-American children at two ages under four different instructional sets. *Developmental Psychology, 5.*

Klein, P. (1985). *More intelligent children.* Translation of a book published in Israel, School of Education, Bar-Ilan University, Ramat Gan, Israel.

Kohli, M. (1989). *The social construction of the life course.* Invited address at Tenth Biennial Meeting of ISSBD in Finland.

Labov, W. (1972). The logic of nonstandard English. *I Pier Paolo Giglioli (Language and Social Context)* New York: Penguin Books.

Lave, J. (1989). *Apprenticeship learning.* Symposium during Tenth Biennial Meeting of ISSBD in Finland.

Lepper, M., Greene, D., & Nisbett, R. E. (1973). Undermining children's intrinsic interest with extrinsic rewards: A test of the overjustification hypothesis. *Journal of Personality and Social Psychology, 28,* 129–137.

LeVine, R. A. (1977). Child rearing as cultural adaptation. In Leiderman, Tulkin, & Rosenfeld, *Culture and infancy: Variations in the human experience.* New York: Academic Press.

LeVine, R. A. (1988, Fall). Lecture at the University of Oslo.

LeVine, R. A., & White, M. I. (1986). *Human conditions.* London: Routledge and Kegan Paul.

Levy Strauss, C. (1987). *Myth and meaning.* London: Routledge and Kegan Paul.

Mercer, N., & Edwards, D. (1981). Ground-rules for mutual understanding: A social psychological approach to classroom knowledge. In N. Mercer (1981). *Language in school and community.* London: Edward Arnold.

Ochs, E., & Schieffelin, B. B. (1985). Language acquisition and socialization. Three developmental stories and their implications. In R. Schweder & R. A. LeVine (Eds.), *Culture theory.* Cambridge, UK: Cambridge University Press.

Pantin, F. G. (1983). *The mobilization of grassroot communities: The experience of Servol.* Keynote Address to the Fourth International Community Education Association, Dunlin, UNECSCO, Paris.

Rommetveit, R. (1974). *Message structure.* New York: Academic Press.

Scheper-Hughes, N. (1985). *Rethinking psychological anthropology.* New York: H. Freeman and Company.

Schweder, R., & Bourne, E. (1986). Does the concept of person vary cross-culturally? In R. Schweder & R. LeVine (Eds.), *Culture theory.* New York: Cambridge University Press.

Schurmans, M. N., Dasen, P., & Vouilloz, M. F. (1989, June). *Social representations of intelligence: Cote D'Ivoire and Switzerland.* Paper presented at Second Regional European Conference of the International Association for Cross-Cultural Psychology, Amsterdam.

Smedslund, J. (1984). The invisible obvious. In K. Niem (Ed.), *Psychology of the 1990's.* Amsterdam: Elsevier.

Vygotsky, L. (1978). *Language in society.* Cambridge, MA: Harvard University Press.

Werner, E. (1979). *Cross-cultural child development.* Monterey, CA: Brooks/Cole Publishing Company.

Whiting, B. B., & Whiting, J. W. (1975). *Children of six cultures: A psychocultural analysis*: Cambridge, MA: Harvard University Press.

Witkin, H., & Berry, J. (1975). Psychological differentiation in cross-cultural perspective. *Journal of Cross-Cultural Psychology, 17* (2), 89–100.

part II

Early Development of Giftedness

chapter **4**

A Developmental View on the Early Identification of the Gifted

Frances Degen Horowitz

The Graduate School & University Center
The City University of New York[1]

It is not unreasonable to ask: How early in life can we identify those individuals who will become gifted and talented? In attempting to address this question it is important to note that everyone who has written about the development of gifted and talented children and adults recognizes the role of environmentally based nurturance on the fullest development of individual talents and gifts (e.g., Feldman, 1986; Horowitz & O'Brien, 1985). If environmental nurturance is critical to the realization of giftedness, then one wants to know for whom such nurturance would be particularly beneficial, when such identification is possible, and what is to be lost in terms of human potential if environmental support and nurturance are not present or not present to a sufficient degree. Currently, the knowledge base is insufficient to provide definitive answers. Yet we suspect that many individuals with the potential for being gifted never achieve that potential. What is lost not only affects the individ-

---

[1] Early drafts of this chapter were written while the author was at the University of Kansas.

ual but deprives society of the contributions that might have been made.

Obviously, the desideratum would be identification of individuals during infancy. If it were possible to know during infancy which children have the potential for being gifted and talented then the environmentally necessary forces could be marshalled to encourage such development to the benefit of both the individual and society. However, given what we know about development and given the various theories of development a number of questions arise. Is infancy a developmental period when we might hope to make a reliable identification? Are there reasons to think that the preschool period after infancy is better? How long a "developmental view" might one take about the identification of gifted and talented individuals and fostering their development? For example, how do issues of identification relate to a developmental view that is informed by a life-span perspective? Can giftedness manifest itself and develop at any age, or is its emergence restricted to a particular age or ages? Does early identification mean we can reliably predict later development?

It is the purpose of this chapter to explore these questions and issues and to address the reasonableness of the desire for reliable early identification of gifted and talented individuals. Our discussion will be made in the context of a developmental focus. We will begin by considering the nature of our database on prediction of developmental outcome and then discuss the questions from the point of view of different developmental theories and models.

PREDICTING DEVELOPMENTAL OUTCOME

The scientific understanding of phenomena typically requires two kinds of basic efforts: description and the attempt to make predictions. There are rich literatures representing both of these traditions in the developmental research concerned with behavioral development and behavioral function over the course of the life span. These literatures sometimes intersect; more often than not, they are quite separate.

Though descriptive efforts wax and wane in the fashion of doing research, descriptions that provide a sense of normative characteristics at different ages become very critical to the question of early identification of children who are or who have the potential to be gifted. Early identification of special ability requires an understanding of the range of individual differences at any point in time with respect to a given behavior, to a set of behaviors, or to the more general nature of developmental status. The earliest descriptive efforts can be found in the work of the baby biographers (e.g., Preyer, 1909a, b) and subsequently in the work of Gesell and his colleagues (Gesell, 1925; Gesell, Amatruda, Castner, & Thompson, 1939), and in Piaget's descriptions of early developmental sequences (Piaget, 1926, 1952). As a result, we have a relatively good overview over the normative course of development in young children, especially in the areas of motor and cognitive development and, more recently, in language development. The normative data for other areas are growing, though once we get much past adolescence, the normative base begins to thin considerably. Additionally, some of our normative databases are distinctly limited with respect to the populations described.

In looking at individual differences, the normative database is complemented by the data we have on successful prediction of developmental outcome. The predictive tradition in developmental psychology is of two kinds. One of these is represented by the standard "what if" experimental paradigm, where the experiment is designed so as to provide a relatively immediate answer. These kinds of studies focus on predictions of outcome that involve relationships of particular variables at a given point in time. Watson and Rayner's (1920) study of conditioned emotional responses and the many studies of children's learning (see Stevenson, 1972) are of this type. Such studies usually represent efforts aimed at trying to understand how the variables chosen for study in an experiment function as opposed to the behavior of individual subjects, though it is possible to use subject characteristics as one of the variables being studied. While it is possible to claim that any study is "developmental" if it tests subjects at two points in time, a stronger developmental focus may be provided in experimental research if age of subject serves as an independent in an experiment.

The second kind of predictive tradition is more fully focused upon direct questions of developmental outcome. This kind of research has typically been lodged in efforts to understand individual differences through testing and assessment of individual subjects over time. Here the question usually relates to whether or not a particular testing instrument predicts later behavior or later developmental status. Such a strategy informed the earliest rationales for the development of infant tests of intelligence. The assumption underlying these efforts was that intelligence was a fixed characteristic. The goal in using such tests to assess intelligence during infancy was the prediction of later childhood intelligence (Bayley, 1933). The practical use of such assessments was often in the service of helping with decisions concerning the placement of infants being considered for adoption.

Eventually it became clear that there was not sufficient evidence to support the idea that later childhood or adult intelligence could be predicted from assessments of intelligence during infancy. A variety of reasons were advanced to explain this failure (Bayley, 1955; Mc-Call, 1976, 1989; McCall, Eichorn, & Hogarty, 1977), including the developmentally changing essential nature of intelligence itself. Recently there have been efforts to revive the idea that early infant assessments can provide reliable predictions of later intelligence. Using measures of infant visual behavior in a novelty preference task, there have been a number of reports showing that performance on a novelty preference task during infancy predicts later intelligence and/or developmental status (Fagan & Singer, 1983; McCall, 1989, 1990; Rose, Feldman, Wallace, & McCarton, 1989; Rose & Feldman, 1990).

The assessment literature is not, however, the only place where one finds an interest in prediction of developmental outcome. The entire literature on the effects of programs of early stimulation on developmental outcome rests on the possibility that the nature of early experience will influence developmental progress and/or outcome. Assessments of early environmental experience and interventions to enhance early experience have been attempted to demonstrate that variations in early experience will enhance developmental outcome (Garber, 1988; Garber & Hodge, 1989; Horowitz, 1980; Horowitz & Paden, 1973; Jensen, 1989; Lazar, Darlington, Murray, Royce, & Snipper, 1982). The implication is that such interventions with certain populations predict enhanced developmental outcome. Yet the results of these efforts have been variable and complex.

Research designed to predict developmental outcome has also been undertaken with respect to high-risk infants. Prenatal conditions, birth conditions, and early postnatal circumstances have been studied to see if any one or set of these can be used for predictive purposes. In their classic review of this literature, Sameroff and Chandler (1975) concluded that, in most instances, the then-standard medical prenatal, perinatal, and early postnatal variables did not predict developmental outcome. They suggested that an understanding of developmental outcome would require a knowledge, not only of subsequent environmental variables, but of the interplay of the organism and those variables over time.

The failure to find the expected strong relationships between early experience and developmental outcome, the modest magnitude of predictive ability in those cases where there has been some success, and the growing awareness of how complex our account of development is likely going to be to account for developmental outcome have led to a considerable amount of discussion and questioning. These discussions and questions have ranged from consideration of the nature of the developmental theory and model from which we derive our research on developmental outcome, to particular issues such as how much continuity and how much discontinuity we might expect to find across developmental periods, what is the relevance of the concept of developmental stage, and what is the nature and relationship of the critical organismic and environmental variables as this relationship pertains to our trying to understand predicting developmental outcome (Clarke & Clarke, 1976; Emde & Harmon, 1984; Horowitz, 1984, 1987; Kagan, Kearsley, & Zelazo, 1978; Wolf, 1989; Zelazo & Barr, 1989).

Though the discussion of the general issue of prediction of developmental outcome is extensive, interest in this question as it pertains to the gifted and talented has waxed and waned over the years (Grinder, 1985). Currently, the gifted and talented are subjects of considerable and increasing attention (e.g., Horowitz & O'Brien, 1985; Storfer, 1990; Wallace & Gruber, 1989; Feldman, 1986; Sternberg & Davidson, 1986). It has become clear in these discussions that all of the issues related to prediction of developmental outcome have particular bearing upon any discussion of early identification of gifted and talented individuals. For example, if there is continuity from early to later development, then early assessment can be seen as a tool for predicting which children have the potential for gifted development; if there is no continuity from early to later development, then trying to develop assessments for identifying the gifted during infancy would not be fruitful. Alternatively, using early assessment to make successful predictions may be possible in some domains but not in others. Prediction from early assessment may be conditioned, not only upon the behavioral domain, but upon the definition of *early*, and so on. Addressing any or all of these requires an examination of basic assumptions about development.

ASSUMPTIONS UNDERLYING DEVELOPMENTAL MODELS

How one begins to consider prediction and early identification of developmental outcome depends entirely upon the model of development that one elects to use and upon the assumptions underlying the model. Three different assumptions are relevant to prediction and early identification: linearity and nonlinearity in development, the existence of stages in development, and the degree to which there is continuity and/or discontinuity in development.

Linearity and Nonlinearity

Few developmentalists assume that development is best represented as a linear process across the life span with additions and subtractions affecting a kind of cumulative balance at any point in time. On the other hand, one might ask the question whether for some areas of behavioral development during some periods of time, behavioral acquisition can best be understood from a linear perspective. For example, to what extent is learning to spell, learning to do arithmetic, or learning to read dependent upon processes of acquisition best described in sequential, additive, and cumulative terms? That is, does the acquisition of these behaviors proceed in a cumulative manner from the simple to the complex, from one response "added" to another until the larger ability is acquired? Or does the acquisition of these behaviors proceed in a nonlinear manner wherein at certain points in time there is an increase in ability that results from qualitative reorganizations of existing responses such that new and more complex abilities "emerge"? Is linearity a more viable assumption in some developmental domains than in others, and during some phases of development but not in others?

The arguments against linearity as a basic assumption for developmental process are currently quite strong. Most significant are observations that there are qualitative differences, and that consolidations and integrations appear to occur with regularity in the development of the normal behavioral repertoire. The same responses in two different individuals may represent two quite different levels of development. For instance, the retarded child who is assessed as having a mental age of 2 years is behaviorally quite different from the normal 2-year-old, even though the particular set of problems successfully solved in the assessment may be similar. Accepting the validity of nonlinearity as an important characteristic of behavioral development is not, however, inconsistent with the possibility that linearity might be an appropriate model/assumption for some of the cumulative aspects of behavioral acquisition and particularly for some aspects of learning.

The discussion of linearity and nonlinearity in development is stronger on the side of rejecting linearity than on the side of specifying exactly what is meant by nonlinearity. There are a number of terms that have been introduced to imply nonlinearity, such as *transactional, systems,* and *dynamical.* In his seminal discussions of system theory, von Bertalanffy's (1968, 1975) major contention was that the development and the functioning of organisms and organizations must be thought of in what he called *open system* terms. Open systems are not linear either with respect to the inter-relation of the parts of the system or with respect to the course of development. However, with development, portions of the system become organized in such a fashion that they become closed. The operational aspects of the closed system have become routinized and function in a linear manner.

It is not necessary for a routinized system to function linearly, though the implication in von Bertalanffy's discussion is that a closed system is more likely to be characterized as linearly organized. In any event, the closed routinized portions of the system operate on an input–output algorithm that can be completely specified. Not so with the open system where input–output relationships are neither routinized nor always completely specifiable—especially during periods when there is dynamic development in the system. System theory has become a popular analogy for describing behavioral development in the human organism.

In thinking about the behavior and development of gifted and talented individuals, one possibility is to suggest that individuals who are or who have the potential to be gifted and talented may look different on a number of dimensions that relate to open and closed system functioning. For example, the routinization characteristic of closed system functioning may develop more efficiently or more fully in the area of particular gifts, with the effect of freeing the system to deploy energies involved with the open system and with producing novel or advanced levels of open system functioning.

System theory has often been invoked as synonymous with transactional theory (Sameroff, 1983). This has been particularly true when the discussion of transactional theory is seen as presenting an alternative to linear models to describe behavioral development. However, the transactional model specifies only that the organism's behavior is both influenced by and influencing of the environment, with resulting effects that are mutually modifying (Sameroff, 1983; Sameroff & Chandler, 1975). There is nothing inherent in such a position that means the influences and the mutuality of the direction of the influences are nonlinear. Indeed, a transactional relationship could, theoretically, be described in entirely linear terms. Further, it is not clear how the transactional approach accounts in any different way for the course of behavioral development other than suggesting that the developmental course is shaped by bidirectional or multidirectional influences.

A larger contender for the theoretical account of development in nonlinear terms is dynamical systems theory as proposed by Thelen and her colleagues (Thelen, 1989, 1990; Thelen, Kelso, & Fogel,

1987). A version of a dynamical systems proposal can be found in some of Gesell's principles, especially as they are applied to motor development (Gesell, 1954), and in Kuo's theory of behavior potentials (Kuo, 1967). Development from this perspective is described in terms of the successive introduction of parameters that can constrain the degrees of freedom of the system and/or that can exert a disproportionate influence on the operation of variables in the system (like von Bertalanffy's notion of a "leading part").

Dynamical systems theory can be used to think about the development of the gifted and the talented. For example, it might be proposed that, in the development of gifted individuals, different parameters operate as compared to normally developing individuals. Or, some parameters may function differently but only in the domains where an individual is gifted. Alternatively, as in the discussion of von Bertalanffy's open systems, specific functions of parametric control may develop more efficiently, leaving more time and energy for the development of unique, different, or advanced behavior in areas of special potential.

Thelen's formulation of dynamical systems theory is, however, very complex (Thelen, 1990). It addresses quite specifically the issues of linearity and nonlinearity, opting totally for a nonlinear model to account for developmental trajectories. Behavioral development, from Thelen's point of view, involves a complex system that functions in terms of principles of thermodynamic nonequilibrium that results in patterned behavior. This patterned behavior, as a result of nonlinear functions over time, produces successive forms of "emergent order." In a somewhat similar manner as von Bertalanffy's leading part, specific variables can have an inordinate influence on the subsequent course of an individual's developmental trajectory. Thelen takes the position that, because of what she calls the "intrinsic noisiness" in dynamical systems, the ability to make long-term predictions of individual developmental outcome from a set of earlier variables is essentially limited. This would obviously apply to both normal and gifted children.

As already noted, nonlinear models of development currently appear to be more attractive than linear models. Accepting the assumption of an essentially nonlinear model as accounting for the developmental course and for developmental outcome provides a large challenge to the design and analysis of developmental research. One response is the growing use of complex multivariate statistical techniques such as LISRL and path analysis to evaluate the mutual effect of variables and the changing influence of variables over time—particularly in the study of mother/infant interaction.

Thelen has focused her application of dynamical systems theory on the study of normative motor development. It remains to be seen whether Thelen's (1990; Thelen et al., 1987) demonstration of the utility of dynamical systems theory for studying motor development is sustained and can be employed in the study of other developmental domains (see Fogel, 1990, for application to infant communicative behavior). It also remains to be seen how dynamical systems theory can be used to address individual differences and the prediction of developmental outcome.

If development is best thought of in nonlinear terms, there are interesting and possibly contradictory implications for early identification of the gifted and for prediction of developmental outcome. On the one hand, in a nonlinear model early characteristics are not necessarily permanent characteristics, and thus early identification of giftedness may not be possible. On the other hand, early characteristics may persist and not be affected by subsequent events such that early behaviors presaging later gifted behavior may be identifiable. The assumption of nonlinearity in development thus says nothing definitive with respect to early identification or with respect to prediction of developmental outcome.

Stages

The notion of stages is deeply embedded in any colloquial, common-sense discussion of development. It is part and parcel of our everyday referential language when talking about children and when thinking about an individual's progress across the life span. Many of our basic textbooks in child development and developmental psychology are organized by "age" and, by implication, stage.

The common-sense use of the term *stage* involves acceptance of the idea that there are developmental epochs and that each developmental epoch has some unifying common characteristics that distinguish one epoch from another epoch. These characteristics include relative size (infants are smaller than preschool children), the range of the behavioral repertoire in particular domains (infants have more limited cognitive abilities than elementary school children, and the aged have less motoric agility than adolescents), as well as differences in rate of development, direction of development, and the lability/stability of particular behaviors.

The concepts involved in the colloquial use of the term *stage* all have some scientific currency and have been built into most of the major developmental theories. Gesell used the notion of stage though, in actuality, his data and ultimately his discussions of those data may be more appropriately described as focusing upon sequences rather than distinct stages in development. The more classic expression of stage as the dominant feature of development can be found in the developmental theories of Baldwin (1906), Piaget (1926, 1952), and Werner (1957a, b). Freud, too, used the concept of stage extensively (Freud, 1905, 1917). Stage concepts have also been employed in all areas of developmental biology (Weiss, 1968, 1971).

When developmentalists discuss stages, they typically assume that such stages occur in given and usually invariant sequences, though there is no logical reason why the concept of stage must necessarily imply a fixed sequence. At the simplest level a stage is a period in development where there is sufficient descriptive commonality within an age period or age span and sufficient descriptive differences between periods. Stage can also involve notions of process or laws that characterize one period but not another. Piagetian stages of cognitive development describe different ways in which the child processes information and interacts with the environment.

The relationships within a stage can fit linear or nonlinear models, and the same can be said for relationships between stages. Few developmental theories have been specific in addressing stages in terms of the linear–nonlinear dimension. There are aspects within Freudian discussions of "within stage" dynamics that appear to assume some degree of linearity while the "between stage" relationships appear to involve less linearity. Discussions of Piagetian stages typically assume nonlinearity within and between stages, though the specifications of the nonlinear dynamics are not very clear. An attempt has been made to combine the nonlinear characteristics of Piagetian stages with the much more linear relationships of behaviorism in Fischer's (1980) theory of the construction of hierarchies of skills.

In dynamical systems theory (Thelen, 1990), and in the structural/behavioral model of development (Horowitz, 1987), a more complex approach to stage has been attempted. The discussion of stage in dynamical systems theory involves the notion of different controlling parameters on the behavioral repertoire that at one and the same time restrict the degrees of freedom for developmental direction and liberate within those degrees of freedom the opportunities for dynamic interaction of concurrent variables.

The structural/behavioral model (Horowitz, 1987) assumes that organismic and environmental contributions to development differ at different points in time in terms of both specific organismic and environment variables and the functional relationship between the variables. Developmental outcome is seen as the result of an equation describing these variables and relationships. A *stage* is defined as a period of time during which the variables and the functional relationships among the variables remain relatively stable. The point at which there is the *possibility* of change or instability in these functional relationships signals a transition period to a new stage. The assumption is that the possibility of a shift in these functional relationships is not possible at any point in development—only at some points. Further, the possibility of a shift in functional relationships does not mean such a shift will necessarily occur. Nevertheless, whether the shift does or does not occur, a new stage pertains and during this period of time a shift in the functional relationships between the interacting organismic and environmental variables is not possible—until the next "nodal" point of possible change.

In the structural/behavioral model, and in the dynamical systems theory, giftedness could be seen as characteristic of only one stage of development or as characteristic of more than one stage. To the extent that there is not an assumed continuity across stages in development, there is no necessary conclusion to be drawn about the possibility of the early identification of giftedness and talent, or of the prediction of such across development.

Continuity and Discontinuity in Development

The question of early identification and prediction is most directly addressed by the assumptions involving continuity and discontinuity in development. The way in which continuity and discontinuity are seen is critical to the question of predicting developmental outcome. Continuity is most often drawn as an issue related to whether the developmental status and/or behavior of an individual at one point in time will remain constant to another point in time. Evidence for continuity in this sense would thus permit prediction of later behavior or developmental status from a measure made at an earlier point in time.

Many assessments of early behaviors such as intelligence and attachment are evaluated for their utility in terms of those assessments predicting later intelligence or attachment. This is a definition of *continuity* that involves focusing on the continuity of the "phenomenon" (Horowitz, 1987). Thus, one is looking for stability in behavior or relative developmental status across time by measuring the behaviors themselves.

Discussion of continuity in development from the point of view of the continuity of developmental phenomena has distinct limitations. First, though some measures are better developmental predictors than others, by and large, the magnitude of the variance accounted for by the predictions—that is, the correlations—is invariably small to modest (Clarke & Clarke, 1988; Horowitz, 1987). The exception is when the two measures occur relatively close in time. Second, the only alternative to a hypothesis about continuity in development, if continuity is defined in terms of the phenomena of development, is discontinuity.

A different approach to the question of whether or not there is continuity in development is to focus upon the processes that account for development. If one does this, then the issue of continuity and discontinuity immediately becomes considerably more complex. If the processes are constant across time, and if all the values and variables that enter into the processes are constant across time, one should see continuity in development. If, however, processes change and/or the values and variables involved in the processes change, then there is no reason, a priori, to expect continuity in developmental status across time (Horowitz, 1987). Thus, prediction of developmental outcome would require, not only measurement of phenomena at two points in time, but an understanding of what has occurred in between in terms of the processes at work that produce continuity across time or discontinuity across time.

There is evidence that such complex models are increasingly represented in discussions of longitudinal studies of developmental outcome involving the relationship of early assessments to later developmental status (e.g., Cicchetti & Aber, 1986; Shoda, Mischel, & Peake, 1990; Sroufe, Egeland, & Kreutzer, 1990).

If one adopts the focus on process in relation to the issue of continuity and/or discontinuity in development, then the matter of linearity and nonlinearity in development can also be put in process terms. Some processes for some periods of development in some domains may be linear; some processes in some periods of development and in some domains may be nonlinear. The power of this general approach is that it makes the questions of continuity/ discontinuity and linearity/nonlinearity empirical. Further, the relationship of linearity/nonlinearity and continuity/discontinuity also becomes an empirical question with the possibility that the answers may differ in different periods of development, for different processes and in different domains.

Nature and/or Nurture

There is no topic in the developmental literature and in the discussions of development (particularly human development) that has received more attention in the field of developmental psychology than the relative influences of nature (heredity) and nurture (environment) on development and developmental outcome. It would be folly to try a brief summary of those discussions. Nevertheless, especially because the nature/nurture question is central to the issue of predicting who will be gifted and who will not be gifted, some consideration of the basic issues is required in this chapter.

Nature sometimes refers to genes, sometimes to the constitution of an individual, sometimes to both. The terms *genetic* and *constitutional* are not synonymous; nor are the terms *genetic* and *biological*. Occurrences of accident, infection, and illness, the adequacy of nutritional intake, smoking, and the use of alcohol and drugs can all affect the biological constitution of an organism and subsequently influence behavior and development. These influences have environmental origin. They are not, themselves, genetic influences, though genetic factors may contribute to the impact of environmental variables on the organism.

The term *nurture* typically involves reference to environmental variables. There are currently many unanswered questions concerning environmental variables and their effect on developmental outcomes. For example, one can ask, Which variables in the environment are relevant, and when and for what behaviors or aspects of development? Another issue involves the question related to the best way to parse environmental variables in order to determine the functional units of environmental variables (Bronfenbrenner, 1979; Bronfenbrenner & Crouter, 1983; Horowitz, 1987; Wachs, 1989, 1990).

The relationship between nature and nurture is, of course, one of the central issues in almost all debates about how development happens. Genetic contributions have typically been assumed to be the "givens" present at the start of life, with the environmental contributions playing a role across the life span and against the genetic givens. Recent evidence suggests a more complex picture, such that environmental and genetic influences may each influence behavior and development differently at different points along the life span (Loehlin, Horn, & Willerman, 1989).

All the issues summarized in relation to predicting developmental outcome have a bearing upon early identification of the gifted and talented. Having presented them, we can now turn to the specific question of whether early identification is a reasonable goal.

PREDICTING WHO WILL BE GIFTED

The developmental context shaped in this chapter can be employed in addressing the question of how early one could hope to identify individuals who will be gifted. It should be obvious that only a model that assumes total continuity and, to some extent, predominant linearity in development, along with the preeminence of genetic influence on development, would permit the question to be framed in this manner in the first place. A more sophisticated approach to the question of early identification of the gifted would be: At what age is it possible to think that it is possible to identify individuals who, under appropriately fostering environmental conditions, have the most potential for developing into individuals judged to be gifted? Additionally, this question needs to be addressed from a life-span perspective.

Framing the question in this manner involves the recognition that there are important qualifications in forming the answer. First, identifying the potential for giftedness may be possible at multiple points during development. For example, identification of musically gifted children may be possible at a number of points during development, though optimal identification for the purposes of the best chance at nurturing that talent may be during infancy. Identifying motorically gifted children may also be possible at multiple points during development, but the preschool period, elementary school period, or adolescence may turn out to be the best periods for such identification in terms of the time when one could provide the best functional environmental support.

Second, the nurturing environment necessary for the realization of giftedness may be quite different for a given domain of giftedness depending upon when in development the identification is made. The nurturing environment for artistic giftedness when such identification is made during the adult years would be different from what would be environmentally best if the identification were made during preschool.

Third, there may be several or many degrees of freedom for the period during which identifying giftedness permits the provision of effective environmental support in some domains; in other domains providing effective environmental support may be possible only when giftedness is identified early (or late?).

Taking a life-span perspective on the development of gifted individuals adds an additional set of qualifications. While early experiences may contribute to the development of giftedness, there is no *logical* reason why environmental influences later in life cannot be as or more potent in fostering giftedness. However, evidence may ultimately be gathered to demonstrate the differential influence of experience at different points throughout the life span. Finally, it must also be recognized that what is considered "gifted" will be influenced by historical time and by the nature of the values and culture that define gifted behavior (Feldman, 1980; Horowitz & O'Brien, 1985; Storfer, 1990; Wallace & Gruber, 1989).

"Best Bets" for Early Identification

Having identified many of the qualifications that surround finding the answer to the question of "how early" we can identify giftedness, it remains a possibility that the earlier the potential for some kinds of talents is identified, the better the chance for the realization of that potential. The reason for saying this is that, if talents and gifts do not develop fully without environmental nurturance, the earliest identification of potential may significantly increase the probabilities of realizing that potential if the appropriate environmental nurturance is then provided.

We know a great deal about normative behavior in infancy in many domains. The traditional tests and measurements approach to individual differences as it has been applied to infants has had limited success in predicting developmental outcomes. However, recent developments have occurred in the study of infant individual differences in laboratory experiments or seminatural setting observations (Colombo & Fagan, 1990; Horowitz, 1990). These research strategies offer a way of asking whether we can study behaviors during infancy that would offer fruitful clues to identifying the gifted.

To give examples of how this might be approached in the area of intelligence, we will draw upon Sternberg's depiction of processes and intelligence (Sternberg, 1985) and Gardner's discussion of different kinds of intelligences (Gardner, 1983). Sternberg, in his book *Beyond IQ*, suggested that intelligence is best conceived as having three major facets: Executive processes that involve problem-solving strategies, or what Sternberg calls *metacomponent* aspects of intelligence; knowledge acquired as a function of experience; performance that can be described in terms of lower order processes used to execute problem-solving tasks. Gardner, in his book *Frames of Mind*, has described what he believes are six different kinds of intelligences: linguistic, musical, logic-mathematical, spatial, bodily kinesthetic, and personal-social.

Many different kinds of laboratory tasks have been devised to study normal infant behavior in relation to auditory and visual information. Using these tasks, it is possible to explore whether Sternberg's components of intelligent behavior can be described for young infants. Further, it is possible to make these explorations separately for various of the intelligence domains described by Gardner. An example of this approach involved using what we know about habituation, novelty preference, and social referencing tasks in infants. The habituation paradigm can be used to study individual differences in processing auditory stimuli employing linguistic and/or musical information (Horowitz, 1974). Various parameters of repeated performance on habituation tasks (such as trials to criterion, duration of peak fixation, magnitude of recovery, etc.) could be seen as measures of Sternberg's executive and lower order processes as they are used in tasks that appear to tap various of Gardner's intelligences. The novelty preference task, with some of its parameters, offers an analogous opportunity in the visual domain. For example, faces as stimuli provide an opportunity to probe the personal-social domain. Social referencing paradigms also permit exploring personal-social intelligence. Sternberg's knowledge component could be manipulated by controlled exposure to and experience with particular stimuli or by assessing the infant's knowledge gained through experiences in the infant's natural environment.

The essential strategy here would be to identify infants whose behavior on one or more of these various tasks appears especially efficient and/or different within a large database gathered from normal infants. A longitudinal study of these infants and a control group over the preschool and early elementary school years offers some rich possibilities. Assessment of the intervening environmental experiences could reveal the environmental conditions that maintain or enhance the different/precocious behaviors observed and the conditions that produce stability or instability in these behaviors. Subsequent designation of some of these children as "gifted" in elementary, junior high, or high school would permit a retrospective analysis to identify which early measures were most informative in predicting giftedness and in what domains.

CONCLUDING OBSERVATIONS

On the one hand, there is no reason to believe that infancy is necessarily the best or most opportune time for identifying those children with the potential for giftedness. A fully developmental point of view leads to a model that recognizes that giftedness is not something that resides and develops solely within an individual to be identified during the early years of life. It is theoretically possible that giftedness can be identified and nurtured at various points in the life span. On the other hand, when identification of the potential for giftedness is identified during the early years, there may be a much greater possibility for the realization of those gifts if the needed processes of environmental nurturance occur in the early years. On still another hand, the processes responsible for the development and maintenance of gifted behavior may be different in different domains and at different developmental points. All of which is to reiterate, in this final comment, that much remains to be understood about identifying and nurturing the development of gifted and talented individuals. And still more remains to be known about how we might apply our knowledge to encourage the fullest realization of individual gifts and talents across a wide variety of situations and cultures.

REFERENCES

Baldwin, J. M. (1906). *Mental development in the child and the race.* New York: Macmillan.

Bayley, N. (1933). Mental growth during the first three years. *Genetic Psychology Monographs, 14,* 1–92.

Bayley, N. (1955). On the growth of intelligence. *American Psychologist, 10,* 805.

Bronfenbrenner, U. (1979). The ecology of human development. *Experiments by nature and design.* Cambridge, MA: Harvard University Press.

Bronfenbrenner, U., & Crouter, A. C. (1983). The evolution of environmental models in developmental research. In P. H. Mussen (Series Ed.), *Handbook of child psychology* (4th ed., Vol. 1, pp. 357–414), W. Kessen (Ed.), *History, theory and methods.* New York: Wiley.

Cicchetti, D., & Aber, J. W. (1986). Early precursors of later depression. In L. P. Lipsitt & C. Rovee-Collier (Eds.), *Advances in infancy research* (Vol. 4, pp. 87–137). Norwood, NJ: Ablex.

Clarke, A. M., & Clarke, A. D. B. (1976). *Early experience: Myth and evidence.* New York: The Press.

Clarke, A., & Clarke, A. D. B. (1988). The adult outcome of early behavioral abnormalities. *International Journal of Behavioral Development, 11,* 3–20.

Colombo, J., & Fagan, J. (Eds.). (1990). *Individual differences in infancy: Reliability, stability, prediction.* Hillsdale, NJ: Erlbaum.

Emde, R. N., & Harmon, R. J. (Eds.). (1984). *Continuities and discontinuities in development* (pp. 41–68). New York: Plenum Press.

Fagan, J. (1984). The relationship of novelty preferences during infancy to later intelligence and later recognition memory. *Intelligence, 8,* 339–346.

Fagan, J. F., & Singer, L. T. (1983). Infant recognition memory as a measure of intelligence. In L. P. Lipsitt & C. K. Rovee-Collier (Eds.), *Advances in infancy research* (Vol. 2, pp. 31–78). Norwood, NJ: Ablex.

Feldman, D. H. (1980). *Beyond universals in cognitive development*. Norwood, NJ: Ablex.

Feldman, D. (1986). *Nature's gambit*. New York: Basic Books.

Fischer, K. W. (1980). A theory of cognitive development: The control and construction of hierarchies of skills. *Psychological Review, 87*, 477–531.

Fogel, A. (1990). The process of developmental change in infant communicative action: Using dynamic systems theory to study individual ontogenies. In J. Colombo & J. Fagan (Eds.), *Individual differences in infancy: Reliability, stability, prediction* (pp. 341–358). Hillsdale, NJ: Erlbaum.

Freud, S. (1905). Three essays on the theory of sexuality. In J. Strachey (Ed.), *The standard edition of the complete psychological works of Sigmund Freud* (Vol. 17). London: Hogarth Press.

Freud, S. (1917). Introductory lectures on psychoanalysis. *The standard edition of the complete psychological works of Sigmund Freud* (Vol. 15 & 16). London: Hogarth Press.

Garber, H. L. (1988). *The Milwaukee Project*. Washington, DC: American Association on Mental Retardation.

Garber, H. L., & Hodge, J. D. (1989). Reply: Risk for deceleration in rate of mental development. *Developmental Review, 9*, 259–300.

Gardner, H. (1983). *Frames of mind: The theory of multiple intelligences*. New York: Basic Books.

Gesell, A. (1925). *The mental growth of the preschool child*. New York: Macmillan.

Gesell, A. (1954). The ontogenesis of infant behavior. In L. Carmichael (Ed.), *Manual of child psychology* (2nd ed.). New York: Wiley.

Gesell, A., Amatruda, C., Castner, B. M., & Thompson, H. (1939). *Biographies of child development*. New York: Paul B. Hoeber, Inc.

Grinder, R. E. (1985). The gifted in our midst—by their divine deeds, neuroses, and mental test scores we have known them. In F. D. Horowitz & Marion O'Brien (Eds.), *The gifted and the talented: Developmental perspectives*. Washington, DC: American Psychological Association.

Horowitz, F. D. (Ed.). (1974). Visual attention, auditory stimulation and language discrimination in young infants. *Monographs of the Society for Research in Child Development, 39*, 5–6.

Horowitz, F. D. (1980). Intervention and its effects on early development: What model of development is appropriate? In R. Turner & H. W. Reese (Eds.), *Life span development; psychology intervention* (pp. 235–248). New York: Academic Press.

Horowitz, F. D. (1984). The psychobiology of parent-offspring relations in high-risk situations. In L. P. Lipsitt & C. Rovee-Collier (Eds.), *Advances in infancy research* (Vol. 3, pp. 1–22). Norwood, NJ: Ablex.

Horowitz, F. D. (1987). *Exploring developmental theories: Toward a structural/behavioral model of development.* Hillsdale, NJ: Erlbaum.

Horowitz, F. D. (1990). Developmental models of individual differences. In J. Colombo & J. Fagan (Eds.), *Individual differences in infancy: Reliability, stability, prediction* (pp. 3–18). Hillsdale, NJ: Erlbaum.

Horowitz, F. D., & O'Brien, M. (Eds.). (1985). *The gifted and the talented: Developmental perspectives.* Washington, DC: American Psychological Association.

Horowitz, F. D., & Paden, L. Y. (1973). The effectiveness of environmental intervention programs. In B. M. Caldwell & H. N. Ricciuti (Eds.), *Review of child development research* (Vol. 3, pp. 331–402). Chicago: University of Chicago Press.

Jensen, A. R. (1989). Raising IQ without increasing g? A review of "The Milwaukee project: Preventing mental retardation in children at risk." *Developmental Review, 9,* 234–258.

Kagan, J., Kearsley, R. B., & Zelazo, P. R. (1978). *Infancy: Its place in human development.* Cambridge, MA: Harvard University Press.

Kuo, Z. Y. (1967). *The dynamics of behavioral development.* New York: Random House.

Lazar, I., Darlington, R., Murray, H., Royce, J., & Snipper, A. (1982). Lasting effects of early education. *Monographs of the Society for Research in Child Development, 47* (1–2, Serial No. 194).

Loehlin, J. C., Horn, J. W., & Willerman, L. (1989). Modeling IQ change: Evidence from the Texas adoption project. *Child Development, 60,* 993–1004.

McCall, R. B. (1976). Toward an epigenetic conception of mental development in the first three years of life. In M. Lewis (Ed.), *Origins of intelligence* (pp. 97–122). New York: Plenum Press.

McCall, R. B. (1989). Issues in predicting later IQ from infant habituation rate and recognition memory performance. *Human Development, 32,* 177–186.

McCall, R. B. (1990). Infancy research: Individual differences. *Merrill-Palmer Quarterly, 36,* 141–157.

McCall, R. B., Eichorn, D. H., & Hogarty, P. S. (1977). Transitions in early mental development. *Monographs of the Society for Research in Child Development, 42* (Serial No. 171).

Piaget, J. (1926). *The language and thought of the child.* New York: Harcourt Brace.

Piaget, J. (1952). *The origins of intelligence in children.* New York: International Universities Press.

Preyer, W. (1909a). *The mind of the child. Part II: The development of the intellect.* New York: Appleton & Co. (Published originally in German 1881–1882.)

Preyer, W. (1909b). *The mind of the child. Part I: The senses and the will.* New York: D. Appleton & Co. (Published originally in German 1881–1882.)

Rose, S. A., & Feldman, J. F. (1990). Infant cognition: Individual differences and developmental continuities. In J. Colombo & J. Fagan (Eds.), *Individual differences in infancy* (pp. 229-245). Hillsdale, NJ: Erlbaum.

Rose, S. A., Feldman, J. F., Wallace, J. F., & McCarton, C. (1989). Infant visual attention: Relation to birth status and developmental outcome during the first 5 years. *Developmental Psychology, 25*, 560–576.

Sameroff, A. J. (1983). Developmental systems: Concepts and evolution. In P. H. Mussen (Series Ed.), *Handbook of child psychology* (4th ed., Vol. I), W. Kessen (Ed.), *History, theory and methods* (pp. 237–294). New York: Wiley.

Sameroff, A. J., & Chandler, M. J. (1975). Reproductive risk and the continuum of caretaking casualty. In F. D. Horowitz (Ed.), *Review of child development research* (Vol. 4, pp. 187–244). Chicago: University of Chicago Press.

Shoda, Y., Mischel, W., & Peake, P. K. (1990). Predicting adolescent cognitive and self-regulatory competencies from preschool delay of gratification: Identifying diagnostic conditions. *Developmental Psychology, 26*, 978–986.

Sroufe, L. A., Egeland, B., & Kreutzer, T. (1990). The fate of early experience following developmental change: Longitudinal approaches to individual adaptation in childhood. *Child Development, 61*, 1363–1373.

Sternberg, R. J. (1985). *Beyond IQ: A triarchic theory of human intelligence.* Cambridge, UK: Cambridge University Press.

Sternberg, R., & Davidson, J. E. (Eds.). (1986). *Conceptions of giftedness.* Cambridge, UK: Cambridge University Press.

Stevenson, H. W. (1972). *Children's learning.* New York: Appleton-Century-Crofts.

Storfer, M. D. (1990). *Intelligence and giftedness.* San Francisco: Jossey-Bass.

Thelen, E. (1989). Self-organization in developmental processes: Can systems approaches work. In M. R. Gunnar & E. Thelen (Eds.), *Systems and development Minnesota symposium on child psychology* (Vol. 22, pp. 77–117). Hillsdale, NJ: Erlbaum.

Thelen, E. (1990). Dynamical systems and the generation of individual differences. In J. Colombo & J. Fagan (Eds.), *Individual differences in infancy: Reliability, stability, prediction* (pp. 19–43). Hillsdale, NJ: Erlbaum.

Thelen, E., Kelso, J. A. S., & Fogel, A. (1987). Self-organizing systems and infant motor development. *Developmental Review, 7*, 39–65.

von Bertalanffy, L. (1968). *General system theory* (rev. ed.). New York: George Braziller.

von Bertalanffy, L. (1975). *Perspectives on general system theory.* New York: George Braziller.

Wachs, T. D. (1989). The nature of the physical environment: An expanded classification system. *Merrill-Palmer Quarterly, 35*, 399–420.

Wachs, T. D. (1990). Must the physical environment be mediated by the social environment in order to influence development? A further test. *Journal of Applied Developmental Psychology, 11*, 163–178.

Wallace, D. B., & Gruber, H. (Eds.). (1989). *Creative people at work*. Oxford: Oxford University Press.

Watson, J. B., & Rayner, R. (1920). Conditioned emotional reactions. *Journal of Experimental Psychology, 3*, 1–14.

Weiss, P. A. (1968). *Dynamics of development: Experiments and inferences*. New York: Academic Press.

Weiss, P. A. (1971). *Hierarchically organized systems in theory and practice*. New York: Hafner Publishing Company.

Werner, H. (1957a). *Comparative psychology of mental development* (3rd ed.). New York: International Universities Press.

Werner, H. (1957b). The concept of development from a comparative and organismic point of view. In D. B. Harris (Ed.), *The concept of development: On issues in the study of human behavior* (pp. 125–148). Minneapolis: University of Minnesota Press. (Reprinted in S. S. Barten & M. B. Franklin (Eds.), *Developmental processes*, 1978, pp. 107–130. New York: International Universities Press.)

Wolf, P. H. (1989). The concept of development. How does it constrain assessment and therapy. In P. R. Zelazo & R. G. Barr (Eds.), *Challenges to developmental paradigms* (pp. 13–28). Hillsdale, NJ: Erlbaum.

Zelazo, P. R., & Barr, R. G. (Eds.). (1989). *Challenges to developmental paradigms*. Hillsdale, NJ: Erlbaum.

chapter 5

The Early Development of Three Profoundly Gifted Children of IQ 200*

Miraca U. M. Gross

University of New South Wales
Sydney, Australia

Someone has said that genius is of necessity solitary, since the population is so sparse at the higher levels of mental ability. However, adult genius is mobile and can seek out its own kind. It is in the case of the child with extraordinarily high IQ that the social problem is most acute. If the IQ is 180, the intellectual level at six is almost on a par with the average eleven-year-old, and at ten or eleven is not far from that of the average high-school graduate. . . . The inevitable result is that the child of IQ 180 has one of the most difficult problems of social adjustment that any human being is ever called upon to meet.

(Burks, Jensen, & Terman, 1930, p. 264)

Ian Baker, at the age of 1, used to enjoy counting his diapers as his mother dropped them into the washing machine. By age 2 he had his own collection of elderly 45 r.p.m. records and cassette

---

* "Christopher Otway" and "Ian Baker," and the names given to their parents, are pseudonyms selected by the children themselves. All other details are factual. "Terence Tao" is Terry's real name. Some of the details regarding Terry's early education and development are reproduced, with thanks, from an earlier paper (Gross, 1986).

tapes, and would entertain himself for hours, selecting his favorite music by reading the labels, as his reading skills had developed early and with remarkable speed. Even as a toddler his vocabulary was rich and mature: he astonished family friends at the age of 2 years 3 months by informing them, "My father is a mathematician and my mother is a physiotherapist." By 3½ he was reading small books, and at kindergarten, which he entered at age 4, Ian was accustomed to assisting his teacher by reading aloud to the rest of the class. He had developed the technique of holding the book away from him and reading upside down so that the other children, seated around him, could follow the words. He was a vibrant, energetic child, enthralled by new knowledge and propelled by a compulsion to learn all he could about everything that crossed his path.

Australian children enter kindergarten at age 4, and school at age 5, 12 months earlier than their American counterparts. By the time Ian entered school he was reading, with keen pleasure and full comprehension, E. B. White's *Charlotte's Web*. Difficulties arose, however, within the first few weeks. Sally Baker, Ian's mother, had tentatively mentioned to his Reception Class teacher that Ian was already a fluent and enthusiastic reader. The teacher refused to believe this, and insisted that Ian should work through reading readiness exercises with the other 5-year-olds. As Ian had long since passed through the stage of needing to "sound out" words and now read silently and absorbedly, his teacher, even when she did notice him reading, assumed he was simply looking at the pictures. As for math, which had been a joy and obsession to Ian since he turned 4, by which age he had already mastered addition and subtraction of numbers up to 1,000—Math in the Reception Class was limited to the recognition of the numbers 1–10!

Ian made two important discoveries in his first few weeks of schooling—firstly, that the school would teach him nothing which he had not taught himself at least 18 months previously; and secondly, that he had absolutely nothing in common with the other children in his class. His reading capacity, his interests, his vocabulary, the games he wanted to play in the schoolyard, the television programs he preferred, were all radically different from those of the other 5-year-olds. Before long he was disliked, resented, and rejected by his classmates. Being a lad of spirit and furious with the school's refusal to let him learn, Ian returned the resentment in full measure.

Ian was bored, deeply unhappy, and restless at school, but his parents were not, at first, informed of any serious behavioral problems. However, some 8 months into the school year, the vice-principal and Ian's teacher asked them to visit the school for an interview. In this meeting Sally and Brock were rather brusquely informed that

Ian was uncontrollable in class, that he was displaying bouts of frightening physical violence towards other children, and that the school wished to have him psychometrically assessed with a view to transferring him to a special school for behaviorally disturbed children. This school was attached to the psychiatric department of a large children's hospital.

"We were totally devastated," says Brock Baker. *"We felt as though we had managed in 5½ years to bring up a violent criminal who was about to be expelled from school before he had completed 1 year."*

In some ways, however, the news of Ian's aggressiveness at school confirmed a concern which Brock and Sally already had about aspects of his behavior at home. *"We had always felt that Ian was reasonably bright, and we had noticed that, whenever he became bored, he stormed around the place like a caged lion looking for a fight. When he was in that mood, he became physically aggressive and verbally nasty towards anyone in reach, especially smaller children. When he was mentally stimulated, then his behavior improved considerably. Accordingly, we were only too happy to have him assessed. We felt sure that if he was indeed identified as bright and in need of further stimulation, then the school would respond to this. In addition, any help the psychologist could give us to improve our handling of Ian at home would be most welcome!"*

Ian was assessed on the *Stanford-Binet Intelligence Scale L-M* at the age of 5 years 11 months and was found to have a mental age of 9 years 10 months and an IQ somewhere in excess of 169. To complement the *Stanford-Binet* testing, the educational psychologist administered a standardized test of reading achievement and found that Ian's reading accuracy and reading comprehension were at the 12-year-old level—more than 6 years in advance of his classmates. Subsequent testing on the *Stanford-Binet L-M* at the age of 9 years 3 months established a mental age of 18 years 6 months and a ratio IQ of 200. Children scoring at this level appear in the population at a ratio of fewer than 1 in 1 million. To require Ian to undertake all his school work with age-peers of average ability was somewhat akin to requiring a child of average intelligence to spend 6 hours a day, 5 days a week, interacting solely with children who were profoundly intellectually handicapped.

RESEARCH ON EXCEPTIONALLY AND PROFOUNDLY GIFTED CHILDREN

Children of truly exceptional intellectual potential are an understudied and underserved population. Educators and psychologists working in gifted education generally recognize that the intellectually gifted differ from their age-peers of average ability in the development of their speech and motor skills, their learning styles and capacities, their friendship choices, their hobbies and interests, and in their social and emotional growth. Many of us, however, are unaware of the vast extent of the differences among the gifted themselves.

Researchers have noted profound differences between moderately gifted and exceptionally gifted children on almost every cognitive and affective variable studied to this date. In terms of intellectual capacity alone, the child of IQ 190 differs from moderately gifted classmates of IQ 130 to the same degree that the latter differ from intellectually handicapped children of IQ 70. If he or she is to come anywhere near to maximizing his or her remarkable intellectual or academic potential, the exceptionally gifted (IQ 160–179) or profoundly gifted (IQ 180+) child requires an educational program which differs quite radically in structure, pace, and content from that which might be offered to moderately gifted age-mates. A pullout program offering "relevant academic enrichment" (Stanley, 1979) for a few hours per week may be an excellent interventive response to the needs of a Grade 4 student who is capable of Grade 6 math; however, enrichment taken by itself would be an inadequate and inappropriate response to a student such as Ian Baker, who in Grade 4 scored 560 on the *Scholastic Aptitude Test-Mathematics (SAT-M)*.

Differences between moderately and extremely gifted children are not, of course, confined to the cognitive domain. Hollingworth (1926) defined the IQ range 125–155 as "socially optimal intelligence." She found that children scoring within this range were well-balanced, self-confident, and outgoing individuals who were able to win the confidence of age-peers. She claimed, however, that, above the level of IQ 160, the difference between the exceptionally gifted child and his or her age-mates is so great that it leads to special problems of development which are correlated with social isolation, and that these difficulties appear particularly acute at ages 4 through 9 (Hollingworth, 1942). DeHaan and Havighurst (1961), examining the differences between what they termed "second-order" (IQ 125–160) and "first-order" (IQ 160+) gifted children, reinforced Hollingworth's findings and suggested that the second-order gifted child achieves good social adjustment because he or she has sufficient intelligence to overcome minor social difficulties but is not "different" enough to induce the severe problems of salience encountered by the exceptionally gifted student.

Several researchers studying the peer relations of extremely gifted children have emphasized that the social isolation to which many of them seem prone is not the self-sought isolation of emotional disturbance, but rather a "separateness" which is imposed on the child through his or her rejection, from an early age, by age-peers of average ability. Sheldon (1959) found that over 50% of his sample of children of IQ 170+ reported feelings of isolation and rejection, but concluded that an extremely high IQ is not by itself sufficient cause for perceptions of isolation; he believed that the negative self-perceptions of his subjects arose in part from factors in the dynamic roles played by teachers and classmates. Janos (1983), comparing the psychosocial development of 32 children aged 6–9 with IQs in excess of 164 with that of 40 age-peers of moderately superior intellectual ability, emphasized that the social difficulties experienced by his highly gifted group did not stem from a preexisting emotional disturbance but rather were caused by the absence of a suitable peer group with whom to relate. There are virtually no points of common experience and common interest between a 6-year-old with a mental age of 6 and a 6-year-old with a mental age of 12. That this social insolation results from an absence of congenial companionship rather than from a tendency to misanthropy on behalf of the exceptionally gifted is demonstrated by the fact that, where socially isolated children have been accelerated to be with intellectual peers, the isolation has disappeared and the exceptionally gifted have been able to form warm and supportive relationships with their older classmates (Hollingworth, 1942; Pollins, 1983; Gross, 1989).

In a comprehensive review of research on the psychosocial development of the intellectually gifted, Janos and Robinson (1985) indicate that research studies regarding favorable personal and social adjustment emanate from studies of moderately gifted rather than highly gifted children. Janos and Robinson claim that, although the special problems of the extremely gifted demand urgent investigation, "the research devoted to exploring them pales in comparison with that devoted to virtually any other maladaptive set of behaviors" (Janos & Robinson, 1985, p. 182).

Exceptionally gifted children comprise a population characterized by its scarcity. The incidence of children scoring at or above IQ 160 on the *Stanford-Binet Intelligence Scale (L-M)*, as predicted by the statistical tables, lies somewhere between 1:10,000 and 1:30,000 (Marland, 1972). It should be noted that researchers over the last 60 years have repeatedly found that the number of children actually identified in the IQ range 160+ far exceeds the theoretical expectations derived from the normal curve of distribution (Terman, 1926; Burt, 1968; Robinson, 1981; Silverman, 1989a; Gross, 1989); nevertheless, even the most generous overprediction must acknowledge that these young people comprise an extremely small minority of the child population.

Because of this factor, research on extreme intellectual precocity in children has comprised, in the main, isolated case studies of individual students (Terman & Fenton, 1921; McElwee, 1934; Witty & Coomer, 1955). Such group studies as do exist are generally of short duration (Gallagher & Crowder, 1957; Barbe, 1964; Flack, 1983), and have examined the academic and psychosocial development of the extremely gifted during only one part of their school lives, rather than tracing their social and emotional growth through childhood and adolescence. Indeed, some of the best-known studies are retrospective, written when the children have attained adulthood, or even after the subject's death (Montour, 1977; Bergman, 1979). Longitudinal studies of extremely gifted children that followed the child's development through adolescence into adulthood, such as Leta Hollingworth's landmark study of children of IQ 180+ (Hollingworth, 1942) or the "study within a study" which traced the development of the Terman subjects of IQ 170+ (Burks et al., 1930) are disturbingly few.

If we are to acquire a fuller appreciation of the needs and characteristics of this understudied minority, it is important that studies of the academic and social development of profoundly gifted young people should be undertaken, not retrospectively, but *in current time*; that is, at the time when the young subjects are actually experiencing the upbringing, the school programs, the social relationships, and other influences that contribute to their overall development. In this way, events and situations that impact on the child's development can be observed as they occur rather than through the filter of an unintentionally biased or selective memory. The changing influence of family, school, and society can be analyzed and discussed with the child himself as well as with others involved in his academic and personal growth. It is especially important, in cases of exceptional or profound intellectual giftedness, where the child's psychosocial development may differ radically from that of his age-peers, that his feelings and perceptions of the world should be recorded at the time when they are influencing his thoughts and actions, rather than related in later years, blurred or altered by his adult recollections.

The case study method is a sound approach for developing specific knowledge about exceptional giftedness. It is ideally suited to the investigation and description of events or individuals characterized by their rarity (Foster, 1986). It can describe intensively the particular and idiosyncratic features of the student's development. It provides a holistic view of the subject (Frey, 1978) and allows the researcher to develop and validate theories grounded in direct observation of individual students. Indeed, close observation of the subject in natural settings, the analysis of subjective factors such as the subject's feelings, views, and needs, and the use of a wide range of observation procedures, all of which are characteristic of good case study research, enable a more comprehensive observation of a subject or process than is possible with any other research methodology (Merriam, 1988).

THREE AUSTRALIAN CASE STUDIES

For some years the author has been pursuing a longitudinal study of 40 exceptionally and profoundly gifted Australian children who score at or in excess of IQ 160 on the *Stanford-Binet Intelligence Scale L-M* (1972 norms). This study will trace the intellectual, academic, social, and emotional development of each subject through childhood and adolescence, until the youngest child, currently aged 6, has graduated from high school. At the time of writing (early 1991), no subject has been in the study for fewer than 2 years, and the author has been closely involved with several of the subjects for more than 8 years.

A major difficulty in the assessment of extremely high levels of intellectual giftedness is the systematic depression of scores at the high end of the scale on all currently used instruments because of ceiling effects. Group IQ tests are notoriously ineffective in discriminating between the intellectual capacities even of moderately and highly gifted children (Pegnato & Birch, 1959), and even certain individual tests such as the *WISC-R*, the *WIPPSI*, and the *K-ABC* do not have items of sufficient difficulty to assess the full range of abilities of extremely gifted students. Indeed, Hagen, in an interview with Silverman on the construction of the new *Stanford-Binet Revision IV* (Silverman, 1986), commented that, in general, items are purposely omitted from IQ tests if they can only be solved by intellectually gifted students.

Until 1986, the *Stanford-Binet L-M* was generally regarded as the best single available measure of general intellectual ability (Martinson, 1974; Stanley, 1977–1978), and the most reliable method of measuring very high levels of intellective ability (Hagen, 1980; Silverman, 1989a). Silverman and Kearney (1989) reported discrepancies of over 50 IQ points in scores of extremely gifted children assessed on the *WISC-R* or *K-ABC* and subsequently tested on the

Stanford-Binet-L-M. Gross (1989) reported similar findings, including an emotionally disturbed 12-year-old girl whose full-scale score on the *WISC-R* was 147 but who scored in excess of IQ 180 on the *Stanford-Binet (L-M).*

In 1986, however, the publication of the *Stanford-Binet Revision IV* replaced the earlier *L-M* version. Unfortunately, the new test is generating significantly lower scores for the entire gifted range. The *Revision IV* manual itself reports that mean composite IQ scores for a group of 82 gifted children (average age 7 years 4 months) were 135 on the *L-M* version, but only 121 on the *Revision IV* (Thorndike, Hagen, & Sattler, 1986). Kitano and De Leon (1988) reported that the *Revision IV* identifies fewer preschool children as achieving IQ scores of 1.5 standard deviations above the mean than did the *L-M* version. Robinson (this volume) reports that the mean IQ of linguistically precocious toddlers aged 30 months was 138, with a standard deviation of 9.6 on the *Stanford-Binet L-M,* but only 125 on the *Revision IV.* This is a significant depression of scores on the newer test. Thus, even moderately gifted children are less likely to be identified through use of the new *Stanford-Binet* than would have been identified by using its predecessor.

An additional problem lies in the construction of the *Revision IV* in that, among other changes, it eliminates the mental age which, in the *L-M* version, could be used to calculate a ratio IQ for exceptionally and profoundly gifted children whose scores went beyond the range of norms in the manual. Psychologists such as Silverman and Kearney, who have a particular interest in the highly and exceptionally gifted, are now recommending that, in cases where a child obtains three subtest scores at or near the ceiling of any current instrument, he or she should be tested on the *Stanford-Binet L-M* and ratio scores computed for any child who scores beyond the test norms (Silverman & Kearney, 1989).

All 40 subjects in Gross's Australian study have been tested using the 1972 norms of the *Stanford-Binet L-M.* Even so, a ceiling effect has operated for no fewer than 8 of the 40 children, and, following the practice advocated by Silverman and Kearney (1989), ratio IQs have been computed for these young people through the formula:

$$\frac{\text{mental age}}{\text{chronological age}} \times 100$$

The ratio IQs thus computed for the eight children range from 175 to a remarkable 220.

This chapter deals with the three most profoundly gifted of Gross's Australian subjects, three young boys currently aged between 10 and 15 who, when assessed on the *Stanford-Binet L-M*, obtained mental ages twice, or more than twice, their chronological ages, and thus ratio IQs of 200 or higher. Ian Baker, Terence Tao, and Christopher Otway are among the most profoundly gifted children identified and studied anywhere in the world (Silverman, 1989b).

Each of the three boys displayed, from their earliest years, quite astonishing intellectual and academic precocity. Each, by the time he entered school, was displaying levels of reading and mathematics achievement not normally attained until the later years of elementary school. However, the significance of this developmental precocity will be more clearly understood when viewed in the light of the children's subsequent school careers and academic successes. Accordingly, a brief profile of each child's school history and scholastic attainments will be presented in the next few pages, prior to commencing a comparative analysis of various aspects of the children's psychomotor, intellectual, and psychosocial development during the first 8 years.

Ian Baker

When the educational psychologist who tested 5½-year-old Ian on the *Stanford-Binet* confirmed that he had a mental age of 9 years 10 months, an IQ in excess of 169, and the reading accuracy and comprehension of a 12-year-old, he emphasized strongly, both to the Bakers and to the school, that Ian's frightening emotional swings were directly related to the amount of intellectual stimulation he was receiving, and asserted the importance, for the emotional health of such an exceptionally gifted child, of providing him with academic work at sufficiently challenging levels. The psychologist also emphasized that Ian desperately needed the companionship of other children who shared his abilities and interests, and referred him to the weekend programs run by the Gifted Children's Association in his State, while strongly recommending that the school establish some form of enrichment and extension program to respond to his intellectual and social needs during the rest of the week.

To the surprise and pleasure of Brock and Sally Baker, the school, and Ian's teacher, responded to the challenge with enthusiasm. *"Ian's teacher, who had never had such a child in her class before, took it upon herself to stimulate Ian, and did not force him to do the same work as the others if he did not want to,"* relates Brock Baker. *"She scoured resource centers looking for suitable curriculum materials and put in a great deal of extra work to ensure that the problem of boredom did not recur. Ian stayed with this teacher right through Grade 1 and Grade 2 and she gave him a variety of really stimulating Math tasks—some of them right up at Grade 8 level. In addition, the principal was very encouraging towards the gifted children in the school. He set up several pull-out sessions, taught both by himself and other staff members, which Ian and several others in the school attended. These 2 years could not have been better for Ian and, as a result the whole family benefitted."*

Unfortunately, this situation was relatively short lived. Shortly after the start of the year in which Ian entered Grade 3, the principal retired. During the few months following his departure the pull-out program was allowed to dwindle and finally die out. In addition, Ian's Grade 3 teacher, who had reluctantly permitted him to do Grade 7 math in the first few weeks of the year, gave him no special teaching, guidance, or assistance, and with no encouragement to continue, Ian gradually reverted to the Grade 3 curriculum of his classmates. At the start of Ian's grade 4 year a new principal was appointed. This was an experienced and politically astute young woman who was aware of the overt hostility of the militant Australian teacher industrial unions towards special programming for the gifted, and the disapproval of gifted programs openly voiced by a number of influential senior administrators in the State Education Department. She was also made aware, by her new staff, that they had "had enough of gifted children and special programs for the gifted," which they felt had been foisted upon them by the old principal. When Brock and Sally sought an interview to ask whether some form of enrichment could be offered to Ian, she refused adamantly to allow him any special provision that was not offered to the other students, and informed the Bakers frankly that it would be "political suicide" for her to re-establish gifted programs in her school.

Ian completed Grade 3 in a quiet fury of anger, intellectual frustration and bitterness. His verbal and physical aggressiveness returned in full spate; however, as he was now 2 years older than he had been in Grade 1, he was able to maintain a tighter control on his emotions while at school, and his teachers remained quite unaware of the emotional toll levied on him. At home, however, he released all his frustration and resentment and became, in Brock's words, "almost impossible to live with." In addition, he began to experience severe headaches, bouts of nausea, and stomach pains. The mornings became a battle to get Ian well enough, and subdued enough, to go to school.

This situation lasted for 2 whole years, through Grades 3 and 4. The Bakers made regular visits to the school to plead with the teachers and the principal to provide some form of intellectual stimulation for Ian, but they were met with vague promises which never materialized. During his Grade 4 year, Brock and Sally decided to have Ian reassessed by an independent psychologist with a special interest in intellectually gifted children. Accordingly, at the age of 9 years 3 months Ian was assessed firstly on the *Wechsler Intelligence Scale for Children (WISC-R)* and subsequently on the *Stanford-Binet (L-M)*, the scale on which he had first been tested at age 5. Ian ceilinged out on the *WISC-R*, scoring scaled scores of 19 on all subscales of both the verbal and performance subtests. On the *Stanford-Binet* Ian, in the words of the psychologist's report, "sailed through all the items through to the highest level of all, Superior Adult Three. Here he did start to fail on some tests, but nevertheless his IQ came off the top of this scale also." Ian scored a mental age of 18 years 6 months, exactly twice his chronological age. As was discussed earlier in this chapter, in cases of exceptional intellectual giftedness where a deviation IQ cannot be calculated, a ratio calculation is recommended in order to obtain some indication of the child's intellectual status. A ratio calculation places Ian's IQ at 200. In addition, the psychologist administered standardized achievement tests of math, reading, and spelling. Ian's reading and spelling were at adult level, and on the *British Ability Scales* math test, he scored more than 5 years above his chronological age.

The psychologist was appalled to hear that a child of such exceptional talent was being forced to plod through a lockstep curriculum with other Grade 4 students. She expressed her concern strongly in her written report.

> I was somewhat concerned to hear from Ian and from his parents that he has been doing Grade 4 maths along with his classmates. We clearly have here a boy who has extreme talent in the math area. . . . I would strongly suggest that Ian most clearly needs acceleration in his math program. He is likely to become quite bored and frustrated by math at his own age level and it seems to be a real waste of true talent.

> Over the years Ian's parents and teachers have had occasional bouts of difficult behavior from Ian. He certainly is not a subtle sort of child. . . . His parents have found, as is true with many other gifted and talented children, that when Ian becomes bored, and does not have his "fix" of intellectual activity, it is then that the difficult behavior begins. . . . It is important to remember that his behavior only deteriorates to unacceptable levels when he is signalling that he is bored and is not getting the intellectual stimulation he needs by legitimate means.

> It needs to be remembered that for Ian to be intellectually stimulated, the activities presented to him need to be of a particularly high level.

He certainly will not be challenged by the types of problems and puzzles which generally interest children of his age. Certainly, working with the Binet, he could dismiss such types of questions without a second thought, and they obviously hold no interest for him, nor any satisfaction when he has solved them.

Psychologist's report on Ian Baker, aged 9

Half way through Ian's Grade 4 year, it became clear to the Bakers that there was little hope of his school, under the new principal, ever reestablishing its programs for, or its interest in, highly able students, and they began to search for a new school to which Ian could be transferred. They approached a number of local schools, both government and private, to determine if any were sympathetic to the plight of gifted and talented children. In almost every case the principal expressed sympathy with their problem but indicated quite definitely that the school made no special provision for gifted students, nor was such provision likely to be established in the foreseeable future.

Finally, the principal of the elementary section of a large and prestigious private (independent) school took an interest in Ian. She had attended several conferences on gifted children, had been involved in the activities of the Gifted Children's Association in the State in which she had previously lived, and knew enough about gifted education and the intellectually gifted to recognize the implications of the psychologist's report. She told the Bakers that, although her school had, at that time, no special programs for gifted students, she intended to establish these the following year, and having such an extremely gifted student as Ian in the school would prove an additional incentive for their establishment. Ian enrolled in her school at the start of Grade 5. Two months later, as part of the regular assessment procedures required for the longitudinal study of exceptionally gifted children in which Ian is involved, the author administered to him the *Scholastic Aptitude Test-Mathematics (SAT-M)*. He made a scaled score of 560M—.6 of a standard deviation above the mean on this test normed on American college-bound high school students 7–8 years his senior.

During the first semester of Grade 5, Ian participated in pull-out programs for mathematically gifted children in Grade 5–7. His Grade 5 class teacher admittedly freely, however, that she simply did not have the skills or knowledge to extend his phenomenal mathematics capabilities within the regular classroom. Accordingly, the school found a mentor for Ian—one of the mathematics teachers from the senior school—and this teacher worked with Ian in a mentorial relationship for the rest of the year, taking him through the Grade 8 and 9 math curriculum, and filling in the gaps in his knowledge. The target was to bring Ian up to the Grade 10 standard in math, so that the following year, 1990, he could work with the Grade 10 students in a program of subject acceleration. This indeed occurred.

At the present time Ian, aged 11, is based with the Grade 8 students having been permitted to skip Grade 7, but undertakes math with the top stream of the Grade 11 students. In addition, he attends pull-out programs developed by the school for mathematically talented students. He still finds much of the Grade 8 curriculum in other subject areas boring and unchallenging, but the Bakers hope that, as the year goes on and the school realizes the academic and emotional benefits that are accruing from Ian's math acceleration, they might consider accelerating him in other areas as well.

During 1989 the school entered Ian, along with other mathematically talented students, in two Australia-wide math competitions. Normally, students are not eligible to enter these competitions before Grade 7; however, in acknowledgement of Ian's remarkable abilities, he was permitted to enter while still in Grade 5. In both competitions he outperformed all other entrants from his school. Ian was jubilant, but slightly dazed. *"His achievements in these competitions finally meant that he received some public recognition for his scholastic abilities,"* says Brock Baker. *"The certificates and trophies were presented at school assemblies, and, in addition, his achievements were referred to during the junior school principal's annual report presented on Speech Day. This was the first time in Ian's life that anyone had publicly acknowledged and praised his abilities. For Ian, and his parents and grandparents, Speech Day was a very high high."*

At the time of writing, part way through Ian's Grade 8 year, his dislike of school has moderated to some extent, he is receiving some degree of intellectual challenge, and the migraines, abdominal cramps, and nausea that plagued him when his intellectual frustration was at his most severe seem to have disappeared. It is unfortunate, however, that Ian had to suffer through 4 years of educational mismanagement before his astonishing intellectual abilities were at last acknowledged and fostered.

Terence Tao

Fifteen-year-old Terence Tao, of South Australia, is a prodigiously gifted young mathematician. Julian Stanley, Director of the internationally renowned Study of Mathematically Precocious Youth (SMPY) at Johns Hopkins University, Baltimore, has stated that Terry has the greatest mathematical reasoning ability of any child he has ever discovered (Stanley, 1985). In May, 1983, at the age of 8 years 10 months, Terry took the (SAT-M) at Stanley's invitation and made the phenomenal score of 760 out of a possible 800. Only 1% of college-bound-17- and 18-year-olds in the United States attain a score of 750 or more.

Terry's remarkable mathematical and scientific reasoning abilities are grounded in a truly phenomenal intellectual capacity. He was assessed on the *Stanford-Binet* at the age of 6, obtaining a mental age of 14 and a ratio IQ of between 220 and 230.

As with Ian Baker, Terry's mathematical precocity had displayed itself at an early age. By the time he was 3, he was displaying the reading, writing, and mathematical ability of a 6-year-old. Billy and Grace Tao, who had both been educated in Hong Kong and had little experience of the Australian school system, decided to allow their brilliant son to enter school at the age of 3½, 18 months earlier than the norm for South Australian children.

> We were so carried away by the speed of Terry's progress between the ages of 2 and 3½ that we took the rather naive and simplistic view that everything would be very easy and rosy and that if we sent Terence to school early, the school would do whatever would be necessary to meet his needs, and he would be able to continue to develop at his own pace. (Billy Tao, 1985)

Numerous studies (e.g., Worcester, 1955; Hobson, 1979; Alexander & Skinner, 1980) have shown that, where underage children are admitted to formal schooling on the basis of intellectual and academic precocity, they perform as well as, or rather better than, their older classmates. Early entry is acknowledged as a practical and appropriate response to the academic and social needs of highly gifted children in cases where the child is intellectually, academically, and socially mature enough to cope with the demands of the school day. A requirement of equal importance, but usually given less consideration, is that the school that enrolls a young child of exceptional intellectual potential must provide a curriculum that is academically rigorous, intellectually stimulating, and flexible enough to meet the demands of the child.

Terry entered a private primary school in February 1979, at the age of 3 years 6 months. The experiment, however, was not a success. Intellectually, Terry was very far in advance of his 5-year-old classmates; socially, however, he would have needed a great deal of support and encouragement from his class teacher if he were to cope successfully with a 6-hour school day. This understanding and flexibility were, unhappily, not forthcoming; his teacher was unable to cope with Terry's intellectual and social needs and complained to the school principal that he distracted the other children. After several weeks the Taos and the school principal agreed that Terry should be withdrawn from school. It should be noted that at no other time in Terry's school and university career of extremely radical acceleration (he completed the requirements for his bachelor of science degree in mid-1990, shortly after his 15th birthday) have the Taos been told that his presence has been a distraction to other students. Proctor, Feldhusen, and Black (1988), in their guidelines for early admission of intellectually gifted children, emphasize that the receiving teacher must have positive attitudes toward early admission and be willing to assist the young child to adjust to the new situation. In Terry's case the receiving teacher was unable to respond to those requirements.

Terry's parents enrolled him in a neighborhood kindergarten (preschool) with children of his own chronological age, and there he remained for the next 18 months. During this period his mathematical ability progressed at a phenomenal pace. Guided by his mother, herself a first-class honors graduate in mathematics and physics, he completed almost all the elementary school math curriculum before his fifth birthday. One of Terry' early mentors, now a lecturer in mathematics education at Deakin University in Melbourne, Australia, has described Grace Tao's role as one of guiding Terry's math development rather than teaching him. "She said that while she sometimes attempts to guide Terry's mathematical learning she doesn't help him much because he 'doesn't like to be told what to do in mathematics' " (Clements, 1984, p. 221). Indeed, most of Terry's knowledge was acquired through his voracious reading of mathematics and mathematics textbooks.

During this period, through reading and talking with educators, Billy and Grace Tao developed the concept of a form of scholastic program that they believed would meet Terry's intellectual and social needs. Although his performance in most subject areas was far above the level of his chronological age, he was not, nevertheless, uniformly advanced across the board. His prodigious mathematical ability was some years beyond his language ability, advanced though the latter was. Billy and Grace conceived a structure whereby Terry would 'ride' several class levels at one time, taking each school subject at the grade level according to his ability. This structure would have the added advantage of permitting him to mix with children of all ages and ability levels as he moved through school.

Billy and Grace investigated a number of local schools, seeking one with a principal who would have the flexibility and open-mindedness to accept Terry within the program structure they had in mind. After Terry's first unfortunate experience of schooling, they could no longer afford to assume that teachers were ready or willing to cope with his prodigious abilities. They were more fortunate than the Bakers had been. The principal of a local government (public) school two miles from their home shared their belief that an age-based progression through school would be educationally and socially disastrous for an exceptionally gifted child. Terry enrolled in this school shortly after his fifth birthday, and after a brief period in the Reception class during which the principal and staff could assess his performance both academically and socially, he was promoted to a split class of Grade 1 and 2 children, where he did most of his work with the Grade 2 students, who were 2 years older than he, except for mathematics, for which he went daily to the Grade 5 classroom. The program was extremely successful, meeting both Terry's intellectual and social needs, and by the time he was 6½, he was attending Grades 3, 4, 6, and 7 for different subjects, and was playing in the schoolyard with friends from each grade level he worked at.

By the time Terry reached the age of 7, he had far outpaced the Grade 7 students in mathematics and was working independently on Grade 10 math at home in the evenings. At age 7½, through the intervention of his elementary school principal, Terry was permitted to attend the local high school (which enrolled students from Grades 8 to 12) for part of each day, working in Math at Grade 11 level with students 7 years older than he. The rest of the day was spent in Grade 5 and 6 in his elementary school. Terry is a modest and unassuming lad with an unusually open and friendly nature, and he became extremely popular with both his elementary and high school classmates. By the time he turned 8, he was taking math, physics, English, and social studies at high school, moving flexibly between classes at Grade 8, 11, and 12 level, while continuing to attend elementary school part time.

At age 8½, having informally sat and passed university entrance mathematics examinations, Terry began first-year university math, initially in independent study but later under the guidance of faculty members at the Flinders University of South Australia. His parents and the principal of his elementary school had, by this time, reluctantly decided that this school had little more to offer him, and just before his 9th birthday he made a smooth transition from elementary school and began to spend one-quarter of his time at university and the other three-quarters at high school, working in several science subjects in Grades 10, 11 and 12 while taking humanities and general studies with Grade 8. By the time he was 12, his studies at university included 4th year algebra, 2nd year physics, and 2nd year computer science.

Like Ian Baker, Terry displayed an absorbing thirst for knowledge from his earliest years. Both he and his parents were anxious that his education should be a broadening experience rather than a purely vertical extension of his prodigious talents in Math and Science. Accordingly, as Terry gained each university qualification he used the time thus saved at school to take on another subject. As the pace with which he masters new work is immeasurably faster even than that of his classmates at university, he has been able to maintain a radically accelerated program that is equally remarkable for the breadth of its content. Currently, at age 15, he has passed university entrance examinations in mathematics, physics, chemistry, biology, and English, and has completed university courses in areas such as mathematical physics, linear and abstract algebra, Lebesque integration, electromagnetic theory, optics, and several areas of computing science. At high school in 1990 he took classical studies, modern European history, and Latin at Grade 12, and German at Grade 10. In 3 successive years he competed in the International Mathematical Olympiad as a member of the Australian team, winning a bronze medal in Cuba in 1986 at the tender age of 10, a silver in Warsaw in 1987, and a gold in Canberra, Australia, at the age of 12.

Terry Tao gained his bachelor of science degree shortly after his 15th birthday and is now taking postgraduate studies in math. There is little doubt that had he chosen to enter university full time at the age of 9, at which time he would certainly have been able to master the academic content of this course, he would probably have graduated with his first degree at the age of 12. It was more important to Terry and his parents, however, that he divide his time between high school and university in such a way that he could progress at a more leisurely pace, where more emphasis could be placed on creativity, original thinking, and the acquisition of a broader knowledge base. *"Later, when he does enter full-time,"* said Billy Tao when Terry was 10 years old, *"he will have much more time for research or anything else he finds interesting. He may be a few years older when he graduates but he will be much better prepared for the more rigorous graduate and post-doctoral work."*

"University is not the best place for a young child to mature socially," added Billy Tao, *"and certainly not before adolescence.*

By continuing to spend part of his time in high school Terry can continue to make friends nearer his own age, learn to sort out the priorities of life, establish a more mature self-perception, and generally cope with the realities of the world" (B. Tao, 1985).

Christopher Otway

From his earliest years Christopher Otway displayed prodigious talents in mathematics and language. He taught himself to read at 2 years of age, and before his 4th birthday he was reading children's encyclopedias and had acquired a level of general knowledge that would be unmatched by the majority of Grade 5 or 6 students. His math abilities developed almost as precociously. Shortly after his third birthday he spontaneously began to devise and complete simple addition and subtraction sums, and by the time he entered kindergarten at the usual age of 4, he was capable of working, in mathematics, at Grade 4 level.

Christopher was tested by a Kindergarten Union psychologist at 4½ years of age and was assessed as having a mental age of at least 7 years. However, his parents did not wish for, or seek, early entrance to school for Chris. By the time he enrolled in the local State elementary school a few weeks after his fifth birthday, he had the math achievement level of a Grade 5 student.

Like the parents of Terry Tao, Elizabeth and David Otway were members of their State's Association for Gifted and Talented Children. They had studied the literature on giftedness and were aware of the educational and psychosocial benefits of acceleration for exceptionally gifted children. Accordingly, they suggested to the principal of Christopher's school that he might be a suitable candidate for grade-skipping or subject acceleration. The principal and teachers had recognized Chris's remarkable abilities within a few days of his enrollment and readily accepted that he required a curriculum considerably differentiated in pace and content from that usually offered to Grade 1 students. Consequently, Chris was withdrawn from his Grade 1 class for a few hours each day to join the Grade 2 children for English and the Grade 5s for math. It soon became evident, however, that even this intervention did not address the full extent of Christopher's advancement, and the following year, as a Grade 2 student, he went to the Grade 7 class each day for math.

For the first two years of Christopher's elementary schooling, radical subject acceleration within his own school building proved an effective and sufficient response to his remarkable gifts in mathematics. As in the case of Terry Tao, however, major difficulties arose when Chris's skill and knowledge in math developed to the point where they could no longer be adequately addressed by the staff of the elementary school. Only a few weeks into Grade 3, it became obvious that even the Grade 7 math extension work he was being offered in private tutorials by the principal was no longer sufficient to meet his needs.

After much thought, the Otways transferred Chris, half way through his Grade 3 year, to a large neighborhood school that enrolled students across all grades from Reception to Grade 12. In response to his accelerated abilities in math and language, the receiving school decided to enroll him in Grade 4 rather than Grade 3—an immediate grade-skip of 12 months. To complement the grade-skip, the school was only too willing to continue his subject acceleration in mathematics, and, as an additional response to his evident musical aptitude, permitted him to start lessons in flute, a curricular offering usually reserved for students in Grade 8 and above. The following year Chris entered Grade 5, but was enrolled in Grade 9 for math, and started Indonesian lessons with the Grade 8 students.

A few days after his 11th birthday, Chris was reassessed on the *Stanford-Binet (L-M)* by the psychologist who had conducted the second assessment of Ian Baker. Her report indicates the phenomenal level of Christopher's ability.

On the Stanford-Binet Intelligence Scale, at the age of 11 years 0 months, Christopher obtained a mental age of 22 years. This meant that he had in fact passed virtually all the items on the test, right up to Superior Adult Three. Even here, however, it was obvious that Chris had not really reached his ceiling on some of the items. This gives him an intelligence quotient of at least 200. . . . To extend the testing established on the Stanford-Binet, I also used the *WAIS-R* which is the adult intelligence scale most widely used. Here Chris performed at the absolute maximum for abstract reasoning and arithmetic, placing him in the "very superior" range even compared with adults. At this level we started to pick up some *relative* weaknesses, in that his spacial skills are in the "superior" rather than the "very superior" range compared with an adult. However, obviously given that he is only just 11 years of age, this too is an exceptional score. My belief is that Chris is a boy of very rare talent. Certainly I think the testing today was limited by the ceilings on the tests, rather than by Christopher's ability.

As discussed with Chris's father, I think that his very orderly way of handling information is of interest in its own right. He works well at trying to put every piece of information or every problem which he has to solve into some sort of category. Perhaps at his level of intellectual activity, this is the most effective way of handling the enormous volume of thinking processes which he is getting through and the multitude of information and ideas which he handles each day. I also observed (as have his parents) that Chris is one of the very rare people who truly seem to be able to process information in parallel. For instance, when he was working on quite a difficult question in the assessment, and was obviously thinking and talking on that particular problem, he suddenly interrupted himself to produce the solution to a previous problem which he felt he could improve on.

Psychologist's report on Christopher Otway, aged 11.

Christopher's program of subject acceleration has been extremely successful. At the age of 12 he was based in Grade 9 with students 2 and 3 years older than he, but took physics, chemistry, economics, and English with the Grade 11 classes. He entered Grade 10 in 1990, a few weeks after his 13th birthday, but rather than accelerate to Grade 12 for individual subjects, he himself chose to "repeat" Grade 11 in different curriculum areas, this time taking humanities and foreign language subjects. By the time he reaches Grade 12, the final grade of high school, at age 14, he will have studied a remarkable range of subjects from which he can choose those in which he wishes to specialize in preparation for university entrance.

Christopher could certainly have sat for university entrance at the end of 1989 and would undoubtedly have achieved extremely high grades. His scaled score on the *SAT-M* at the age of 11 years 4 months was a remarkable 710M; fewer than 2% of college-bound 18-year-olds could expect to gain such a score. However, both Chris and his parents feel that, for social reasons, it is best that he postpone part-time university entrance until he is at least 15 years of age.

The relative merits of acceleration and enrichment have been much debated. Many researchers (Goldberg, Passow, Camm, & Neill, 1966; Sisk, 1979; Feldhusen, 1983) conclude that the most effective interventive technique is a combination of acceleration and enrichment, enhanced by other intervention strategies. Christopher has been fortunate in that his school has married his program of radical acceleration to an enrichment program in English, creative thinking, and problem solving, contained within pull-out classes. Additionally, he has participated in a cluster grouped program for academically gifted Year 8 and 9 students, organized by a local teachers' college. Further enrichment and extension in mathematics has been provided, as in the case of Ian and Terry, by allowing him to enter State and national math competitions at much younger ages than is generally permitted. At the age of 10 he placed second in his State's section of the national IBM math competition, in which he was competing at Grade 10 level.

Terman and Oden (1947), in their follow-up research on the young adults of Terman's gifted group, argued forcefully that, for students who display truly exceptional levels of intellectual giftedness, the more conservative accelerative procedures, such as a grade-skip of a single year, are unlikely to be sufficient to meet their intellectual or social needs; for such students Terman and Oden, like Hollingworth (1942), advised several grade-skips spaced appropriately throughout the student's school career. The individualized educational programs offered to Terry and Christopher, which have combined grade skipping with a graduated program of subject acceleration over several years answer the requirements of Terman and Oden, and respond effectively to the intellectual, academic, and social needs of these profoundly gifted young men. By contrast, it is only during the last year that Ian Baker has been permitted any form of intellectual or social interaction with students who approach his level of mastery and interest in mathematics, the physical sciences, and computing. He spent the first 5 years of his school career interacting solely with children with whom he had nothing in common save the accident of chronological age.

DEVELOPMENT OF SPEECH AND MOVEMENT

The literature on giftedness suggests that intellectually gifted children tend to speak earlier, and develop more complex speech patterns at an earlier age, than do their age-peers of average ability. Lenneberg (1967) reported that the mean age at which a child of average ability speaks his or her first word is 12 months. By around 18 months the child has a vocabulary of between 3 and 50 individual words, but little attempt is made to link these into meaningful speech until the child is approaching 2 years of age.

By contrast, Terman (1926) noted that the average child in his sample of over 1,500 intellectually gifted children had a vocabulary of at least three words by the age of 11 months, and that the mean age at which these children were speaking in short sentences was 17½ months. Jersild (1960), comparing the speech patterns of bright and average children, found that, at the age of 18 months, children of average ability were uttering a mean number of 1.2 words per "remark," whereas the mean for their gifted age-peers was 3.7 words. At 4½ years the mean number of words per remark for average children was 4.6, whereas for the gifted it was 9.5. The gifted children were able to link words into meaning earlier and with greater degrees of complexity than were their age-peers.

Individual case studies of profoundly gifted children report some fascinating examples of early speech. Baker (1987) reported on a young girl who began to speak at 7 months of age and who, on her first birthday, greeted her grandparents with, "Hello, Nanna and Pop, have you come to wish me a happy birthday?" Goldberg (1934) described "K" of IQ 196, who at 2 years of age could recite the addresses and telephone numbers of 12 members of his family. Hollingworth (1926) reported on "David," who was talking in sentences at the age of 11 months and who, at the age of 8 months, exclaimed "Little boy!" when his shadow appeared on a wall. The mean age at which Gross's 40 subjects of IQ 160+ uttered their first word was 9 months, three months earlier than the average for the general population, with several of the children beginning to speak at 5 or 6 months of age.

Surprisingly, none of the three profoundly gifted boys described in this chapter were particularly early speakers. Ian Baker spoke his first word at 12 months, Terry Tao at 13 months, 3 and 4 months later than the mean for the sample. The speech of Christopher Otway developed very late indeed. When Christopher was 18 months of age and showed no inclination to produce meaningful speech, his mother, Elizabeth, was warned by the Mothers and Babies Health Clinic which she attended that this significant delay might well be an indication of intellectual retardation. Chris did not utter his first word until 21 months!

It is difficult, however, to assess when these three children began to speak in phrases, because their parents report that the children moved from single words to complete sentences without passing through the usual transition stages which, in children of average ability, may take several months. The parents of Ian and Christopher remarked on the precision and speed of self-correction in their children's speech. "His speech as such may not have developed particularly early," says Sally Baker, "but once he decided he was going to talk he went from single words to complete sentences with incredible speed and with virtually no transition stage. And there were very few pronounciation errors: 'koaka' for 'koala' and 'manadin' for 'mandarin' are the only two I can remember. As for correctness of grammar; most children carry on for some time saying 'he comed' or 'I falled,' but Ian only had these stages momentarily and then it was straight on into absolute accuracy. Grammar was just instinctive." By the age of 23 months Ian could sing, from start to finish, the song My Grandfather's Clock.

As with speech, mobility develops in the intellectually gifted significantly earlier than in the normal population. The mean age at which a child of average ability sits up unsupported is 7–8 months, while effective mobility through crawling is attained around 10 months (Mussen, Conger, & Kagan, 1956). The average child walks supported by an adult at 11 months, and unsupported at 15 months. By contrast, the mean age for sitting unsupported in Gross's Australian subjects of 160+ was 6 months, while these children, on average, crawled at just under 8 months, walked supported at 10 months, and walked unsupported at 12 months. Interestingly, the skill gap between walking supported and walking unsupported, which in the normal population approaches 4 months, was bridged in these gifted toddlers in 6–8 weeks (Gross, 1989).

Although Ian and Terry were relatively slow to begin talking, in comparison with their gifted age-peers, while Chris was significantly slower than even children of average ability, all three boys achieved mobility at very early ages. Terry was sitting up unsupported by 4½ months, while both he and Ian were walking by themselves at 13 months, at least 3 months earlier than could be expected. Chris took his first steps at 9 months, supported by his mother, and by 10½ months was walking around quite freely by himself. By 10 months of age he could independently navigate short flights of stairs.

As can be seen, not only did these three boys develop the capacity to move around and explore for themselves several months earlier than their age-peers of average ability, but the complexity and sophistication of their speech as it developed enabled them to express their ideas, seek information through questioning, and interact verbally with their parents and other family members at an age when other children are still learning to put sentences together. This precocity in mobility and speech contributed significantly to these children's capacity to acquire and process information, and served to strengthen crystallized intelligence. A third contributor to the children's enhanced capacity to acquire knowledge was the astonishingly precocious development of literacy and numeracy.

EARLY DEVELOPMENT OF READING

Early reading has long been recognized as one of the most powerful indicators of exceptional intellectual giftedness in young children. Terman found that one of the very few variables on which the exceptionally gifted children (IQ 170+) in his gifted group differed from the moderately gifted subjects was the very early age at which they learned to read. Almost 43% of Terman's IQ 170+ group was reading before age 5, compared with 18.4% in the sample as a whole, while 13% of the IQ 170+ group had learned to read before age 4 (Terman & Oden, 1947). Even more remarkably, 80% of the children of IQ 180+ studied by Hollingworth (1942), and 80% of the finalists in the 1982 Mid-West Talent Search (VanTassel-Baska, 1983) were reading by age 4.

Terry, Ian, and Chris learned to read at remarkably early ages. In common with a number of other intellectually gifted children (Salzer, 1984), Terry taught himself to read before his second birthday through watching *Sesame Street*. His reading came as a complete surprise to his parents; they found him playing with another child's alphabet blocks, arranging the letters in alphabetical order. Some of the blocks had numbers, and the Taos discovered that Terry could arrange these in numerical order and, shortly after, do simple addition and subtraction (Gross, 1986). A few months after Terry's second birthday, the Taos found him using a portable typewriter that stood in Dr. Tao's office; he had copied a whole page of a children's book laboriously with one finger. At this stage his parents decided that, although they did not want to "push" Terry, it would be foolish to hold him back. They began to borrow and buy children's books for him, and soon found it hard to keep pace with the boy. They encouraged Terry to read and explore but were careful not to introduce him to highly abstract subjects, believing, rather, that their task was to help him develop basic literacy and numeracy skills so that he could learn from books by himself and thus develop at his own rate. *"Looking back,"* says Billy Tao, *"we are sure that it was this capacity for individual learning which helped Terry progress so fast without ever becoming bogged down by the inability to find a suitable tutor at a crucial time."* By the age of 3, Terry was displaying the reading, writing, and mathematical ability of a 6-year-old.

Ian, as with other self-taught readers, received much of his stimulation from street signs, labels in supermarkets, and names of shops. As has been described, Ian at age 2 was able to differentiate among the labels of his beloved collection of old 45 rpm records and audio cassette tapes, and entertain himself by playing his favorite music. The development of his reading was quite remarkable. Before his third birthday he became fascinated with road maps, and by 3½ his mastery of reading was such that he would use the street directory of the large city in which he lives to plot a new route from his home to preschool or to a friend's house, and then, with the directory closed on his lap, he would navigate his father through the new route as his father drove in accordance with Ian's directions. "Second on the right will be Cedar Avenue; then take the first right down Wallace Street and left again on Park Street and you'll be there." At the age of 4½ his knowledge of the neighborhood was so encyclopedic that he was able to direct a stranger, who was lost, to a destination several streets away. Nor was his reading confined to road maps; as a 4-year-old at kindergarten Ian was able to read stories to the other children to entertain them while his teacher prepared for the next activity session.

David Otway, the father of Christopher, reports that even before the age of 2 Chris had realized that letters could be grouped into words; he would line up letters from his plastic alphabet and besiege his parents with requests to read aloud the "words" he was forming. His actual skill in decoding words became evident at around 2 years 3 months, and by age 3 Chris was reading small books. Before the age of 4 he had graduated to children's encyclopedias which he devoured with keen enjoyment. *"By the age of 4½,"* reports David Otway, *"he knew what countries were in what continents and what the capitals were."* When he entered school at age 5, Christopher had the reading accuracy and comprehension levels of a child of 10 and was reading the daily newspaper each evening when he came home from school.

Although early reading is generally recognized as a powerful predictor of intellectual giftedness, some educators question its validity as a predictor of scholastic success. Braggett (1983) proposed that many children who display unusually accelerated reading development in early childhood may not retain this capacity but may, rather, be "developmental spurters" whose early promise is not fulfilled as the child progresses through elementary school. However, the persistence of exceptional reading accuracy and comprehension skill in Gross's Australian subjects of IQ 160+ indicate that these children are by no means "developmental spurters." In all 40 cases the reading development of these children has followed the pattern reported in the studies of Burks et al. (1930), Hollingworth (1942), Durkin (1966), and VanTassel-Baska (1983), and in the numerous individual case studies of precocious readers (Terman & Fenton, 1921; Hirt, 1922; Witty & Coomer, 1955; Feldman, 1986; Gross, 1986); that is, the precocity which was such a salient feature of the child's early development has persisted, and in many cases increased, through the children's elementary school years.

What has decreased, however, has been the opportunity accorded to these children to display their precocity in the classroom situation. In the majority of cases these exceptionally gifted children have been required, from Grade 3 onward, to read from the same school texts and materials as their chronologically aged peers (Gross, 1989). Thus, their continuing exceptionality in reading is displayed, not in the classroom, but at home, or in weekend programs for gifted children organized by advocacy groups, where their unusual reading abilities and reading interests are accepted and valued. In several cases the child has appeared, to his classroom teacher, to have developed a new, and apparently unrelated, gift or talent.

An important insight into the continuity, but transmutability, of precocity in reading is offered by Jackson (this volume). Jackson proposes that, since the challenge of learning to read exceptionally well may lose its excitement as the young gifted child progresses through primary into elementary school, he or she may seek other avenues for the expression of his or her precocious talent for decoding and encoding what is, in essence, a complex and sophisticated symbol system. Some precocious readers may translate this facility into an enhanced capacity for learning mathematics or computer programing. Others may retain their decoding capacity within the field of linguistics, and turn their hand to oratory or creative writing. In a school environment which depresses, rather than facilitates, accelerated reading development, the child may deliberately choose to transfer his or her skills to another area in the hope that this new expression of talent may be accepted more readily by her teacher and classmates.

Rather than assuming, with Braggett, that giftedness is transient and that developmental spurters are "possibly the largest single group of gifted children we may identify in the school" (Braggett, 1983, p. 14), we should seek to understand the continuity of giftedness through its diverse manifestations and transitions as the child matures. Perhaps those children who are able to translate their exceptionality in one field of performance into an equally felicitous production in a second field are those who have developed, to an unusual degree, what Sternberg, in his "componential" theory of intellectual giftedness, would term *transfer components*—these skills required for generalizing information from one context to another (Sternberg, 1981). Unfortunately, Braggett's caveats regarding the prevalence of developmental spurters (Braggett, 1983), and the repeated admonitions of Renzulli that, rather than seeking to identify *giftedness*, we should search for "gifted behavior," which may surface "in certain students (not all students), at certain times (not all the time) and in certain circumstances" (Renzulli, 1986, p. 63), may turn our attention from the underlying abilities that have contributed to the development of the gift or talent and lead us to view giftedness as transient rather than transferable.

EARLY DEVELOPMENT OF NUMBER

In Ian, Terry, and Christopher the precocious development of reading was accompanied by an equally remarkable precocity in math. By the age of 4, Terence Tao was able to multiply two-digit numbers by two-digit numbers in his head. The author observed Terry, 1 month before his fifth birthday, working with a group of gifted 7–9-year olds at a math workshop held by the South Australian Association for Gifted and Talented Children (SAAGTC). The teacher challenged the students to find the next four numbers in the sequence 9182736. Terry thought briefly and responded, "4554." He was, of course, correct. The number sequence consisted of consecutive multiples of 9 (Gross, 1986).

Ian Baker became fascinated with number before he was 4 years old. *"He had quite a good understanding of numbers up to 1,000 at this age and was constantly asking us to set him sums that he could do,"* says Sally Baker. *"We went through a stage which lasted for many months when his first question on waking up in the morning was a request for some sort of sum."* Christopher's prodigious talent for number showed itself shortly after the age of 3; when he started kindergarten at age 4, he was capable of Grade 4 math work and, as has been related above, when he started formal schooling at age 5, he was permitted to attend the Grade 5 class for an hour each day for math.

At the age of 11 years 4 months, Christopher sat the *Scholastic Aptitude Test-Mathematics* (SAT-M) and achieved the remarkable score of 710. He was disappointed with this score, as his scores on the two practice tests which he had taken had been 760 and 780, and he felt that test anxiety had reduced his test score to what, for him, was a less than acceptable level. To restore his spirits, the author attempted to explain to him the significance of having scored 2.1 standard deviations above the mean on a test standardized on students 6–7 years his senior. The conversation between the author (MG) and Christopher (CO) is recorded verbatim.

MG: Look, Chris, do you know what the mean of a set of scores is?
CO: Oh yes, it's the average of the scores.
MG: Okay, now do you know what I mean if I talk about a standard deviation?
CO: Not really, but I can make a guess. I think it would be the average of all the differences from the mean.
MG: Chris, how on earth did you come at that? You're not quite there but you're awfully close.
CO: Well, the standard is sort of the *expected* score, isn't it, so it would be

a kind of average in a way; and deviations are differences from the average, so standard deviations would have to be the average of all the differences of the different scores from the mean.

From a child of 11 with no experience of statistics, this is a remarkable response. The author related this incident to Professor Julian Stanley of the *Study of Mathematically Precocious Youth* (SMPY) at Johns Hopkins University, who promptly sent Christopher a letter commending him on his "cleverly close" solution, and enclosing a proof that the sum of the deviations of measures about their arithmetic mean is always zero (J. C. Stanley, personal communication, June 8, 1988).

SPECIAL INTERESTS OF THE PROFOUNDLY GIFTED

Christopher, Terry, and Ian had each developed, at least 12 months before they entered school, the reading accuracy and reading comprehension skills of children at least 4 years older than they. By the time they were 5 years of age they had access, through the books, magazines, and newspapers in their homes, to information, views, and attitudes that many of their age-peers would not encounter until half-way through elementary school. The accelerative influence of this early access to an "information bank" normally reserved for children several years their senior is reflected in many areas of childhood development: their preferred reading materials, their hobbies and interests, their enthusiasms, their play interests, and even their friendship choices resembled those of children 4 or 5 years their senior.

Terry Tao pursued his advanced mathematical studies with enthusiasm and dedication both at home and at school. By the age of 6, having taught himself BASIC language by reading a manual, he had written several computer programs to solve mathematical problems. Terry is a lively creative child whose puckish sense of humor comes over in the introduction to his Fibonacci program, which is quoted in full by Clements (1984).

```
8 print J. (This symbol means "clear the screen".)
10 print "here comes mr. fibonacci."
20 print "can you guess which year was mr. fibonacci born?"
30 print "write down a number please . . .": input c
31 if c = 1170 then print "you are correct: now we start!" go to 150
```

50 if c>1250 then print "no, he is already in heaven: try again": go to
30
60 if c<1170 then print "sorry, he wasn't born yet! try again": go to 30
70 if c>1170<1250 then print "he would be c-1170 years old."
71 print "now can you guess?"

The program goes on to produce all the Fibonacci numbers up to the
level requested by the player. At the age of 8 years 3 months Terry
achieved his first publication, a BASIC program to calculate perfect
numbers (T. Tao, 1983).

Terry has always been a wide and avid reader. Math and physics
texts delighted him from an early age, as did the more complex and
challenging science fiction and science fantasy novels more usually
enjoyed by highly able adolescents. In common with many other
exceptionally gifted children, he is not content to be simply a con-
sumer of knowledge (Tannenbaum, 1983); even his spare time
amusements involve creative production. At the age of 12 he began
to translate *The Hitch-Hiker's Guide to the Galaxy* into Latin, a
language he had been learning for less than 3 years.

Another spare-time occupation which gave Terry keen pleasure
and a deep emotional satisfaction was acting as a mentor to his two
younger brothers. *"I discovered I could learn better and remember
more if I taught my brothers what I had learned. So I taught one
brother chess and the other music. My music has never been very
good—in fact I hated it until I gave myself the motivation to teach
Trevor. Now I actually quite enjoy playing duets with him. I spent
a lot of my spare time working out interesting ways to teach them,
and I probably learned more from teaching them than they did
from me!"* (Terry Tao, aged 9, 1985).

Like many other exceptionally gifted children Christopher Otway
displays unusually high levels of ability in music as well as in mathematics. While still in Grade 4, Chris was permitted to start learning
flute, a subject offering which his school normally reserved for Year
8 students. He has studied piano since the age of 5, and his piano
and flute teachers say he is very talented on both instruments. He
loves stamp collecting, swimming, and the study of economics, particularly since taking this subject in his accelerated Grade 11 class
at the age of 12. When completing the Renzulli *Interest-a-Lyzer*
(Renzulli, 1977) at the age of 11, he said that, if he were given the
opportunity to write a newspaper or journal column on a topic of his
choice, he would choose to develop a column on stock-market analysis. This, he commented, would give him the opportunity to synthe-
size the knowledge gained from his three great interests, math,
economics, and current affairs.

Christopher's reading interests have always been far beyond his years. His tastes, however, are highly eclectic; at the age of 11 his interests ranged from Dickens and the Brontes through to Arthur C. Clarke's science fiction novels, Australian history, mystery novels and short stories, a wide range of newspapers and journals and, for light relief, the *Asterix* and *Garfield* comics. Chris chooses to keep several books "in play" at any time; at the age of 11½, during a 4-week period during which Elizabeth Otway recorded his reading habits for the author's research purposes, he read from an average of 22 sources per week. During the same period Chris made, for the author, a list of books he had read, and particularly valued, over the previous 6 months; the list included *David Copperfield* and *Nicholas Nickleby, Jane Eyre, Wuthering Heights, Tess of the D'Urbervilles*, and the collected short stories of American author O. Henry.

Much of Ian Baker's intellectual enjoyment is derived from mastering new challenges. He studies piano, and his teacher describes him as talented. However, his pleasure in the lessons seems to be derived from overcoming the difficulties of acquiring a new piece or a new technique; when he has learned a new work to his satisfaction, he shows little interest in continuing to play it. His parents liken this to his attitude toward chess, in which Ian is intensely competitive—but only in relation to himself.

"We gave him an electronic chess game for his ninth birthday," says Brock Baker, *"and he set it on the easiest level and beat it on the third game. As soon as he had beaten it he showed no interest in playing any further at that level—he just raised the difficulty level and played on. That lasted for about a week, by which time he had beaten it at all eight levels of difficulty and when he had done that he simply put it back on the shelf and didn't look at it again for months."*

It is in Ian that one can see most clearly the transference of exceptional ability and interest from one field of performance to another. Ian's fascination with number has remained with him, despite the school's failure to respond to and foster his talent in this field; his love of reading, however, could seem, at first glance, to have almost disappeared.

"I don't know, though," qualifies Sally Baker. *"Ian always seemed to look for different things in reading, compared with other kids. For example, he's never been interested in fantasy or imaginative stories. The sort of things that excited him were factual books, books on computing or logic, or compendiums of math puzzles. He had a craze, at one stage, for "Choose Your Own Adventure" stories, because he liked working out the different permutations of changes and endings. But even in writing, he doesn't go in*

for imaginative stories. When he was 7 his teacher said to me that she would throw a party on the day he wrote an imaginative story because anything she asked him to do he would convert into a diagram, a maze, a flow-chart, a timetable, calendar—everything had to be set out and analyzed."

Earlier in this chapter we briefly alluded to Ian's passion for street directories and road maps. By the age of 9, Ian, who at age 4 had been reading stories to his kindergarten class mates, had reduced his personal reading to a mere 2 hours per week. His preoccupation with road maps had developed to the point where it dominated his waking hours. Cartography became his joy and his obsession. At 9 years of age he could identify and classify, in terms of Department of Main Roads descriptors, any major or minor road in his home city of one million people. He was almost as skillful in his analyses of the road systems of other Australian states. When he was not absorbed in his collection of Australian street directories, he drew maps to demonstrate his theories of how the road systems and traffic flow of various suburbs could be improved.

This fascination with structural analysis extended to an absorbing study of the transport systems of the large city in which Ian lives. In August 1989, when Ian was 10 years 4 months of age, his father wrote to the author:

> When I last wrote to you, I didn't mention the latest passion that His Nibs has taken up with his usual total dedication. WATCH OUT, STATE TRANSPORT AUTHORITY, YOU'RE BEING HEAVILY SCRUTINIZED! Yes, he's taken up learning all the bus, train, and tram routes. He can now tell you how to get from anywhere to anywhere right across the city by public transport. This includes the route numbers, the roads travelled on and the stop numbers to board and alight. He has produced a document on the Word Processor called "All You Need to Know About the S.T.A.", which he has built up from the S.T.A. route maps and his street directories. Every route is listed, with the roads along which the bus travels. In the case of trains and trams, he includes the stops. His latest trick is to produce route timetables for routes of interest.

One of Ian's greatest delights is to travel with his mother and father, by bus, through the outer suburbs of his city, experiencing for the first time in reality the rides which he knows so well from his theoretical studies. On a recent trip, the bus driver, who was new to the route, became lost, and Ian had the pleasure and excitement of directing him through the maze of side-streets back to the correct road. Although Ian had never travelled that route before, he knew it intimately!

Ian's talent for decoding and encoding complex symbol systems, which permitted the development of reading before the age of 2, is clearly visible in his passion for analyzing and synthesizing the spatial and temporal links of his city's transport system; yet when Ian was 8 years old the diminution of his interest in prose reading was seen by his school as much more significant than his continuing interest in math, and through the reasoning identified by Jackson (1990) and discussed earlier in this chapter, it was assumed that his cognitive development had plateaued. In the eyes of the school he had been a developmental spurter, a child who was no longer displaying gifted behavior and thus no longer needed to be viewed as gifted.

It is sometimes assumed that, although the learning capacities of exceptionally gifted children are far beyond those of their age peers, their hobbies and interests will be linked more to their chronological than to their mental age and will form a bridge between the extremely gifted child and his or her classmates of average ability. In reality, the interests of exceptionally gifted children are so very different from those of their age-peers that they accentuate, rather than blur, the differences between them. The profoundly gifted child's enjoyment of leisure activities that are completely outside the realms of interest or capability of the average child may present a significant barrier to normal socialization with age peers. "Seymour," a boy of IQ 192 reported by McElwee (1934), was given a chemistry set at age 7½ and immediately tried to establish a chemistry club among the boys in his neighborhood; to his chagrin, he found not one child to share his interest. Zorbaugh and Boardman (1936) described a boy, "R," of Stanford-Binet IQ 204, who began to design and make books at the age of 3 and who had applied to the United States patent office for two patents by the time he was 8 years old. Hollingworth's "Child D," of IQ 184, was, at the age of 7, composing and selling a regular playground newspaper; yet he was unable to make normal social contacts with other children until he was permitted to enter Junior High School at the age of 9 (Hollingworth, 1942). Terry Tao's passion for computing, and his expertise in this field, which enabled him to achieve his first publication at the age of 8, were utterly foreign to his 8-year-old age peers. Ian Baker has no one with whom he can share his pleasure and excitement in redesigning the roads and transport system of his city. *"He finds it all so fascinating,"* says Brock Baker, ruefully, *"and naturally is a bit miffed when no one else is interested. The relations, however, show interest and consequently end up being snowed under by the vast quantities of documents he heaps upon them."*

FRIENDSHIP CHOICES OF THE EXTREMELY
GIFTED

A major factor affecting the social and emotional development of
Terry, Chris, and Ian is that, while the two older boys have been
permitted programs of radical acceleration that bring them into
daily contact with children several years older than they, Ian has
been kept, for most of his school career, in the regular classroom,
working in a lockstep program with his chronological age peers.
Chris and Terry are able to work and socialize with students who
share their ways of thinking, their levels of achievement, their reading interests, and their hobbies. To both boys, the fact that these
students, to whom they relate as equals, are 5, 6, or more years
older, is quite irrelevant. What counts for these lads is that they are
able to form friendships with other children who like, accept, and
understand them. Ian has not been so fortunate.

The need to develop intimate, supportive relationships with others is a deep and ongoing psychosocial drive. In adult society we seek
the companionship of people with like values and interests. In childhood relationships, this translates into a seeking after people at the
same developmental stages as oneself. Many researchers have noted
the tendency for intellectually gifted children to seek out, for companionship, either older children several years older, or children of
their own age who have similar levels of intellectual development
(Davis, 1924; Hollingworth, 1931; O'Shea, 1960). O'Shea (1960)
noted that, in several studies conducted over a number of years, no
variable correlated more highly with friendship choices in children
than mental age, and that this stood considerably above any other
factor. Hubbard, recording the spontaneous play of children at
nursery school, before friendships were artificially engineered on
the basis of chronological age as they are at grade school, found
that, when she calculated the correlation between mental age and
spontaneous group participation, the correlation for those children
who played together longest was a remarkable .62 (Hubbard, 1929).

At a chronological age of 7 years, the mental ages of Terry, Christopher, and Ian were approximately 14. Let us examine what was
happening to the three boys at this time. Christopher, in Grade 2,
was being permitted radical subject acceleration in Math, which he
took each day with the 12-year-olds in the Grade 7 class. Terry had,
for the past 2 years, enjoyed his program of flexible progression and
was attending Grades 3, 4, 6, and 7 for different subjects; at the age
of 7½ he was to commence his math studies at high school with the
Grade 11 students for one or two subject periods each day. Both

boys had access, on a daily basis, to children whose mental ages were roughly comparable to theirs and whose achievement levels in math approached their own. Ian, on the other hand, was forced to interact, day by day, by children who were only just approaching the levels of intellectual and academic development he had himself attained before the age of 4. He had no access, at school, to children of his own mental age.

THE INFLUENCE OF SELF-ESTEEM
ON THE MOTIVATION TO EXCEL

Terman and Fenton (1921), Bloom (1985), Feldman (1986), and others in their studies of young people who have demonstrated remarkable achievements in their fields of talent, have emphasized the motivational impact of the drive to excel, to reach the highest standards of which the individual is capable. Foster (1983) proposed that a necessary condition for the development of this drive is a healthy and secure self-concept. Feldhusen (1986) reviewing the research on the self-concept and self-esteem of gifted individuals, concluded that self-concept should, indeed, be viewed as an integral component of giftedness or talent. Developing this argument further, Feldhusen and Hoover (1986) proposed that the interlinkage of intelligence, self-concept, and self-esteem may engender the strong motivational force essential for high-level production. "This conceptualization therefore implies a relationship, in gifted individuals, between self-concept, self-esteem and a realization of intellectual ability or potential" (Feldhusen & Hoover, 1986, p. 141).

The literature on gifted education contains a number of useful studies of the relationships between self-concept and intellectual giftedness. It would be pointless to deny, however, that the literature also contains many self-concept studies that are of limited value to researchers interested in the psychosocial development of the gifted, because the researchers have restricted themselves to reporting the global summary score, rather than analyzing the subjects' scores on various subscales.

The *Coopersmith Self-Esteem Inventory (SEI)* (Coopersmith, 1981) was designed to measure evaluative attitudes toward the self in social, academic, family, and personal areas of experience. The School Form of the *SEI* yields a total score for overall self-esteem as well as separate scores for four subscales: home–family, school–academic, social self–peers, and general self. The subscales allow for variance in perception of self-esteem in different areas of experience.

The self-esteem of all children aged 8 years and over in Gross's Australian study of exceptionally and profoundly gifted children was tested on the *SEI*. An analysis of the global self-esteem scores shows 60% of the subjects as having a global score within the normal range, that is, within one standard deviation above or below the mean for children of their age, while only a small minority appear to score significantly below the mean score for age-peers (Gross, 1989). At first glance, therefore, these extremely gifted children appear to have healthy levels of self-esteem.

When the subscale scores are analyzed, however, a very different picture emerges, with significant differences appearing between the radical accelerands such as Terry and Chris, who have been fortunate enough to enjoy a school program specially designed to serve their intellectual and social needs, and the majority of the subject children who, like Ian, have been required to spend the majority of their school lives with age peers, or who have been permitted a token acceleration of 12 months.

Perhaps surprisingly, the children who achieve high scores—more than one standard deviation above the mean—on the school–academic subscale of the *SEI* are not those who have been permitted to develop at their own pace. Rather, they are children who have been retained with age peers, working at levels that do little to challenge their intellectual or academic abilities. They complete the work with ease, and their performance is well beyond that of their classmates. Their academic superiority has never been challenged, and they have no classmates whose intellectual ability approaches their own, with whom they may compare themselves. Their academic self-concept is high, because they have never had to struggle for success.

By contrast, radical accelerands such as Terry and Christopher, who have been permitted a combination of grade skipping and subject acceleration, and who have been academically and intellectually challenged for most of their lives, display more modest, although still positive, levels of academic self-esteem. Terry obtained a z-score of .09 on the school-academic subscale of the *SEI*, and Chris a z-score of .68. These boys compare their academic performance with that of their classmates who are several years their senior. They still outperform their classmates, but they have to work to achieve their successes. The school–academic self-esteem scores of the radical accelerands in Gross's study contradict the belief that children who are accelerated will become conceited about their academic ability.

On the social self–peers subscale of the *SEI*, however, the pattern is reversed. The children who have been retained with age-peers, and have had little or no chance to interact with children of like abilities and interests, display low levels of social self-esteem. Indeed, over two-thirds of the nonaccelerands obtained a z-score of less than −1.00 on the social self–peers subscale, with one young girl, Anastasia, obtaining the disturbingly low score of −2.59. Anastasia, at age 8, was reading, at home, an English translation of *Les Miserables*; having seen the show, she wanted to read the book! At 7½ she was enjoying Richard Adams' *Watership Down*. Anastasia was permitted a token grade-skip of 1 year but is required, at school, to read books appropriate to the grade-level in which she is now placed—with 9-year-olds. Like Ian Baker, whose social self–peers z-score was an extremely low −1.97, she has no child companions with whom she can share her hobbies, her reading interests, her ideas, or even the way she feels.

Five of the eight items on the social self–peers subscale of the *SEI* address the issue of social acceptability. The nonaccelerands in Gross's study are poignantly aware of the extent to which they are rejected and disliked by their age-peers. Over three-quarters of the nonaccelerands responded "Unlike me" to subscale items such as "I'm popular with kids my own age" and "Kids usually follow my ideas." Over two-thirds identified with the statement "Most people are better liked than I am," and, disturbingly, over half responded "Like me" to the statement "Kids pick on me very often." Hollingworth (1931) noted the tendency for school bullies, particularly those of below average intelligence, to reserve their particular venom for young children of exceptional intellectual ability.

By contrast, it is the radical accelerands such as Terry and Christopher, who display the healthiest social self-concept. The schools attended by these young people have tried to create for them a peer group of children whose levels of intellectual, academic and emotional development approach their own. As a result, these accelerands are able to work and socialize with other children who share, or can at least empathize with, their interests, their delight in intellectual enquiry, and their ways of viewing the world. These children are confident in their relationships with classmates. They are no longer rejected for being different. They know they are liked and their opinions valued. They have been able to assume positions of social leadership. They are enjoying the social pleasures of childhood while, at the same time, experiencing the intellectual satisfaction of challenging academic work.

In a study of self-concept, self-esteem, and peer relationships among intellectually gifted children, Janos, Fung, and Robinson

(1985) found that self-esteem scores of children who saw themselves as being "different" from age-mates were significantly lower than those of children who did not. The authors proposed that it is possible that the mere awareness of their intellectual superiority and atypical interest patterns might be sufficient to diminish self-esteem in the intellectually gifted. It is interesting that social self-esteem scores in the exceptionally and profoundly gifted young people of Gross's study are significantly higher among children who associate on a regular basis with students of similar achievement levels and similar interests.

Many studies over the last 20 years have reported alarming incidences of deliberate underachievement among the intellectually gifted (Pringle, 1970; Painter, 1976; Whitmore, 1980). Under-achievement for peer acceptance, to attempt to lessen the sense of "difference" and alienation from one's age-peers, is disturbingly common among extremely able students. Of Gross's sample of exceptionally and profoundly gifted students, only one child, Terry Tao, claimed that he had never, at any time, moderated his academic achievement for the sake of peer-group acceptance. Other children who have been radically accelerated generally claimed that the pressure to underachieve diminished sharply, or ceased completely, on their acceleration to a more appropriate grade placement. It is the children who have been retained with chronological age-mates who report that they regularly play down their abilities, refrain from answering questions in class, conceal their interests, and pretend to adopt the values, attitudes and achievement levels of their age-peers, in pursuit of social acceptance. In each case, interviews with the child's parents have elicited the parental perception that, whereas the child had demonstrated a strong motivational drive in early childhood, that drive seemed to have dissipated over the years of schooling.

As discussed earlier, Feldhusen and Hoover (1986) proposed that giftedness consists of a conjunction of intelligence, self-concept, and self-esteem, which interact to engender the strong motivational force which is necessary for high-level production. A corollary to this model might propose that, where a child who is known to be gifted is *not* demonstrating high-level performance, we might have cause to suspect that her exceptional cognitive abilities are not supported by healthy levels of self-concept or self-esteem. The nonaccelerands in Gross's (1989) study generally have low levels of social self-esteem, are aware of the dislike and resentment of their age-peers, have chosen to underachieve deliberately in an attempt to be accepted by their classmates, and have lost the enthusiasm for learning, the motivation to succeed, which characterized them in youth. This finding strengthens and enhances the Feldhusen-Hoover conception of intellectual giftedness. An inappropriate and undemanding curriculum, and the requirement to work at the level of age-peers, have not only imposed underachievement on these children, but have also engendered the conditions of low self-esteem and poor motivation, which serve to insure that underachievement continues.

Ian Baker's parents believe that, in the 4 years of educational mismanagement that preceded his current school's willingness to recognize and foster his astonishing mathematical abilities, Ian came very near to completely losing his motivation to learn. *"He is having to start all over again and learn to work in school,"* says Brock Baker. *"It's years since he had to think about anything that was presented to him in class. Consequently, when he was first presented with the Grade 8 and 9 math material in Grade 5 he would write down the first answer that occurred to him. Of course he could get away with that with the Grade 5 math because he could do it standing on his head, and it has come as quite a shock to him to have to apply himself. However, his attitude towards school has definitely improved. A few times in the last few weeks he has come home with the gleam in his eye that we remember from when he was little. Only now have we realized how much he had turned off. I think we've arrested the slide, but I also think we went very close to him switching off altogether."*

THE IMPORTANCE OF PEER GROUP INTERACTION IN EARLY CHILDHOOD

Educators concerned for the academic and social needs of the intellectually and physically handicapped often argue that these children should be placed in the "least restrictive environment." For many advocates of integration, this is viewed as placement in the regular classroom, where the handicapped child may interact in work and play with age-peers and be exposed to a broader and more enriched curriculum than might be possible in the environment of a special class or special school. Ironically, however, the regular classroom is not necessarily the least restrictive environment for the intellectually gifted, and for the profoundly gifted it is probably the *most* restrictive environment any school or system could devise. From her lifetime of study of the extremely gifted, Leta Hollingworth was sure of this.

In the ordinary elementary school situation, children of IQ 140 waste half their time. Those of IQ 170 waste practically all their time.

(Hollingworth, 1942, p. 299)

Exceptionally and profoundly gifted children differ from their age-peers of average intellectual ability on virtually every cognitive and affective variable studied to this date. The precocious development of speech and movement contributes significantly to their capacity to acquire and process information. This also means, however, that the child's "difference" from his or her age-peers is identifiable from an unusually early age, not only to his or her parents but also to neighbors and other community members. This "difference" is accentuated by early reading, the early development of numeracy, and a joy and excitement in learning that compels the child to seek after knowledge wherever it might be found. By the time he or she enters school, the profoundly gifted child may well have the achievement levels, the reading interests, and the knowledge base of a child in the upper grades of elementary school. Even his or her interests are different, and totally foreign to his or her age-peers'. This discrepancy intensifies as the child progresses through school. Few 12-year-olds would have the urge, let alone the capacity, to translate *The Hitch-Hikers Guide to the Galaxy* into Latin. The average Grade 3 student would be hard-pressed to decipher one of Ian Baker's beloved street directories; his interest in traffic flow, road design, and other aspects of civil engineering are utterly beyond the comprehension of his age-peers.

In the quote which began this chapter, Terman discussed the problems of social isolation which may confront the highly gifted, and proposed that "the child of IQ 180 has one of the most difficult problems of social adjustment that any human being is ever called upon to meet" (Burks, et al., 1930, p. 264). Hollingworth (1942) concurred, identifying an IQ of 160 as being the "danger point" above which the differences between the highly gifted child and his or her age peers so far outweigh the similarities as to hinder the formation of productive social relationships; she noted that problems of social isolation seemed particularly acute between the ages of 4 and 9.

It cannot be sufficiently emphasized, however, that the problems of social isolation, peer rejection, loneliness, and alienation that afflict many extremely gifted children arise, not *out of* their exceptional intellectual abilities, but *as a result of* society's response to them. These problems arise when the school, the education system, or the community refuses to create for the profoundly gifted child a peer group based, not on the accident of chronological age, but on a commonality of abilities, interests, and values. Only through the creation of such a group can the extremely gifted child be freed from the taunts and jeers of age-peers, the pressure to camouflage his or her abilities in a desperate and futile struggle to conceal his or her difference, and the frightening sense of being the one-eyed man in the country of the blind who is rejected because he has vision. The literature on the exceptionally and profoundly gifted abounds with histories of children like Hollingworth's "Child C," a boy of IQ 190 who was consistently rejected by other children until he was transferred to a special class for gifted children where the median IQ was 164. In this class he was able, for the first time, to make social contacts with his classmates, and after a year or so he was one of the most popular class members (Hollingworth, 1942).

As Terman emphasized, "adult genius is mobile, and can seek out its own kind" (Burks, et al., 1930, p. 264). The capacity of profoundly gifted children to meet others like them is determined by the adults who are responsible for their schooling. Terence Tao and Christopher Otway are blessed with educational programs that address not only their need for intellectual stimulation and academic rigor, but also their need for the social companionship of like minds. They are happy, well-adjusted, self-confident lads who are being encouraged and assisted to achieve their remarkable potential. Ian Baker, by contrast, has been segregated from his intellectual peers in the restrictive environment of the regular classroom. Not surprisingly, he has responded with anger, frustration, and bitter resentment. In the crucial years of age 4–9 he had no access to children who shared, or could even understand, his interests, his values, or his way of thinking. His abilities were only identified when his teachers attempted to refer him, at the age of 5½, to a school for behaviorally disturbed children.

Hollingworth, in her landmark work on children of IQ 180+, warned that profoundly gifted children have to learn to accept that the majority of persons they will encounter in life are very different from themselves in thought and action. "The highly intelligent child must learn to suffer fools gladly—not sneeringly, not angrily, not despairingly, not weepingly—but *gladly* if personal development is to proceed successfully in the world as it is" (Hollingworth, 1942, p. 299).

There is no doubt that, no matter how appropriate are the interventions made for Terry, Chris, and Ian in school, they will live as adults in a world where the vast majority of people they will encounter will find it difficult to relate to their remarkable intellectual capacities, their atypical interests, and their different values and perceptions. This does not mean, however, that our schools should absolve themselves from the requirement to make the extremely gifted child's passage through childhood as trouble free as possible; a child who receives affection and approval from other children is learning and practicing the skills that will assist him or her to form sound relationships in adulthood. A child who is ostracized by his or her peers has little opportunity to practice these skills.

As this chapter is written, Terry Tao is 15 years old, Christopher is 14, and Ian is 11. How they will develop through the years of adolescence will be largely determined by the foundations that have been laid in early childhood.

REFERENCES

Alexander, P. J., & Skinner, M. E. (1980). The effects of early entrance on subsequent social and academic development. *Journal for the Education of the Gifted, 3,* 147–150.

Baker, J. (1987, December 1). Gifted children. *Warragul and Drouin Press,* p. 5.

Barbe, W. B. (1964). *One in a thousand: A comparative study of highly and moderately gifted elementary school children,* Columbus, OH: F. J. Heer.

Bergman, J. (1979). The tragic story of two highly gifted, genius-level boys. *Creative Child and Adult Quarterly, 4,* 222–233.

Bloom, B. (1985). *Developing talent in young people.* New York: Ballantine.

Braggett, E. J. (1983). Curriculum for gifted and talented children: Needs. In Commonwealth Schools Commission (Ed.), *Curriculum for gifted and talented children* (pp. 9–30). Canberra, Australia: Commonwealth Schools Commission.

Burks, B. S., Jensen, D. W., & Terman, L. M. (1930). *Genetic studies of genius (Vol. 3), The promise of youth.* Stanford, CA: Stanford University Press.

Burt, C. (1968). Is intelligence normally distributed? *British Journal of Statistical Psychology, 16,* 175-190.

Clements, M. A. (1984). Terence Tao. *Educational Studies in Mathematics, 15,* 213–238.

Coopersmith, S. (1981). *Self-Esteem Inventories: Manual.* Palo Alto, CA: Consulting Psychologists Press.

Davis, H. (1924). Personal and social characteristics of gifted children. In G. M. Whipple (Ed.), *Report of the Society's Committee on the Education of Gifted Children* (The Twenty-Third Yearbook of the National Society for the Study of Education, pp. 123–144). Bloomington, IL: Public School Publishing Company.

DeHaan, R. F., & Havighurst, R. J. (1961). *Educating gifted children.* Chicago: University of Chicago Press.

Feldhusen, J. F. (1983). Eclecticism: A comprehensive approach to education of the gifted. In C. P. Benbow & J. C. Stanley (Eds.), *Academic precocity: Aspects of its development* (pp. 192–204). Baltimore: Johns Hopkins University Press.

Feldhusen, J. F. (1986). A conception of giftedness. In R. J. Sternberg & J. E. Davidson (Eds.), *Conceptions of giftedness* (pp. 112–127). Cambridge: Cambridge University Press.

Feldhusen, J. F., & Hoover, S. M. (1986). A conception of giftedness: intelligence, self-concept and motivation. *Roeper Review, 8*(3), 140–143.

Feldman, D. H. (1986). *Nature's gambit.* New York: Basic.

Flack, J. (1983). *Profiles of giftedness: An investigation of the development, interests and attitudes of 10 highly gifted Indiana adolescents.* Unpublished doctoral dissertation, Purdue University.

Foster, W. (1983). Self-concept, intimacy and the attainment of excellence. *Journal for the Education of the Gifted, 6*(1), 20–27.

Foster, W. (1986). The application of single subject research methods to the study of exceptional ability and extraordinary achievement. *Gifted Child Quarterly, 30*(1), 333–37.

Frey, D. (1978). Science and the single case in counselling research. *The Personnel and Guidance Journal, 56,* 263–268.

Gallagher, J. J., & Crowder, T. (1957). The adjustment of gifted children in the regular classroom. *Exceptional Children, 23,* 306–312, 317–319.

Goldberg, M. L., Passow, A. H., Camm, D. S., & Neill, R. D. (1966). *A comparison of mathematics programs for able junior high school students* (Vol. 1). Washington, DC: U.S. Office of Education, Bureau of Research.

Goldberg, S. (1934). A clinical study of K., IQ 196. *Journal of Applied Psychology, 18,* 550–560.

Gross, M. U. M. (1986). Radical acceleration in Australia: Terence Tao. *G/C/T, 45,* 2–11.

Gross, M. U. M. (1989). *Children of exceptional intellectual potential: Their origin and development.* Unpublished doctoral dissertation, Purdue University.

Hagen, E. (1980). *Identification of the gifted.* New York: Teachers College Press.

Hirt, Z. I. (1922, June). A gifted child. The *Training School Bulletin,* pp. 49–54.

Hobson, J. R. (1979). High-school performance of under-age pupils initially admitted to kindergarten on the basis of physical and psychological examination. In W. C. George, S. J. Cohn, & J. C. Stanley (Eds.), *Educating the gifted: Acceleration and enrichment* (pp. 162–171). Baltimore: Johns Hopkins University Press.

Hollingworth, L. S. (1926). *Gifted children: Their nature and nurture.* New York: Macmillan.

Hollingworth, L. S. (1931). The child of very superior intelligence as a special problem in social adjustment. *Mental Hygiene, 15*(1), 3–16.

Hollingworth, L. S. (1942). *Children above IQ 180.* New York: World Books.

Hubbard, R. (1929). A method of studying spontaneous group formation. In D. Thomas et al. (Eds.), *Some new techniques for studying social behavior.* New York: Teachers College Bureau of Publications.

Janos, P. M. (1983). *The psychological vulnerabilities of children of very superior intellectual ability.* Unpublished doctoral dissertation, Ohio State University.

Janos, P. M., Fung, H. C., & Robinson, N. M. (1985). Self-concept, self-esteem and peer relations among gifted children who feel "different." *Gifted Child Quarterly, 29*(2), 78–82.

Janos, P. M., & Robinson, N. M. (1985). Psychosocial development in intellectually gifted children. In F. D. Horowitz & M. O'Brian (Eds.), *The gifted and talented: Developmental perspectives* (pp. 149–195). Washington, DC: American Psychological Association.

Jersild, A. T. (1960). *Child psychology.* London: Prentice-Hall.

Kitano, M. K., & De Leon, J. (1988). Use of the Stanford-Binet Fourth Edition in identifying young gifted children. *Roeper Review, 10*(3), 156–159.

Lenneberg, E. H. (1967). *Biological functions of language.* New York: Wiley.

Marland, S. P. (1972). *Education of the gifted and talented.* Washington, DC: U.S. Government Printing Office.

Martinson, R. A. (1974). *The identification of the gifted and talented.* Ventura, CA: Office of the Ventura County Superintendent of Schools.

McElwee, E. (1934). Seymour, a boy with 192 IQ. *Journal of Juvenile Research, 18,* 28–35.

Merriam, S. B. (1988). *Case study research in education: A qualitative approach.* San Francisco: Jossey Bass.

Montour, K. (1977). William James Sidis: The broken twig. *American Psychologist, 32,* 265–279.

Mussen, P. H., Conger, J. J., & Kagan, J. (1956). *Child development and personality* (3rd ed.). New York: Harper and Row.

O'Shea, H. (1960). Friendship and the intellectually gifted child. *Exceptional Children, 26*(6), 327–335.

Painter, F. (1976). *Gifted children: A research study.* Knebworth, UK: Pullen Publications.

Pegnato, C. W., & Birch, J. W. (1959). Locating gifted children in junior high schools: A comparison of methods. *Exceptional Children, 23,* 300–304.

Pringle, M. L. K. (1970). *Able misfits.* London: Longman.

Pollins, L. D. (1983). The effects of acceleration on the social and emotional development of gifted students. In C. P. Benbow & J. C. Stanley (Eds.), *Academic precocity: Aspects of its development* (pp. 160–178). Baltimore: Johns Hopkins University Press.

Proctor, T. B., Feldhusen, J. F., & Black, K. N. (1988). Guidelines for early admission to elementary school. *Psychology in the Schools*, 25(1), 41–43.

Renzulli, J. S. (1977). *The Interest-a-Lyzer*. Mansfield Center, CT: Creative Learning Press.

Renzulli, J. S. (1986). The three-ring conception of giftedness: a developmental model for creative productivity. In R. J. Sternberg & J. E. Davidson (Eds.), *Conceptions of giftedness* (pp. 53–92). Cambridge, UK: Cambridge University Press.

Robinson, H. B. (1981). The uncommonly bright child. In M. Lewis & L. A. Rosenblum (Eds.), *The uncommon child* (pp. 57–81). New York: Plenum Press.

Salzer, R. T. (1984). Early reading and giftedness: Some observations and questions. *Gifted Child Quarterly*, 28(2), 95–96.

Sheldon, P. M. (1959, January). Isolation as a characteristic of highly gifted children. *The Journal of Educational Sociology*, pp. 215–221.

Silverman, L. K. (1986). An interview with Elizabeth Hagen: Giftedness, intelligence and the new Stanford-Binet. *Roeper Review*, 8(3), 168–171.

Silverman, L. K. (1989a). The highly gifted. In J. F. Feldhusen, J. VanTassel-Baska, & K. R. Seeley (Eds.), *Excellence in educating the gifted* (pp. 71–83). Denver: Love.

Silverman, L. K. (1989b, November). *The continuing legacy of Leta Hollingworth*. Paper presented at the 36th Congress of the National Association for Gifted Children, Cincinnati.

Silverman, L. K., & Kearney, K. (1989). Parents of the extraordinarily gifted. *Advanced Development*, 1, 1–10.

Sisk, D. A. (1979). Acceleration versus enrichment: A position paper. In W. C. George, S. J. Cohn, & J. C. Stanley (Eds.), *Educating the gifted: Acceleration and enrichment* (pp. 236–238). Baltimore: Johns Hopkins University Press.

Stanley, J. C. (1977–78). The predictive value of the SAT for brilliant seventh- and eighth-graders. *The College Board Review*, 106, 31–37.

Stanley, J. C. (1979). Identifying and nurturing the intellectually gifted. In W. C. George, S. J. Cohn, & J. C. Stanley (Eds.). *Educating the gifted: Acceleration and enrichment* (pp. 172–180). Baltimore: Johns Hopkins University Press.

Stanley, J. C. (1985). Inter-departmental memo, Johns Hopkins University.

Sternberg, R. (1981). A componential theory of intellectual giftedness. *Gifted Child Quarterly*, 25, 86–93.

Tannenbaum, A. J. (1983). *Gifted children: Psychological and educational perspectives*. New York: Macmillan.

Tao, B. (1985, April). *Reflections on Terry's education*. Paper presented at Purdue University.

Tao, T. (1983). A BASIC program to calculate perfect numbers. *Trigon, the School Mathematics Journal of the Mathematics Association of South Australia*, 21(3), 7.

Terman, L. M. (1926). *Genetic studies of genius: Vol. 1. Mental and physical traits of a thousand gifted children.* Palo Alto, CA: Stanford University Press.

Terman, L. M., & Fenton, J. C. (1921). Preliminary report on a gifted juvenile author. *Journal of Applied Psychology, 5,* 163–178.

Terman, L. M., & Oden, M. H. (1947). *Genetic studies of genius* (Vol. 4). *The gifted child grows up.* Palo Alto, CA: Stanford University Press.

Thorndike, R. L., Hagen, E. P., & Sattler, J. M. (1986). *The Stanford-Binet Intelligence Scale: Fourth Edition. Technical Manual.* New York: The Riverside Publishing Co.

VanTassel-Baska, J. (1983). Profiles of precocity: The 1982 Midwest Talent Search Finalists. *Gifted Child Quarterly, 27*(3), 139–144.

Whitmore, J. R. (1980). *Giftedness, conflict and underachievement.* Boston: Allyn and Bacon.

Witty, P., & Coomer, A. (1955). A case study of gifted twin boys. *Exceptional Children, 22,* 104–108.

Worcester, D. A. (1955). *The education of children of above average mentality.* Lincoln: University of Nebraska Press.

Zorbaugh, H. W., & Boardman, R. K. (1936). Salvaging our gifted children. *Journal of Educational Sociology, 10,* 100–108.

part III

Precocious Mental Powers and Processes in Young Children

chapter 6

The Use of Standardized Tests with Young Gifted Children*

Nancy M. Robinson
Halbert Robinson

*Halbert Robinson Center for the Study of Capable Youth
University of Washington*

An abundant technology exists for assessing cognitive development in young children. Numerous standardized tests are available to tap general (or undifferentiated) mental ability as well as more specific abilities, particularly language. These measures are clearly a valu-

* The longitudinal research concerning toddlers precocious in language was supported by funds available to the Seattle node of the John D. and Catherine T. MacArthur Foundation Network on the Transition from Infancy to Early Childhood. The participation and assistance of Gladys Sears, psychometrist and of co-investigators, Philip Dale and Sharon Landesman, and the colleagues in that network is gratefully acknowledged.

The longitudinal research concerning preschool children identified by their parents as gifted in one or more domains was supported by a series of grants from the Spencer Foundation to the late Halbert B. Robinson. A great many people worked with dedication on that project. Especially instrumental were Gladys Sears, Nancy E. Jackson, Charles Stillman, Wendy Roedell, and Sandra Marks, as well as many student assistants. Subsequent to Robinson's death in 1981, assistance in analysis was provided by Charles Stillman, Clifford Lunneborg, Mark Greenberg, Philip Dale, and Kenneth Tangen.

able asset in research with young children, but have they other legitimate uses with toddlers and preschoolers as well? This chapter will consider some issues that bear upon a decision about when, if, and how to use such measures with individual children thought to be advanced in development.

This discussion will focus on children in the age range 3 to 6 years, with some excursions to findings with children as young as 18 months. Although there is no magic age at which reliable test scores suddenly emerge (Humphreys & Davey, 1988), prior to toddlerhood, tests of normal children are of limited reliability and show weak relationships with factors such as familial background (Bayley, 1970) and intervention efforts (Bryant & Ramey, 1987). For children suspected of developmental delays, testing in infancy may well be warranted and may predict later status effectively (Siegel, 1989), but for those "at risk for precocity," neither the reasons for testing nor the power of the tests justify standardized assessment, unless the goal is purely a scientific one.

Anecdotal, retrospective studies of persons who have achieved eminence suggest that, if tests had been administered during the preschool years, the scores of these individuals would have been impressive. One of the most intriguing studies, by Catherine Cox (1926), was an attempt to estimate early childhood IQ by comparing biographic information with test items, a methodologically very shaky but provocative enterprise. She found evidence of extreme precocity in many of her subjects, especially those destined to become philosophers or scientists. Such studies can, though, do little more than indicate a direction; hindsight is much clearer than foresight. The prospective studies required to produce dependable answers are much more difficult, very expensive, and subject to their own biases in selection and attrition of samples. Before we consider the prospective evidence available, however, let us first examine the purposes for which testing may in practice be sought for gifted young children.

TYPICAL QUERIES TO WHICH TESTING
IS DIRECTED

Requests for individual testing generally come from one of three sources: (a) parents and, indirectly, teachers seeking developmental evaluation of a child who appears precocious and whose advancement, if confirmed, would indicate the need for changes in the home and/or preschool environment; (b) occasional kindergarten, more frequently primary schools and programs for bright children, with testing as part of their admissions screening; and (c) consideration for early entry to first grade or kindergarten. Frequent in the folklore, but rare in our experience, is the parent who merely wants the prestige of a high IQ. In other words, requests for testing nearly always come from concerned adults seeking to meet children's needs—parents and teachers who hope that, by identifying and documenting the extent and nature of children's precocity, ways can be supplied or devised to support their optimal development and a satisfying quality of life.

Such requests, whatever their level of sophistication, often reveal a working definition of giftedness which is not unlike that of professionals. Despite their differences, theorists of many persuasions (Sternberg & Davidson, 1986) tend to agree that the promise of childhood will be realized only if the child's own abilities are stimulated and encouraged by an interesting, responsive, and probably somewhat demanding environment. They see such experience as essential, not only to cognitive development, but also to motivation for achievement, the zest and wisdom to be an intellectual risk taker, and the skills to express one's creative ideas. Starting this process in the right direction for the young child with precocious development is appropriately seen as a significant challenge by adults who care both for the happiness of childhood and the fulfillment of adulthood.

AVAILABLE STANDARDIZED MEASURES

There is no dearth of reasonably well-standardized developmental measures for young children. Among those with a broad cognitive developmental focus are the Bayley Mental Scales of Infant Development (Bayley, 1969) (birth to 30 months), the Stanford-Binet, Form L-M (Terman & Merrill, 1973) (now outdated), the Stanford-Binet Fourth Edition (Stanford-Binet IV) (Thorndike, Hagan, & Sattler, 1986a) (ages 2 years to adult), the Wechsler Preschool and Primary Scales of Intelligence, Revised (WPPSI-R) (Wechsler, 1989) (ages 3 to 7 years), the Kaufman Assessment Battery for Children (K-ABC) (Kaufman & Kaufman, 1983) (30 months to 12 years, 5 months), the McCarthy Scales of Children's Abilities (McCarthy, 1972) (2.5 years to 8.5 years), and the Woodcock-Johnson Psycho-Educational Battery, Revised (Woodcock & Johnson, 1989) (2 years to 90 years).

Language development is salient and rapid during the toddler and preschool years, and plays a central role in the kinds of reasoning skills that will later be reflected in school achievement. There are, therefore, numerous scales by which to assess early language skills, of which some of the best are the Peabody Picture Vocabulary Test, Revised (PPVT-R) (Dunn & Dunn, 1981) (ages 2.5 years to adult); the Reynell Developmental Language Scales (Reynell, 1981) (ages 12 months to 7 years), a scale long used in Britain and now under U. S. standardization; and the MacArthur Communicative Development Inventories for Infants (8-16 months) and Toddlers (16-30 months) (Fenson et al., 1991) which utilize parents or other informants. Many testers also collect a spontaneous language sample to analyze for mean length of utterance (Miller, 1981).

Young children's competence in social and everyday skills as well as communication can also be assessed by parent report with the Revised Vineland Adaptive Behavior Scales (Sparrow, Balla, & Cicchetti, 1984). Finally, the grade equivalent of early reading and mathematical skills can be assessed using the Peabody Individual Achievement Test, Revised (Markwardt, 1989) or the Woodcock-Johnson Psycho-Educational Battery, Revised (Woodcock & Johnson, 1989) even with children younger than the normative population.

This range of instruments was not developed primarily to assess that small proportion of the population thought to be gifted. Some of the instruments, notably the Bayley Scales, were developed primarily for research purposes. Most were developed in response to practical concerns about children thought to be at risk for developmental impairment. A fundamental goal of these instruments is the early identification of developmental lags so that intervention can be instituted promptly; in addition, they are available to assess the child's subsequent progress. Even so, most of the scales have sufficient "top" for precocious children, so long as one avoids using them with children in the upper age range for that test.

CONCURRENT VERSUS PREDICTIVE QUESTIONS

Issues of continuity in development as reflected in psychological tests really embody several different questions, only some of which can be addressed by test data. Uzgiris (1989) is one author who has discussed these aspects of *continuity*, which itself implies some persistence of functions or processes during development. Functional continuity may have different manifestations at different ages, showing what Kagan (1971) called *heterotypic* continuity. For example, the bright toddler may be early to combine words; the bright adolescent may be quick to grasp abstract relationships. Uzgiris maintains that we cannot look at continuity of development as a whole, but must look at continuity of specific dimensions of behavior. Uzgiris uses the term *constancy* to refer to "unchanging behavioral patterns or some underlying elements producing those behavior patterns" (p. 125), while the term *stability* refers to regularity in the rate of progress within a group of individuals over time, with those who have attained the highest level of development continuing to progress fastest. Such stability leads to *predictability* in the standings of individuals from one time to another. Other authors use somewhat different terms.

As applied to psychological tests and young children, we then have several questions to answer. Some of these must be directed at the tests themselves: Are they measures we can count on to be both dependable and meaningful? Some questions have to do more directly with issues of predictability, within-domain versus heterotypic continuity, and stability: Using tests, can we improve our guesses about the relative standing children will exhibit in the future? Are there perhaps unexpected linkages between one set of skills and abilities in the preschool years and another at school age? Will children who are relatively more mature as preschoolers continue to develop intellectual abilities at a more rapid rate than average age peers?

In this section, we will examine evidence for the reliability and validity of some of these instruments as they have been used with young, precocious children. Two time perspectives are usually involved in the questions posed: First, how well do tests describe or relate to the child's current behavior? Do they provide a reliable and accurate picture? Do they reflect the abilities they were intended to measure? Second, what do the test results suggest about the child's future development? How well, and over what period of time, do they predict outcomes? Such evidence yields information, not only about the measures, but, in aggregate, about variability/stability of cognitive development itself.

Concurrent Reliability

Young children are notoriously variable in their response to unfamiliar situations and they are vulnerable to disorganization by hunger, fatigue, competing interests, incomplete socialization, and rampant hedonism. Experienced testers with specialized skill at dealing with children in structured situations are needed to elicit the child's sustained attention and optimal response. Published accounts of research results seldom provide information concerning these variables.

Most of the information about concurrent test reliability is to be found these days in the manuals published by test authors themselves. The easiest but most misleading way to calculate reliability is a split-half method, for example correlating the results on odd-numbered items with even-numbered items. Such results are likely to be inflated; situational effects will affect both halves equally, and establishing a basal and ceiling guarantees that there will be matching strings of successes at the bottom and of failures at the top.

Re-administration of the same scale within a short period of time is likely to produce practice effects (although bright children may resist repeating something they have already done). For example, readministration of the Stanford-Binet Fourth Edition to an average group of 4- and 5-year-olds yielded an initial Composite Score of 98.8 and a second one of 107.0, after an intervening period of 2 to 8 months. Retest reliability of the composite score was .91, with stability coefficients of domain scores ranging from .71 (Quantitative) to .88 (Verbal Reasoning) (Thorndike, Hagan, & Sattler, 1986b).

With the exception of the Peabody Picture Vocabulary Test, Revised, however, alternate forms of recently standardized tests are not available. For the two Peabody scales, which are brief multiple-choice measures of receptive vocabulary, retest within a month with the other form yielded correlations ranging from .54 to .77 in the 2–5 year age range, compared with .81 to .90 in the 9–12 year range. Same-day alternate form correlations were higher, but still ranged only between .71 and .89 at any given age. Relatively low reliability probably stems from the brevity of the task, which is roughly equivalent to one subscale of a test such as a Stanford-Binet or Wechsler.

It is instructive to examine some old data from the standardization of the much more comprehensive 1937 Stanford-Binet, Forms L and M. Table 6.1 presents findings reported by McNemar (1942,

Table 6.1.   Correlations between Form L and Form M obtained during standardization of the 1937 Revision of the Stanford–Binet*

IQ Range	Ages 2.5–5.5	Ages 6–13	Ages 14–18
130–139	.85	.90	.94
110–119	.89	.92	.93
90–99	.91	.93	.94
70–79	.92	.96	.97

*From McNemar (1942). *The revision of the Stanford–Binet Scale.* Boston: Houghton Mifflin, pp. 62–63. Reprinted by permission.

pp. 62–63) that show the correlation between scores on the two forms, administered within 1 week, and the standard error of measurement for several age and ability groups. It is clear from this table that correlations between the scores on the two forms during the preschool era were substantial, but lower than those obtained later, and lower for bright than for dull children.

Concurrent Validity

Though the same satisfactory reliabilities cannot be claimed for every scale, there is enough reliability here even with young children to justify inquiring into the validity of the measures, that is, to question what it is that the scales are measuring. This question forces us to deal with measures of real-world behavior or, as a substitute, other psychometric measures of children's development. To consider the question of whether early tests measure meaningful and identifiable characteristics, we will call upon two studies with very young precocious children conducted at the University of Washington Center for the Study of Capable Youth.

One study (Dale, Robinson, & Landesman, in preparation; Robinson, Dale, & Landesman, 1990) focused upon the patterns of abilities shown by young children with precocious language. Parents of toddlers up to age 18 months were recruited by means of a few radio announcements and newspaper articles that mentioned criteria such as speaking words by 8 or 9 months, making new word combinations by 15 months, exhibiting unusually broad vocabulary, or understanding adult language at a very early age. We were especially interested in whether children with precocious language showed a characteristic pattern of language usage and acquisition, and, in the process, we administered a broad battery of psychometric measures and recorded the children's language. Their mothers completed the Early Language Inventory (see Dale, Bates, Reznick, & Morisset, 1989), a forerunner of the MacArthur Communicative Development Inventory for Toddlers. The children, who qualified for the study by reported or observed language (vocabulary, advanced grammatical development, or performance on standardized measures of language at least two standard deviations above the mean for their age), were seen at ages 20, 24, and 30 months and were observed in spontaneous play with their mothers as well as being given a variety of psychometric measures.

Of particular interest here are the correspondences between various measures given at the same age. For example, several language measures were obtained at 20 months, when, on the basis of preliminary parental report, 49 children had been invited for an initial visit prior to selection for the longitudinal study. The mothers' inventories of their children's vocabulary corresponded moderately well with the children's actual behavior in the laboratory: with the language items of the Bayley Mental Scale, .63; with Stanford-Binet IV Vocabulary, .53; with the child's mean length of utterance in free play, .37. The mothers' reports of combinatorial language (remember that most toddlers of this age are just beginning to combine words), correlated with the same criteria .44, .43, and .59, respectively. (Note the correspondence of reported and observed combinatorial language.) Correlations with mothers' reports of communication skills via the Vineland scale were of the same order. Thus, the standardized observations by the psychometrician in the laboratory related moderately well to maternal reports via two structured instruments.

At age 30 months, the broadest set of standardized tests was administered. The 28 children seen at that age were invited to the laboratory twice within a 2-week period. At one session, the Stanford-Binet (1972 revision) and the PPVT-R were administered; at the other session, Stanford-Binet IV was administered. The sessions were counterbalanced in order. The significant correlations are seen in Table 6.2. Note that there were no significant correla-

Table 6.2. Means, standard deviations, and significant correlations at age 30 months among measures given to children selected as toddlers with precocious language[a]

| | Stanford–Binet, 4th Edition | | | | | |
	Composite	Verbal	Abstract/ Vis.	Quant.	Memory	PPVT-R
Mean	124.7	127.2	112.5	114.0	128.5	127.9
S.D.	6.5	8.5	10.3	11.8	8.3	11.1
Correlations						
S-B IV Verbal						.49*
S-B Form L-M IQ	.63***	.50**		.59**		
Language items	.48*	.60***				.46*
Performance items			.41*	.44*		
Memory items	.45*			.54**	.59**	

*p < .05. **p < .01. ***p < .001
[a]Adapted from Robinson, Dale, & Landesman (1990). Validity of Stanford–Binet IV with linguistically precocious toddlers. *Intelligence, 14,* 173–186. Reprinted by permission.
Note. Language, performance, and memory items were extracted from Stanford–Binet, Form L-M (1972 revision). Subject sample size varied from 22 to 27. Correlations were not corrected for attenuated range of scores.

tions among the four domain subscales of Stanford-Binet IV (Verbal Reasoning, Abstract/Visual Reasoning, Quantitative Reasoning, and Memory), but that across tests, the within-domain measures did show interesting correspondences. The verbal measures tended to vary together, as did the performance/spatial and memory measures, although the specific tasks within each domain were diverse. Although these correlations are only moderate in size, in view of the restricted range of the scores and the brevity (and therefore the limited reliability) of the subscales, these relationships are impressive. The measures do seem to be tapping abilities of some scope and, furthermore, those abilities show distinctive test patterns. Correlations across cognitive domains were seldom significant, nor were there significant correlations between cognitive domains and gross motor skills (Bayley Psychomotor Development Index) or temperament (measured by the Emotionality, Activity, Sociability Scale [EAS], Buss & Plomin, 1984). Even within the cognitive realm, these very young children were showing a level of differentiation which has usually not been found until somewhat later ages.

The second major study from this laboratory, an earlier large-scale longitudinal investigation by the late Halbert B. Robinson and his colleagues (unpublished), was undertaken with children ages 2–5 who were identified by their parents in response to newspaper notices. The invitations mentioned specific criteria such as speaking in sentences before a year or showing fascination with numbers or puzzles. Parents were urged to contact the laboratory if they believed their child to be advanced.

Most of the children lived in the Puget Sound region of the State of Washington; their average age when first seen was 3 years, 5 months. Of the sample; 49% were female. In racial composition, 80% were White, 6% Black, 4% Asian, 8% of mixed parentage, and 2% were from other backgrounds. Most (70%) were first-born or only children (possibly because parents with more children were less likely to volunteer); 24% were second-born, 5% third-born, and only a few were from larger sibships. Because the children were young, many sibships were incomplete. Only 4.4% of the children were adopted. Parental education was high, with 27% of the fathers holding a doctoral-level degree, 28% with masters or some graduate school, and only 8% with no more than high school education. Mothers' education was somewhat less advanced, but, again, only 7% were high school graduates or less, and 26% held at least a masters degree.

Of relevance to the concurrent validity question is the comparison of parental report with the children's initial skills as demonstrated on psychometric measures. Parents who telephoned the laboratory were given a two-part questionnaire. Part I asked general questions about the children's interests and skills in verbal reasoning, mathematics, reading, spatial reasoning, and memory, and invited anecdotal information. Part II, which has come to be known as the Seattle Project Parent Questionnaire (see Renzulli, Reis, & Smith, 1981), consisted of 40 very specific questions about children's current skills, and invited additional comment as well. Coding of the parent information was carried out by trained coders who reached a mean percentage agreement of 89% during training. A complex method was developed for determining the degree of the child's precocity in each of the five domains mentioned above. Brief tests in each domain were also administered in addition to the abbreviated Stanford-Binet.

Comparing parent reports of overall development with initial IQs, a significant but low correlation ($r = .22$, $N = 396$) was found. Parents were considerably better at describing children's behavior in some domains than in others. For example, their descriptions of early reading recognition and mathematical reasoning skills matched the children's Peabody Individual Achievement Test scores fairly well (r's of .56 [$N = 236$] and .34 [$N = 195$], respectively). (Ns varied because, on initial visit, some of the children were too immature to be given a standardized measure in some domains.) In contrast with these more easily observable academic skills, for which parents probably had established age expectations, there were low but statistically significant correlations between parental report and measured spatial skills (.23 [$N = 333$] with WPPSI Block Design but only .09 [$N = 290$] with Mazes) and memory (.18 with McCarthy memory for digits forward [$N = 375$] and .19 with digits backward [$N = 114$]), and a negligible correspondence ($r = .04$, $N = 396$) in the verbal domain with Stanford-Binet vocabulary.

It is interesting to speculate why these parental reports did not show higher correlations with the children's test scores, especially when one contrasts Robinson's findings with those of Dale et al., who found higher correlations between parental report of toddler language and actual measurements in the laboratory. There are at least two possible explanations. First, the instruments for the parent report were technically less elegant in the first study than the later one, and there may have been slips in communication. Second, and more likely, however, is the fact that parents' observations may be most accurate just when a skill is emerging. Dale et al. gathered parental reports at 18–20 months, a critical era for the emergence of language; by age 3 to 4 years (the mean age at which children entered Robinson's study), the same parents might not have been so accurate in their descriptions of the children's levels of competence in using much more complex language and reasoning. Note that in Robinson's study, precocious reading (emerging during the preschool years) was described with greater accuracy. Quite possibly, parents have poorer subjective norms and more limited opportunities to observe spatial and quantitative skills, accounting for the low correlations in those areas.

Looked at from another vantage, however, these parents were rather accurate in their assessment that their children's development was precocious. As many as 550 children were tested at least once on the abbreviated form of the Stanford-Binet, 1972 revision (i. e., four starred items at each age). Of these, approximately half of the children (N = 259) attained initial IQs of 132 or higher, that is, IQs in the top 2.5% of the population. Moreover, for 340 children tested at yearly intervals, IQs were more likely to rise than fall, so that by age 5, the average IQ of those retested was 139 (SD = 18.7) and at age 6, 137 (SD = 21.6). In addition, a number of children with somewhat lower IQs showed clearly precocious behavior of other kinds, such as reading. In other words, parents who had been asked to identify precocious children did identify a group of children whose test scores were, on average, two or more standard deviations above the mean of children their age and, furthermore, continued high to at least age 6. (Note that the issue here is the validity of the tests and not the stability of individual scores, a matter which will be discussed in a later section.)

With regard to patterns of test scores within the group, Stillman (1982) summarized the preliminary analyses as consistent with a multifactor view of intelligence. Many of the children, over repeated testing, consistently demonstrated superior performance on particular measures while earning lower IQ scores. Only low to moderate correlations were found between many of the specific abilities test and Stanford-Binet IQ, although test-retest reliabilities over a 9-month period were adequate on all the measures except the digits test (Robinson, Jackson, & Roedell, 1977).

Stillman (1982) tested 80 of the same subjects (41 boys and 39 girls) at approximately age 6 on a special test battery including several spatial and several language subtests. He found a far greater proportion of the variance was accounted for by a general factor (37%) than the verbal (6%) or spatial (9%) factors for the group as a whole. Evidence for the spatial factor was stronger in the boys, whose performance was also higher on the spatial tasks, but equivalent to that of the girls on the verbal tasks.

This study was not the first to discover differentiated aptitudes in young, gifted children. Tannenbaum (1986) points out that a study by Davis, French, and Lesser (1959) had not only identified a group of children ages 4.5 to 5.5 with special aptitudes for vocabulary, number, reasoning, science, and space but had instituted an experimental class for them at the Hunter College Elementary School. Although the average IQ of these children was only 132, they did as well on the Thurstone Primary Mental Abilities Test as a control class at the same school with an average IQ of 153. Tannenbaum suggests that, at the upper ranges of tested intelligence, measures of special abilities may reveal more about rate and direction of growth than do measures of more general abilities.

A recent study by Louis and Lewis (1992) sheds a little further light on the concurrent relationship between parent report and current intellectual status. Louis and Lewis found that, of 118 parents who brought young children (mean age 33 months) to a specialized clinic, believing them to be "gifted," those describing exceptional memory, creativity–imagination, and abstract thinking actually had children with higher IQs (mean IQ = 149) than those who mentioned knowledge of body parts, alphabet, and numbers (whose children had a mean IQ of 118). Interestingly, early interest in reading did not significantly differentiate the groups, although this quality, together with word and symbol recognition, was mentioned somewhat more often by parents of the brighter children.

Taken together, these studies suggest that, indeed, during the preschool years, psychometric instruments can have substantial, though certainly imperfect, validity when used with children who are precocious in their development. Not only overall levels of development, but specific domains of ability and skill, may be described even for the very young child.

Do the tests reveal anything not already known about the children? None of the research available has addressed this issue. Just as with older children, the psychometric instruments probably provide a short-cut for observers who are not yet well acquainted with the children or who themselves have limited developmental knowledge, and they serve as one way to objectify information. The research we have quoted suggests that the tests also yield useful information within domains such as verbal reasoning, spatial reasoning, and memory; children's scores on different tasks tend to cluster within domains more than across domains. The tests are, however, imperfect and limited in scope. To what extent it is useful and responsible to use these measures with individual children is a discussion we will postpone for the final section of this chapter.

Predictive Reliability

Now we turn to information about the stability of test scores over time. Innumerable variables can affect such stability, some of them inherent in the tests and some inherent in the developing child. Overall, however, there are four trends in predictive power that are of primary importance. First, higher IQs tend to be less stable than lower ones (McCall, Appelbaum, & Hogarty, 1973; McNemar, 1942). Second, the younger the child, the less stable the scores (Bayley, 1949; McCall et al., 1973). Third, the longer the interval between tests, the less stability can be expected (Humphreys & Davey, 1988). Finally, the interaction of family environment with the child's developmental rate makes its mark increasingly between about age 2 and early school years and then levels off (Bayley, 1970; Bradway & Robinson, 1961); similar results have been found for the effects of early intervention programs (e.g., Bryant & Ramey, 1987). None of these rules of thumb bodes well for the long-range predictive power of tests used with very young, bright children.

   Predictions from infant development. There is ample evidence from a number of longitudinal studies that developmental quotients observed in the first year of life bear little resemblance to later cognitive progress, except for children who show developmental retardation (e. g., Bayley, 1970; Bee et al., 1982; Broman, Nichols, & Kennedy, 1975; Knobloch & Pasamanick, 1967; McCall, 1979; VanderVeer & Schweid, 1974; Wilson, 1983). Indeed, several authors find, within the first few months, a slight *negative* relationship between developmental status and later IQ (Bayley, 1970)! By the second half of the first year, however, correlations have typically become statistically significant, but are of little practical predictive value to, say, the early school years.

   A dissenting view has been voiced by Siegel (1989), who has studied preterm infants and comparison fullterm infants. She maintains that the proper use of early tests is to detect developmental problems, so that a categorical prediction (problems vs. normal) is appropriate. Using either a correlational or a categorical approach, her own research shows the early tests to be predictive of later IQs and school achievement data at ages 5 to 8 years (correlations) as well as of learning disabilities (categorical relationships).

   There may, moreover, be some aspects of development in early infancy that, in the long run, will prove predictive of advanced development in childhood. Abroms (1982) argued, on the basis of her literature review, that several above-average groups tested early in infancy had shown behaviors predictive of their later status. The most promising variables appeared to be cry counts (i. e., number of cry bursts following a flick on the sole at 4 days of age), early visual preference for novel stimuli, rapid habituation to visual stimuli (i. e., rapid cognitive processing), and visual attention. Later investigations by Fagan on early preference for novel stimuli (Fagan & McGrath, 1981) and by Bornstein (1989) on early attention and information processing have demonstrated substantial correlations with language and cognition in childhood. Note that these studies demonstrate the heterotypic continuity (Kagan, 1971) mentioned earlier. Despite these provocative findings, we will not delve further in this chapter into the relationship between infant tests and later intelligence.

How stable are test scores? Longitudinal studies of the same populations over time are the only way to secure information about the predictive value of scores for individuals. For relatively unselected populations, preschool test scores are, in general, only moderately predictive of subsequent test scores (e. g., Pinneau, 1961; Wilson, 1983).

Pinneau (1961, pp. 209–225), analyzing data from the longitudinal Berkeley Growth Study, listed the subsequent median changes in deviation IQ for children tested at various ages beginning in infancy. For example, the median change (up or down), compared with the children's test score at age 4, was 8 points to age 5, 12 points to age 8, 15 points to age 12, and 12 points to age 17. After age 6, the magnitude of change did not increase with age, though some children went steadily up, some went steadily down, and others showed stable or mixed patterns. The range of IQ changes was substantial, from 0 to 37 points.

Kangas and Bradway (1971) reported one of the few studies that has followed the same subjects from the preschool era to middle adulthood. They managed, by dint of unusual effort, in 1969 to locate 48 of the California segment of the original preschool (ages 2.5–5 years) standardization sample of the 1937 Stanford-Binet, first tested in 1931. In 1941, Bradway had tested 110 of the sample, and in 1956, 111 of them. The 1931 test scores, which represented the mean of Form L and Form M of the Stanford-Binet, had correlated .65 ($N = 110$) with junior-high Stanford-Binet Form L IQs in 1941, .59 ($N = 111$) with young-adult Stanford-Binet Form L IQs in 1956, but, in 1969, remained only moderately related to middle-age adult IQs ($r = .41$ with Stanford-Binet Form L-M, $N = 48$). Mean test scores for the 48 subjects tested first in 1931 at a mean age of 4 years were 110.7 (1931), 113.3 (1941), 124.1 (1956), and 130.1 (1969), although WAIS IQs, standardized on adult populations, did not show the same adult IQ inflation (109.6 in 1956 and 118.1 in 1969).

One of the most recent longitudinal studies is that reported by Wilson (1983), who has studied the synchrony of test score patterns in a large sample of twin pairs in Louisville. Because no single test at that time was both standardized over a wide age range and designed to yield a pattern of scores as opposed to a single score, Wilson had to shift tests (Stanford-Binet at age 3, WPPSI or McCarthy at age 4, WPPSI at ages 5 and 6, and WISC at ages 7, 8, and 9). With age 9 WISC IQs as the end point, preschool IQs were correlated with that outcome as follows: age 3 years, .65; age 4 years, .71; age 5 years, .79; age 6 years, .84. Again we see here that the shorter the interval, the higher the correlation. These correlations mean that the earlier scores predict only a part of the variance of the 9-year IQs (at 4 years, 50%; at 5 years, 62%; at age 6, 70%), but indeed a rather substantial part.

Studies in our own laboratory have covered much shorter time spans, but they are nearly the only longitudinal data available on sizable groups of very young children who have been selected not simply by test score, but because of precocious behavior.

Robinson et al. (1990), as we have noted earlier, administered, to a selected group of toddlers with precocious language, the Bayley scales at 20 months, Stanford-Binet IV and PPVT-R at 24 months, and both Stanford-Binet L-M and Stanford-Binet IV as well as PPVT-R at 30 months. The 30 toddlers followed longitudinally were the most advanced of a group of 49 seen at 20 months of age. Stanford-Binet IV for several reasons proved inappropriate even for precocious toddlers at 24 months, and only marginally appropriate at age 30 months. Many tasks were unattractive to small children; in some cases, the nature of the task was opaque even to very bright children this young; and age spans in the scoring tables are unacceptably broad. Age-adjusted scores on Stanford-Binet IV were appreciably lower at 24 months than 30 months, and few correlations were found between those scores and any other behavioral indices. For these reasons, the 30-month data are of greater interest. At 20 months, the children had attained a mean Bayley Mental Developmental Index of 141 (s.d. = 10.1) and a mean Psychomotor Developmental Index of 112 (s.d. = 15.3). Means for most of the 30-month tests are listed in Table 6.2. Not listed is the mean Stanford-Binet Form L-M IQ of 138 (s.d. = 9.6), which is significantly higher than the mean of 125 for Stanford-Binet IV but represents a less recent standardization. While the sizes of the correlations shown in Table 6.3 are only moderate at best within domains, the restricted range of

Table 6.3.   Correlations between 20-month measures and 30-month measures for children selected as toddlers with precocious language[a]

30-month	20-month Bayley measures		
	MDI	Language items	Nonlanguage items
S-B IV Composite	.55**	.25	.42*
S-B IV Verbal	.21	.54**	−.03
S-B IV Abst/Visual	.44*	−.28	.52**
S-B IV Quantitative	.44*	.12	.37
S-B IV Memory	.16	.32	.03
S-B L-M (1972) IQ			
PPVT-R	−.09	.34	−.23

*p < .05, **p < .01
[a]Adapted from Robinson, Dale, & Landesman (1990). Validity of Stanford–Binet IV with linguistically precocious toddlers. *Intelligence, 14,* 173–186. Reprinted by permission.

scores (limiting the magnitude of the correlation) must be kept in mind. Because we cannot, except by fiat, declare which of the Stanford-Binet IQs is more accurate, we are unfortunately unable to say to what degree the level of cognitive advancement remained stable from age 20 months (MDI = 141.0) to age 30 months, but we do note that 30-month scores on Verbal Reasoning, Short-Term Memory (Memory for Sentences & Bead Memory), and the PPVT-R are consistently in the range of 127-128, suggesting a possible drop in rate of development. On the other hand, scores on the Memory for Sentences subscale were the group's highest attainment, averaging the equivalent of a domain score of 136.

In this language-precocious sample, cognitive development in nonverbal domains was above average but not as advanced as in verbal domains, and the cross-domain correlations were nonsignificant (see Table 6.3). In this, our findings are similar to the conclusions of Bates, Bretherton, and Snyder (1988), who followed a middle-class but somewhat more heterogeneous sample of children from 10 to 28 months of age. Unfortunately, their only measure of intelligence was the PPVT, an index of receptive single-word vocabulary, which at 28 months correlated .45 with observed vocabulary and .54 with mean length of utterance. Bates et al. (1988) found considerable evidence of continuity in intellectual development and in both power and style of language development during the 10–28 month range, though the developmental tasks and therefore the specific kinds of behaviors changed from one age to another. Our data have not yielded such findings but the time span with which we have dealt is small.

Most of the language-precocious children in our study were seen again at age 4.5 years in an investigation which focused on language and early reading abilities (Crain-Thoreson, 1990). Very few of the children were reading, though most recognized letters and initial consonant sounds. Generally speaking, they were still ahead of their peers, particularly in language. On the PPVT-R, mean scores had dropped only slightly from 128 to 124 ($r = .49$). Their memory for sentences on the Stanford-Binet IV was still advanced but lower than their earlier score (124, down from 136, $r = .64$). On the WPPSI-R Information scale, they attained a scaled score which extrapolated to a Verbal IQ of 133, while on WPPSI-R Block Design, their scaled score extrapolated to a Performance IQ of 104. Interestingly, the Quantitative scale of Stanford-Binet IV given at 2.5 years was the scale most predictive of reading skills at 4.5 years, while Memory for Sentences at both ages was related to WPPSI-R Information scores at 4.5 years. (No measure of mathematics was included, unfortunately, at the later round of testing.) Perhaps we are seeing here some evidence of the heterotypic continuity one might expect at these transitional ages.

Now we turn again to the longitudinal study by H. B. Robinson and his colleagues of preschool children identified as advanced by their parents. Recall that these parents were asked to contact Robinson's laboratory if their children's development was advanced in one or more areas. Robinson was interested in discovering whether precocious children could be identified at an early age by their parents, whether such children remained precocious over time (or perhaps became even more so), whether parental descriptions in conjunction with test scores could improve the predictability of development, and whether children who were advanced in specific cognitive abilities such as spatial reasoning or memory, or in academic skills, would remain advanced in those specific areas. Robinson was also interested in whether the psychometric properties of the test scores resembled those of older children (of similar MA) in stability and differentiation, or whether they were more characteristic of those of CA-matched children. Of interest here, then, are the stability of abbreviated Stanford-Binet IQs over the preschool era, the role of parental descriptions, and evidence for or against stability of within-domain estimates of precocity.

The correlational data in Table 6.4 demonstrate moderate stability over time, but are certainly no higher than those of children of similar age in the Louisville Twin Project. Despite the group's high average IQs, the correlations were not attenuated by reduced variance; indeed, the standard deviations were 17.5 to 18.7, compared

Table 6.4. Stability coefficients for precocious toddlers tested with the short-form Stanford–Binet Form L-M first during the preschool years and again at age 6, compared with twin sample from Louisville study (tested with different instruments)[a]

| | Robinson sample | | Louisville twin sample | |
Age at first test	Correl.	N	Correl.	N
2 years	.75	16	.61	385
3 years	.59	117	.66	324
4 years	.61	74	.73	468
5 years	.79	25	.87	590

[a]Louisville data from Wilson (1983). The Louisville twin study: Developmental synchronies in behavior. *Child Development, 54*, 198–216. In that study, the Bayley was administered at age 2, the Stanford–Binet at 3, the McCarthy or WPPSI at 4, the WPPSI at age 5, and the WISC at age 6. Most children entered the study as infants. In Robinson's study, the short-form Stanford–Binet was administered at all ages, but here we report only the correlation between first test (on entry to the study) and the 6-year test.

with a standard deviation of 16 in the standardization sample. An additional regression analysis, which took into account initial IQ, sex, age at first test, and time between first and last test, did not greatly improve prediction of final IQ over the simple correlation between initial IQ and final IQ alone. Robinson's hypothesis that stability might be a property of MA rather than CA can, then, be confidently rejected; the expectation (McCall, 1970; McNemar, 1942) that high scores will be somewhat less stable than low scores, cannot. Even so, it is important to remember that, as a group, these children retained a marked degree of advancement.

For the subsample of 50 children tested by Stillman (1982) mentioned previously, there was interesting within-domain consistency over time. Comparison of subtest scores at about age 4.5 (mean age 52 months) with those at about age 6.5 (mean age 77 months) revealed generally stronger correlations of earlier verbal performance (Stanford-Binet vocabulary) with later verbal scores (vocabulary, syntax, auditory closure, auditory associations) and of earlier spatial scores (WPPSI block design and mazes) with later spatial scores (block designs, mazes, Primary Mental Abilities spatial subtest) than across the verbal and spatial domains.

With respect to the role of parental report, the results of Robinson's longitudinal study were interesting. A multiple regression analysis was conducted for each measure in the final test battery, administered to all children within the age span 48 to 89 months, by far the majority near their sixth birthday (72 months). The question was whether parental information could improve upon the predictions made from early test scores alone. All the ratings of the initial parental descriptors of their children's precocity in each of the five domains were first standardized for the entire group, and those standard scores used as predictors. Entered first into each equation was the initial Stanford-Binet IQ; a stepwise regression model then permitted the parental predictors in the domains to enter in order of their relationship with the test outcome variable.

The significant correlations resulting from this analysis are to be found in Table 6.5. Initial parent information about reading as it predicted final test performance was the only consistent variable. It related most strongly to subsequent reading skill but predicted other academic skills as well. It is difficult to discern from this study, for which families volunteered, whether this is because parents initially were better able to recognize and describe their children's advanced performance in this area, or whether early reading is actually the most effective predictor of later academic achievement at school entry. Note that, except for reading, two of the strongest relation-

Table 6.5. Bivariate Correlations between First IQ (FIQ) and Parental Information as Predictors of Final Test Scores and R² Resulting from Regression Analysis

Final Test	FIQ	Memory	Spatial	Math	Read	Verbal	R²	N
Stanford–Binet								
S-B IQ	.56						.346	274
Vocabulary	.42						.199	273
McCarthy								
Forward Dig.	.33	.27				.07	.245	108
Backwd. Dig.					.29		.144	86
WPPSI/WISC-R								
Block Design	.20				.30		.159	272
Mazes							.154	177
PIAT								
Math				.28	.32		.119	177
Reading Rec.	.22		.28		.55		.227	185
Reading Comp.	.29				.40		.241	117
Spelling	.21		.24		.53		.199	185
Information	.50					.22	.215	179
Total PIAT	.32				.51		.266	183

The header spans: Bivariate Correlations / Initial IQ and Parent Report over the columns FIQ, Memory, Spatial, Math, Read, Verbal.

Note: All correlations listed above were significant at the .01 level or better. Subjects were 48–89 months at final test, but most were tested close to their 6th birthday. For children functioning above the level of the WPPSI subscales, WISC-R items from the same subscale were added.

ships were between initial and final IQ, and initial IQ and subsequent fund of general information (PIAT).

One other longitudinal study has recently been reported by Eaves and Subotnik (1989), who retested a group of 48 highly gifted children who, at an average age of 3 years, 8 months, had been admitted to the preschool of Hunter College Elementary School. Presumably, applications were entered only by parents who thought their children to be gifted; children attaining a Stanford-Binet Form L-M IQ of 135 or higher were tested further and observed. At age 10, they were administered the Cognitive Levels Test (Algozzine, Eaves, Mann, & Vance, 1988). The correlation between the earlier Stanford-Binet and the Cognitive Index at age 10 was .48 (corrected for curtailment to .73). Mean IQ at age 3 was 155 (s.d. = 8.2) and mean Cognitive Index at age 10 was 143 (s.d. = 16.5), interpreted by Eaves and Subotnik as regression toward the mean. Unfortunately, the change of tests clouds the picture; readministration of the Stanford-Binet at age 10 would have been helpful.

Do test scores predict subsequent rate of development? The familiar IQ has long stood as an expression of rate of development. In its original, ratio IQ form (= MA/CA x 100), that was precisely its meaning, at least during early and middle childhood. A child with a mental age of 6 at a chronological age of 4 (IQ = 150) had acquired in one sense the developmental competence of a child half again his or her age, or a growth rate of 150%. Such figures could not be taken literally; yearly increments were known to diminish over time (Bayley, 1949, 1970). Furthermore, the original ratio IQ had a number of statistical problems (Pinneau, 1961) that led to its being abandoned in favor of the deviation IQ, a form of standard score. The two are not equivalent, although statistically they have the same mean and standard deviation. Nevertheless, in a very practical sense, some estimate of developmental rate is almost indispensable, and testmakers currently tend to report developmental age equivalents for raw scores.

The question then becomes whether an IQ not only describes development to the current age, but predicts rate of development as well. Will the precocious child continue to learn at an advanced rate? This is an important question fundamental to the optimal provision of educational options for gifted children. Unfortunately, here the evidence is controversial.

Humphreys and Davey (1988), following a suggestion by Anderson (1940), have reanalyzed data from the Louisville Twin Project (Wilson, 1983) with the premise that progressive instability in test performance over time is a product of a lack of correlation between developmental status at Time 1 and rate of growth after that time; the stability that exists is, in this view, a persisting effect of status at Time 1. (Imagine a basketball game in which one team is ahead 20 points at the half. Within a loss-limit of 19 points, that team need not outscore their opponents in the second half to win the game.) Using this model, Humphreys and Davey find a good fit with the Louisville data as well as that reported by McCall (1979). Stability across adjacent ages can be high and yet correlations will deteriorate over time.

Humphreys and Davey's view is, then, that IQ does *not* predict rate of new development from Time 1 to Time 2. A correlate of this interpretation is that the mean score of an atypical group of children selected because of high scores should gradually diminish over time. This phenomenon is the familiar regression toward the mean, and may well hold for a group of children chosen for high scores alone. Willerman and Fiedler (1974, 1977), for example, identified, from a large collaborative study, a group of 114 children in Boston with abbreviated Stanford-Binet IQs of 140+ at age 4. At age 7, their mean IQ had dropped from 148 (Stanford-Binet) to 123 (WISC), a drop of 1.5 standard deviations. Interestingly, at 8 months of age, these children had not shown advancement on the Bayley Mental Scale. The children had not been identified because of precocious behavior but because of test scores at a single age.

Similarly, Shapiro, Palmer, Antell, Bilker, Ross, and Caputo (1989) assessed a predominantly upper middle-class cohort repeatedly from birth to age 7.5. Of the 200 children so followed to age 7, 36 (18%) attained WISC-R verbal, performance, *or* full scale IQs greater than 135 and were called "gifted." (Mean WISC-R scores for this group were not reported.) Examining their earlier performance, Shapiro et al. found the "gifted" group only 5 points higher on the Bayley Mental Scale administered at 13 months and 8 points higher on the Stanford-Binet administered at age 3 years than the "nongifted" group, though the correlations of those tests with the 7-year WISC-R Full Scale IQs were .35 and .52, respectively. The gifted group also walked a little earlier though they were not more advanced on other motor milestones, and spoke two-word sentences two months earlier. Shapiro et al. concluded that while some continuity of developmental rate was revealed by these findings, the level was far too modest to permit individual prediction.

Contrast these findings with those of other longitudinal studies of gifted children which have not relied on test scores alone but other indices of development. As we have seen, the longitudinal study of H. B. Robinson and his associates identified a group of children who *increased* slightly in IQ over the brief preschool era, to age 6. Pinneau (1961), reanalyzing the data from the Berkeley Growth Study, a sample from advantaged families who at age 6 attained a mean 1916 Stanford-Binet IQ of 128, found most successive mean deviation IQs on the 1937 Stanford-Binet very slowly declining to a final mean IQ of 124 at age 17, a higher score than would have been expected had the children's learning after age 6 been unrelated to their advanced development.

It may be possible to reconcile such findings with the position of Anderson and of Humphreys and Davey. Above-average groups appear to maintain above-average status when more than test scores play a role in the selection process, the testing following nomination by parents or teachers.

The preschool children from all of these longitudinal studies also came from homes which were above average in resources, high in parent education and occupational status, and able to support the children's development in a variety of ways in addition to whatever genetic advantage they may have conveyed at conception. Maternal education is strongly correlated with child IQ, emerging as the most powerful of a long list of predictors of the preschool test performance of 26,000 children in a large collaborative study (Broman et al., 1975). (Father education was not used as a predictor.) Education and occupation of parents and grandparents are, moreover, powerfully predictive of IQ changes from preschool to junior-high age (but not beyond), as Bradway and Robinson (1961) reported for the California preschool-age standardization sample of the 1937 Stanford-Binet.

Educational level of the family is, of course, a marker for a complex of related variables that impinge more directly on the life of the child. Aside from hereditary effects (see, e.g., Plomin, 1986), parental education is also correlated with the ways in which parents rear their children—the kinds of stimulation and support they provide, for example, and the appropriateness of the pace and developmental level of that stimulation (e.g., Bradley & Caldwell, 1976; Yarrow, Rubenstein, Pedersen, & Jankowski, 1972). The quality of the parent–child interaction is extraordinarily powerful in determining intellectual outcomes and child achievement (Baumrind, 1967; Clarke-Stewart, 1973). Sometimes the effects are not discernible right away. Kagan and Moss (1962), for example, found that relatively "pushy" mothers of infants, particularly boys, later on had brighter children. They also found that boy babies of happy, loving mothers had relatively low IQs during the first year of life while those with hostile mothers had relatively high scores, but that by age 5 the patterns had reversed and remained stable thereafter. Paradoxically, the girls' scores were more independent of their mothers' early behavior. Particularly interesting is a study by Bee et al. (1982), who followed the development of 190 working-class and middle-class mothers and infants over a 4-year period. They found assessment of mother–infant interaction and general environmental quality to be among the best predictors at each age tested, and, at 24 and 36 months, as good as the children's own test scores at predicting IQ and language measures at age 4 years.

White and Watts (1973) observed extensively a group of mothers who had already successfully reared a bright preschool child and were now rearing a second preschooler. They found that these mothers talked with their children a great deal at a level the children could understand; they provided interesting experiences and expressed their own interest in the child's activities; they were responsive to the child's questions but not pedantic; they let the children know that tasks were worth doing, and worth doing well; with firmness and consistency, they made their children feel secure.

The child's own personal qualities, too, relate to intellectual outcomes. For example, passive children are more likely to decline in intellectual status as they grow older, while more active, curious ones are more likely to show a rise (Sontag, Baker, & Nelson, 1958). Yet the passive, conforming child is valued in many families and schools, and is likely to be rated a much easier child to rear.

We are, then, left with the finding that, even though there may well be individual variation within a group of bright children in the rate of their acquisition of new skills and abilities, as a group they can be expected to maintain most if not all of their accelerated rate of development. The more we are able to learn about the facilitating effects of parenting styles and about children's own style of interacting with their environment, the better we will probably become at using such information in conjunction with test scores to predict later outcomes.

A PRACTICAL TEST: ASSESSMENT FOR EARLY ENTRY TO KINDERGARTEN OR FIRST GRADE

As we noted initially, one of the major sources of parental requests for testing occurs in conjunction with applications for early admission to school. Early school entrance is an attractive option for the bright young child who is well prepared intellectually, who is socially and emotionally mature, and who possesses the requisite fine motor skills and beginning academic skills. Although for the very bright child this option will need to be supplemented by further curriculum adjustment, early school entry often permits the child to be better matched with mental peers and school experiences than if he or she had waited another year.

There is abundant evidence that bright children carefully selected for early entrance tend to do very well indeed, both academically and socially (Proctor, Black, & Feldhusen, 1986; Robinson & Weimer, 1991; Shepard & Smith, 1986). The key lies in the selection process. Unselected children who are young for grade have been found with great regularity to achieve poorly in comparison with their classmates and to exhibit social and behavioral problems more frequently.

While testing usually plays an important role in the placement decision, only one study (Obrzut, Nelson, & Obrzut, 1984) attempted (unsuccessfully) to correlate the results of preadmission evaluation with subsequent performance in school. Relying on their own clinical experience, Robinson and Weimer (1991) recommended a battery of tests that cover a wide range of functions, including general intelligence, academic skills, auditory and visual discrimination (for prereaders), social and self-help skills, fine motor skills, and gross motor skills. They stressed, however, that test results be taken in conjunction with as much collateral information as can be developed about the child in order to arrive at a reasoned judgment, recognizing that, for the child who is "deviant," life will be a series of compromises.

All of the questions of reliability, validity, and predictive power raised in this chapter bear upon decisions such as this. It is unfortunate that so little research has been directed at elucidating the appropriate contribution of testing to this practical situation. In a sense we must say, "The proof is in the pudding." Tests have been used; for the most part, good decisions have been made. That is not quite good enough.

AN OVERVIEW

Intelligence testing as we know it today has a long and rich tradition and is part of the fabric of our efforts to provide appropriate matches for the needs of children who demonstrate precocity of development. Intelligence testing simultaneously has a tarnished reputation, which emanates in large part from strong beliefs about the human worth and dignity of everyone, whatever his or her performance on such instruments.

This out-of-hand rejection of the use of tests with children has many sources, among which are the following:

1. Unrealistic expectations about the potential contributions of psychological tests (Robinson & Chamrad, 1986). On the basis of 1 or at best 2 hours' experience with a child, the psychologist is expected to predict, not only the child's ability to cope with the academic aspects of the school situation in the near future (the purpose for which such tests were derived), but to take into account all those myriad factors that will determine life satisfaction in the distant future as well, all this in isolation from other information about the child, the family, and the school. Such expectations are of course doomed to failure. The appropriate question is not whether testing is a sufficient basis for description of the child today and prediction about his or her behavior in the future, but whether testing *adds to* the accuracy and meaningfulness of the picture.

2. Comparing known test shortcomings with an ideal, unrealized notion of the efficacy of other (largely hypothetical) methods which might be invoked for the same purposes. As we have seen in Halbert Robinson's longitudinal study of gifted children identified during the preschool years, even a very comprehensive picture of a children's skills given by concerned and informed parents was of limited help in predicting that child's test performance some years hence, reading skills being the only exception. All the other potential sources of information, including school grades, performance on "creativity" measures, and teacher nominations, are subjective.

> There is not a single instance in the literature on academic talent, so far as we know, of a selection system based on such subjective ratings that is demonstrably more effective for any purpose than a system which includes and weighs test performance. Indeed, those studies that have pitted teacher ratings against test scores have generally favored the intelligence test scores.
>
> (Robinson & Chamrad, 1986, p. 162)

3. A persistent naive expectation of perfect constancy in children's rate of development and/or test scores. As we have seen, predictive power for the individual deteriorates over time, certainly the more so when there have been changes in life circumstance. In today's society, particularly in light of the instability of family constellations, even young children often experience stresses which profoundly affect their developmental trajectories and, for many other reasons, unanticipated changes of developmental rate occur. Especially when young children are concerned, we must remain open to new information.

Keeping these caveats in mind, we can review the results of the major studies reported here as suggesting that testing during the preschool years can yield a reasonably valid picture of the child's current pattern and level of functioning provided that the child was comfortable and motivated to succeed on the tasks presented. We saw in the study by Philip Dale, Nancy Robinson, and Sharon Landesman, for example, that test scores earned by children with precocious language tended to show differential patterns at an unexpectedly early age, and some stability over a short period of time.

The adults who care for children often seek support for their parenting and information about appropriate resources for their children. Tests, used conservatively by the experienced clinician, can serve as a relatively brief way to gain some knowledge about a child which can be taken in conjunction with the parents' description of development and behavior.

With regard to longer range predictions, the correlations obtained are of a magnitude which suggests that the tests can reduce errors compared with chance alone, but that there will be significant variation for individual children. As one tool, then, the tests can be an adjunct in decision making (such as the decision for or against entering a child early into school). They cannot, however, do the whole job. Life is not that simple.

REFERENCES

Abroms, K. I. (1982). The gifted infant: Tantalizing behaviors and provocative correlates. *Journal of the Division for Early Childhood, 5,* 3–18.

Algozzine, B., Eaves, R. C., Mann, L., & Vance, H. R. (1988). *The Cognitive Levels Test.* Norristown, PA: Arete.

Anderson, J. E. (1940). The prediction of terminal intelligence from infant and preschool tests. *Yearbook of the National Society for the Study of Education, 39* (I), 385–403.

Bates, E., Bretherton, I., & Snyder, L. (1988). *From first words to grammar.* Cambridge, UK: Cambridge University Press.

Baumrind, D. (1967). Child care practices anteceding three patterns of preschool behavior. *Genetic Psychology Monographs, 75,* 43–88.

Bayley, N. (1949). Consistency and variability in the growth of intelligence from birth to eighteen years. *Journal of Genetic Psychology, 75,* 165–196.

Bayley, N. (1969). *Manual for the Bayley Scales of Infant Development.* New York: Psychological Corporation.

Bayley, N. (1970). Development of mental abilities. In P. H. Mussen (Ed.), *Carmichael's manual of child psychology* (Vol. 1, pp. 1163–1209). New York: Wiley.

Bee, H. L., Barnard, K. E., Eyres, S. J., Gray, C. A., Hammond, M. A., Spietz, A. L., Snyder, C., & Clark, B. (1982). Prediction of IQ and language skill from perinatal status, child performance, family characteristics, and mother-infant interaction. Child Development, 53, 1134–1156.

Bornstein, M. H. (1989). Stability in early mental development: From attention and information processing in infancy to language and cognition in childhood. In M. H. Bornstein & N. A. Krasnegor (Eds.), Stability and continuity in mental development: Behavioral and biological perspectives (pp. 147–170). Hillsdale, NJ: Erlbaum.

Bradley, R. H., & Caldwell, B. M. (1976). Early home environment and changes in mental test performance in children from six to thirty-six months. Developmental Psychology, 12, 93–97.

Bradway, K. P., & Robinson, N. M. (1961). Significant IQ changes in twenty-five years: A follow-up. Journal of Educational Psychology, 52, 74–79.

Broman, S. H., Nichols, P. L., & Kennedy, W. A. (1975). Preschool IQ: Prenatal and early developmental correlates. Hillsdale, NJ: Erlbaum.

Bryant, D. M., & Ramey, C. T. (1987). An analysis of the effectiveness of early intervention programs for environmentally at-risk children. In M. J. Guralnick & F. C. Bennett (Eds), The effectiveness of early intervention for at-risk and handicapped children (pp. 33–78). Orlando, FL: Academic Press.

Buss, A. H., & Plomin, R. (1984). Temperament: Early developing personality traits. Hillsdale, NJ: Erlbaum.

Clarke-Stewart, K. A. (1973). Interactions between mothers and their young children: Characteristics and consequences. Monographs of the Society for Research in Child Development, 38 (6–7, Serial No. 153).

Cox, C. M. (1926). Genetic studies of genius. Vol. 2: The early mental traits of three hundred geniuses. Stanford, CA: Stanford University Press.

Crain-Thoreson, C. (1990, April). Early adult/child story reading interactions and emergent literacy. Paper presented at the annual meeting of the American Educational Research Association, Boston.

Dale, P. S., Bates, E., Reznick, J. S., & Morisset, C. (1989). The validity of a parent report instrument of child language at 20 months. Journal of Child Language, 16, 239–249.

Dale, P. S., Robinson, N. M., & Landesman, S. J. (in preparation). Patterns of language, cognitive, and social development in children selected for linguistic precocity.

Davis, F. B., French, E., & Lesser, G. S. (1959). The identification and classroom behavior of elementary school children gifted in five different mental characteristics. Mimeographed research paper, Hunter College, New York.

Dunn, L. M., & Dunn, L. M. (1981). Peabody Picture Vocabulary Test—Revised. Circle Pines, MN: American Guidance Services.

Eaves, R. C., & Subotnik, R. F. (1989). A longitudinal, criterion-related validity study of the Cognitive Levels Test for a group of highly gifted students. *Diagnostique, 14* (2), 79–88.

Fagan, J. F., & McGrath, S. K. (1981). Infant recognition memory and later intelligence. *Intelligence, 5,* 121–130.

Fenson, L., Dale, P. S., Reznick, J. S., Thal, D., Bates, E., Reilly, J. S., & Hartung, J. P. (1991) *Technical Manual for the MacArthur Communicative Development Inventories.* San Diego, CA: San Diego State University.

Honzik, M. P., Macfarlane, J. W., & Allen, L. (1948). The stability of mental test performance between two and eighteen years. *Journal of Experimental Education, 17,* 309–324.

Humphreys, L. G., & Davey, T. C. (1988). Continuity in intellectual growth from 12 months to 9 years. *Intelligence, 12,* 183–198.

Kagan, J. (1971). *Change and continuity in infancy.* New York: Wiley.

Kagan J., & Moss, H. A. (1962). *Birth to maturity: A study in psychological development.* New York: Wiley.

Kangas, J., & Bradway, K. (1971). Intelligence at middle age: A 38-year follow-up. *Developmental Psychology, 5,* 333–337.

Kaufman, A. S., & Kaufman, N. L. (1983). *K-ABC: Kaufman Assessment Battery for Children.* Circle Pines, MN: American Guidance Service.

Kitano. M. K., & De Leon, J. (1988). Use of the Stanford-Binet, Fourth Edition in identifying young gifted children. *Roeper Review, 10,* 156–165.

Knobloch, H., & Pasamanick, B. (1967). Prediction from the assessment of neuromotor and intellectual status in infancy. In J. Zubin & G. A. Jervis (Eds.), *Psychopathology of mental development.* New York: Grune & Stratton.

Louis, B., & Lewis, M. (1992). Parental beliefs about giftedness in young children and their relation to actual ability level. *Gifted Child Quarterly, 36,* 27–31.

Markwardt, F. C., Jr. (1989). *Peabody Individual Achievement Test— Revised: PIAT-R Manual.* Circle Pines, MN: American Guidance Service.

McCall, R. B. (1979). Stability-instability of individual differences in mental performance. In J. Osofsky (Ed.), *Handbook of infant development* (pp. 707–741). New York: Wiley.

McCall, R. B., Appelbaum, M. I., & Hogarty, P. S. (1973). Developmental changes in mental performance. *Monographs of the Society for Research in Child Development, 38* (Serial No. 150).

McCarthy, D. (1972). *Manual for the McCarthy Scales of Children's Abilities.* New York: Psychological Corporation.

McNemar, Q. (1942). *The revision of the Stanford-Binet Scale.* Boston: Houghton-Mifflin.

Miller, J. F. (1981). *Assessing language production in children.* Baltimore: University Park Press.

Obrzut, A., Nelson, R. B., & Obrzut, J. E. (1984). Early school entrance for intellectually superior children: An analysis. *Psychology in the Schools, 21,* 71–77.

Pinneau, S. R. (1961). *Changes in intelligence quotient.* Boston: Houghton Mifflin.

Plomin, R. (1986). *Development, genetics, and psychology.* Hillsdale, NJ: Erlbaum.

Proctor, T. B., Black, K. N., & Feldhusen, J. F. (1986). Early admission of selected children to elementary school: A review of the research literature. *Journal of Educational Research, 80,* 70–76.

Renzulli, J. S., Reis, S. M., & Smith, L. H. (1981). *The revolving door identification model.* Mansfield Center, CT: Creative Learning Press.

Reynell, J. (1981). *Reynell developmental language scales* (rev. ed.). Windsor, UK: NFER-Nelson.

Robinson, H. B., Jackson, N. E., & Roedell, W. C. (1977). *Identification and nurturance of extraordinary precocious young children. Annual report to the Spencer Foundation.* Seattle, WA: University of Washington Child Development Research Group.

Robinson, N. M., & Chamrad, D. L. (1986). Appropriate uses of intelligence tests with gifted children. *Roeper Review, 8,* 160–163.

Robinson, N. M., Dale, P. S., & Landesman, S. (1990). Validity of Stanford-Binet IV with linguistically precocious toddlers. *Intelligence, 14,* 173–186.

Robinson, N. M., & Weimer, L. (1991). Selection of candidates for early admission to kindergarten. In W. T. Southern & E. D. Jones (Eds.), *Academic acceleration of gifted children.* New York: Teachers College.

Roedell, W. C., Jackson, N. E., & Robinson, H. B. (1980). *Gifted young children.* New York: Teachers College.

Shapiro, B. K., Palmer, F. B., Antell, S. E., Bilker, S., Ross, A., & Capute, A. J. (1989). Giftedness: Can it be predicted in infancy? *Clinical Pediatrics, 28,* 205–209.

Shepard, L. A., & Smith, M. L. (1986). Synthesis of research on school readiness and kindergarten retention. *Educational Leadership, 44,* 78–86.

Siegel, L. S. (1989). A reconceptualization of prediction from infant test scores. In M. H. Bornstein & N. A. Krasnegor (Eds.), *Stability and continuity in mental development: Behavioral and biological perspectives.* Hillsdale, NJ: Erlbaum.

Sontag, L. W., Baker, C. T., & Nelson, V. L. (1958). Mental growth and personality development: A longitudinal study. *Monographs of the Society for Research in Child Development, 23* (2, Serial No. 68).

Sparrow, S. S., Balla, D. A., & Cicchetti, D. V. (1984). *Revised Vineland Adaptive Behavior Scale.* Circle Pines, MN: American Guidance Service.

Sternberg, R. J., & Davidson, J. E. (1986). *Conceptions of giftedness.* Cambridge, UK: Cambridge University Press.

Stillman, C. M. (1982). *Individual differences in language and spatial abilities among young gifted children.* Unpublished dissertation, University of Washington.

Tannenbaum, A. J. (1986). Giftedness: A psychosocial approach. In R. J. Sternberg & J. E. Davidson (Eds.), *Conceptions of giftedness.* Cambridge, UK: Cambridge University Press.

Terman, L. M., & Merrill, M. A. (1973). *Stanford-Binet Intelligence Scale: Manual for the third revision with 1972 norms tables by R. L. Thorndike.* Boston: Houghton Mifflin.

Thorndike, R. L., Hagen, E. P., & Sattler, J. M. (1986a). *Stanford-Binet Intelligence Scale: Fourth edition, Guide for administering and scoring.* Chicago: Riverside.

Thorndike, R. L., Hagen, E. P., & Sattler, J. M. (1986b). *The Stanford-Binet Intelligence Scale: Fourth edition. Technical manual.* Chicago: Riverside.

Uzgiris, I. C. (1989). Transformations and continuities: Intellectual functioning in infancy and beyond. In M. H. Bornstein & N. A. Krasnegor (Eds.), *Stability and continuity in mental development: Behavioral and biological perspectives* (pp. 123–143). Hillsdale, NJ: Erlbaum.

VanderVeer, B., & Schweid, E. (1974). Infant assessment: Stability of mental functioning in young retarded children. *American Journal of Mental Deficiency, 79,* 1–4.

Wechsler, D. (1989). *Manual for the Wechsler Preschool Primary Scale of Intelligence—Revised.* San Antonio, TX: The Psychological Corporation, Harcourt Brace Jovanovich.

White, B. L., & Watts, J. C. (1973). *Experience and environment: Major influences on the development of the young child* (Vol. 1). Englewood Cliffs, NJ: Prentice-Hall.

Willerman, L., & Fiedler, M. F. (1974). Infant performance and intellectual precocity. *Child Development, 45,* 483–486.

Willerman, L., & Fiedler, M. F. (1977). Intellectually precocious preschool children: Early development and later intellectual accomplishments. *Journal of Genetic Psychology, 131,* 13–20.

Wilson, R. S. (1983). The Louisville twin study: Developmental synchronies in behavior. *Child Development, 54,* 198–216.

Woodcock, R. W., & Johnson, M. B. (1989). *Woodcock-Johnson Psycho-Educational Battery, Revised.* Allen, TX: DLM Teaching Resources.

Yarrow, L. J., Rubenstein, J. L., Pedersen, F. A., & Jankowski, J. J. (1972). Dimensions of early stimulation and their differential effects on infant development. *Merrill-Palmer Quarterly, 18,* 205–219.

chapter 7

Precocious Reading of English: Origins, Structure, and Predictive Significance*

Nancy Ewald Jackson

College of Education,
University of Iowa

Descriptions of precocious reading ability have appeared many times in biography and autobiography and in the psychological and educational literatures (e.g., Clark, 1976; Cox, 1926; Durkin, 1966). However, these descriptions appear to have had little influence on theorists concerned with understanding child development, reading acquisition, or intellectual giftedness. Scanning the indexes of three comprehensive textbooks that I have used recently in my own courses (Mayer, 1987; Shaffer, 1989; Tannenbaum, 1983), I found not even a single reference to the topic of precocious reading or to the major studies in the field. The educational (Mayer, 1987) and developmental (Shaffer, 1989) psychology texts included few refer-

---

* Much of the research reviewed here was supported by grants to the author from the National Science Foundation Memory and Cognitive Processes Program (BNS 8509963) and the University of Washington Graduate School Research Fund.

ences to any aspect of giftedness. The text about gifted children (Tannenbaum, 1983) did not mention precocious readers as part of that population.

The purpose of the present chapter is to propose that precocious reading is a phenomenon worth considering both because it is an important form of giftedness in young children and because analyses of precocious reading can contribute to the development of general theories of cognitive development, giftedness, and reading acquisition.

Why Study Precocious Reading?

Learning to read early is an achievement that is important within the context of children's everyday life. For young children in a literate society, beginning to read is a developmental milestone as dramatic as becoming ambulatory or beginning to produce oral language. Just as children who are able to walk and talk can gain access to a larger world, children who have learned to read have a powerful new tool for learning about their physical and cultural environment.

We expect children to be able to read by the age of 6 or 7 years. We worry if the acquisition of reading is substantially delayed, and we are impressed if it is accelerated by several years. When a child of preschool age demonstrates precocious (i.e., unusually advanced) reading ability, knowledge that the child is ahead of schedule may influence adults' perceptions of and expectations for the child. Thus, precocious reading ability may influence a young child's development, not only by its direct effects in opening up new modes of learning, but also by changing adults' expectations and the child's social environment.

When precocious readers enter a public school system, the system faces the challenge of accommodating kindergarten and primary pupils who already have mastered a significant component of the early school curriculum. Precocious readers test the schools' ability to provide appropriately differentiated education for exceptionally able young children.

The study of precocious reading can contribute to our theoretical understanding of both reading acquisition and intellectual giftedness. Most studies of individual differences in beginning reading have involved contrasts between children who are progressing reasonably well and those who are progressing slowly. Without studies of precocious readers, theories of individual differences in reading acquisition have failed to encompass the full range of those differences. Extrapolation is always risky in science, and examination of the most able beginning readers may contribute to the modification of general conclusions about the nature of reading acquisition. For example, identifying the range of characteristics and component skill patterns found among precocious readers may suggest that some characteristics thought to be necessary for success in beginning reading are not universally essential (Clark, 1976; Coltheart, 1979; Jackson & Biemiller, 1985).

In comparison with other domains in which young children can demonstrate giftedness, such as mathematics, music, or the graphic arts, reading is relatively well understood. Standard tests provide norms (at least for children of school age) against which the progress of precocious readers can be evaluated. Cognitive theories of reading processes are sophisticated and powerful, and cognitive theories of reading acquisition are beginning to emerge (e.g., Perfetti, 1985; Stanovich, 1986). The reading researcher has access to well-documented measures of components of reading skill. In these respects, the study of precocious reading ability provides a "best case scenario" for studies of giftedness in young children. What we learn from our research in this relatively rich investigative domain should help us develop theories and methods for the study of more exotic and less well-understood gifts.

If substantial precocity in beginning to read were extremely unusual, it would be interesting to developmental and reading theorists, but there would not be much practical need to understand its significance in children's development or to determine how schools can work most effectively with precocious readers. However, precocious readers, although exceptional, are not freakishly rare. Estimates of the incidence and prevalence of precocious reading ability will depend on the definition of precocity used and will vary across communities and eras, but children with this advanced ability seem to be as common as other special populations for whom specific educational provisions have been made.

Durkin's (1966) prevalence data are especially valuable, because she screened defined populations of school children rather than relying on parent or teacher nominations to generate her samples. After excluding children who were repeating first grade or who had some instruction in reading during kindergarten, Durkin found that 3.5% of the New York first graders she screened in 1961 qualified as precocious readers by identifying at least 18 words on a 37-word test and achieving a minimal raw score on a paragraph reading test. In her 1958 Oakland study, similar procedures had yielded a sample of precocious readers that was about 1% of the population screened. The more than threefold increase in prevalence of reading precocity from the first to the second study could have reflected geographic differences, but Durkin speculates that changes in scholarly and public perceptions of the "readiness" of young children for reading instruction may have contributed to the increase.

To my knowledge, there are no current statistics available on the prevalence of prekindergarten or pre-first-grade reading precocity in the United States. Changes in public values, widespread enrollment in preschool education programs, and the availability of popular educational toys and television programs may have made precocious reading more common, or the degree of precocious reading attained more extreme. We do know that precocious readers remain easy for researchers to find. For example, in Summer 1987, my colleagues and I generated an initial sample of 124 precocious readers by using the screening test records of a gifted education program selection system in Seattle, Washington, and by contacting kindergarten teachers in five nearby suburban public school districts (Jackson, Donaldson, & Mills, 1990). In previous years, kindergarten teachers in Seattle had nominated 80 precocious readers, and those in smaller suburban districts typically nominated about 10 or 15 children per district (Jackson, Donaldson, & Cleland, 1988; Jackson & Donaldson, 1989b). Because we did not survey private schools or the first-grade teachers of children who had skipped kindergarten, and because we were relying on both teachers' nominations and parents' decisions to volunteer, our sample size probably underrepresented the number of precocious readers among the area's kindergarten-age population at that time.

When I talk to teachers and parents about my research with precocious readers, I find that most people in my audiences have known at least one such child. In the suburban school districts from which I have drawn the participants for several of my studies, several end-of-the-year kindergarten classes yielded two or three precocious readers. These were children whose postkindergarten reading comprehension levels were at least at the norm for beginning second graders and typically were much higher. Most of them had been effective word readers from the age of 4 or even earlier. Clearly, precocious reading is too common to be ignored by theorists who wish to explain the development of all children or practitioners who wish to provide appropriate education for every individual.

Because learning to read is important and many precocious readers exist, understanding reading precocity has considerable practical significance. Is beginning to read early a desirable achievement that should be encouraged by as many parents, preschools, and kindergartens as possible, or are there negative consequences associated with early reading? If precocious achievement in reading is desirable, how likely is it that parents or schools *can* create more precocious readers by special nurturance or instruction? What about the precocious readers who already exist—do they need special instruction to fill in gaps in their skill patterns? In the long run, what kind of performance in reading and other academic areas can be expected of a child who has entered school with advanced reading skill? Should precocious readers be placed in programs for the gifted? Preliminary answers to practical questions such as these are beginning to emerge from research on precocious reading.

The nontrivial prevalence of precocious reading ability has methodological as well as practical implications. Precocity in reading is a form of giftedness in young children that is common enough to be studied using research designs that require large samples. Whereas some forms of giftedness in young children can be studied only by examining individuals or small groups of cases, the study of reading precocity can involve multivariate and even multiple-indicator techniques (e. g., Jackson et al., 1988). Case studies of gifted individuals can be richly informative, but the use of large-N designs permits traditional hypothesis testing and facilitates the integration of studies of gifted populations with mainstream research in developmental psychology.

Sources and Scope of the Chapter

Several fairly comprehensive reviews of the pre-1980 literature on precocious reading ability are available elsewhere (Baghban, 1984; Coltheart, 1979; Jackson, 1988a; Torrey, 1979). However, the most recent of these reviews were written for broad audiences and minimize the theoretical and technical issues that are central to the development of a scientific body of literature. Those issues will be emphasized in the present chapter. I will focus on the program of research that my colleagues and I have conducted since the late 1970s (Jackson, 1988a; Jackson & Biemiller, 1985; Jackson & Donaldson, 1989a,b; Jackson et al., 1988, 1990; Jackson & Myers, 1982; Mills & Jackson, 1990). However, I also will cover other investigators' work as it relates to issues I feel are central to understanding the psychological and educational implications of precocious reading ability.

The family backgrounds, early experiences, and cognitive and personality characteristics of precocious readers provide some clues to the origins or causes of precocious reading ability. Studies of the reading skill patterns and strategies used by precocious readers address the general question of whether reading ability that has developed early (and, in most cases, without formal instruction) is different from reading ability that has been developed in elementary school. Longitudinal studies of the later development of precocious readers provide insights into the long-term predictive significance of this form of early childhood giftedness.

Precocious reading ability may be related to precocity in the development of oral language or writing and spelling skills. However, there is little evidence available on possible relations among these different forms of early giftedness in communication skills, and this chapter includes only passing references to skills other than reading.

ORIGINS OF PRECOCIOUS READING ABILITY

Family Characteristics

Children who are born to, or raised by, parents who are well educated and who have abundant material and psychological resources are more likely to show many forms of intellectual competence than are children from disadvantaged backgrounds (e.g., Scarr & Weinberg, 1977; Terman & Oden, 1947). One might, therefore, be tempted to think of the extremely high degree of competence demonstrated by precocious readers as the exclusive provenance of children from middle- or upper-class homes. However, precocious readers have been identified from all socioeconomic and major ethnic groups in American society. In one of our own recent studies (Jackson & Donaldson, 1989b), 14% of the postkindergarten precocious readers in our volunteer sample came from homes with incomes low enough to qualify the child for free or reduced-price lunches. Studies of precocious readers have included Black children from low-income homes (Durkin, 1982; Torrey, 1979); children who learned to read English early despite coming from homes in which English was not the primary language used (Jackson, 1988a; Jackson & Donaldson, 1989b); and Scottish children whose parents had left school at ages as young as 14 years (Clark, 1976).

Parents' expectations for their preschool-age children's mastery of academic skills and the press they impose for early achievement would be expected to contribute to the development of precocious reading ability, but the limited data available suggest that any relationship is not a straightforward linear one. Several investigators have described precocious readers' parents as concerned and committed to fostering their children's general development and devoting considerable time to childrearing (Clark, 1976; Durkin, 1966; Hirsh-Pasek, 1989; Jackson, 1988a). However, Thomas (1984) found that the only demographic variable on which education-level-matched parents of precocious readers and nonreaders differed was the amount of time fathers spent working, an average of 10 hours less per week for fathers of precocious readers.

Parents' Attitudes and Behaviors

As is evident in Table 7.1, parents of precocious readers almost universally report that they have engaged in activities that would be expected to facilitate reading development (Jackson et al., 1988), even though they may deny having taught their children to read (Bus & van IJzendoorn, 1988). However, many parents who have provided facilitating experiences similar to those offered by parents of precocious readers have children who do *not* read early (Durkin, 1966; Thomas, 1984). Many precocious readers have nonprecocious siblings (Clark, 1976).

In one recent longitudinal study of middle class families (Hirsh-Pasek & Cone, 1989), there was a small positive relationship (r = .29) between mothers' scores on the academic subscale of an "Edu-

Table 7.1. Parent Reports of Teaching Activities Related to Reading

Activity	Number of Parents		
	Yes	No	Not Sure
Before your child started kindergarten, when you or anyone else read to your child, did that person			
— discuss the pictures?	85	2	0
— point out letters and words?	79	6	2
— explain meanings of words?	87	0	0
— check the child's comprehension of the story?	79	5	3
— (other activities)	40	—	—
Before your child started kindergarten, did you or anyone else help the child by			
— identifying letter names?	85	2	0
— identifying numerals?	86	1	0
— identifying letter sounds?	83	2	2
— helping with spelling?	76	10	1
— discussing the meanings of words?	85	2	0

cational Attitudes Scale" and 4-year-olds' concurrent performance in such preacademic skills as learning letters and numbers. However, this association had disappeared when the children were retested at kindergarten age, perhaps because of a ceiling effect from the kindergarteners' consistently high achievement. Hirsh-Pasek and her colleagues concluded from the overall pattern of their data that there "does not appear to be any advantage to accelerating the academic environment of preschool children."

Thomas (1984) also found a relationship between parents' attitudes toward their children and precocious reading ability in four year olds. Parents of precocious readers were more likely to describe their children in positive rather than negative terms and to specify cognitive/creative rather than emotional/social characteristics. As in the Hirsh-Pasek study, this concurrent relationship could reflect the influence of children's achievements on their parents' attitudes rather than the reverse.

Parent–Child Interaction Patterns

Identification of family characteristics strongly related to the development of precocious reading ability may require abandoning status and trait variables in favor of a more fine-grained analysis of parent–child interactions. In a cross-sectional study of 1½-, 3½-, and 5½-year-old Dutch children, Bus and van IJzendoorn (1988) found that dyads in which the child's attachment to the mother was rated as securely attached showed more harmony during reading-related interactions, more frequent protoreading (activities such as attempting to spell words or name letters) by the child, and more instruction by the mother in the formal aspects of written language. Performance on measures of emergent literacy administered to the two older groups also was related to aspects of mother–child interactions. Mothers of children who earned higher literacy test scores spent less time on interpretation of illustrations and stories. These more literate children also devoted less of their time during the interactions to story exploration and more to protoreading.

Bus and van IJzendoorn's intriguing pattern of results has several possible interpretations. The authors conclude that mothers of securely attached children may be able to demand more of their children, who are less likely to be distracted or require discipline during learning interactions. Alternatively, one or more additional factors may be the source of the observed relation. Competent parents or temperamentally easy children may be more likely to demonstrate both secure attachment and productive learning interactions.

Bus and van IJzendoorn correctly note that the observed relations between mothers' teaching activities and children's skill levels could reflect causal links in either or both directions: mothers' activities could both foster and reflect their children's skill development. All of these alternatives are interesting. Unfortunately, Bus and van IJzendoorn's analysis of their data does not exclude yet another possibility—that chronological age differences in performance on their three classes of measures contribute to the observed relations among them.

In a study that complements Bus and van IJzendoorn's, Crain-Thoreson and Dale (1992) found a positive relationship between child behaviors observed during mother–child storyreading interactions at 24 months and the child's performance on several standardized tests administered at 54 months. Within this sample of 25 American children, who had all been selected because of precocity in their oral language development, children's attentiveness to the story was positively associated with later performance on a test of print awareness and on both verbal and nonverbal subtests selected from an intelligence test. Their data did not permit Crain-Thoreson and Dale to determine the extent to which the child's early attentiveness to storyreading was a stable characteristic of the child, a response to the mother's behavior during the session, or both. However, they suggest that further observations of adult–child interactions during storyreading may help us identify individual differences in emerging literacy very early in development.

Books, Toys, and Television

Most children in industrialized nations encounter many forms of print in their everyday environments. Traffic signs, advertising, and product labels provide exposure to written language even for children whose parents do not provide them with books to look at and who are not themselves frequent readers. However, virtually all precocious readers are like many nonreaders in that, from infancy onward, they have been given books, been read to, and observed their parents reading (Baghban, 1984; Durkin, 1966; Jackson et al., 1988).

Durkin (1966) and others who have asked parents of precocious readers about their children's early play interests have described these children as "pencil-and-paper kids" who had early access to and enjoyed using a variety of drawing and writing materials. The writing and drawing skill of one precocious reader whose development has been described elsewhere (Jackson, 1988b) is evident in

Figure 7.1. Drawing completed at preschool by a precocious reader shortly before his fourth birthday. His name has been deleted from the dedication at the left. The combination of text and graphics is typical of this child's artwork.

Figure 7.1. However, not all precocious readers seem precociously inclined to graphic expression (Jackson, 1988a).

In one of the most recent comparisons of the interests of precocious readers and nonreaders matched for family background and intelligence, Thomas (1984) found that the parents of precocious readers reported more enjoyment of "reading readiness" toys such as alphabet books, audiotape story cassettes, and letter sets and puzzles. This was the only category of toys on which precocious readers and nonreaders differed consistently across the full age span of their parents' retrospective reports, although there were some other differences at particular age periods. On the whole, similarities between the groups' reported interests were more striking than differences.

Educational television programs such as "Sesame Street," which introduces some key prereading and beginning reading concepts such as letter names, and the more advanced "Electric Company," may contribute to the development of precocious reading ability. Children who watch "Sesame Street" frequently have been found to be more knowledgeable about the preacademic concepts covered in the program than less frequent viewers are (Bogatz & Ball, 1972) and "Electric Company" has had positive effects on learning when watched in a supporting educational setting (Ball & Bogatz, 1973). Many precocious readers are frequent viewers of these programs.

When parents of 87 precocious readers in one of our studies (Jackson et al., 1988) were asked about their child's viewing, only one parent reported that her child never had seen "Sesame Street," and well over half reported that their child began watching at or before the age of 2 years. Thirty-three children were reported to have begun watching "Electric Company" at or before age 2. Reports from parents of precocious readers suggest that some of them have been fanatic "Sesame Street" watchers, viewing the program several times each day (Jackson, 1988b). However, Thomas (1984) found no difference between 4-year-old precocious readers and nonreaders in frequency of viewing "Sesame Street." Precocious readers did watch "Electric Company" more frequently.

As a whole, the literature on precocious readers' early interests suggests they frequently have had access to and enjoyed toys, books, and television programs that could have facilitated their learning, but that also have been available to and enjoyed by nonreaders. Interests in some activities, such as watching "Electric Company" may be results of more than contributors to precocious development in reading.

Gender

Boys are much more likely than girls to have unexpected difficulty learning to read (Stanovich, 1986). Thus, girls might be expected to be disproportionately represented in samples of precocious readers. On the other hand, the tendency for boys to be more variable, in both directions from the mean, on many cognitive characteristics (e.g., Benbow, 1988) suggests that they might be more likely than girls to be unusually precocious as well as unusually delayed in reading. No clear-cut pattern has emerged from the data. Some samples of precocious readers have been predominantly female (Durkin, 1966; Tobin & Pikulski, 1988; Jackson et al., 1988), others have been predominantly male (Clark, 1976; Jackson & Donaldson, 1989b), and still others have contained approximately equal numbers of boys and girls (Jackson et al., 1990).

One possibility that merits further investigation is suggested by Terman and Oden's (1947) retrospective parent report data. Within their sample of children selected for high IQs, about equal numbers of boys and girls were reported to have begun reading at the age of 4 or 5 years. Boys were especially likely to be precocious readers if their IQs were above 170. IQ and reading precocity were less strongly associated among the girls. Clark's (1976) Scottish sample of children who were extremely advanced in reading when identified close to their initial school enrollment at about 5 years of age included 20 males and only 12 females. However, we have not found any significant relationship between gender and degree of reading precocity within our own research samples (Jackson et al., 1988).

Cognitive and Personality Characteristics

Intelligence. Across the full range of ability, success in beginning reading shows a modest positive relationship with general, and especially verbal, intelligence (e.g., Curtis, 1980; Stanovich, 1986). Therefore, one would expect precocious readers typically to be above average in verbal intelligence, and they are. In five studies, each of which involved at least 30 precocious readers nominated by a procedure that would not obviously bias IQ estimates (Clark, 1976; Durkin, 1966; Jackson et al., 1988; Tobin & Pikulski, 1988), mean group verbal IQs ranged from 121 (Durkin, 1966, California sample) to approximately 145 (Clark, 1976) but centered at about 130. There is a tendency for samples whose reading precocity was more extreme to have had higher mean IQs.

The mean IQ data suggest that a substantial proportion of precocious readers could qualify as gifted in verbal intelligence according to the criteria used in many school districts. However, half or more would not so qualify, and the variability in precocious readers' verbal IQs is striking. One of our own studies was typical in that Wechsler Intelligence Scale for Children-Revised (WISC-R; Wechsler, 1974) Verbal IQs, estimated from performance on three subtests, had a standard deviation of 13.5 (mean = 128). This figure approaches the standard deviation of 15 for the norming population of the test. Precocious readers with verbal IQs in the average range are not uncommon (e. g., Durkin, 1966; Mills & Jackson, 1990; Tobin & Pikulski, 1988; Torrey, 1969).

The most dramatic exceptions to the typical finding that precocious readers have above-average verbal intelligence are "hyperlexic" autistic children, who have learned to pronounce written words accurately before reaching normal school age despite being substantially below average in their oral language production and comprehension skills (Healy, 1982). The existence of hyperlexic children proves that advanced oral language development is not necessary for the precocious emergence of reading skill.

Neither is linguistic precocity sufficient for precocious reading achievement. In a longitudinal study of children identified as precocious in oral language at the age of 2 years, Crain-Thoreson and Dale (1992) found that only one had made substantial progress in word recognition by the age of 4½, and degree of precocity in reading was not positively related to degree of oral language precocity. This result is consistent with findings from an earlier study of intellectually gifted preschoolers (Jackson & Myers, 1982).

Within samples of 5–6-year-old precocious readers tested during the summer after their kindergarten year, my colleagues and I have found moderate positive relations, correlations ranging between .30 and .43, between verbal intelligence and various reading measures including performance on a standard test of reading comprehension, oral text reading speed, and isolated word identification accuracy (Jackson et al., 1988, 1990). These figures are consistent with the correlation of .40 between degree of reading precocity and Stanford-Binet IQ in Durkin's (1966) California sample and higher than the .24 correlation for the same measures in her New York sample.

The modest correlations between reading and verbal intelligence found within samples of postkindergarten and first-grade precocious readers are compatible with the finding that most preschoolers selected for high verbal intelligence are not precocious readers. However, individual differences in verbal ability may be more related to the extent of progress in reading that a young child makes after developing the rudiments of word identification ability than to the age at which those rudiments first appear.

Other cognitive abilities. A diverse array of specific cognitive abilities have been investigated as possible concomitants or precursors of precocious reading achievement, with most attention directed to abilities that have been found to be weak in specifically disabled readers. Few associations have been found consistently across samples (Torrey, 1979).

Anecdotal reports (Jackson, 1988b; Torrey, 1979) suggest that precocious readers sometimes also are precocious in the acquisition of beginning number skills. However, other data suggest that extreme mathematical precocity is much rarer than a comparable degree of reading precocity during the preschool years (Jackson, Krinsky, & Robinson, 1977; Roedell, Jackson, & Robinson, 1980).

Disabled readers have sometimes been characterized as deficient in auditory short-term memory (e. g., Stanovich, 1986). According to most cognitive theories of reading, short-term memory can be the locus of a bottleneck in text processing, because incoming information must be held there long enough to be synthesized into larger units of meaning—letters and their sounds into words, words into sentences. Therefore, the hypothesis that superior short-term memory contributes to the development of precocious reading skill is reasonable. However, findings have been inconsistent across studies (Jackson et al., 1988, 1990; Jackson & Myers, 1982). Associations between memory span may be strongest within samples of young children just moving into reading (Jackson & Myers, 1982). Span typically is measured by having children repeat a series of digits either exactly as presented or in reverse order. Therefore, the association may be attributable to precocious readers' greater familiarity with number names and greater facility, as a result of their reading experience, in creating and "reading" a mental image of the series of digits they have heard and been asked to repeat. On the other hand, parents of precocious readers often comment on their children's general ability to recall and repeat long strings of information.

Concurrent relationships also have been found between reading precocity and reading-related skills or knowledge such as awareness of print concepts and awareness of or ability to manipulate word sound components (Backman, 1983; Evans & Smith, 1976; Torrey, 1979). For example, Backman (1983) found that kindergarten-age precocious readers performed substantially better than age-matched nonreaders on a sound deletion task that involved saying what word would be formed by a deletion, such as saying *nest* without the *s*. Within her sample of 24 precocious readers, performance on the sound deletion task was moderately related to individual differences in pseudoword reading accuracy and spelling, but not to other aspects of reading skill.

While the general literature on beginning reading has yielded many suggestions that ability to do oral phonological tasks such as sound deletion contributes to success in beginning reading (e. g., Blachman, 1984), the correlational findings available for precocious readers do not permit the conclusion that advanced phonological awareness causes accelerated development of reading ability. Findings have been specific to particular phonological measures and particular reading subskills, and there is sufficient variance among precocious readers to dismiss the possibility that reliable performance on phonological tasks is prerequisite for precocity in reading (Backman, 1983).

The speed with which children name letters is a concurrent and longitudinally predictive correlate of word reading accuracy among intellectually gifted preschoolers (Jackson & Myers, 1982) as well as a reliable, if modest, correlate of several measures of text-reading ability among postkindergarten precocious readers (Jackson & Biemiller, 1985; Jackson et al., 1988, 1990). Precocious readers' postkindergarten letter-naming speed is modestly related to individual differences in time taken to complete a reading comprehension test 5 or 6 years later (Mills & Jackson, 1990). Although the ability to name letters rapidly may appear to be a component of reading skill rather than a distinct cognitive ability, research with other populations suggests that individual differences in letter-naming speed reflect a more general difference in ability to retrieve name information rapidly from long-term memory (Blachman, 1984; Jackson et al., 1988).

Extremely precocious readers name letters faster than moderately precocious readers do. However, the group as a whole is substantially slower at naming letters than reading-level-matched older children are (Jackson & Biemiller, 1985; Jackson et al., 1990). Investigators working with other populations also have found that performance on letter-naming tasks is strongly influenced by chronological age, perhaps because of age limits on the efficiency of articulatory processes that are a component of letter-naming response time but unrelated to reading ability (Stanovich, Nathan, & Zolman, 1988). Therefore, the within-age and cross-age data are not contradictory. The components of letter-naming performance that are relevant to reading may be masked in cross-age comparisons.

Given other evidence suggesting that efficient operation of basic memory processes may be an important aspect of intelligence and intellectual giftedness in young children (Borkowski & Peck, 1986), the possibility that potential for precocious achievement in reading is indicated by a general or letter-specific ability to name visual stimuli rapidly merits further investigation. If general name retrieval efficiency is the effective predictor, some sort of broadly based, possibly neurological, individual differences in readiness would be suggested.

Effects of Early Formal Instruction

Preschool and kindergarten experiences of precocious readers. Reports from parents of precocious readers suggest little influence of formal instruction in preschool on the development of their children's skills. Parents of the children in one of the samples studied by my research group (Jackson et al., 1988) rarely reported any preschool instruction in reading beyond identification of letter names, and several parents commented that the prereading instruction their child had received at preschool was well behind the pace of the child's learning at home.

Instruction during children's kindergarten year may contribute in more important ways to pre-first grade reading achievement. However, in the samples we have studied, kindergarten instruction appears to have functioned to facilitate the further development of already advanced reading skills rather than to "create" precocity. The *standard* kindergarten curricula in the school districts in which my colleagues and I identified several samples of postkindergarten precocious readers provided only for the development of very elementary skills such as "decode monosyllabic words containing short vowels" such as 'pan' and 'tip' and "read sight words in context such as "The dog is big" (Jackson & Donaldson, 1989b). Mastery of these standard objectives would not have been sufficient to bring a child to the reading level required for inclusion in our samples. On the other hand, parents of about half of the 87 precocious readers studied by Jackson et al. (1988) reported that their children had received some sort of individual or small-group instruction tailored to the child's already advanced skill level.

Short-term effects of experiments in early instruction. Early school instruction in reading can cause precocious mastery of beginning reading skills. When children have been randomly assigned to programs offering instruction in reading beginning at 4 or 5 years, the experimental groups typically have shown statistically significant and sometimes substantial gains relative to uninstructed controls (Durkin, 1970, 1974–1975; Feitelson, Tehori, & Levinberg-Green, 1982; Fowler, 1971). For example, after two years of instruction beginning at age 4, Durkin's (1970, 1974–1975) experimental group could identify an average of 125 words (compared with 18 for the control group) and knew 15.5 of the 22 letter sounds taught. The effectiveness of some programs may have been limited by reliance on a worksheet and drill-oriented curriculum designed for older children (Feitelson et al., 1982).

Summary: Origins of Precocious Reading

No single family characteristic, home or school experience, or child characteristic appears to be necessary or sufficient for the emergence of precocious reading ability. Diverse factors have shown some relation with reading precocity, but a comprehensive multivariate study identifying how these factors might work together has yet to be done. Because the emergence of precocious reading ability changes a child's environment and cognitive skills and may alter parents' recollections of past events, description of the origins of precocious reading should be based on prospective longitudinal research.

STRUCTURE: WHAT READING SKILLS
DO PRECOCIOUS READERS HAVE?

Distinguishing Characteristics of Precocious Readers

Strengths. Reading subskill or component process strengths found to be more characteristic of precocious than of other readers are interesting because they are plausible sources of precocious readers' rapid development. The most extreme strengths of precocious readers merit investigation as potential keys to reading success, just as the most extreme deficits of disabled readers have been considered as potential causes of reading failure (Jackson & Butterfield, 1989).

In a series of studies of different large samples of precocious readers (Jackson & Biemiller, 1985; Jackson & Donaldson, 1989b; Jackson et al., 1990), we repeatedly have found text-reading speed (oral in three studies, both oral and silent in one) to be precocious readers' greatest strength, relative to the skill patterns of reading-level-matched older children and relative to their own out-of-context word-reading speed. An attempt to explain precocious readers' fast text-reading speeds as a result of superior ability to use information from prior context to facilitate word identification was not successful (Jackson & Donaldson, 1989b). A plausible alternative hypothesis is that precocious readers' rapid text reading reflects a strategic preference for rapid reading rather than any unusual processing of specific kinds of information.

Reading text rapidly facilitates comprehension by increasing the odds that the idea units (propositions) that need to be linked to one another in order for the reader to build up a coherent mental representation of a text will all be available in short-term memory at the same time (Kintsch & van Dijk, 1978). Perhaps precocious readers, on the average, are more likely than school-taught readers to have learned that plunging through text at the most rapid pace possible is a good way to absorb and enjoy its content. One 5-year-old reader, when asked by her mother to "sound out" an unfamiliar word, replied, "You're making me forget the story. Just tell me, I'll remember it next time." (Baghban, 1984, p. 105). The astuteness of this young reader's preferred strategy has been demonstrated by Breznitz (1987), who found that first graders who were presented with text at their maximum normal reading rate showed improved comprehension and a reduction in oral reading errors.

When they are reading isolated words, precocious readers tend to be more distinguished by the accuracy than by the speed of their pronunciations (Jackson & Donaldson, 1989b; Jackson et al.,

1990). When words are presented one at a time, there is no intrinsic payoff for speed, and taking ample time to identify new or difficult words accurately is a developmentally adaptive strategy.

Potential weaknesses. Relative weaknesses in the skill patterns of precocious readers would be most interesting if they occurred in skill areas thought to be essential for success in learning to read. For example, early mastery of phonological decoding rules has been proposed as a prerequisite for successful progress in reading (Stanovich, 1986), in part because disabled readers sometimes are found to be especially weak in ability to use those rules. In one of our studies, parents of 95% of postkindergarten precocious readers reported that they had discussed letter sounds with their children. However, many precocious readers may have had little formal instruction in decoding rule use. If they make rapid progress despite weak phonological decoding skills, their progress would be evidence that alternative word identification strategies can be sufficient for reading success.

Anecdotal reports suggest that at least some preschool-aged precocious readers have learned to identify words " by sight" without being able to "sound them out." Clark (1976) suggested that, for precocious readers, the identity of a word "just clicks." Baghban (1984) reports a similar impression, which is also consistent with my own informal observations of some 3- and 4-year-old readers. However, my students and I also have observed 3- and 4-year-olds who were highly skilled at sounding out unfamiliar words and pseudowords. By the time precocious readers are 5 or 6 years old, their phonological decoding skills (measured by the ability to pronounce phonologically legitimate pseudowords such as *islop*) are, on the average, about as strong as other aspects of their word identification skills (Jackson et al., 1990). Whether precocious readers' pseudoword-reading ability reflects mastery of rules or of connections with components of real words that have been identified by analogical reasoning (Baron, 1979), they have mastered the essence of English grapheme–phoneme correspondences by the time they are postkindergarteners reading, on the average, at the late third-grade level (Jackson et al., 1990). The development of their mastery to that point merits further investigation.

Precocity or difference? We have not identified any other significant deficits or strengths in precocious readers' component skills. With the exceptions noted above, the group's average performance is consistent with a "developmental advance" model that mirrors the consistent delays in skill development found among "garden variety" poor readers (Stanovich et al., 1988). The data in

Table 7.2 show that advanced development begins early. Parents' retrospective reports of the first ages at which their children mastered prereading and reading skills suggest an accelerated version of a sequence found by Mason (1980) to be characteristic of more typical preschoolers. Their performance on standard tests of reading comprehension may be less advanced than their performance on other measures of word and text reading, but this discrepancy probably reflects the contribution of nonreading factors such as general knowledge and verbal ability to comprehension test scores (Jackson et al., 1977, 1990).

There is no evidence that precocious readers are identifying words or reading text using strategies that are qualitatively different from those of other readers. For example, precocious readers and level-matched second graders' word identification speeds are influenced in similar ways by a word's frequency and by the regularity of its grapheme–phoneme correspondences (Jackson & Donaldson, 1989a). Similarly, Malicky and Norman (1985) found that patterns of oral reading errors shown by precocious readers were similar to those of school-taught readers.

Table 7.2.   Reading History Milestones Reported by Parents

	Percentage Distribution by First Age in Years				
Accomplishment	2 or before	3	4	5	6 or not yet
Recited most of alphabet	59	37	5		
Identified several capital letters	57	36	7		
Identified own name in print	36	59	6		
Recognized words on signs or in advertisements	30	38	28	5	
Spelled words using blocks, magnetic letters, printing, or other means	6	38	49	7	
Printed most capital letters	1	41	49	8	
Began reading simple books such as One Fish, Two Fish or Hop on Pop	5	25	55	15	
Sounded out unfamiliar words	2	13	31	46	8
Began reading long books with few pictures, such as Charlotte's Web		3	17	38	41

Note. Modal ages are underlined. Percentages within rows sum to approximately 100%, allowing for rounding.

Differences Among Precocious Readers

Even if precocious readers, as a group, have skill patterns similar to those of older average readers, the possibility remains that individuals may differ from one another in ways that have theoretical and practical significance. For example, while the group as a whole is characterized by solid word identification skills and exceptional fluency in text reading, there might be individual precocious readers who are weak in one or both skill areas. The existence of even a few children within the group who are weak decoders but manage nonetheless to read text fluently and comprehend it well would indicate the same kinds of alternative pathways to reading success as would be suggested by such a performance pattern for the group as a whole. There appear to be diverse ways in which children can fail to learn to read (e. g., Olson, Kleigl, Davidson, & Foltz, 1985). Are there also diverse ways in which they can succeed? Indeed, Backman (1983, p. 476) reports that while "as a group [kindergarten-age precocious readers] . . . did not differ from . . . older readers in their ability to decode nonsense words, there was evidence that at least a subgroup of early readers was successfully using a visual word-recognition strategy to read."

Analysis of the performance of 87 postkindergarten precocious readers on 11 measures of oral word- and text-reading skills (Jackson et al., 1988) revealed individual differences in patterns of performance that could be described as differences in reading style. The children differed from one another in the level of their overall performance on this set of measures, and it was this superordinate factor, which we called General [Reading] Ability, that was correlated with performance on a standard test of reading comprehension and with Verbal Ability. However, as indicated in Figure 7.2, these precocious readers also differed from one another on a complex of subordinate factors that we labeled Speed, Decoding Rule Use, and Graphic Precision. These factors contributed substantially to explanation of the total variance in the set of scores. For example, performance on the two pseudoword reading measures was determined as strongly by Decoding Rule Use as by General Reading Ability.

The subordinate style factors were correlated with one another in a way that suggested a dimension of style difference ranging from slow, precise reading and strong mastery of decoding rules to fast, imprecise reading and relative weakness in use of decoding rules. This set of differences is similar to a plodder–explorer dimension of reading style difference that Olson et al. (1985) identified among disabled readers but failed to find among average readers. In our own research, some longitudinal stability of reading styles was indi-

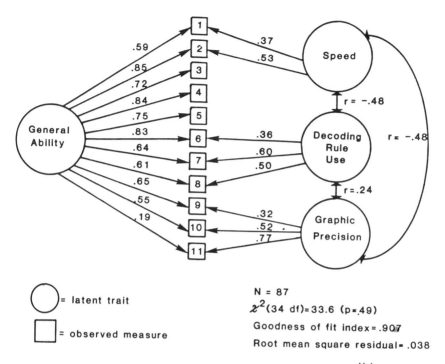

N = 87

χ^2(34 df)=33.6 (p=.49)

Goodness of fit index=.907

Root mean square residual=.038

○ = latent trait

□ = observed measure

Number	Description of measure	Unique Variance
1	Speed reading Biemiller word list	.51
2	Speed reading 4 text passages	.00
3	Accuracy, 2 cloze passages	.49
4	Contextual constraint of errors, text passages	.29
5	Accuracy, Baron irregular words	.44
6	Accuracy, Baron regular words	.19
7	Accuracy by regular rule, Baron pseudowords	.23
8	Accuracy, Woodcock–Johnson pseudowords	.38
9	Graphic constraint of errors, text passages	.48
10	Absence of omission errors, text passages	.42
11	Absence of insertion errors, text passages	.37

Figure 7.2. Best LISREL V solution describing the factor structure of a set of 11 reading tasks. The unique variance for Measure 2 was set at zero. (Reprinted with permission from the _Journal of Educational Psychology_, 1988, 80, 234–243.)

cated by a modest but specific relationship between postkindergarten reading Speed and time to complete a standard test of reading comprehension administered 5 or 6 years later (Mills & Jackson, 1990).

In a subsequent study of 116 postkindergarten precocious readers and 123 reading-level-matched second graders that involved a more comprehensive task battery, we did not identify exactly the same structure of abilities (Jackson et al., 1990). However, the results were consistent with our previous research and with Olson's in that there was more independence among sets of word-reading and text-reading skills within the sample of precocious readers than there was for second graders.

The data from this most recent of our studies are consistent with our earlier conclusion that there are substantial individual differences in the extent to which precocious readers rely on grapheme-phoneme correspondences to identify words. Word identification based on processing orthographic information ("sight" recognition), and word identification based on phonological decoding, were only moderately correlated, but both kinds of word identification skills were related to aspects of text reading (Jackson et al., 1990).

Summary. On the average, precocious readers seem to read much as older average readers do, but more fluently. However, group averages conceal a remarkable degree of diversity in precocious readers' individual subskill patterns or reading styles. Considerable variation in individual strengths and weaknesses is compatible with precocity in beginning to read.

PREDICTIVE SIGNIFICANCE OF PRECOCIOUS READING ACHIEVEMENT

The developmental sequelae of precocity in beginning reading have been difficult to identify conclusively. However, one can make some sense of the research findings by noting that they vary systematically with the exact nature of the predictive question asked and the design used.

Retrospective Case Histories

Biographies of eminent men (and, occasionally, women) frequently mention that the subject was a precocious reader (Albert, 1971; Cox, 1926). Children identified as intellectually gifted in their elementary school years often are reported to have been precocious readers (Cassidy & Vukelich, 1980; Price, 1976; Terman & Oden, 1947). However, many intellectually gifted schoolchildren and eminent adults were not precocious or even average beginning readers (Terman & Oden, 1947; Schulman, 1986). Moreover, retrospective reports tell us nothing about the *prospective* odds that children iden-tified as precocious readers will achieve excellence in later school years or eminence in adulthood (Jackson, 1988a).

Prospective Correlational Studies

Two related questions have been addressed in prospective, longi-tudinal correlational studies of the predictive significance of reading precocity: (a) To what extent do precocious readers remain excep-tionally good at reading? and (b) Is precocious readers' later reading achievement different from what would have been expected if they had not started early? The first question is a simpler one for which longitudinal correlational research can provide solid answers; the second is more problematic.

Several investigators have found that, on the average, precocious readers continue to be good readers in their later elementary school years (Durkin, 1977; Mills & Jackson, 1990; Tobin & Pikulski, 1988). The 49 precocious readers in Durkin's (1966) California study earned a median grade-equivalent score of 5.3 in May of their third-grade year. As they continued through school, 15 of these children performed well enough to be double promoted, and the remaining 34 had a median grade-equivalent score of 9.0 in May of their sixth-grade year. In Durkin's (1966) New York sample of 156 precocious readers, the median reading grade-equivalent score in May of their third-grade year (fourth grade for the 25 who had been double-promoted) was 6.1. More recently, 17 precocious readers studied by Tobin and Pikulski (1988) earned a mean Basic Reading Inventory instructional level score of 6.5 when they were tested at the beginning of fourth grade.

Grade-equivalent scores may be the only index available to inter-pret the performance of excellent readers whose abilities can only be expressed fully when they are given tests designed for older children. However, these scores can be misleading, and do not indicate how unusual a child's performance is relative to his or her agemates. Contemporary methods of test design sometimes allow statistical estimation of children's performance relative to age-appropriate norms even when they have been administered a test not directly standardized for their age group. Mills and Jackson (1990) used such estimated normal-curve-equivalent (NCE) scores to describe the out-of-level California Achievement Test (CAT) performance of 42 precocious readers who were retested at the end of their fifth-grade year and 17 precocious readers (from a different cohort) tested at the end of their sixth-grade year. Both groups had median Reading Comprehension NCE scores about 1.5 standard deviations above their respective age/grade norms, which corresponds to a late tenth grade equivalent score for the fifth graders and a "beyond high school" (12.9 plus) score for the sixth graders. These precocious readers' CAT scores are typical of postprimary reading achievement test scores in that the grade-equivalent scores seem much more remarkable than the NCE deviation scores. The NCE scores provide a more realistic and useful index of performance.

The median NCE scores of Mills and Jackson's (1990) sample on the CAT (reading) Vocabulary and Spelling subtests were similar in level to their Reading Comprehension scores. Language Mechanics scores (capitalization and punctuation) were lower, especially for the younger group, but still more than one standard deviation above average. As a whole, then, these precocious readers continued to read well, but their performance was no longer as exceptional as it had been at the end of kindergarten (Jackson et al., 1988).

The variation in precocious readers' later achievement also deserves note. In all four of the longitudinal studies summarized above, individual followup reading achievement scores ranged from about average to exceptionally high levels. Within Mills and Jackson's (1990) sample, individual differences in later reading comprehension accuracy were predicted as well or better by postkindergarten verbal intelligence as by postkindergarten reading achievement. This is not surprising, given that reading comprehension is increasingly dependent on linguistic and general knowledge as decoding basics are mastered and the material children are asked to comprehend becomes more complex.

In summary, precocity in beginning reading almost guarantees that a normal child will continue to be an above-average reader, and it most likely indicates that a child's achievement in reading will continue to be substantially above average throughout the elementary school years. However, exceptionally precocious readers do not always remain *exceptionally* good readers (Mills & Jackson, 1990).

The second question addressed by some prospective correlational studies of precocious readers is hypothetical: To what extent do precocious readers continue to achieve *better than they would have done if they had not begun to read early?* Investigators such as Durkin (1966) and Tobin and Pikulski (1988) have addressed this question by matching precocious readers with nonprecocious comparison groups on attributes such as verbal intelligence and family background, and comparing the groups' progress. Matching represents an attempt to control for the fact that precocious readers typically are above average in general or verbal intelligence and comes from homes that would be expected to produce above-average students. The purpose of matching, then, is to test (explicit or implicit) causal hypotheses about the extent to which precocious reading *in itself* contributes to later school achievement.

On its face, the evidence from matched-group studies suggests that a precocious start in reading does give a child lasting benefits. In at least two studies (Durkin, 1966; New York sample: Tobin & Pikulski, 1989), precocious readers continued to surpass comparison groups on measures of reading achievement collected in later elementary school years. In Tobin and Pikulski's study (1988, computations from Tables 1 and 3), precocious readers surpassed a comparison group on Gates-MacGinitie Reading Vocabulary and Reading Comprehension scores and on five measures derived from an informal battery of reading tasks (range of effect sizes in standard deviation units, $ES = 0.62$ to 1.25). The biggest effect sizes were for Gates-MacGinitie Reading Vocabulary ($ES = 1.25$) and oral reading rate ($ES = 1.23$).

These results have several possible interpretations. Pikulski and Tobin (1989) have proposed that a head start in reading has enduring and cumulative effects because precocious readers have the opportunity for more (and more advanced) reading both in and out of class, and they use this opportunity to enhance their reading and language skills. If this is the case, then efforts to give more children a head start in reading are called for. Unfortunately, matched comparison group studies such as Durkin's (1966) and Tobin and Pikulski's (1988) never make intrinsically unequal groups equal on "everything else" besides the factor of interest (Coltheart, 1979; Jackson & Butterfield, 1989), and they cannot provide sufficient evidence that a precocious start in reading in itself confers enduring benefits. For example, parents who provide the kinds of experiences that facilitate a precocious start in reading may continue to be especially effective in supporting their child's school progress. Alternatively, some aspect of the child's temperament, interests, or motivational pattern may contribute both to reading precocity and to sustained achievement. True experiments, which can make "everything else" equal, provide better evidence regarding the long-term effects of reading precocity.

Experiments in Early Reading Instruction

Encouraged by the results of her correlational research, Durkin (1970, 1974–1975) began a 6 year study in which children who had been randomly assigned, at the age of four years, to two pre-first-grade years of reading instruction were compared with a minimally instructed control group. As noted above, the experimental group did learn to identify words and letter sounds, and their initial achievement surpassed that of the controls. However, by the time the children reached the end of third grade, the reading achievement of those who had received early instruction was no longer significantly above that of the controls (Durkin, 1974–1975). Other studies, similar in their lack of long-term effects, are summarized by Coltheart (1979).

Like other null results, failures of early, advanced instruction in reading to produce long-term gains should be interpreted cautiously. Classes may not have been taught using the kinds of methods most appropriate for very young readers, or the match between the children's initially high skill levels and the classes in which they spent their subsequent years may have been so poor as to dampen their progress. Perhaps early instruction in reading would have enduring effects if preschool and kindergarten teachers could individualize reading instruction as parents do, or if "follow through" programs were coordinated with early instruction. However, the existing experimental evidence stands in striking contrast to the results of correlational studies. "Naturally occurring" precocious readers may have some strengths or background resources that give them a lasting boost (Pikulsi & Tobin, 1989; Tobin & Pikulski, 1988), but these characteristics have yet to be identified and created "artificially" by teaching reading early.

Summary

All the available evidence converges on the conclusion that precocious readers continue to do well. However, a precocious start in reading is neither necessary nor sufficient for exceptionally strong achievement in later years. Furthermore, beginning reading instruction unusually early does not itself appear to confer lasting benefits.

None of the research summarized above is relevant to evaluating the effectiveness of early reading instruction as a component of broadly based compensatory preschool or kindergarten programs for disadvantaged children. Such programs are not designed to teach the exceptionally advanced reading skills that are the focus of this chapter, but some of the precocious readers we have studied have attended them. Long-term benefits of even a modest head start in reading may be greatest for children who are at the greatest risk for school failure (Durkin, 1982).

CONCLUSIONS

In introducing this chapter, I claimed that the study of precocious reading can contribute to a better understanding of both reading acquisition and intellectual giftedness. I also proposed that research evidence about the sources, structure, and predictive significance could have practical implications. In concluding, I review the ways in which our current knowledge addresses these theoretical and practical issues.

Implications for Understanding Individual Differences in Reading Acquisition

Research to date has not yet yielded a clear picture of the experiences or child characteristics that provide the basis for precocious reading achievement, but longitudinal research may soon begin to disentangle the causes and consequences of children's precociously emerging literacy.

To a considerable degree, the results of studies of precocious readers have supported and extended the results of studies of individual differences in beginning reading achievement focused on differences between children of low and average ability. Here again, we see the moderate, limited relationship between verbal intelligence and success in beginning reading (cf. Curtis, 1980).

On the average, precocious readers seem to have the range of component skills one would expect of very good readers. The exceptional fluency of precocious readers' text reading, both early in their development and later on (Jackson & Biemiller, 1985; Jackson & Donaldson, 1989; Mills & Jackson, 1990; Tobin & Pikulski, 1988) mirrors a lack of fluency sometimes noted in studies of disabled readers (Breznitz, 1987) and suggests that further research on the effects of instruction designed to maximize children's text-reading speeds is warranted.

The diversity evident in precocious readers' skill patterns reminds us that there may be multiple ways in which an individual child can succeed in learning to read, and that a relative weakness in a particular component skill need not always set limits on a child's reading progress (Jackson et al., 1988, 1990; Mills & Jackson, 1990). Precocious readers' skill patterns or reading styles seem to vary in ways similar to the variation that has been observed among disabled readers (Olson et al., 1985). If precocious readers, and all other good readers, were more consistent in their skill patterns than disabled readers are, we might conclude that a certain pattern of skills was necessary for learning to read English. However, the diversity that has now been detected at *both* extremes of the ability continuum implies that the relative consistency of average readers' skill patterns is not a cause of their (moderate) success. Perhaps this consistency is an artifact of homogenizing effects of standard classroom instruction.

Implications for Understanding the Development of Giftedness

The study of precocious reading reminds us that one useful approach to the conceptualization of giftedness in young children is to define such giftedness as the precocious completion of major developmental tasks (Jackson & Butterfield, 1986). When one thinks of giftedness in this way, the nature of long-term continuity in giftedness becomes a manageable, if yet unanswered, question. Learning to read is an important challenge for young children to master, but those who have met this challenge precociously do not all remain exceptionally good readers. Reading exceptionally well does not present the same kind of challenge to children in the later elementary school years as beginning to read does during the preschool and kindergarten years. Where, then, should we seek continuity in this kind of giftedness? One possibility is that continuity in basic aptitudes will express itself in developmentally appropriate, but superficially very different, forms as children mature. Perhaps some precocious readers are especially facile at learning new code systems, and later will express this facility in learning mathematics, computer programming, or foreign languages. In other cases, precocious reading may reflect a more general ability and interest in using language, which may be expressed in later years as a gift for writing or speaking.

Researchers seeking continuity in the development of intelligence from infancy onward have found a surprising degree of stability by considering individual differences in basic processes, such as efficiency in processing novel information, that are expressed in superficially different forms at different ages (Fagan, 1985). Perhaps those of us who study the development of specific forms of giftedness such as reading and mathematical precocity and musical and artistic talent also need to focus on both the changing requirements for excellence as gifts (and children) develop and on the underlying abilities that have contributed to the emergence of giftedness at a particular time. Aldous Huxley (1924) tells the fictional story of a young child whose precocious talent in music was gradually supplanted by a passion for mathematics. How much we would know about the development of giftedness if we could predict and explain such transitions!

Practical Implications

We now know enough about precocious reading to reassure parents and teachers that an early start in reading does not pose any threat to the child's later academic success, and that precocious readers are a competent group who read in fairly conventional ways. These children do know what they are doing, and their competence should not be devalued because it was acquired outside of school. At the same time, the diversity evident in early readers' skill patterns suggests that individual diagnostic testing might identify particular strengths and weaknesses that merit further attention, even though these children do seem to be capable of working around weaknesses on their own.

Research on relationships between precocious reading, current intelligence, and future achievement suggests that school personnel developing identification criteria for gifted education programs need to think carefully about what they expect of precocious readers. Precocious readers have the kind of unusual skills that merit differentiated programming, which is especially hard to find during the kindergarten year when precocious readers are likely to need it most. On the other hand, precocious readers will not always be the best candidates for permanent inclusion in a program designed for children with exceptionally high verbal intelligence.

Parents of precocious readers often are concerned, and justifiably so, about how their children will fit into public school (Jackson et al., 1977). Acknowledging that precocious reading is an important and reasonably common gift is the first step in developing ways to identify and serve these children.

In this era of high parental expectations for their young children (Zigler & Lang, 1985), the literature on precocious reading provides both good and bad news for parents eager to produce literate 3-year-olds. So far, despite the exaggerated claims of some zealots (Doman, 1983), no reliable formula for raising a precocious reader is evident in the literature. The good news for ambitious parents of late bloomers is that many children who do not start reading early catch up with and surpass the reading achievement of many precocious beginners (Mills & Jackson, 1990). Precocious reading is a delightful and fascinating accomplishment, but the still-preliterate 5-year-old is not doomed to academic failure.

REFERENCES

Albert, R. S. (1971). Cognitive development and parental loss among the gifted, the exceptionally gifted, and the creative. *Psychological Reports, 29,* 19–26.

Backman, J. (1983). Psycholinguistic skills and reading acquisition: A look at early readers. *Reading Research Quarterly, 18,* 466–479.

Baghban, M. (1984). *Our daughter learns to read and write.* Newark, DE: International Reading Association.

Ball, S., & Bogatz, C. (1973). *Reading with television: An evaluation of The Electric Company.* Princeton, NJ: Educational Testing Service.

Baron, J. (1979). Orthographic and word-specific mechanisms in children's reading of words. *Child Development, 50,* 60–72.

Benbow, C. P. (1988). Sex differences in mathematical reasoning ability in intellectually talented preadolescents: Their nature, effects, and possible causes. *Behavioral and Brain Sciences, 11,* 169–232.

Bissex, G. L. (1980). *GNYS at work: A child learns to write and read.* Cambridge, MA: Harvard University Press.

Blachman, B. A. (1984). Relationship of rapid naming ability and language analysis skills to kindergarten and first grade reading achievement. *Journal of Educational Psychology, 76,* 610–622.

Bogatz, G. A., & Ball, S. (1972). *The second year of Sesame Street: A continuing evaluation.* Princeton, NJ: Educational Testing Service.

Borkowski, J. G., & Peck, V. A. (1986). Causes and consequences of metamemory in gifted children. In R. J. Sternberg & J. E. Davidson (Eds.), *Conceptions of giftedness* (pp. 182–200). New York: Cambridge University Press.

Breznitz, Z. (1987). Increasing first graders' reading accuracy and comprehension by accelerating their reading rates. *Journal of Educational Psychology, 79,* 236–242.

Briggs, C., & Elkind, D. (1973). Cognitive development in early readers. *Developmental Psychology, 9,* 279–280.

Bus, A. G., & van IJzendoorn, M. H. (1988). Mother-child interactions, attachment, and emergent literacy: A cross-sectional study. *Child Development, 59,* 1262–1272.

Cassidy, J., & Vukelich, C. (1980). Do the gifted read early? *The Reading Teacher,* 578–582.

Clark, M. M. (1976). *Young fluent readers.* London: Heinemann Educational Books.

Coltheart, M. (1979). When can children learn to read—and when should they be taught? *Reading research: Advances in theory and practice* (Vol. 1, pp. 1–30). New York: Academic Press.

Cox, C. M. (1926). *Genetic studies of genius* (Vol. 2). *The early mental traits of three hundred geniuses.* Palo Alto, CA: Stanford University Press.

Crain-Thoreson, C. & Dale, P. S. (1992). Do early talkers become early readers? Linguistic precocity, preschool language, and emergent literacy. *Developmental Psychology, 28,* 421–429.

Curtis, M. E. (1980). Development of components of reading skill. *Journal of Educational Psychology, 72,* 656–669.

Doman, G. (1983). *How to teach your baby to read.* Garden City, NY: Doubleday.

Durkin, D. (1966). *Children who read early.* New York: Teachers College Press.

Durkin, D. (1970). A language-arts program for pre-first grade children: Two-year achievement report. *Reading Research Quarterly, 5,* 534–565.

Durkin, D. (1974–75). A six-year study of children who learned to read in school at the age of four. *Reading Research Quarterly, 10,* 9–61.

Durkin, D. (1982, April). *A study of poor black children who are successful readers.* Reading Education Report No. 33, Center for the Study of Reading, University of Illinois at Urbana-Champaign.

Evans, J. R., & Smith, L. J. (1976). Psycholinguistic skills of early readers. *The Reading Teacher, 30,* 39–43.

Fagan, J. F., III. (1985). A new look at infant intelligence. In D. K. Detterman (Ed.), *Current topics in human intelligence. Vol. 1. Research methodology.* Norwood, NJ: Ablex Publishing Corp.

Feitelson, D., Tehori, B. Z., & Levinberg-Green, D. (1982). How effective is early instruction in reading? Experimental evidence. *Merrill-Palmer Quarterly, 28,* 485–494.

Fowler, W. (1971). A developmental learning-strategy for early reading in a laboratory nursery-school. *Interchange, 2,* 106–125.

Healy, J. M. (1982). The enigma of hyperlexia. *Reading Research Quarterly, 17,* 319–338.

Hirsh-Pasek, K., & Cone, J. (1989, April). *Hurrying children: How does it affect their academic, creative, and emotional development?* Paper presented in the symposium, Learning environments in early childhood: Challenge or pressure?, K. Hirsh-Pasek, Chair. at the biennial meeting of the Society for Research in Child Development, Kansas City, MO.

Huxley, A. (1924). *Young Archimedes and other stories* (pp. 250–312). New York: G. H. Doran.

Jackson, N. E. (1988a). Precocious reading ability: What does it mean? *Gifted Child Quarterly, 32,* 200–204.

Jackson, N. E. (1988b). Case study of Bruce: A child with advanced intellectual abilities. In J. M. Sattler (Ed.), *Assessment of children* (3rd ed., pp. 676–678). San Diego: Jerome Sattler, Publisher.

Jackson, N. E., & Biemiller, A. J. (1985). Letter, word, and text reading times of precocious and average readers. *Child Development, 56,* 196–206.

Jackson, N. E., & Butterfield, E. C. (1986). A conception of giftedness designed to promote research. In R. J. Sternberg & J. E. Davidson (Eds.), *Conceptions of giftedness* (pp. 151–181). New York: Cambridge University Press.

Jackson, N. E., & Butterfield, E. C. (1989). Reading-level-match designs: Myths and realities. *Journal of Reading Behavior, 21,* 387–412.

Jackson, N. E., & Donaldson, G. (1989a). *Effects of frequency, decodability, and versatility on word identification by precocious and second-grade readers.* Paper presented at the biennial meeting of the Society for Research in Child Development, Kansas City, MO.

Jackson, N. E., & Donaldson, G. (1989b). Precocious and second-grade readers' use of context in word identification. *Learning and Individual Differences, 1,* 255–281.

Jackson, N. E., Donaldson, G., & Cleland, L. N. (1988). The structure of precocious reading ability. *Journal of Educational Psychology, 80,* 234–243.

Jackson, N. E., Donaldson, G., & Mills, J. R. (1990, April). *Skill patterns of precocious and level-matched second grade readers.* Paper presented at the annual convention of the American Educational Research Association, Boston, MA.

Jackson, N. E., Krinsky, S. G., & Robinson, H. B. (1977). *Problems of intellectually gifted children in the public schools: Clinical confirmation of parents' perceptions.* Seattle, WA: University of Washington. (ERIC Document ED 143 453).

Jackson, N. E., & Myers, M. G. (1982). Letter naming time, digit span, and precocious reading achievement, *Intelligence, 6,* 311–329.

Kintsch, W., & van Dijk, T. A. (1978). Toward a model of text comprehension and production. *Psychological Review, 85,* 363–394.

Malicky, G., & Norman, C. (1985). Reading processes of 'natural' readers. *Reading-Canada-Lecture, 3,* 8–20.

Mason, J. M. (1980). When do children begin to read? An exploration of four-year-olds' letter and word reading competencies. *Reading Research Quarterly, 15,* 203–277.

Mayer, R. E. (1987). *Educational psychology: A cognitive approach.* Boston: Little, Brown.

Mills, J. R., & Jackson, N. E. (1990). Predictive significance of early giftedness: The case of precocious reading. *Journal of Educational Psychology, 82,* 410–419.

Olson, R. K., Kleigl, R., Davidson, B. J., & Foltz, G. (1985). Individual and developmental differences in reading disability. In G. E. MacKinnon & T. G. Waller (Eds.), *Reading research: Advances in theory and practice* (Vol. 4, pp. 1–64). New York: Academic Press.

Perfetti, C. A. (1985). *Reading ability.* New York: Oxford University Press.

Pikulski, J. J., & Tobin, A. W. (1989). Factors associated with long-term reading achievement of early readers. In S. McCormick & J. Zutell (Eds.), *Cognitive and social perspectives for literacy research and instruction. Thirty-eighth yearbook of the National Reading Conference* (pp. 123–124). Chicago: National Reading Conference.

Plessas, G., & Oakes, C. R. (1964). Prereading experiences of selected early readers. *The Reading Teacher, 17,* 44–48.

Polk, D., & Goldstein, D. (1980). Early reading and concrete operations. *Journal of Psychology, 106,* 11–116.

Price, E. H. (1976). How thirty-seven gifted children learned to read. *The Reading Teacher, 30,* 44–48.

Roedell, W. C., Jackson, N. E., & Robinson, H. B. (1980). *Gifted young children*. New York: Teachers College Press.

Salzer, R. T. (1984). Early reading and giftedness—Some observations and questions. *Gifted Child Quarterly, 28*, 95–96.

Scarr, S., & Weinberg, R. A. (1983). The Minnesota adoption studies. Genetic differences and malleability. *Child Development, 54*, 260–267.

Schulman, S. (1986). Facing the invisible handicap. *Psychology Today, 20*, (2), 58–64.

Shaffer, D. R. (1989). *Developmental psychology: Childhood and adolescence* (2nd ed.). Pacific Grove, CA: Brooks/Cole.

Snow, C. E. (1983). Literacy and language. Relationships during the preschool years. *Harvard Educational Review, 53*, 165–189.

Stanovich, K. E. (1986). Matthew effects in reading: Some consequences of individual differences in the acquisition of literacy. *Reading Research Quarterly, 21*, 360–406.

Stanovich, K. E., Nathan, R. G., & Zolman, J. E. (1988). The developmental lag hypothesis in reading: Longitudinal and matched reading-level comparisons. *Child Development, 59*, 71–86.

Tannenbaum, A. J. (1983). *Gifted children: Psychological and educational perspectives*. New York: Macmillan.

Terman, L. M., & Oden, M. H. (1947). *The gifted child grows up. Genetic studies of genius* (Vol. 4). Palo Alto, CA: Stanford University Press.

Thomas, B. (1984). Early toy preferences of four-year-old readers and non-readers. *Child Development, 55*, 424–430.

Tobin, A. W., & Pikulski, J. J. (1988). A longitudinal study of the reading achievement of early and non-early readers through sixth grade. In J. Readance & R. S. Baldwin (Eds.), *Dialogues in literacy research. Thirty-seventh yearbook of the National Reading Conference*. Chicago: National Reading Conference.

Torrey, J. W. (1969). Learning to read without a teacher: A case study. *Elementary English, 46*, 550–556.

Torrey, J. W. (1979). Reading that comes naturally: The early reader. In T. G. Waller & G. E. MacKinnon (Eds.), *Reading research: Advances in theory and practice* (Vol. 1, pp. 117–144). New York: Academic Press.

Wechsler, D. (1974). *Manual for the Wechsler Intelligence Scale for Children—Revised*. New York: Psychological Corporation.

Zigler, E., & Lang, M. E. (1985). The emergence of "superbaby:" A good thing? *Pediatric Nursing, 11*, 337–341.

chapter 8

The Learning Game*

Lannie Kanevsky

Simon Fraser University
Vancouver, British Columbia, Canada

THE LEARNING GAME

Children's early experiences play a fundamental and powerful role in the development of the abilities they enjoy later in life. The early years are a period of rapid growth and continual change and excitement. The dynamic nature of the relationship between learning and the development of intellectual competence is apparent in the daily increases in the knowledge and skills a child has for interacting with their environment. As time passes, children know more. They know more about how to learn more and about how to think about what they know. They use what they know more efficiently and more flexibly. Somehow, bright children do this better and gain an accumulating advantage in knowledge and skill in knowing when, how

---

* This research could not have been completed without the support and cooperation of the administration and participating teachers of the Hollingworth Preschool (at Teachers College, Columbia University), Hunter College Elementary School, New York City, and the Coquitlam School District, British Columbia, Canada.

and why to apply it. They become playful masters of the learning game. This is particularly apparent when they are working in their area of special talent or interest.

Until recently, all children younger than 6 years of age were characterized as unsophisticated and inefficient problem solvers (e.g., Piaget, 1976). Empirical evidence is now accumulating to support naturalistic observations that indicate that this is not an accurate representation of their capabilities (Blank, Rose, & Berlin, 1977; Crisafi & Brown, 1986; Klahr, 1981; Klahr & Robinson, 1981) and that quantitative and qualitative differences in the learning and problem solving of young average and high-IQ children also exist (Kanevsky, 1990). Developmentally appropriate methodologies for assessing learning and problem solving are providing new insights on individual differences in these dynamic behaviors. These techniques permit young children to demonstrate the nature of their competence, rather than the extent of their deficiencies in comparison to older children (Brown, in press; Gelman, 1979; Kanevsky, 1990; Kanevsky & Rapagna, 1990).

Do bright children learn differently from their peers of average ability? This chapter will explore the literature that addresses this question and is improving our understanding of individual differences in learning ability and the role these individual differences may play in the development of intellectual competence. Initially, the theoretical and empirical foundations of current research will be discussed. This will be followed by an empirically based description of differences found in the cognitive and affective behaviors of average and high IQ children (ages 4 to 8) as they generalized a newly acquired problem-solving strategy. The chapter will close with a brief discussion of the educational implications of the research and a synthesis of the past and current findings with recommendations for future research.

LEARNING, INTELLIGENCE, AND COGNITIVE DEVELOPMENT

The interactive relationship between learning and intelligence has fascinated researchers for years. In 1921, the *Journal of Educational Psychology* presented a written symposium on the measurement of intelligence. The learning process appeared prominently in the contributions and recommendations of seven of the 14 contributors. Since that time, studies investigating the relationship between individual differences in learning potential and individual differences in intelligence have approached it from scattered perspectives. Each has reflected the most popular theories and techniques of their time.

Early in the century research focused on the assessment of over-learned facts or the mastery of extremely simple tasks in practice or training paradigms, such as those of Woodrow (1917, 1938a, b). Two consistent features of the methodology employed in these studies were that the learner worked independently and learning was considered equivalent to the increase in the number of products or the speed of their production. Comparative studies found no ability-related differences in acquisition and transfer of a variety of skills including backward writing, adding horizontally, and estimating lengths, among others.

The blossoming psychometric tradition operationalized the definition of intelligence as the score derived from a standardized assessment of the accumulated products of learning at any moment in a child's life. These tests relied heavily on snapshot-like, static impressions of what a child knew about a restricted range of content and utilized scoring criteria which were often laden with the values of the majority culture. Although, like the earlier research, they also ignored the role that learning and other cognitive processes might play in the development of the knowledge base that was being evaluated, they did succeed in differentiating individuals of the same age along a continuum of "ability." That continuum, however, was based on how much knowledge they had been able to accumulate up to that moment in time.

Efforts to uncover the nature of the rich, dynamic relationship between processes like problem solving, learning, and intelligent thinking eluded these attempts to understand and distinguish their contributions to development. This may be due to the distinct contrast that exists between the standardized procedures and environments employed in these studies and the natural, social, problem-solving-based learning activities and settings in which young children extend what they know into new contexts and discover new knowledge. As a result, few useful insights on the learning process were gained.

Recently, learning, problem solving and intelligence have been treated as qualities of the same construct (Gagné, 1977; Resnick & Glaser, 1976), and their dynamism has been reflected in the development of more appropriate assessment procedures in efforts to understand them. Examinations of the growth of accessible, flexible, dynamic understandings of concepts, relationships, principles, and so on, hold a much greater potential for improving our under-

standing of the nature of the learning and its role in the development of the exceptionally bright, the average, and the "developmentally delayed" child. Thus, it is not only the process of knowledge
acquisition, but the flexible use or generalization of knowledge
gained from active engagement with people and things that have
become central issues in current theories and research addressing
individual differences in intelligence (Brown & Campione, 1981;
Feuerstein, 1979; Kanevsky, 1990; Spitz, 1982). This adaptive,
goal-directed conception of intelligence (Sternberg, 1985) underlies
the discussion presented here.

TRANSFER, GENERALIZATION,
AND INTELLIGENCE

Like learning, the roles of the processes of transfer and generalization (which are critical features of the learning process) in
intelligent behavior have wandered in and out of the literature on
intelligence since early in this century (Intelligence and Its Measurement: A Symposium, 1921). McGeoch (1946) believed that transfer
played a critical role in the lifelong development of knowledge and
ultimately the actualization of potential:

> After small amounts of learning early in the life of the individual every
> instance of learning is a function of the already learned organization
> of the subject; that is all learning is influenced by transfer. . . . The
> learning of complex, abstract, meaningful materials and the solution
> of problems by means of ideas (reasoning) are to a great extent a
> function of transfer. Where the subject "sees into" the fundamental
> relations of a problem or has insight, transfer seems to be a major
> contributing condition. (p. 42)

Subsequently, Ferguson (1954) insisted that any ecologically valid theory of individual differences in ability must reflect the fact that
all learning occurs within the context of experience. In the midst of
the psychometric frenzy of the 1950s and 1960s, these concerns had
little influence on the research taking place in the name of developmental and differential psychology. Researchers were more concerned with quantifying the size of individual differences related to
age or ability than they were with understanding the nature of the
sources of the differences. The more dynamic dimensions of intelligence, such as the acquisition and application of knowledge, were
noticeably absent from the most popular tests of intelligence.
McNemar's (1964) critical examination of testing traditions led him

to comment, "studies of individual differences never come to grips with the processes, or operations by which a given organism achieves an intellectual response" (p. 881).

More recent investigations of ability-related differences in learning and transfer and generalization have found that intellectually superior learners will apply their skills and knowledge more broadly and flexibly than normal children (Campione, Brown, & Ferrara, 1982; Jackson & Butterfield, 1986; Kanevsky, 1990) or retarded children (Feuerstein, 1979). Research efforts to support this position can be traced to two types of studies which are characteristic of comparative investigations of the learning process in the 1970s and 1980s: strategy training studies and prompted learning studies. The contributions of these research paradigms as well as the contributions of Feuerstein's (1979) work with mediated learning, although not comparative, will be described briefly.

In strategy training studies, the learner is taught, via direct instruction, a predetermined learning or problem-solving strategy. Then a series of similar, but increasingly different tasks are provided in order to assess a learner's ability to apply the strategy in new contexts. Although these studies have demonstrated that bright, school-age children are able to transfer a trained strategy (Anderson, 1965; Klausmeier & Check, 1962; Scruggs, Mastropieri, Monson, & Jorgensen, 1985) and may be able to transfer a trained strategy when their average ability agemates cannot (Scruggs, Mastropieri, Monson, & Jorgensen, 1986), the methodology does not allow examination of the process of strategy acquisition or the strategies each learner might have developed for accomplishing the task if left to his or her own devices (Scruggs, 1986). It is likely that qualitative differences in the manner in which strategies are spontaneously developed and applied by the children will contribute more to our understanding of ability-related differences in *how* children use their learning, rather than *how often* they use what they learn.

Prompted learning studies interpret a subject's dependence on the assistance of a tutor as they acquire and transfer a learning or problem-solving strategy as an index of individual differences in intelligence (Brown, in press; Brown & Campione, 1981; Brown & Ferrara, 1985; Campione & Brown, 1984; Campione, Brown, Ferrara, & Bryant, 1984). This line of research has been founded on a methodology for the dynamic assessment of learning potential proposed by Vygotsky (1978). Students have varied in the nature of the assistance provided and its relationship to the strategy being developed. In some cases, the prompts were parts of an expert's strategy, while in others they were general cues about how to conceptualize the problem. The majority of these studies have considered samples of average and below-average school-age children, however, a few (Brown, in press; Crisafi & Brown, 1986) have focused on preschoolers. Consistent IQ-related differences were found in subjects' potential to generalize what they have learned.

The dynamic assessment of the nature of the learning potential of retarded individuals has also been the central issue in Feuerstein's (1979) endeavors to describe and remediate the sources of the deficient cognitive functions of low functioning individuals. He has stated that a lack of, or impairment in, one or more of three phases of mental activity (input, elaborational, and output), or in the affective-motivational factors, is responsible for less efficient learning. He has reported that it is possible to assess deficiencies if one approaches them in context, dynamically. Once identified, the impaired cognitive functions are "accessible and modifiable through specified strategies of training and enrichment" (p. 70). Thus the goal of assessment is the development of mediated learning experiences that train children to compensate for the deficits in cognitive functions. Some of the cognitive weaknesses Feuerstein describes within each phase and in the affective dimensions bear a strong resemblance to areas of strength identified as characteristics of the performance of high-IQ groups in the purely empirical work. The inverse of the weaknesses in low functioning individuals that could be expected to be strengths of the high functioning individuals include:

1. Inadequacy in the perception of the existence and definition of an actual problem
2. Inability to select relevant versus nonrelevant cues in defining a problem
3. Lack of spontaneous comparative behavior or limitation of its application. (Feuerstein, 1979, p. 59)

Sternberg (1985) has identified these same features as areas of strength in highly effective intellectual functioning.

The results of Feuerstein's work, the strategy training and prompted learning studies all depend on their own versions of a dynamic assessment methodology. All allow the learner to interact with the examiner. All require tasks that are novel for the learner and are able to be learned with the support of the tutor. The prompted learning studies and Feuerstein's work shift the focus of the evaluation of learning from the product to the process (strategy training studies were still product-oriented). The difference in the work based on Vygotsky's and Feuerstein's approaches can be found in two areas: the interpretation and the use of the results. While the research based on Vygotsky's beliefs interprets the degree of assistance required by the learner to master a task as an indication of his or her learning potential, Feuerstein (1979) recommends that the "peaks in the pattern of results should be used as an indication of the cognitive potential of the examinee" (p. 56). Feuerstein uses these results as the basis for the development of an extensive training program while a Vygotskian strategy has been used primarily in empirical settings to explore the specific nature and sources of the differences which naturally occur in individuals having different ages and IQs.

Vygotskian Dynamic Assessment Methodology

Because it provides a theoretical and methodological framework for the research to be presented later in this chapter, a brief introduction to the basic tenets of Vygotsky's beliefs regarding the mechanisms which contribute to intellectual development and appropriate means of assessing them will be provided.

Vygotsky felt that cognitive development occurred through the progressive internalization of knowledge gained through social interaction. All higher mental processes originate as social processes through a transition from other-regulation of behavior to self-regulation:

> Children first experience problem solving activities in the presence of others and slowly come to perform these functions for themselves. The process of internalization is gradual; first the adult and child come to share the problem solving functions, with the child taking the initiative and the adult correcting and guiding when the child falters. Finally the adult cedes control to the child and functions primarily as a supportive and sympathetic audience. (Campione et al., 1982, p. 438)

Vygotsky (1978) expressed the view "that the only 'good learning' is that which is in advance of development" (p. 89). Therefore the series of tasks selected for use in the interactive learning sessions must be beyond the child's current level of independent problem-solving skill. In this context, the researcher has an opportunity to observe the process of strategy development and generalization.

This approach is a clear contrast to the majority of past investigations that had explored ability-related differences in cognitive development. Because, in the past, the dependent variables were measures of a subject's independent performance on a single presentation of a problem, their findings reflected IQ-related differences in the levels of development *already achieved* by the children. Although this information can provide baseline information for studies of learning ability it does little to explain the mechanisms that underly that performance. Thus, a distinction between this "static" approach and the interactive, "dynamic" approach to assessing learning potential has arisen in the literature.

Both styles of learning assessment offer important information and play important roles in education and psychology; however, "it is the dynamic approach that provides a more accurate sense of an individual's potential to learn and their ability to use knowledge gained previously to learn from later challenges. Unlike static approaches, it also allows observations of a learner's attitudes and feelings about facing intellectual challenges and learning from them. The affect observable in static assessment sessions is more likely to reflect levels of text anxiety than attitudes toward the content of the items. For these reasons, the dynamic assessment methodology has been selected for use in this attempt to understand the nature of the differences in the learning processes that contribute to the development of intellectual functioning.

Vygotsky insists that opportunities for enriching and extending a child's cognitive sophistication must provide challenges beyond the child's "actual level of development," in the *zone of proximal development* (ZPD). He defines the ZPD as "the distance between the actual developmental level as determined by independent problem solving and the level of potential development as determined through problem solving under adult guidance or in collaboration with more capable peers" (p. 86). Figure 8.1 provides a graphic representation of the individual differences one would expect to find in the breadth of the ZPDs of children of different levels of intellectual ability. It is considered oversimplified because the constructs of task complexity and the nature of how learning occurs in the ZPD are both much more complex than the two-dimensional, linear representation can indicate. Still, it is important to recognize the relationship between ability and the breadth of the ZPD. As one increases so does the other. Thus, the ZPD for a high-ability child is broader than that of an average ability or developmentally delayed child.

In order to assess or "diagnose" the ZPD, a series of analogous problem-solving tasks is selected, all of which are expected to be beyond the child's independent problem-solving capability. The child is asked to solve the first task, but is told that assistance will

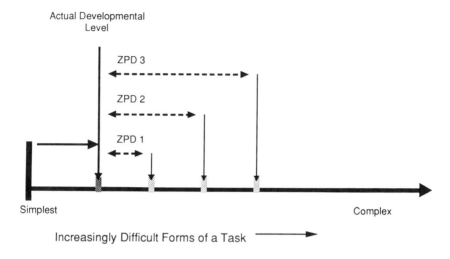

ZPD 1 = zone of proximal development for a developmentally delayed child.
ZPD 2 = zone of proximal development for a child with average ability
ZPD 3 = zone of proximal development for a child with high ability

Figure 8.1. Individual differences in the breadth of the ZPD for three children who are currently at the same actual developmental level.
Adapted from Csikszentmihalyi (1982). Reprinted by permission.

be provided by the experimenter, or tutor, if needed. The tutor offers as many hints in as many trials as necessary for the child to achieve the solution independently. Once the child masters the solution strategy, additional versions of the task are offered which are different and often more difficult. If the child is able to generalize what was learned on the first task to subsequent versions, this will reduce the need for hints on the later versions. Thus, the degree of change in the amount of assistance required to master subsequent tasks is believed to be inversely related to the ZPD for that type of task. The greater the need for help, the narrower the child's ZPD. Conversely, the smaller the need for aid on the harder tasks, the broader the child's ZPD.

AFFECT: A NEGLECTED FEATURE
OF LEARNING ABILITY

The developmental literature has treated overall development as if cognitive, perceptual, psychomotor, social, and emotional development progress on parallel, independent tracks. In reality, the dimensions of a child's life experiences are all developing *inter*dependently. The pace and pattern of their development may vary for many reasons; these individual variations will have implications for the potential development of the whole child.

The interaction of perceptual and psychomotor development with the development of cognitive skill has been given much more attention than the interaction of social and emotional development with the development of other domains of ability. Children have often been empirically characterized as lone, passive recipients of information—learning machines, without emotions—as they grow. The weaknesses in this conceptualization of the young learner can be seen in many efforts to build artificially intelligent computers that are able to emulate human learning. They have been frustrated by their inability to manifest the humanness that arises out of the interaction of the four aspects of behavior with learning and cognitive development.

Vygotsky believed the development of higher mental processes takes place within a social and cultural context, similar to an apprenticeship. In this way, knowledge and skill, as well as other behaviors (values, attitudes, and feelings) are modelled by the tutor and internalized by the learner. It is not uncommon to see young children mimic and adopt the mannerisms and speech patterns of older siblings and adults in their homes. In this way, they "try on" the intellectual life of another, gradually internalizing it.

While the Vygotskian approach to development integrates the social and cognitive aspects, Csikszentmihalyi's (1982) conceptualization of learning offers an affective dimension. His "flow" construct is founded on the belief that learning and growth can be intrinsically motivating when tasks are of an appropriate level of difficulty for a child's current level of skill (see Figure 8.2). Thus, an individual gains a sense of pleasure, or "flow," as well as new knowledge when a challenging task or understanding is mastered.

Csikszentmihalyi feels the most important implications of the "flow" chart are for understanding the dynamics of growth. In order to maintain the flow experience, the level of challenge in a task must increase as the child's level of skill increases, but not too much or too little. If the balance can be maintained, the intrinsic pleasure of learning in the flow channel will continue. If the challenge becomes too great for a child's current skill level, the child may feel anxious and worried about his or her ability to succeed and find himself or herself too high on the task difficulty axis, outside of the flow channel. If the reverse is true, the child's skill level has developed beyond the demands of the task, the child will drop below the flow channel

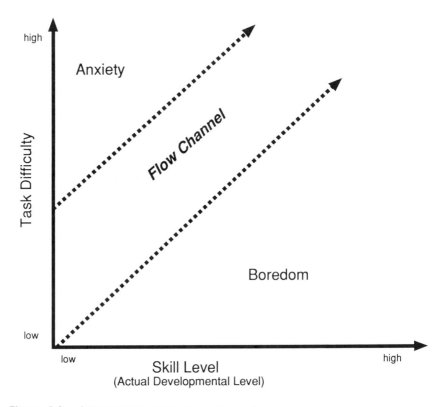

Figure 8.2. Csikszentmihalyi's flow channel.
Adapted from Csikszentmihalyi (1982). Reprinted by permission.

and will feel bored. In either of the latter two cases, the benefits of the experience diminish.

A shared feature of Vygotsky's and Csikszentmihalyi's dynamic representations of growth is the dimension of task difficulty. As a result the breadth of a child's ZPD may have implications for the breadth of the "flow channel." Children with wider ZPDs may also have broader flow channels. As a result, the increments in task difficulty may be greater for brighter children, and concomitantly, a relatively greater increase in skill development will result. Figure 8.3 indicates the relative differences in the sizes of the "steps" that could be taken by an average versus a high-IQ child.

Personality trait, perceptual, and psychomotor skill development are also likely to influence the breadth of the range of task difficulty a child at a given skill level will enjoy. Interest, self-confidence, short-term memory capacity, and eye–hand coordination could each, or all, be factors depending upon the nature of the task. Therefore the

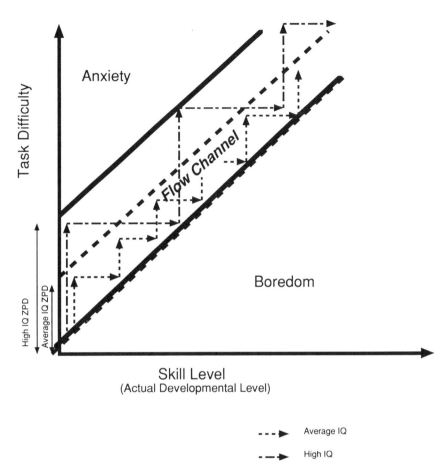

Figure 8.3. A comparison of the learning increments, or "steps" an average IQ child and a high IQ child in their respective flow channels.
Adapted from Csikszentmihalyi (1982). Reprinted by permission.

width and depth of a child's flow channel could be expected to vary greatly across tasks depending upon the role each of these, and possibly other factors play in a child's ability to master the task.

Few parents and educators who have witnessed a young child's pursuit of a curiosity, a solution, or a challenge can deny that there is obvious intrinsic motivation, particularly when the child achieves a new sense of understanding of one of an infinite number of the world's mysteries. There is just *so* much to know, *so* much to be learned! It is often the intensity of the pursuit of this pleasure that is one of the clearest and earliest manifestations of individual differences in intellect. To distinguish the cognitive, affective, and other dimensions of a young child's learning experiences in order to investigate them would be equivalent to serving a dinner guest a meat patty, a bun, a pickle, and catsup as separate courses of a meal and then asking him or her if the hamburger was enjoyable. The integrity of the experience is lost.

THE RESEARCH

In the following section a comparative examination of age and IQ-related differences in the results of dynamic analyses of young children's learning will be presented. Within the context of a Vygotskian dynamic assessment methodology, the interactive contributions of cognition and affect will be examined as children acquire and generalize a problem-solving strategy. As they operate in their zones of proximal development and flow channels, the behaviors that appear to distinguish the groups of average and high-IQ children will be described. Portions of this research have been published elsewhere and provide more extensive descriptions of the tasks, procedure, and quantitative analyses (Kanevsky, 1990; Kanevsky & Rapagna, 1990). Previous interpretations have focused heavily on the cognitive aspects of performance and only touched lightly on the more integrated orientation offered here. These reports have depended on quantitative analyses of the qualitative aspects of children's performances. Here, however, the intent is to complement that work with an examination of some of the less quantifiable behaviors that appeared to differentiate the high from the average IQ children. These observations will be discussed within the context of related literature from differential, developmental, and educational psychology.

The overall purpose of the study was to gain new insights into the nature of differences in the quantitative and qualitative aspects of the performance of young average and high IQ children as they applied a newly acquired problem-solving strategy to an analogous task. Participants in the study were 20 average IQ (YA), 22 high-IQ (YH) 4- and 5-year-olds, and 22 average IQ (OA) and 25 high-IQ (OH) 7- and 8-year-olds. Table 8.1 provides the mean IQs, chronological ages (CA), and mental ages (MA) for the groups. The IQ range for children in the average IQ groups was 90–110 on the Slosson Intelligence Test, and in the high-IQ groups it was 135–160+ on the Stanford-Binet (Form L-M). The mean mental age (MA) of the high IQ 4- and 5-year-old, and the average IQ 7- and 8-year-old groups (94.7 and 97.8 months, respectively) had been matched to permit later comparisons. This 2×2 design (chronological age $\times$ IQ)

Table 8.1.   Group means for IQ, CA and MA*

IQ groups

		Average	High
		YA	**YH**
	4 & 5	IQ = 105.2 (6.0)	IQ = 153.5 (8.4)
	year-olds	CA = 58.3 (5.1)	CA = 59.3 (4.0)
Chronological		MA = 60.8 (6.1)	MA = 94.7 (6.2)
Age		N = 20	N= 22
Groups		**OA**	**OH**
		IQ = 103.2 (5.6)	IQ = 155.4 (7.1
	7 & 8	CA = 94.5 (6.3)	CA = 94.8 (3.7)
	year-olds	MA = 97.8 (9.2)	MA=153.3(10.8)
		N = 22	N = 25

* expressed in months

Source: Kanevsky, L. S. (1990). Pursuing qualitative differences in the flexible use of a problem-solving strategy by young children. *Journal for the Education of the Gifted, 13*(2), 115–140. Reprinted with permission.

permitted three types of group comparisons: age-related differences, IQ-related differences, and MA-related differences.

Children were given two tasks to learn. Both were versions of a task employed frequently in problem-solving and intelligence research, the Tower of Hanoi. In its traditional form (see Figure 8.4),

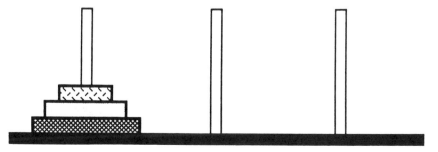

Figure 8.4.   The traditional Tower of Hanoi Puzzle.

the "problem" is to move the three disks that form the tower from the far-left post to the far-right by moving only one disk at a time, without placing a larger disk on top of a smaller disk. The minimum number of moves needed to transfer the tower is seven. The Tower of Hanoi was selected for use in this study because it was believed to be beyond the "actual developmental level" and within the ZPD of all of the subjects.

The first version of the Tower of Hanoi that a child was presented was the Monkey Cans (MC; see Figure 8.5). In this version, three

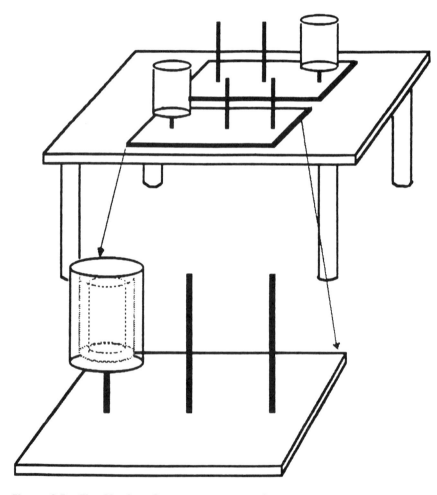

Figure 8.5.   The Monkey Cans game apparatus.

Source: Kanevsky, L. S. (1990). Pursuing qualitative differences in the flexible use of a problem-solving strategy by young children. *Journal for the Education of the Gifted, 13*(2), 115–140. Reprinted with permission.

nested cans were positioned on one of three posts. The cans represented three members of a monkey family, and the posts represented three trees. Children were asked to make their monkey family (which was positioned on the far-left post) look like the tutor's, which were on the far right. The story and apparatus were developed by Klahr and Robinson (1981) for use with young children.

The second version, the Layer Cake game (LC; see Figure 8.6) was a computer simulation of the traditional Tower of Hanoi. It had been developed specifically for use in this research. The layers of the 'cake' were made up of rows of the letters that the children needed to know in order to control their movement (As, Bs, and Cs). The object of the game was to move the cake from one post to another without breaking the rules.

Children were provided as many trials, with as much assistance, as necessary, to master the optimal, seven-move solution strategy for each of two tasks on the MC and then the LC game. The first task required that the child learn to move the tower of monkeys or cake layers, depending upon the task, from the far left to far right. The

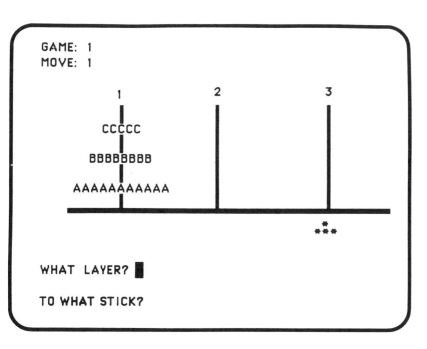

Figure 8.6.   The Layer Cake game screen display.

Source: Kanevsky, L. S. (1990). Pursuing, qualitative differences in the flexible use of a problem-solving strategy by young children. *Journal for the Education of the Gifted, 13*(2), 115–140. Reprinted with permission.

second task required a reversal of that solution, moving the monkey family or cake from right to left. Mastery was defined as two consecutive, independent, seven-move solutions. Once both MC tasks were mastered, the child was offered the Layer Cake game, under the same conditions.

Quantitative data were collected throughout each trial of each task. Variables included the number of legal moves used, the number of times a game rule was violated, the number of hints used, and the number of trials required to achieve mastery on each task. The extent to which a child was able to use what had been learned from the MC tasks on the LC tasks was interpreted as his or her ZPD, or the ability to generalize learning. Children with a broader ZPD were expected to need less assistance, use fewer moves and less time, and break fewer rules on the LC task than children with a narrower ZPD. Their greater independence would be due to more efficient use of the knowledge gained from mastering the MC task.

Data was also collected on qualitative variables as they appeared in children's performances on the generalization tasks (the LC game). These were reported as the number and percentage of children in each group that behaved in particular ways after being offered a hint or breaking a rule, or commented on aspects of the task that they noticed were common to one or more of the tasks. A child's use of the hints available from the tutor was noted as acceptance or rejection of an offer, or as having been requested by the child. Rule violations were followed by a query to give the child an opportunity to explain which game rule had been violated. If she or he was unable to explain, an explanation was offered by the tutor. These were also tallied. If, during the LC tasks, a child commented on the similarity or similarities of the tasks, the content of the comment was classified as being related to the game rules, apparatus or solution strategy.

A FIRST LOOK AT THE RESULTS: THE QUANTITATIVE PERSPECTIVE

The analysis of the data collected on the quantitative variables described above provided quantitative evidence of the statistically significant and separate influences of age and IQ on a child's ZPD or learning potential. The older and higher IQ groups demonstrated superior generalization of their learning from MC to LC as measured by each of the quantitative variables. These findings provide additional support for the relationships found to exist between age and learning potential, and IQ and learning potential, in samples of children and adults having low, average, and slightly above average

IQs. The results derived from the qualitative variables complemented these relatively superficial findings. They indicated that children of different ages differ, not only in the speed and accuracy of their generalization, but in how they behave as they generalize. The high-IQ children were more likely to deny an offer of assistance, regardless of age. This might have been interpreted as a preference for working alone, except that more of the high-IQ 4- and 5-year-olds requested help than any of the other groups. Although these two findings initially appear to be in direct conflict, they may suggest that the YH children were more able to evaluate their own need for assistance. They asked for it when they felt they needed it and denied it when they felt they could, eventually, decide on a good move. In contrast, the average IQ 4- and 5-year-olds seldom denied help and generally accepted the tutor's offer to help as an indication that they needed it. Therefore, the availability of a supportive tutor is as important for the YH children as the YA but for different reasons. Working alone on a challenging task does not appear to be the preferred learning environment for either the average or high-IQ 4- and 5-year-olds.

The analysis of children's understanding of their rule violations reflected the same overall age differences in the number of rules broken as had been found in the quantitative analysis. Older children broke fewer rules than younger children. Differences in the children's ability to explain the violations were found, but only between the performances of the average and high-IQ 4- and 5-year-olds. So, although the YH children broke more rules than their mental age-mates (the OA children), more were able to explain their violation when asked.

Group differences in children's recognition of the similarities in the MC and LC tasks suggested some interesting patterns related to the inequivalence of the mental age-matched YH and OA children. Consistently, a greater number of the high-IQ 4- and 5-year-olds commented on the similarities in the game rules and apparatus than the OA children. The same numbers of each group (YH and OA) recognized the similarity of the MC and LC solution strategy. From the small number of YH children who made these types of comments, the numbers grew substantially in the OH group. Thus, the OA and OH children differed to an even greater extent than the YH and OA indicating that the interest in spontaneously comparing the tasks appears to increase with age in the high IQ children.

The findings based on these quantitative and qualitative variables support and extend trends identified in the findings of previous research involving and comparing groups of individuals with lower IQs, most of whom were older than those in this study. Still, after collecting and analyzing the data it was apparent that efforts to quantify the qualitative differences in the children's performances had cheated the differences of their importance. They deserve a more descriptive, less quantitative approach.

A SECOND LOOK: THE FUN OF LEARNING

The purpose here is to complement the more quantitative descriptions of the children's behaviors and attitudes reported in previous analyses (Kanevsky, 1990; Kanevsky & Rapagna, 1990) with the results of a more qualitative analysis. Any analysis of this type is always vulnerable to criticisms of subjectivity due to the variety of alternative interpretations of each behavior. As a result, efforts have been made to link the findings of this investigation with previous research that has addressed similar issues but with older subjects or subjects of different levels of ability than those considered here. The inferences drawn from the observations are offered as tentative interpretations that will be tested and scrutinized in future studies.

Four types of behavior that distinguished the performances of children in different age and ability groups on the Layer Cake game (the generalization task) will be described: gamesmanship, efficiency, the search for complexity, and breaking rules.

Gamesmanship

One of the most fascinating differences in the performances of the high- and average IQ groups, regardless of age, was in the sense of "gamesmanship" the high-ability children added to the activity. These children seemed to consider the game rules and goals, as described by the tutor, to provide a baseline level of challenge. Once these were clearly understood, in the first or second trial, the high-IQ children introduced additional targets for their performance that enhanced their enjoyment of the game. This appears to have been an intentional effort to maintain the "flow" in the experience. In this way, their engagement in the task retained an intrinsically motivating level of task difficulty, or fun.

In general, the average IQ children did not demonstrate this type of intellectual playfulness. They were willing to complete the prescribed task and enjoyed the computer but did not appear to introduce any appreciation for the process of achieving mastery beyond that of simply having mastered it in a manner that satisfied the experimenter. Essentially, they appeared more extrinsically motivated by the researcher's interest in their success.

The groups also seemed to differ dramatically in the nature of their understanding of "The Game." Although introductions to the tasks followed standardized scripts, the children seemed to focus on different aspects of the game to differing degrees depending on their age and ability. The YA children took their pleasure from manipulating the layers of the cake on the computer screen, i.e., controlling their movements, rather than from mastering a solution strategy. Due to the number of children in this group who never mastered LC (there was a failure rate of 55% for the children in this group), and the difficulties experienced by many of the successful children, it is doubtful whether the knowledge they had acquired on the first task, Monkey Cans, was at all strategic in nature, or simply a sequence or pattern of moves. Remembering the pattern of moves that pleased the researcher was of secondary importance to the fun they were having by controlling the objects on the computer screen. This would explain the task-specificity and inflexibility of their solution and the relative difficulty they experienced when asked to reverse their solution strategy to solve the second LC task.

These differences between the YA and YH groups appear to be similar in nature to the age differences Harter (1975) found when she investigated the mastery motivation of 4-year-olds and 10-year-olds. Without considering IQ, she found these two age groups differed in their reasons for continuing to attempt to complete solvable and unsolvable color discrimination tasks, although they did not differ in the amount of time they were willing to play. The latter was contrary to her expectations. Harter suggested that the 4-year-olds persisted enthusiastically because they enjoyed producing and watching "interesting sensory events which they could control through their own actions" (p. 376). In contrast, the 10-year-olds continued due to "the desire to solve cognitively challenging problems for the gratification inherent in discovering the solution" (p. 376). Thus, in terms of mastery motivation, the 4-year-olds in Harter's study and the YA children in this study were similar, and Harter's 10-year-olds were similar to both high-IQ groups in this study.

Children in both of the high-IQ groups also appeared to elaborate the basic task structure in a number of ways. A few gave the layers of the cake flavors appropriate to their keyboard designations (Apple for 'A'; Banana for 'B'; Chocolate for 'C'), or they made the cake analogy for the tower more explicitly by calling it a wedding cake. Comments like these indicate that the children went beyond the basic task representation to actively seek connections with their prior knowledge. Other high-IQ children sought means to challenge themselves in ways that were both within and beyond the scope of the task as it had been described to them. They would make announcements like "I'm going to do it faster this time" or "Now I'll do it without any mistakes." This may indicate that they searched their prior experience, not only for knowledge related to their understanding of the task, but also for intrinsically motivating aspects of prior problem solving or game experiences, such as speed and accuracy.

The last two types of comments created an interesting dilemma for the experimenter, one frequently experienced by teachers. Statements encouraging the children to reduce their time, or the number of illegal moves they attempted, were to be introduced by the researcher later in the procedure. Teachers consistently report their amusement (or irritation) with the bright child who poses the teacher's next question, or presents a synthesis of the week's work on Monday, long before the rest of the class is ready. Although this is often interpreted as evidence of precocity (simply mastering the same material more quickly), these observations of differences between the high- and average IQ children suggest that the high-IQ children approach challenges with an additional set of goals. These goals included making connections with prior knowledge and intrinsically rewarding characteristics of problem solving. If this were simply a matter of precocity, one would have expected to hear more comments about the similarities of the tasks from the OA children who had been matched to the YH for mental age. This was not the case.

Many children in the YH group expressed sentiments similar to that of one 4-year-old girl. She repeatedly stated, "This is hard . . . really hard . . . mmm. I won't give up!" and persisted, apparently to experience the pleasure associated with conquering a "really hard" task, a task in the upper reaches of the flow channel. If just felt good. Again, this type of comment, and its associated level of task commitment, were not apparent in the behavior of the OA children. In fact the high-IQ children in both age groups were the only children making such comments. Thus it appears that this gamesmanship may reflect a difference in task orientation that cannot be accounted for in terms of the same skills and behaviors as are found in children of the same mental age, but older chronologically.

The sense of the game developed by both groups of high-IQ children appeared to have provided them with an orientation to the task that was more facilitative for achieving speedy mastery and their brand of fun. They constructed a more elaborate, integrated, accurate task representation more quickly, which left them more mental work space to select moves, evaluate them, and plan an optimal sequence of moves. Some of this additional mental workspace may also have been created to allow them to pursue the additional features of their learning that they also found personally rewarding (efficiency, complexity, and feedback). These will be discussed next.

Efficiency

The quantitative analysis of children's generalization indicated the high-IQ children in each age group made more accurate move selections and were more efficient in their strategy development. Beyond this superficial analysis, the group differences in move accuracy and solution efficiency reflected age- and ability-related differences in the aspects of problem-solving children found intrinsically motivating that interacted with their fundamental understanding of "The Game." This affected the decisions children made in order to achieve their version of success and fun. Without being prompted, the high-IQ children decided to pursue a quick (in terms of time), independent solution in the least number of moves. For the OH children, this was apparent immediately, in the first trial on each task. It was all part of "The Game," as they had defined it. For the YH children, it appeared in comments in the third and fourth trials, once they were comfortable with the task procedures, goals, and constraints. This reduction in task demands from the first and second trials provided them with additional resources to devote to efficiency.

The average ability children did not spontaneously add these features of success to their performance. They did not appear to value the accuracy, independence, and speed aspects of their performance until the researcher drew attention to their importance. In fact, the OA children were less accurate, and less concerned about it, than any other group (Kanevsky & Rapagna, 1990). They made more moves in the early trials of the LC game than any other group. The brief pauses between their moves suggested that they were being less reflective, planful, or evaluative than their high-IQ peers. Their definition of success was to complete the puzzle, somehow, without appearing to need help. Apparently, the OA child would rather continue making moves, which may or may not be accurate, than ask for help that would provide them with the best next move. Although they appear independent, it is at the cost of efficiency.

The YH children demonstrated their interest in move accuracy in a compromise between the approaches of the average and OH children. Their concern for accuracy, like the OH children's, but less efficient information-processing skills, forced them to ask for, or accept, more hints rather than taking the risk of breaking a game rule. They appeared to have developed a hierarchy of move acceptability. A self-selected move was most preferable, followed by a hint from the researcher, and finally an attempted move that could not be executed (an illegal move). In this sense, the YH children were more economical (using fewer moves) as well as efficient (using fewer trials) in their strategy development when compared to the OA children. Each move appears to have been more thoroughly evaluated by the young high-IQ children than by their average ability peers of the same chronological or mental age.

These findings suggest a pattern similar to that found by Klausmeier and Loughlin (1961) in their comparison of the problem-solving behaviors of high- (IQs = 120–146), average (IQs = 90–110) and low- (IQs = 55–80) IQ 10- and 11-year-olds. The high-IQ children's performance demonstrated a number of behaviors that the researchers felt contributed to their superior problem-solving efficiency: they offered fewer incorrect solutions, verified more of their solutions independently, and were more likely to use a logical approach to solving the problems. Thus Klausmeier and Loughlin's high-IQ children, and those in this research, appear to be more reflective and methodical.

Although they mastered the solution strategy in fewer trials than the 4- and 5-year-olds, the interest OA children in this study showed for keeping the layers of the cake moving reflects remnants of the pleasure the YA children found in controlling the movements of the layers and Harter's (1975) findings (discussed earlier). Perhaps, where controlling or manipulating the objects was the most rewarding aspect of the activity for the YA children, control and efficiency were of equal importance for the OA children. In contrast, for the YH and OH groups, efficiency was of primary importance, and moving the layers was of secondary importance for the YH children and of minimal interest to the OH. As a result, moving the cake efficiently became a larger part of the game the high-IQ children were playing than the average.

The high-IQ children's interest in efficiency, as expressed in their words and actions, may be manifestations of the differences in metacognition that have been found to contribute to individual differences in memory, learning, and problem-solving abilities. *Metacognition* is "the active monitoring and consequent regulation of processes in relation to the cognitive objects or data on which they bear, usually in the service of some concrete goal or object" (Flavell, 1976, p. 232). As a result, while the OA child was asking herself, "What is *any* move I can make?" the high IQ child would be asking herself, "What is the *best next* move I can make?" This does not mean that all children did not have both questions in their repertoire of metacognitive skills. The high-ability children simply appeared to choose to address the latter question rather than the former, and this was reflected in the smaller number of self-initiated moves executed by the high-IQ groups than the average to achieve each solution.

Beginning with Flavell's (1970) description of the metacognitive aspects of cognitive performances, the importance of using what one "knows" is becoming an increasingly prominent feature of efforts to explain individual differences in intelligence and problem solving. He felt the efficacy of execution of a strategy in an individual's repertoire ranges from "flawless execution" to "no attempt to execute it at all." Robinson and Kingsley (1977) provided evidence that the factors underlying differences in the performances of Grade 3 and 4 children on a recall task were more dependent on the efficiency of strategy use rather than simply having the strategy. Brown and Deloache (1978) also felt that metacognitive failure was an appropriate explanation for differences in the problem solving performances of an even younger group of children. This accumulating body of evidence indicates, "It's not only what you know, but how you use it (if at all) that matters" (Schoenfeld, 1987, p. 192).

Studies such as that of Moss (1985, this volume) suggest that IQ-related differences in the metacognitive behavior of preschoolers may be partially due to differences in the nature of mothers' interactions with their children while problem solving. Mothers of high-IQ preschoolers model, and their children respond with more metacognitive content than mother–child dyads involving average IQ preschoolers and their mothers. Borkowski and Peck (1986) suggest that parents of youngsters with high IQs observe the exceptional perceptual efficiency of their children and as a result parents

likely respond with greater intellectual stimulation, including game playing and early encouragement to take on challenging tasks and puzzles. Attention to these stimulating activities requires the child to become more deliberate, effortful and strategic.

Emerging from this enriched environmental context—originally prompted by signs of perceptual efficiency—the gifted preschool child gains the metacognitive advantages that we observed at ages 7 and 8, and that probably are present as early as 3 or 4. (p. 198)

Thus, the differences in the efficiency of children's efforts to master the solution strategy suggest a difference in the decisions children make at various points along the road to mastery. In fact the observed differences may be the combined result of underlying differences in the way the children understand the task and in the ways they monitor their learning, which may result from their interactions with family members and other more knowledgeable individuals.

Complexity

As described earlier, the high-IQ children introduced additional criteria for success to the LC game (accuracy, independence, and speed) before they were identified as valuable by the tutor. They also sought opportunities to increase the complexity of the LC task that would make it more difficult (if not impossible) by adding layers and pegs, and varying the start and goal positions of the layers. These were not idle suggestions. They wanted to try them—immediately! Many of their ideas have been considered in a more extensive task sequence that is currently being developed. While solving the assigned problem, the children were simultaneously devising variations of the task as entertainment. This may have been an attempt to prevent boredom as their skill level increased. This maintained the "flow." In order to maintain the fun of learning, action needed to be taken. What could be done to make this activity more challenging? Do it faster. Do it better. Make it harder. Scruggs (1986) also observed this pursuit of complexity in his examination of the learning strategies employed by average and high ability seventh- and eighth-grade students. He reported: "The results were remarkable. These gifted students had transformed what appeared to be a rote learning task into a problem solving activity, in which the problem was: 'How can I learn these nonsense words most effectively?' " (p. 294).

Another behavior that suggested the high-IQ children had a fascination with more abstract levels or internal representations of the task was the number of children in the high-IQ groups who spontaneously expressed some form of recognition of the similarities of the MC and LC tasks (Kanevsky, 1990). In addition to attempting to remember the rules, successful move sequences, and so on, these children were comparing features of the current task with prior learning to assist them in their efforts. As a result, in the midst of the LC task a number of children realized, "Oh! You just do it like the Monkeys!" It was interesting to find that 6 YH and 17 OH children commented on some form of similarity in the tasks, while none of the YA and only 4 of the OA did. Theorists have identified this "spontaneous comparative behavior" (Feuerstein, 1979) or "selective comparison" (Sternberg, 1985) as characteristic of more intelligent problem-solving behavior. This provides further evidence of a qualitative difference between the high- and average IQ children's orientation to the tasks.

The need for intellectual challenge is much less of a problem before one enters the public school system. Opportunities abound in the backyard, the kitchen, the car, a closet—anywhere! Once children enter a structured learning environment, opportunities are often restricted or eliminated due to the social conventions or classroom management strategies imposed by the educational system. The fact that Scruggs (1986) was able to find elements of this behavior in the learning performances of seventh- and eighth-grade students is encouraging. These must be extremely durable behaviors if they are able to survive years of efforts to discourage them.

Breaking the Rules

Following an attempt to execute a move that violated one of the game rules, the tutor probed the child's understanding of the computer's refusal to move the layer of the cake that had been selected by asking, "Do you know why the computer wouldn't do that?" If the child was not able to explain the rule violation, the experimenter provided an explanation. The older high-IQ, and younger average IQ, children's performances were consistent with expectation. For the OH children, who committed the fewest errors, learning from their mistakes did not play a major role in their learning, as the experimenter had fewer opportunities to explain a rule violation to these children than any other group (they seldom broke a rule). All children appeared mildly apprehensive after breaking a rule. This was likely due to the pass/fail orientation they had toward evaluating their own performance, or expected of the tutor, as if the learning tasks were test items. Either they did it correctly, all on their own, or they had failed. In contrast, all of the YA children attempted substantially more illegal moves and they all needed explanation as they struggled with the task.

IQ-related differences arose in the rates at which the children moved away from a "failure" interpretation of their errors toward the orientation modeled by the researcher, that is, figuring out which rule had been broken so that the error would not be repeated. Gradually the children recognized that the purpose of tasks was not to test their knowledge but to provide an opportunity, complete with assistance and feedback, to improve. As a result, they shifted from a fear of being wrong to asking themselves what could be learned from being wrong. This is another area where the high IQ children, in both age groups, distinguished themselves from the average IQ groups. The high-IQ children used their mistakes as learning experiences sooner.

Although the children in the groups matched for mental age, the YH and OA, committed the same number of rule violations, and as many children needed explanations in both groups, they differed in their ability to explain why the computer refused to move the layer of cake they had selected. Almost twice as many YH as OA children were able to explain at least one violation (13 YH versus 7 OA). It appears that the younger children, of the same MA, had developed an understanding of the game rules that made the rules more accessible than that of the older children. If one only considered the number of rules broken by the same two groups, or their need for explanations of the broken rules, this difference would never have been recognized. Thus, the MA advantage the YH children have over their YA peers is not a sufficient explanation for their superior understanding of the task. The understanding the YH children possess may permit them superior access for explanation; however they still commit as many errors as their mental age-mates. What this may indicate is that the YH and OA children are equally challenged by the task, but that the YH are more aware of the strengths and weaknesses in their performance, and are therefore more able to reflect on it verbally.

Two possible explanations for the advantage of the high IQ children in this aspect of their learning are that it may have been due to a greater sensitivity on the part of the high-IQ children to the researcher's expectations, or to the compatibility of this constructive attitude with a preexisting, self-questioning orientation toward mistakes. In her analysis of ability-related differences in problem-solving performance, Porath (1988) found a similar trend. On tasks that provided opportunities to integrate feedback and utilize cues, the younger gifted children performed more like their older, mental age peers of average ability.

In summary, the YH children had superior access to their understanding of the game rules they had broken and they were better able to improve their performance by learning from their mistakes when they were offered constructive feedback from the tutor. In addition, all of the high-IQ children adjusted from an evaluation-oriented mode of interaction (tester/testee) to a learning-oriented mode of interaction with the tutor.

WITHIN-GROUP VARIATIONS

Up to this point, consistencies in the children's behavior among groups have been discussed as they relate to age and IQ. Now it is necessary to highlight a few of the inconsistencies in the performances within the groups and within individuals. These factors are believed to have affected each child's willingness to bring his or her full learning potential to bear on the tasks as they were presented. The age and IQ scores used to assign children to groups account for a large enough proportion of the variability in performance to achieve statistical significance in most of the quantitative analyses; however, these analyses leave much unexplained. Klausmeier and Loughlin (1961) also raised this concern. They reported noticeable but unexplored differences in the problem-solving behaviors within their groups of low-, average, and high-ability 10- and 11-year-olds. Three variables that are believed to contribute to intragroup differences in the results of the present study consist of (a) interest, (b) fatigue, and (c) prior knowledge.

Interest

For their own reasons, all children were not equally interested in the MC and LC games, the computer, or learning. Undoubtedly this influenced the extent to which they became engaged in the activities. One YA and two YH children made clear the effect that interest could have on their performance. The YA child was a particularly enthusiastic problem solver and was also thrilled to be able to play on the computer. She earned a performance profile that was far superior to her average IQ peers and similar to an 'average' high IQ 4- or 5-year-old. This was an extreme case, but other milder cases of "overachievement" were found.

As a contrast, two of the YH children, who had computers at home, showed little interest in any aspect of the tasks. Efforts to cajole and motivate them were fruitless. They simply were not interested. Although they both earned extraordinary scores on the Stanford-Binet, their potential was not invested in this learning activity. Their performances were still slightly superior to the majority of the successful YA children and were the most inferior of the YH group. Follow-up discussions with their preschool teachers often concluded with statements like "Well, when he's on, he's amazing, and when he's not, he's just like any other 4-year-old."

This indicates that interest level also contributes to the position a child chooses for himself or herself inside or outside the flow channel, and the child's willingness to manage his or her position in and around it. If interested, a child will invest in monitoring his or her performance and will ask for help if he or she finds the task is too difficult to solve independently. Or, if the task is too easy, but still intriguing, he or she may introduce new goals in order to raise the challenge level. These actions will provide an appropriate level of task difficulty for the child's skill level so that flow, the intrinsic pleasure of learning, is maintained. If he or she is not interested, it is unlikely that the child will monitor his or her performance, and therefore he or she is less likely to recognize the need for any adjustments to be made in order to achieve or maintain a flow experience.

Fatigue

In addition to mood, Hayes, Scott, Chemelski, and Johnson (1987), and most parents, have found that 3- and 4-year-olds realize that fatigue can influence their ability to learn. As the Layer Cake tasks progressed, the intensity of the focus of the young children diminished, as did the speed and accuracy of their performance. Some let their minds wander and became chatty, telling stories unrelated to the task at hand. Others became cranky or began fiddling with the equipment and materials within reach. Essentially, for high-IQ children to appear gifted, they needed not only to be interested but alert. The extent of the decline in concentration was much steeper for the YH than YA children, as the YH were relatively more intense initially. They changed from appearing "gifted" for a 4-year-old, to looking like most 4-year-olds.

It should also be noted that the 4- and 5-year-olds showed much greater variations in their attention span and intensity of concentration than the 7- and 8-year-olds across the sessions and within sessions. The younger children often needed extensive encouragement to complete the session although they had a clear understanding of the task. Due to their superior initial skill level related to gaming, puzzles, computers, learning, letters, size, and so on, the demands of the task on the older children were reduced. As a result, they did not tire as quickly, and the fatigue factor had a minimal effect on their performance.

This suggests that, if a child engages in a task that is substantially beyond his or her actual level of development, this will require a relatively large step into his or her ZPD, to the top edge of the flow channel. While attempting to master that task, a child will tire more quickly than when attempting tasks that are at his or her actual developmental level or close to it. Again, this raises the issue of an optimal match. When the goal of an activity is optimal learning, the increases in the task difficulty may need to be reduced as the session progresses in order to prevent a loss of interest or motivation, or discouragement as the child tires.

Prior Knowledge

One cannot ignore the importance of the role children's prior knowledge played in their learning performance. It was particularly apparent in the 55% failure rate in the YA group. Although all of these children had earned IQ scores of 90–110, many of those who could not complete the LC task within the time limit (10 minutes) failed because they had difficulty locating the letters A, B, and C on the keyboard. Some also failed to understand the size relationship between the layers of the cake and the role this played in solving the puzzle. Without these basic foundations, the tasks were beyond the ZPDs of the majority of the YA children. Children "failed" due to a lack of knowledge and processes for managing their learning. Cumulatively, this resulted in their inability to learn to solve LC at that moment in time. The challenge posed by the level of task difficulty was too far beyond these YAs' current skill level, therefore flow was out of the question for them.

EDUCATIONAL IMPLICATIONS

In the midst of constantly evolving educational policies and practices that call for appropriately challenging educational opportunities for all children, educators of precocious young children have had their efforts to achieve this goal frustrated by a lack of literature that provides a sound rationale for how and why to adapt learning experiences to make them suitable for these children (Shore, Cornell, Robinson, & Ward, 1991). This is a direct result of a lack of theoretical and empirical literature that addresses the nature of ability-related differences in the learning process and its contributions to cognitive development. Without an understanding of the nature of these differences, educators will be poorly prepared to create educational experiences or to modify learning activities that have been developed for average learners so that they will be of optimal developmental benefit to bright children. The research just described is an attempt to address this need in terms that may have theoretical and practical relevance.

The phrase *appropriate education* can be interpreted in a number of ways in order to serve a number of purposes. The version most often found in educational contexts is to match the level of difficulty of the task to the child's current level of performance. Vygotsky stated: "learning which is oriented toward developmental levels that have already been reached is ineffective from the viewpoint of the child's overall development" (1978, p. 89). In light of the ZPD and the flow channel, one can see that matching task difficulty to the actual developmental level has the potential to bore any child, a bright child much sooner than the average student. If the goal of an educational activity or educational system is to promote development of higher level mental processes in addition to simply expanding the child's general knowledge base, activities should be created or selected that are slightly beyond the child's current level of performance, in their zone of proximal development. In fact, this strategy is appropriate for all learners, when a goal of the task is to promote development within a particular domain.

The findings of the research just described indicate that one difference between learning activities designed for average ability children and those for high-ability children would be the extent of the difference between what the child is able to do now, independently, and what he or she is being asked to learn to do. The average child should proceed in smaller steps, with the opportunity for more practice with more support, than the brighter child. This does not mean the intellectually brighter child should work without assistance. Learners of all ages and ability levels need to feel support, of some sort, will be provided if they feel their skills and knowledge are not sufficient. It is the extent and the nature of the support they want that will vary with an individual's maturity and learning potential.

Many proponents of special educational opportunities for bright children recommend that the individual child's interests be reflected in the development of experiences intended to engage and nurture his or her potential. Although teachers cannot neglect other domains in efforts to encourage children to optimize their learning, it is apparent that interest level can have a substantial effect on a child's performance. In addition, interest may also affect a child's willingness to monitor his or her "flow" as well. Even 3- and 4-year-olds are able to recognize the effect that mood (sad versus happy) can have on learning (Hayes et al., 1987). Thus it is not surprising that the appeal of a task can result in a level of performance more indicative of a child's level of interest than of his or her level of ability. A second implication of this finding is that the YA children, given the appropriate opportunity, can exceed the performance an

IQ score would lead us to expect. In both cases, there is a dire need for further investigation of techniques for optimally matching interest, challenge, and skill for all children.

The spontaneous and more effective monitoring of the flow experience demonstrated by the high-IQ children indicates that this is an area of intellectual strength that we would be wise to encourage. Self-regulation of the learning process may be a key to freeing teachers and parents from the guilt they experience when a bright child says, "I'm bored." It appears that the bright child may be much more able than the average IQ child to take some responsibility for reducing his or her boredom. The child can be asked to suggest which aspects of a task might be extended or altered to raise its level of difficulty so that it becomes sufficiently challenging to lift him or her back into the flow channel. In a school setting, these task modifications can be negotiated with the teacher so that the goals and objectives of an activity can be achieved as well as the flow experience and good learning. By sharing responsibility for flow and learning, the teacher can maintain his or her accountability for the curriculum while promoting the development of a set of skills that will enable a bright child to take a more active role in managing boredom.

The second advantage of this approach is that the bright child may also explore and come to understand the limitations of his or her skill level when confronted with a task that is too difficult and anxiety arises. For a child to be able to recognize the feelings associated with having been offered "too much of a good thing" can be a great life skill. Bright children are often expected (unjustly) to be equally able in all subject areas, and are often asked to perform equally amazing feats of academic brilliance without support when they are not able. This can produce a variety of worries for the child that are seldom expressed and may result in a generalized school anxiety. Instead of overall brilliance, if a child feels his or her relative strengths and weaknesses are understood, he or she is in a much better position to ask for help on a task or to decline a learning task that will pull him or her above the flow channel. Thus, encouraging self-regulation has its benefits for the bright child on both borders of the flow channel.

CONCLUSION

If one is willing to accept that Vygotsky's conceptualization of "good learning" and Csikszentmihalyi's "flow" are important goals for an appropriate education, then it becomes important that we understand the nature of individual differences in what and how children are *able to learn*, in addition to what they already know. The extent to which research has been and will be able to uncover similarities and differences in the development of intellectually average and superior children has been dependent on the nature of the tasks and procedures employed. An examination of the body of research literature on the relationships among learning, intelligence, and development produces an appreciation for the diversity of methods used to investigate the nature of individual differences in learning ability and its relationship to intellectual development. But one also leaves with many unanswered questions, particularly if one happens to be a parent or educator.

To bring a sense of order to the apparent inconsistencies in the findings of these studies, they can be grouped in terms of their learning assessment methodologies. Training or practice paradigms found no ability-related differences in the outcomes of some kinds of learning experiences. Static assessment methods found that high-IQ children achieved 'levels of cognitive development' early but did not tell us if there were differences in the processes that contributed to their achievement. Now studies using dynamic assessment methods are providing evidence of quantitative and qualitative differences in how children think and learn. As a result of the nature of the differences in the results provided by the different methodologies, educational researchers, teachers, and parents need to explore the child characteristics, task characteristics, and instructional strategies and settings that will tap or stimulate each type of behavior. The challenge continues to be to find ways to understand and to assist each young child in his or her efforts to recognize settings and tasks in which thoughts and feelings will be appropriate to optimize the benefits to be gained from playing the learning game.

In this study and previous investigations, it was found that, in some ways, young high-IQ children behave like their average agemates; in some ways they behave like their older, average IQ mental agemates; and in some ways they behave like their older high-IQ peers. It depends on the nature and goals of the activity, and on how behavior and performance are evaluated.

In this study and others, the 4- and 5-year-old high-IQ children acted like their average ability agemates when:

1. They were tired or uninterested, or
2. Their perceptual and memory capacities were evaluated (see also Borkowski & Peck, 1986; Porath, 1988).

They acted like their mental age-mates (the average ability 7- & 8-year-olds) when:

1. The outcomes of learning were compared; or
2. They were given one opportunity to solve each problem and their performance was evaluated on a pass or fail basis (see also Lempers, Block, Scott, & Draper, 1987); or
3. Their learning was assessed in terms of its quantitative dimensions, for example, number of trials needed to achieve mastery, number of errors committed, and so on (see also Kanevsky, 1990); or,
4. They are asked to adopt a "learn from your mistakes" attitude.

They acted like the older high IQ children when:

1. The qualitative aspects of the process of learning or problem solving was assessed, such as spontaneously elaborating a task to increase the level of challenge it provides, seeking complexity in a task (see also Kanevsky, 1990; Klausmeier & Loughlin, 1961); or
2. They were offered multiple trials on a task, with feedback (see also Porath, 1988).
3. They were asked to explain the rule violations they had committed.

Thus it is not surprising that studies employing traditional, static forms of developmental assessments, such as Piagetian tasks, have provided evidence in support of explanations of the development of high ability in terms of the precocious or early development of the same mental structures as those that are characteristic of relatively older children of average ability. The development of age-appropriate dynamic analyses of the learning process, as it contributes to cognitive development, are providing evidence of the qualitative age and IQ-related differences in the ways that young children learn that had eluded researchers in the past. This is further proof of the importance of creating and employing research methodologies appropriate to research questions that address developmental processes.

In the search for universal principles in the development of outstanding intellectual ability, two neglected concerns have been raised here:

1. The importance of the interaction between the affective and cognitive dimensions of growth with the maturation of other systems, and
2. Intragroup and intraindividual differences in performance.

In research and practice we cannot ignore the integrated nature of real growth, nor can we neglect the peaks and valleys in each individual's performances. It is just these features of behavior, the integration and the inconsistencies, that contribute to the wondrousness of development, and yet they confound our empirical efforts to understand the general principles of that same development.

Research has been relatively successful in locating quantifiable differences in how much has been learned or how quickly. In order to further improve our understanding in theoretically and practically relevant terms, future research addressing the nature and nurture of the qualitatively different aspects of the learning and other intellectual behaviors must continue to examine these activities as they occur rather than after they are completed. Vernon (1969) observed, "it is indeed curious that we use intelligence tests mainly to predict capacity for learning . . . yet none of our subtests involves any learning; instead they give a cross-section of what has been learnt" (p. 106). The dynamic analysis of learning offers a window on the learning game and an opportunity to consider other personality, motivation, and physical variables that may play a role in optimal development of a child's innate potential.

Like the high-IQ children, researchers and practitioners must continue to pursue an understanding of learning and development in their natural forms. With this knowledge, perhaps educators and parents will be able to encourage all young minds to pursue challenges in appropriate ways for the fun of knowing.

REFERENCES

Anderson, R. C. (1965). Can first graders learn an advanced problem-solving skill? *Journal of Educational Psychology, 56*, 283–294.

Blank, M., Rose, S. A., & Berlin, L. J. (1981). In M. Friedman, J. P. Das, & N. O'Connor (Eds.), *Intelligence and learning* (pp. 231–236). New York: Plenum.

Borkowski, J. G., & Peck, V. A. (1986). Causes and consequences of metamemory in gifted children. In R. J. Sternberg & J. E. Davidson (Eds.), *Conceptions of giftedness* (pp. 182–200). New York: Cambridge University Press.

Brown, A. L. (in press). Analogical learning and transfer: What develops? In

S. Vosniadou & A. Ortony (Eds.), *Similarity and analogy reasoning*. Hillsdale, NJ: Erlbaum.

Brown, A. L. (1982). Learning and development: The problems of compatibility, access and induction. *Human Development, 25,* 89–115.

Brown, A. L., & Campione, J. C. (1981). Inducing flexible thinking: A problem of access. In M. Friedman, J. P. Das, & N. O'Connor (Eds.), *Intelligence and learning* (pp. 515–529). New York: Plenum.

Brown, A. L., & Deloache, J. S. (1978). Skills, plans and self-regulation. In R. S. Siegler (Eds.), *Children's thinking: What develops?* (pp. 3–35). Hillsdale, NJ: Erlbaum.

Brown, A. L., & Ferrara, R. A. (1985). Diagnosing zones of proximal development. In J. V. Wertsch (Ed.), *Culture, communication and cognition: Vygotskian perspectives* (pp. 273–305). New York: Cambridge University Press.

Campione, J. C., & Brown, A. L. (1984). Learning propensity and transfer as sources of individual differences in intelligence. In P. H. Brooks, R. Sperber, & C. McCauley (Eds.), *Learning and cognition in the mentally retarded* (pp. 265–293). Hillsdale, NJ: Erlbaum.

Campione, J. C., Brown, A. L., & Ferrara, R. A. (1982). Mental retardation and intelligence. In R. J. Sternberg (Ed.), *Handbook of human intelligence* (pp. 392–585). New York: Cambridge University Press.

Campione, J. C., Brown, A. L., Ferrara, R. A., & Bryant, N. R. (1984). The zone of proximal development: Implications for individual differences in learning. In B. Rogoff & J. V. Wertsch (Eds.), *Children's learning in the zone of proximal development* (pp. 77–91). San Francisco: Jossey-Bass.

Crisafi, M. A., & Brown, A. L. (1986). Analogical transfer in very young children: Combining learned solutions to reach a goal. *Child Development, 57,* 953–968.

Csikszentmihalyi, M. (1982). Learning, "flow," and happiness. In R. Gross (Ed.), *Invitation to lifelong learning* (pp. 167–187). Chicago: Follett.

Ferguson, G. A. (1954). On learning and human ability. *Canadian Journal of Psychology, 8,* 95–112.

Feuerstein, R. (1979). *The dynamic assessment of retarded performers.* Baltimore, MD: University Park Press.

Flavell, J. H. (1970). Developmental studies of mediated memory. In H. W. Reese & L. P. Lipsitt (Eds.), *Advances in child development and behavior* (Vol. 5, pp. 181–211). New York: Academic.

Flavell, J. H. (1976). Metacognitive aspects of problem solving. In L. B. Resnick (Ed.), *The nature of intelligence* (pp. 231–235). Hillsdale, NJ: Erlbaum.

Gagné, R. M. (1977). *The conditions of learning* (3rd ed.). New York: Holt, Rinehart & Winston.

Gelman, R. (1979). Preschool thought. *American Psychologist, 34,* 900–905.

Harter, S. (1975). Developmental differences in the manifestation of mas tery motivation on problem solving tasks. *Child Development, 46,* 370–378.

Hayes, D. S., Scott, L. C., Chemelski, B. E., & Johnson, J. (1987). Physical and emotional states as memory-relevant factors: Cognitive monitoring by young children. *Merrill-Palmer Quarterly, 33,* 473–487.

Intelligence and Its Measurement: A Symposium. (1921). *Journal of Educational Psychology, 12,* 123–147, 195–217, 271–275.

Jackson, N. E., & Butterfield, E. C. (1986). A conception of giftedness designed to promote research. In R. J. Sternberg & J. E. Davidson (Eds.), *Conceptions of giftedness* (pp. 151–181). New York: Cambridge University Press.

Kanevsky, L. S. (1990). Pursuing qualitative differences in the flexible use of a problem-solving strategy by young children. *Journal for the Education of the Gifted, 13,* 115–140.

Kanevsky, L. S., & Rapagna, S. O. (1990). Dynamic analyses of problem-solving by average and high ability children. *Canadian Journal of Special Education, 6*(1), 15–30.

Klahr, D. (1981). Goal formation, planning and learning by pre-school problem solvers or: "My socks are in the dryer". In R. Siegler (Ed.), *Children's thinking: What develops?* (pp. 181–212). Hillsdale, NJ: Erlbaum.

Klahr, D., & Robinson, M. (1981). Formal assessment of problem solving and planning processes in preschool children. *Cognitive Psychology, 13,* 113–148.

Klausmeier, H. J., & Check, J. (1962). Retention and transfer in children of low, average and high intelligence. *Journal of Educational Research, 55,* 319–322.

Klausmeier, H. J., & Loughlin, L. J. (1961). Behaviors during problem solving among children of low, average, and high intelligence. *Journal of Educational Psychology, 52,* 148–152.

Lempers, L., Block, L., Scott, M., & Draper, D. (1987). The relationship between psychometric brightness and cognitive developmental precocity in gifted preschoolers. *Merrill-Palmer Quarterly, 33,* 489–503.

McGeoch, J. A. (1946). *The psychology of human learning.* New York: Longmans Green.

McNemar, Q. (1964). Lost: Our Intelligence? Why? *American Psychologist, 19,* 872–882.

Moss, E. (1985, April). *Informational content of verbal exchanges between mothers and gifted preschoolers.* Paper presented to the Society for Research in Child Development, Toronto, Ontario.

Piaget, J. (1976). *The grasp of consciousness.* Cambridge, MA: Harvard University Press.

Porath, M. (1988, April). *Cognitive development of gifted children: A neo-Piagetian perspective.* Paper presented at the Annual Meeting of the American Educational Research Association, New Orleans, LA.

Resnick, L. B., & Glaser, R. (1976). Problem solving and intelligence. In L.

B. Resnick (Ed.), *The nature of intelligence* (pp. 205–230). Hillsdale, NJ: Erlbaum.

Robinson, J. A., & Kingsley, M. E. (1977). Memory and intelligence: Age and ability differences in strategies and organization of recall. *Intelligence*, *1*, 318–330.

Schoenfeld, A. H. (1987). *Cognitive science and mathematics education*. Hillsdale, NJ: Erlbaum.

Scruggs, T. E. (1986). Learning characteristics research: A personal perspective. *Journal for the Education of the Gifted*, *9*, 291–300.

Scruggs, T. E., Mastropieri, M. A., Monson, J., & Jorgensen, C. (1985). Maximizing what gifted students can learn: Recent findings of learning strategy research. *Gifted Child Quarterly*, *29*, 181–184.

Scruggs, T. E., Mastropieri, M. A., Monson, J., & Jorgensen, C. (1986). Effective mnemonic strategies for gifted learners. *Journal for the Education of the Gifted*, *30*, 105–121.

Shore, B. M., Cornell, D. G., Robinson, A., & Ward, V. S. (1991). *Recommended practices in gifted education: A critical analysis*. New York: Teachers College Press.

Spitz, H. H. (1982). Intellectual extremes, mental age, and the nature of human intelligence. *Merrill-Palmer Quarterly*, *28*, 167–192.

Sternberg, R. J. (1985). *Beyond IQ: A triarchic theory of human intelligence*. New York: Cambridge University Press.

Vernon, P. E. (1969). *Intelligence and cultural environment*. London: Methuen.

Vygotsky, L. S. (1978). *Mind in society: The development of higher psychological processes*. Cambridge, MA: Harvard University Press.

Woodrow, H. (1917). Practice and transference in normal and feeble-minded children: Transference. *Journal of Educational Psychology*, *8*, 151–165.

Woodrow, H. (1938a). The relation between abilities and improvement with practice. *Journal of Educational Psychology*, *29*, 215–230.

Woodrow, H. (1938b). The effect of practice on groups of different initial ability. *Journal of Educational Psychology*, *29*, 268–278.

part IV

Enriching the Environments of Gifted Young Children

chapter **9**

Mediating the Cognitive, Social, and Aesthetic Development of Precocious Young Children*

Pnina S. Klein

Bar Ilan University
Ramat Gan, Israel

Giftedness denotes extraordinary brainpower, or a collection of extra abilities that seem to vary endlessly in unique and subtle combinations, all of them treasured in our society. Developmentally, it is an age-stage concept in the sense that children are "gifted" only in comparison with other children, as are adults in relation to adult standards. Psychometrically, it is a relative concept in the sense that it deviates from age norms in *degree*, rather than in *kind*. To the extent, then, that relative mental strength can be measured at all in children of various ages, it is possible to recognize signs, or at least hints, of individual excellence among them. This applies in the

---

* This chapter describes several unconventional and disparate experiments conducted under the author's direction at the Early Childhood Center, Bar-Ilan University in Israel. The samples were drawn mostly from a pool of 3- and 4-year-olds identified as developmentally accelerated on the basis of direct observation and parental assessment of the nominees.

earliest years of life as well, even though the aptitudes assessed at that age level are unlike those of older children. Individual differences between infants as early as immediately following birth have focused on perceptual skills, responsiveness, alertness, rate of activity, intensity, and other psychomotor variables. Scientists seem to compete in the race to find new, yet unknown, capacities of infants, or to demonstrate how early infants are capable of perceiving and responding differentially to various stimuli.

Research on intellective attributes of the very young gifted is still rare, and whatever evidence exists deals primarily with children over age 3. The frequently quoted studies on younger subjects are Brown's two case studies (1964, 1970). However, the most extensive research has been conducted on older children, the prime example being Terman's longitudinal studies of high-IQ, elementary school samples (Oden, 1968). Since early Baley measures of young gifted children were not predictive of later tested intelligence (Willerman & Fiedler, 1974), the use of other measures, specifically attention, memory, and language development, was recommended for the identification of very young gifted children (Willerman & Fiedler, 1974). However, no longitudinal studies designed to test the Willerman-Fiedler hypothesis have yet been reported. As early as in 1954, Hofstaetter suggested that independent variables change in predicting tested intelligence from infancy onward. He reported that sensorimotor alertness accounts for most of the variance in children's intelligence test performance up to the age of 20 months; from 20 to 40 months the dominant source of intelligence test variance is persistence; and beginning at 48 months most of the variance is accounted for by the factor he labeled "manipulation of symbols."

A striking feature of intellectually gifted children is their ability to acquire relatively large amounts of knowledge and varieties of skills far more rapidly than do most age-mates. Gifted youngsters seem to learn easily, efficiently, and willingly, and they retain what they learn for a long time. The brighter the child, the more he or she seems able to extract ideas from the environment (Freeman, 1985). In fact, the unusual cognitive and nonintellective traits of some children alert us to the possibility of their being gifted. For example, Feldman (1982) reported that gifted children have a near-photographic memory, a large vocabulary, a vivid imagination, lots of hobbies and collections, and an insatiable curiosity. One additional characteristic associated with their verbal precocity is the high frequency in which they formulate questions to satisfy their curiosity (Guilford, Scheuerle, & Shonburn, 1981; Torrance, 1962). Some signs of these traits can be found in children long before they are of an age to enter school.

In addition to the cognitive characteristics reported as typical of gifted children, some research has focused on the emotional and social characteristics of this special population. There is no doubt that emotional and motivational factors play an important role in determining giftedness (Tannenbaum, 1983; Renzulli, 1978). Good socioemotional adjustment at the preschool age was found to characterize gifted children (Lehman & Erdwins, 1981). Birns and Golden (1972) showed that the amount of pleasure infants expressed during a test predicted their later performance on abstract thinking measures better than did the actual test scores. It was concluded that the level of joy expressed by the infant is as important a forecaster of eventual giftedness as is his or her test performance. Elkind (1987) seems to regard the thrill of learning as a key to giftedness at *any* age when he asserts: "With gifted and talented individuals, as with children in general, the most important thing is an excitement about, and enthusiasm for, learning" (p. 22).

Abroms and Gollin (1980) found gifted 3-year-olds to show more than average sharing and helping behaviors, more reactions to other children's signs of distress, and more affection for others. Along the same lines, Jacobs (1971) found that gifted children showed (on the Rorschach test) a greater capacity for emotional reactions to the environment and greater sensitivity to the emotional pressures of the environment than did nongifted children.

The scarcity of published research on the nature of young gifted children is accompanied by a relatively richer literature on suggested programs, activities, checklists, and other structured "formulae" for parents and practitioners. A recent search of APA and ERIC retrieval systems for programs servicing the young gifted in the last 10 years yielded some 36 documents, most of which include general statements of the needs of, and on policy towards, gifted young children. About 25% deal with the gifted among other children with special needs, including the gifted handicapped. The remaining programs, with few exceptions, outline materials, and procedures for the enhancement of various thinking skills (e.g., Berg, 1985; Karnes & Johnson, 1987; Koopman-Dayton & Feldhusen, 1987; Leonard & Causler, 1980; Willard, Hartwell, & Marson, 1985), as well as social skills (e.g., Roedell, 1985).

CHARACTERISTICS OF 3—4-YEAR-OLD ISRAELI GIFTED CHILDREN

As a cumulative 3-year total, 26 gifted children have been identified and continue to participate in a special program at Bar-Ilan University's Early Childhood Center. At the outset of each of the past 3 academic years, the Center has advertised, in community centers located around the university, for parents who think they have gifted offspring no older than 4 years of age, to apply for participation with their children in weekly afternoon sessions designed to enhance the cognitive and emotional growth of these young boys and girls. Despite initial expectations that many parents would consider their children gifted enough to qualify for the program, only 8 applied the first year, 8 the second year, and 11 the third year. The subjects' ages ranged from 2 years, 7 months to 4 years. Even though the program announcement did not specify any particular definition of giftedness, all applicants, with only few exceptions, described their children as having the following characteristics:

1. Precocity in early *language development* (noted by all parents). Most parents of gifted children could specify the age at which their children started to speak, how many words they spoke at 1 year, and when they began to speak in sentences. The children had highly developed verbal ability, specifically a rich vocabulary and an excellent capacity to express themselves orally.
2. A superior *memory* for places, objects, stories, poems, and so on.
3. A highly *inquisitive attitude* about things and people in the environment.
4. An *appetite for learning*. All of the children were perceived by their parents as eager to learn new things; the target of their wish to learn varied considerably including, for example, technical, physical, biological, artistic, language, and chess skills.
5. All but two of the children liked to *draw*, to *play imaginary games*, and to *build with Lego*.
6. With the exception of three, all children liked to *listen to stories*, to *make up new endings*, and to *suggest rhymes*.
7. They all had *good spatial orientation* and could identify well and reach familiar places, that is, visit a friend or relative or reach a local store unaided.
8. All children could *identify numbers up to 10 and add numbers up to a sum of 9*.

9. All children could *cite the names of the days of the week* and could *recite at least one complete children's song or poem.*
10. They were very *alert* and *easily noted the smallest changes made in a familiar story* read to them.

In summary, the cognitive and motivational characteristics of young gifted children reported in the professional literature were confirmed by the Israeli sample. Individual testing of all children, with the exception of one, confirmed that the parents were accurate in their appraisal of their children's capacities, interests, and personal wishes. The children's average verbal IQ, as measured by the Peabody Picture Vocabulary Test, was 138 (as compared to 105 in the population of middle-class children in their neighborhood). Similarly, their visual reception and visual and auditory association (abstract reasoning), as well as their sequential memory, as measured by the Illinois Test of Psycholinguistic Abilities (ITPA), were all at least one standard deviation and frequently two standard deviations above the norm for their age. All children were eager to learn and expressed interest about every object displayed or new person at the Center. These findings confirmed the accuracy of parental evaluations of their gifted preschoolers for U.S. samples (Hanson, 1984). It may thus be concluded that verbal precocity, appetite for learning, and excellent memory are salient traits among young gifted (or at least high-IQ) children.

Are young children identified by their parents as gifted based on specific outstanding aptitudes other than verbal? A survey conducted by a group of our students revealed that, in 60 middle-class families with 3–4-year-old children: identified by their parents as gifted (unpublished data), not one case was found in which parents considered their child gifted in art, independent of language precocity. It stands to reason that at such an early stage, some kinds of giftedness are determined by what Tannenbaum (1983) and others see as the general ability factor, rather than by specific performance aptitudes that require an amount of time for cultivation that preschoolers are generally too young to have had. There are, of course, exceptions who are celebrated widely as prodigies, or *Wunderkinder* (wonder children) with rare gifts, but these subjects generally manifest their early talent in instrumental music (Bamberger, 1986), language, mathematics, chess (Feldman, 1982), and possibly science as well. But early precocity in art is generally not represented in the research literature, either because it is not (yet) possible to measure it in the first 6 years of life, or because the artist has to experience life for a longer period of time before reflecting that experience through art. The most obvious, and perhaps best, explanation is that fine psychomotor skills are not developed enough in young children to facilitate artistic technique at that age, although prodigious young violinists and pianists *are* capable of demonstrating extraordinary digital dexterity.

Following the testing of the Israeli sample of gifted children, parents were asked to play with their children on a puzzle task. The parent–child interaction was observed for 10 minutes and analyzed, using the observation criteria for assessing the quality of parent–child interaction (Klein, 1984, 1988). With no exception, all participating parents were found to mediate their children's perception and understanding of the environment effectively, as determined by low-inference observation methods (Klein, 1988). They all scored high on *transcendence* (i.e., explaining and expanding experiences to their children), and they frequently generated excitement in relation to their children's experiences. Parents varied in the extent to which they urged their children to undertake new tasks, but all were found to use some form of encouragement and expression of affect.

Most of the parents who observed the formal testing asked to repeat the presentation of several test items, claiming that their children "could do it" or knew the answer. When allowed, they were highly active in modifying the test items to match their child's understanding or needs, and linked the present experience with past and future ones (e.g., "You know the answer, it is like what Rony has given to Grandpa" or "We have one like it; ours is smaller and it is yellow").

Parents of gifted children are not necessarily more active or more loving than other parents. They do, however, provide their children with what may be considered a quality interaction, in the sense that they make the most of every opportunity to help them learn all they can about the world surrounding them with insight and enthusiasm.

Do young intellectually gifted children outgrow their promise? Oden (1968) summarized her 40 years' follow-up of the 1,000 school-age high-IQ subjects in Terman's study and concluded that there can be no doubt that, for the overwhelming majority of subjects, the promise of youth has been more than fulfilled, despite the fact that no geniuses of the Shakespeare, Mozart, or Picasso type were found among them.

Tannenbaum (1989) summarizes the research on this question by stating, "From the bulky evidence on the relationships between high-IQ and giftedness . . . it is easy to appreciate why intelligence testing is so popular in screening for able children and why superior general intellectual ability is one of the signs of high potential and one of the links to its fulfillment . . . . Despite the many cases of *aborted* genius, Terman's data provide some assurance that children with high potentialities and reasonably stable personalities who are given the right opportunities to hone their skills, stand a better-than-average chance to excel eventually in their careers."

What are the right opportunities? Psychologists and educators working with young children, gifted or otherwise, tend to repeat a misconception regarding the evaluation of infants, especially those who are developmentally at risk. Most commonly, these evaluations focus on the infant's test performance, with little or no direct assessment of the *quality* of his or her interaction with the environment, particularly the human environment, which no doubt affects development and adds significantly to the predictive power of such an evaluation. In order to identify giftedness in young children, it is necessary to focus on both the child's psychological state and on the dynamics of interaction with the important others in his or her life.

There is hardly any doubt today that genius does not originate solely from genetic characteristics (Feldman, 1982). Mozart's early musical ability is frequently used to demonstrate the role of genetics in the formation of genius. Yet it cannot be overlooked that Mozart was surrounded from birth by a family of talented musicians. The rate and quality of development of retarded, normal functioning, and gifted children is determined by a rare and subtle interplay of both genetic and environmental variables. The critical role of the environment and the lack of defined characteristics of the optimal environment for all children is emphasized in the theory of "goodness of fit" (Thomas & Chess, 1977; Lerner, 1982). This notion implies that optimal development occurs in the process of interaction between the child's behavioral style and the environment's response to it.

RISK FACTORS IN THE MODERN HOME ENVIRONMENT

In 1986, the U.S. Census Bureau published data suggesting that the young child growing up in the U.S. in recent years is under extreme pressure (*U.S. News & World Report*, 1986). Sixty percent of 2-year-olds of the 1980s will have lived in single-parent households sometime before reaching their 19th birthday. Very young children are thrust into *independence* and *self-reliance* before they are cognitively and emotionally ready for it. Children are constantly *pushed* ahead, *driven* to be competitive rather than cooperative, and grow up with virtually no time to stop and smell the roses or pause and wonder. At least some of the current stresses are inflicted by parents and teachers who are concerned about the children's achievement and status. Middle-class parents enroll their toddlers and young children in various programs, pushing them to keep up with the Joneses. Benjamin Spock (1986) is reported as saying that today's children are under stress because we have given up many of the comforts and sources of security of the past, such as the extended family, the small, tightly knit community, and the comfort and guidance that people used to get from religion. He states further that our emphasis on competition minimizes the importance of cooperation, helpfulness, kindness, and love. These qualities are badly needed to make our social milieu a more accepting and less stressful one.

Elkind (1987) speaks of the evils of what he calls "hurried education of the 1960s" and compares these with the "miseducation of the 1980s." The hurried education consisted primarily of starting schooling early, rushing to give the child what was falsely believed to be an earlier, and therefore better, start. Miseducation includes some types of so-called "enrichment" courses, training programs, and other extracurricular activities that fill up the days of young children from infancy. This sense of drivenness obsesses well-meaning parents who wish to insure their child's place in the competitive world and to enhance their own status as parents of these children. Elkind quotes research suggesting that parents today, busy filling up their children's time with various "enrichment" activities, spend little time in quality interaction with them. On the average, mothers are reported to devote only 11 minutes a day during the week and 30 minutes a day on weekends in quality interactions with their children. In Israel, the resemblance to these reported American childrearing practices is striking, especially in the middle classes of the two cultures. Furthermore, the gifted young child seems often to bear a double burden of "hurried education" and "miseducation." Many young children showing precocity in language and thinking skills are placed in formal education earlier so they do not waste any more time in kindergarten, and even when reading and other basic skills are acquired, the "enrichment" proceeds in the form of ill-planned, make-work, extracurricular experiences.

One growing problem in early childhood education is that gifted young children are sometimes subjected to overintensified compensatory programs, as if they were an undermotivated, high-functioning minority in need of special brands of "remedial" intervention, as do undermotivated, low-functioning minorities. As a result, "the image of the competent child introduced to remedy the understimulation of low-income children now serves as a rationale for overstimulation of middle class children" (Elkind, 1986, p. 70). Elkind warns of the dangers of miseducation and suggests a return to a more natural child centered, less stressful education of young children. However, it seems unrealistic to expect parents of young children, especially parents who think their youngsters are gifted, to stop the race toward more and more demanding education (or miseducation) simply because it is sensible to call such a halt, even if this common sense were supported by research evidence. Parents feel the beat of time and hear the sounds of competitive crowds pushing their young children onward and upward. What is needed is not merely the suggestion to stop and relax but a clear definition of what a quality interaction with young children consists of, what parents really want for their children, an identification of distant goals in education, and how to achieve them in a less pressured and less "rehearsed" manner.

Elkind (1986) describes, for example, the important learning that is going on naturally while parents and their young children prepare a vegetable soup together: "The children are learning social cooperation, the names, colors, and shapes of the vegetables, as well as the difference between peeled and unpeeled vegetables . . . crisp, limp, soggy, and that boiling softens the vegetables . . . . They are also learning about weights and measures as they follow recipe directions regarding the weights or numbers of vegetables to be put into the soup" (pp. 143–144). Indeed, children can learn all these facts and skills but this learning does not occur just because someone is preparing a soup with them. That particular someone has to be a good mediator who deftly shapes and interprets the experience to young children. He or she has to know what the children already know, what can be of interest to them, and how to focus their attention on the relevant aspects of the situation, in order for the soup making to become a rich learning event.

Children do manage to learn without adults' direct involvement in the process. But, what accounts for much of the variability in cognitive performance is the quality of human mediation they receive. Children's learning how to learn and whether it is worthwhile to do so is shaped by the adults with whom they interact (Moss, this volume).

THE MORE INTELLIGENT (INSIGHTFUL) AND SENSITIVE CHILD (MISC)

Developing a Stress-Free Quality Environment for Young Gifted Children

The MISC program for enhancing the environment of young gifted children (MISC-G) is one of a series of MISC programs implemented with infants and young children with special needs. The program was originally created in Israel, but since it is relatively independent of specific contexts or materials, it is applicable across a variety of cultures, living conditions, and populations with special needs. Its design is based on a series of research studies carried out on U.S. and Israeli populations (Klein, Weider, & Greenspan, 1987; Klein, 1988; Klein, Raziel, Brish, & Birenbaum, 1986), and it has been adopted for use also in Sri Lanka, Indonesia, Portugal, Norway, and Sweden (Klein & Hundeide, 1989). The major objective of the program is to highlight and clarify to the child's caregivers those basic criteria that are necessary and sufficient for any adult–child or child–child interaction to be considered a unit of *quality* interaction and learning for the child. Feuerstein (1979) refers to this kind of learning as a *mediated learning experience* (MLE), namely, the kind of learning that prepares the child, with the help of an adult intervener, or mediator, to benefit from future experiences of learning.

Numerous attempts have been made to identify maternal nurturant behaviors that affect infants' or young children's cognitive development (e.g., Beckwith, 1971; Belsky, Good, & Most, 1980; Clarke-Stewart, 1973; White, Kaban, & Attanucci, 1979; Yarrow, Rubenstein, & Pedersen, 1975). However, there is still a lack of clarity about some of these interactional processes that facilitate a quality learning experience for the child.

Leading theories pertaining to cognitive development do not elaborate on strategies through which an adult mediates between children and their environment. Piaget, for example, described the experiences of adult–child interactions which lead to the construction of logico-mathematical knowledge; however, he did not attempt to characterize the basic determinants of the quality of such interactions. Commonly used observations of mother–child interactions (e.g., those introduced by Caldwell, 1967; Clarke-Stewart, 1973; and Yarrow et al., 1975) focus on maternal behaviors that are predictive of various kinds of childhood performance, but they do not offer a clear understanding of which specific behaviors, occurring during parent–child interaction represent necessary and sufficient conditions for a learning experience, regardless of the subject matter on which these interactions focus.

One way of answering this basic question can be derived from the theoretical framework of Feuerstein's (1979, 1980) mediated learning experience (MLE). Mediated learning, as distinct from direct learning through the senses, occurs when the environment is interpreted for the child by another person who understands the child's needs, interests, and capacities, and who takes an active role in making components of that environment as well as of past and future experiences, compatible with the child. Mediation affects the individual's present learning and may improve his or her opportunity to learn from future experiences.

As part of Feuerstein's theory of cognitive modifiability, MLE has been in use in special education, mostly for handicapped learners, over some 30 years, and its clinical value has already been demonstrated (Brainin, 1984; Feuerstein, 1979, 1980). Originally designed for training adults to help adolescent populations overcome learning deficits, MLE has more recently been tested for application with infants, toddlers, and preschoolers (Klein & Feuerstein, 1984; Klein, 1985; Klein et al., 1987).

Feuerstein's list of MLE criteria now includes 11 variables, only 5 of which were used by the author as the basis for constructing an observational scale for the assessment of the quality of adult–infant interaction. The other criteria were either of questionable reliability, or were empirically determined to correlate highly with the selected five criteria, which may be described as follows.

Focusing (Intentionality and Reciprocity). Any act, or sequence of acts on the part of an adult, that appears to be directed toward achieving a change in the child's perception, processing, or response (e.g., selecting, exaggerating, accentuating, scheduling, grouping, sequencing, or pacing stimuli). An intentional behavior is considered reciprocal when the infant or child in the interaction responds vocally, verbally, or nonverbally, even by visual focusing, to an adult's behavior. Talking to a child or handing an object to him or her, for example, is counted as intentionality and reciprocity only when it is clear that the parent's behavior is purposeful, not accidental, and when there is an observable response from the child that he or she saw or heard the parent's action. What the observer sees in this instance is a parental effort to change the child's behavior and environment by bringing a toy to the child, moving it back and forth, observing the child, and continuing to adjust the stimulus until the child focuses on it; or moving a bottle or a particular food item in front of the infant's eyes until he or she focuses on it; or placing toys into the bath water; or placing oneself in front of the child, obtaining eye-to-eye contact; or placing objects in front of the child and eliciting the child's attention to them. Whereas Feuerstein stresses the role of the adult as initiator of the intentional interaction, it should be noted that quality interaction in relation to focusing must include instances in which the adult responds to the child's initiative and is guided by it to consequent action.

Exciting (Mediation of Meaning). An adult's behavior that expresses verbal or nonverbal appreciation or affect in relation to objects, animals, or concepts and values. These behaviors may include facial gestures (e.g., exaggerated opening of the eyes and mouth), sounds (e.g., a sigh or a scream of surprise), verbal expressions of affect, classification or labeling, and valuing the child's or adult's experiences. It is interesting to note that Rimm and Loew (1988), summarizing their study on differences between achieving and underachieving gifted children, conclude that "parents' interest in, and satisfaction with, personal careers and intrinsic learning must be specifically communicated to children in order to provide appropriate achieving role models" (p. 353).

Expanding (Transcendence). An adult's behavior directed toward the expansion of a child's cognitive awareness, beyond what is necessary to satisfy the immediate need which triggered the interaction (e.g., talking to a child about the color or taste of food during feeding is beyond what is necessary to assure provision of nutrition; exploring parts of the body or the characteristics of water during bathing is not necessary for cleansing the child in a bath). Transcendence can be expressed through inductive and deductive reasoning, spontaneous comparisons (e.g., "What does this [thing, person, event] remind you of?"), clarifying spatial and temporal orientation, pointing out strategies for short- and long-term memory, and through memory search and recall.

Rewarding (Mediated Feelings of Competence). Any verbal or nonverbal behavior of an adult that expresses satisfaction with a child's behavior and which identifies a specific component or components of the child's behavior as successful. This process of identification can be carried, for example, through timing of the verbal or gestural expression of satisfaction, through repetition of the desired behavior, or through its verbal identification (e.g., saying "good," "wonderful," "great," "yes," or clapping hands and smiling when the child completes a task, or part of it, successfully).

Organizing and Planning (Mediated Regulation of Behavior). Adult behaviors that model, demonstrate, and/or verbally suggest to the child a regulation of behavior in relation to the nature of the task, or to any other cognitive process prior to overt action. Mediated regulation of behavior may be expressed, for example, through processes of matching the task requirements with the child's capacity and interests as well as through organizing and sequencing steps toward success. "Let's wash your face, slowly, so no soap will get into your eyes;" "Slowly, not so hard, it is delicate, do it softly," or "First, turn all the pieces over, then search for the right piece." Mediated regulation of behavior may be related to processes of cognition (i.e., systematic exploration); to the process of elaboration (i.e., planning behavior); or to the processes of expressive behavior (i.e., reducing egocentric expressions and regulating intensity and speed of behavior).

The aforementioned five criteria for monitoring the quality of mediation provided by an adult to a child were found to be stable across time (from infancy to ages 3 and 4), and across various situations of caregiving such as feeding and bathing, among nongifted samples (Klein et al., 1987; Klein, 1988). It was also found that the use of these basic criteria of a quality interaction explains variability in nongifted children's cognitive performance at least until age 4, better than do some commonly used status variables such as SES, birth weight, AGPAR, or early psychomotor test scores of these children (Klein et al., 1986).

In addition, improving the quality of parent–child interaction by using the MLE orientation resulted in greater parental awareness of the need to be active in modifying the environment so that it could better match the children's needs and interests in sharing excitement about their experiences. It also produced more frequent parental explaining, relating, contrasting, praising, and organization of phenomena in the environment for the benefit of their children. Consequently, these children scored higher on various measures of language and reasoning, they asked more questions, requested more information about their environment, were more aware of their own success, and were more likely to reward the success of others (Klein & Alony, 1991). It may thus be concluded that a major factor affecting variations in the modifiability of children's cognitive functioning is the kind and amount of quality interaction they experience, and thus, an attempt to increase a child's capacity to benefit from new experiences must focus on improving the kind of mediation to which he or she is exposed.

APPLICATION OF MISC TO THE GIFTED (MISC-G)

Judging from our hands-on experimentation in home and clinic settings, it has been demonstrated that high-quality mediation will lead to better learning. Most available intervention programs are designed to improve a child's behavior in a number of cognitive domains. The MISC program views improved performance as an objective, but this goal is secondary to one of affecting the child's *need system*, creating in the child a greater urge to focus clearly on stimuli, to search for meaning, to associate, relate, compare, and contrast perceptions, to seek explanations, relations, and general information beyond what is perceived through the senses. Other salient aims are to strengthen the need to afford pleasure to others, to summarize one's own behavior, to plan ahead, and to match one's behavior with the task at hand. A sample of cognitive and social-emotional needs in relation to basic MLE criteria is presented in Table 9.1.

As can be seen in Table 9.1, the MISC program for the gifted is based on the criteria determining the quality of mediation and defining how an interaction should be carried out if it is meant to affect the child. In addition, four general areas of functioning relating to the question, "What should be focused on in the program?" are highlighted. It should be stressed that the specific contents were chosen by the children, with the mediator frequently responding to the children's initiative in the following domains of behavior:

1. Social–Emotional

The mediators in the program highlighted ongoing processes of interaction among the children and between the children and their parents or other adults. Prior to the onset of the program, all of the children learned to identify, label verbally, and imitate facial expressions of emotions and what triggers these emotions. They then identified those in drawings and sculptures and in everyday human interactions, including devoting attention to their consequences and precedents. The variables that were noted in the mediators' summary card were as follows: (a) showing signs of affection for another person, (b) reaction to another child's distress, (c) helping others physically or verbally, and (d) sharing materials and workspace.

During various sessions, when it was appropriate in terms of the content of the ongoing session and children's interest, attempts were made by the mediators to introduce games such as cartoon fill-ins, pictures that allow interpretations of alternate social interactions, and other materials and games designed to enhance children's social-emotional learning.

2. Language

The use of new vocabulary was introduced when appropriate. Following word introduction, efforts were made to use each word again in different situations. Excitement was expressed with regard to the "beautiful new word," "just the word for it," "perfect word." The children were encouraged to verbalize thought. The mediator shared with them his or her own thoughts and feelings. Sentence structure was not corrected immediately; instead, it was duly noted, and the correct structure was brought to the child's attention in a different context. A similar approach was used for grammatic closure. Verbal fluency and verbal expression were encouraged in general, and particularly in relation to feelings.

3. Thinking Processes

Usually, the mediator identified and raised the child's awareness of cognitive processes involved in the child's own behavior, using metacognitive methods to highlight techniques for focusing attention, memory; sorting out relevant vs. irrelevant information; presenting divergent thinking through different people's point of view; pointing out the need to see things clearly, to plan ahead, to assess the challenge of a task or a problem, and to consider all aspects of a problem. Raising the children's awareness to the processes of mediation or to the "instructional secrets" was a frequently used strategy to improve children's awareness of the need to plan and regulate behavior as well as to become familiar with cognitive processes. Hunkins (1987) suggests that "explaining teaching strategies to students allows them to derive more meaning and enjoyment from their classes and to have greater control over their learning" (p. 65).

4. Aesthetics and Art

The objective of the focus on aesthetics and art was to enrich the child's channels of expression, and to enable him or her to differentiate and enjoy the aesthetic qualities of the environment. The mediators highlighted and raised the children's awareness of objects that are aesthetically pleasing, giving reasons for and describing their aesthetic qualities. The mediators shared with the children criteria for aesthetic choices through joint decisions that required aesthetic considerations (e.g., where to place a flowerpot or where to hang a picture on the wall). Children were asked to choose works of art, household utensils, clothing, and so on, which they liked, and to say why they liked them.

Based on the outstanding features of the population of young gifted children and their assumed needs, the general structure of the MISC-G Program was designed with a focus on the five basic

Table 9.1. MISC Program: Intellectual and Social-Emotional Needs in Relation to Mediation

Mediation Processes	Examples of the Process	Intellectual needs	Social Emotional needs
1. Focusing (Intentionality & reciprocity)	Making the environmental stimuli compatible to the child's needs, e.g. bringing closer, covering distractions repeating, sequencing, grouping helping the child focus, see, hear, feel, clearly.	Needs related primarily to intellectual performance. Need for precision in perception (vs. scanning exploration). Need for precision in expression.	Need to focus on and decode, facial and body expressions of emotion. Need to modify one's own behavior or the environment in order to mediate to others (to make the other person see or understand).
2. Exciting (Meaning)	Expressing excitement vocally, verbally or non-verbally over experiences, objects, people, etc. Naming, identifying.	Need to search for meaningful new experiences (i.e. listen, look, taste things that remind one of past meaningful experiences). Need to respond in a way that conveys meaning and excitement (sound, look and feel excited). Need to invest energy in meaningful activities (along the lines of intrinsic motivation).	
3. Expanding (Transcendence)	Explaining, elaborating, associating and raising awareness to metacognitive aspects of thinking.	Need to go beyond what meets the senses. Seek out further information through exploration.	Need to think about one's own feelings and the feeling of others.

		Request information from other people and from other sources. Need to link, to associate, to recall past information and anticipate future experiences.	Need to link cause and effect sequences in social interaction.
4. Encouraging (Feelings of Competence)	Praise in a way that is meaningful to the child. Clear isolation and identification of the reasons for success. Well timed in relation to the experience.	Need to seek more success experiences. Need to summarize one's own activities and determine what led to success.	Need to please others and gain more mediated feelings of competence. Need to identify what pleases different people. Need to provide others with mediated feelings of competence.
5. Organizing & Planning (Regulation Behavior)	Regulation with regard to speed, precision, force and preferred sequence of activities.	Need to plan before acting, e.g. need to consider possible solutions prior to responding. Clarifying goals, meeting subgoals. Need to pace one's activities. Need to regulate the level of energy invested in any task.	Need to control one's impulses in social situations. Learn acceptable ways of expressing one's emotions (i.e., regulate the pace and intensity of one's social responses to anger and joy).

Table 9.2.   General summary card of the MISC program for gifted young children

How \ What	Social/ Emotional	Language	Thinking processes (Meta Cognition)	Esthetics & Art
Focusing (Intensionality & Reciprocity)				
Exciting (Meaning)				
Expanding (Transcendence)				
Rewarding (Competence)				
Organizing & planning (Regulation of Behavior)				

criteria of a quality mediation, defining how the interaction with these children should be carried out, and another focus across four major content areas: social–emotional, language, thinking processes, and aesthetics and art. Following each meeting with a gifted child, the mediator (most frequently an early childhood education student) was required to fill out a summary card reflecting the structure of the program (see Table 9.2). At every meeting different content areas could be dealt with depending on the needs and interests of each individual. Monthly summaries had to include some repeated reference to all four content areas and to be carried out through the application of all five basic criteria of mediation. These summary cards were discussed with the parents, who were encouraged to add to the summary table examples from their own interactions with their children.

As stated earlier, gifted young children are characterized by their appetite for learning, and their unusual capacity to benefit from new experiences. It stands to reason that these children have probably experienced good mediation. Their parents or other adults in their lives have spontaneously provided them with quality interaction. However, in order to ensure continued quality mediation across various situations and time, the MISC-G Program was designed to improve parental awareness and application skills of the basic criteria that define early enrichment through mediation.

EFFECTS OF THE MISC PROGRAM ON A LOW-SES SAMPLE IN ISRAEL

In this longitudinal study it was found that all families, regardless of their initial pattern of mediation, were capable of increasing the incidence of mediated learning experiences they were providing for their young children. Families with high flat profiles and families with uneven profiles of MLE frequently showed more rapid modifiability than did families with low flat profiles. In other words, good mediators who learn to identify the criteria of quality mediation become even better mediators.

It is interesting to note that of the two criteria selected as indicators of change—(a) parent verbal ability to recite the basic MLE criteria, and (b) observed increase in the frequency of these criteria in parent–child interactions—it was found that parental behavior changed before there was a parallel change in their verbal capacity to recite the criteria.

The length of time it took a family to modify significantly the MLE provided for their children depended on a number of variables, some of which are often reported in the literature in relation to changes of attitude (e.g., Bee et al., 1982). However, parental motivation to improve their child's cognitive development was clearly present in all homes, and was unrelated to parental level of education, income, or ethnic background. It must be noted that there was significant variability between parents with regard to their own belief in the modifiability of their child and in their self-perception as agents of the desired change. Assessing these parental attitudes and beliefs may serve as an indicator of the need to spend more time convincing parents of their power to affect the child's abilities and of their child's potential for change. Parents' pessimistic attitudes or beliefs should not be perceived as indicators that MLE cannot be effected in their homes.

Assessments of the preintervention and postintervention conditions in the homes, as well as an assessment of the children, were carried out following 1 and 3 years of intervention. Significant differences in parental mediation and in the children's cognitive performance were found between the pre- and postintervention conditions. Parents were found to initiate more activities directed towards mediating to their child. More of the observed behaviors clearly transcended the satisfaction of the child's basic needs, and more affect and meaning were expressed and mediated to the child. Some forms of expressing mediation of competence were affected by the program (e.g., praise and demonstration of the reason for success).

In a recent 3-year follow-up (Klein & Alony, 1991) of a group of low-SES families, 44 in an experimental and 18 in a control group, who participated in one of the MISC programs, it was found that parental behaviors towards their children, as well as children's learning behavior, changed dramatically following the intervention. The quality of mediation of the parents improved over the 3 years following intervention. The children of these parents were observed to request more information (as opposed to control group children, who requested general attention). They also associated and expressed more excitement about things around them.

Five of the children in the experimental group (N = 44) and none of the control children (N = 18) scored one standard deviation above the norm on the PPVT; three of the children who participated in the program scored over 130, and an additional two scored above 120. Significant differences between the groups were likewise found with regard to auditory reception and abstract reasoning. These differences could be explained by contrasts in the quality of mediation observed in the children's homes. All mothers mediated more to their children at age 4 than they had in infancy; the increase in mediation was, however, more marked for the group that had learned how to mediate 3 years earlier. Significant correlations were found between parental quality and style of mediation and children's actual behavior. For example, in experimentals and controls (N = 59), a correlation of .61 was found between parental expression of excitement (mediation of meaning) and that of the children; a correlation of .49 between the amount of explaining and expanding done by parents and that of the children; a correlation of .59 between giving encouragement to others (mediating competence) provided by parents and that provided by the children.

It is interesting to note that, at the onset of the program, parents in both the experimental and control groups showed a similar bias toward their daughters as compared to their sons. In general, the daughters were expected to be disciplined, educated, and "good girls." Following the intervention, the differences in attitude towards boys and girls diminished. Girls were also expected to be as smart as boys. Mothers of the experimental group expressed a more differentiated view of what smart means, they used more concepts to describe it, relating to memory, perception, and reasoning.

YOUNG GIFTED AND DOWN SYNDROME CHILDREN—A NEW APPROACH

The MISC-G-DS Program is a new development of the basic MISC Program, in which the gifted work and play with Down Syndrome

(DS) children under careful instruction from the Center staff. Young high-IQ children are reported to be more sensitive to the needs of other children, more helpful, and more affectionate than others (Abroms & Gollin, 1980). Based on our observations and on parental reports, young DS children tend to be more interested in, focus their attention longer on, and show that they prefer other young children to older children or to adult models. Many parents of children in Western societies, especially parents of the gifted, are highly motivated to push their children ahead, particularly in areas of cognitive functioning, often at the expense of rich social- and emotion-laden experiences.

In a program involving two groups of children interacting with each other, only one of which is precocious, parents of both groups must be convinced that their children are benefitting from the interaction. Mainstreaming the developmentally handicapped with "normal" children frequently raises opposition from parents of the latter group who claim that the "normals" are being held back because of this interaction. In the MISC-G-DS program, the objective is to enhance the development of both the retarded and the gifted children emotionally and cognitively.

Psychologists and anthropologists have recently begun to inquire into competencies that children might acquire during the time they spend performing household tasks required by their parents. Edwards (1986) focuses on the sociocognitive structures involved in nurturance, specifically, the reasoning about "rational" and "conventional" moral rules that is given a developmental impetus in the caretaking experience. Edwards claims that children in multiage dyads or groupings negotiate constantly with one another the rights and wrongs of acts and who should do what and when. Piaget suggests that peer interaction (which he viewed primarily in play) provides the optimal experience of conflict and reciprocity that children need in order to develop moral autonomy and a sense of justice. The process through which caretaking children learn rules and social norms is an active one and involves both knowledge that is self-acquired and knowledge that is socially transmitted by others (Shweder, 1982). It has thus been concluded that the responsible, nurturant young child becomes not merely a caring and feeling person, but also a thinking child with special social-cognitive competence (Edwards, 1986).

The self-teaching, or even guided learning of social rules and morals of caretaking children, is only a fragment of the rich fabric of learning possibilities inherent in an interaction between two children, in which one assumes the role of the caregiver or teacher. Such a situation may be especially potent if one can construct an interaction in which young children are motivated to care for, and promote, the development of other children whose cognitive development has been retarded. Such a situation requires the presence of an adult mediator who *arouses* bright young children with the prospect of providing special help for a child who needs it, focusing on the joy in making another person happy, or teaching another person; *reinforces* them in their initial attempts to do so; *focuses* their attention on components of the targeted child's behavior that has *communicative* value (e.g., "Let's see what he or she is telling us," "How can we tell?").

The guided, constructive encounters of the gifted with a young retarded child who needs such services also provide fertile ground for various forms of metacognitive learning. Once a week the gifted and DS preschool-age children meet at the Early Childhood Center. The meeting takes place in the presence of the parents and an adult mediator (a student or Center staff member). The mediator guides both groups of children to focus on each other's signs of communication (e.g., smiles, vocalizations, eye contact, head movements, body postures, etc.), pace, and intensity of action, including reaction time, rate, and intensity of response (the latter is particularly relevant for interaction with DS children whose responses may be delayed and vary in intensity).

The gifted are guided to focus on the thinking processes that occur even prior to simple responses; they are instructed to slow down their own rate of response and to adjust it to that of their DS partners. They are assisted to plan activities ahead, set objectives, and test hypotheses regarding the other child. Gifted children become increasingly aware of the need to be active and conscious of learning processes, particularly of the strategies involved in focusing attention and memory. They learn to be good mediators by concentrating on how to focus the other child's attention on various stimuli, how to express excitement that can capture the other child's interest, and how to explain and expand ongoing experiences for the DS child. In so doing, the young gifted are helped to grow out of their egocentric view of themselves and the world around them. The aim is to enable them to become increasingly more sensitive to another's perspective, to learn how others understand and do things, and to consider the changes necessary in their own behavior that can make others understand or experience what is intended for them to understand or experience.

The DS children learn to enjoy their interaction with a nonhandicapped peer, and to be active learners. They learn to focus better on stimuli around them, to search for the names and meanings of things, to construct sequences of experiences, and to feel more secure about imitating and relating to other children of their age. In addition to the cognitive objectives of the MISC-G-DS Program, the gifted learn to care for DS children, to empathize with them, and to enjoy their successes as well as other aspects of their relationship with them. The DS children, through these guided interactions with gifted peers who are interested in them as human beings, gain a unique opportunity for learning through a combination of modelling and mediation. The DS children are the center of attention and receive quality interactions with others. Regular educational settings in which DS children are mainstreamed are often lacking in guided attempts to make intact children better mediators and to become better learners themselves. The gifted are not slowed down by the DS children; on the contrary, the interaction between the two provides a unique opportunity for all children to become more insightful, yet more feeling and caring individuals as well.

In order to maximize the effects of the interaction between the gifted and the DS children, their parents are present at the interaction, and they gain both metacognitive knowledge and mediational skills that they can use in their daily interactions with their children.

AESTHETIC EDUCATION FOR THE VERY YOUNG AND GIFTED

The general criteria of a quality interaction with young children can be applied to various dyadic experiences, independent of their content or context. However, in order to be a good mediator, one has to convey real excitement about what is mediated, a genuine interest in the child, and a general idea of possible educational sequences in the content area in question. Aesthetic education represents still another effort by the Early Childhood Center to cultivate cardinal yet neglected areas of learning for gifted preschoolers.

Adults are often fascinated by the freshness and originality of children's art and by the opportunity it provides to look into a child's inner life. Children's art can be viewed as another language for self-expression. However, precocious development of the graphic forms of artistic expression is not considered to be a sign of giftedness until it includes pictorial representations of the environment. There is a meaningful consistency in toddlers' and young children's self-taught art. The artistic creations at that early age appear to follow definite developmental stages, reflecting concern for placement, shape, and aesthetically balanced design (Kellog, 1970). Most parents and educators, however, are unaware of the developmental stages in children's art and evaluate their drawing by its level of representation of familiar forms. Before children develop to the stage when they can produce representational art, they are rarely rewarded for their achievements in their own form of expression. They are not rewarded for using a variety of colors, for using up much of the drawing space on a page, for producing aesthetically balanced designs, or for using artistic nonpictorial representations in creative ways.

Children's spontaneous scribbles become explicitly pictorial at only about the age of 3, when they may identify in their scribbles recognizable shapes, label them, and elaborate on them. There seems to be a general lack of awareness of the possible existence of artistic precocity before the age of three. Although Kellog and others suggest leaving a child alone to pass through all stages of self-taught art, it is clear that parents could significantly affect a child's need to express himself or herself artistically and to choose a specific mode of self-expression.

Gardner (1982) cautions against an overgeneralization of Piaget's developmental stages as a model explaining development in children's art. He suggests that artistic development may follow a different sequence and claims that the first 7 years in the child's life are years in which children develop insights into the world around them, as well as ways to understand and use symbols. According to Gardner, at 6–7 years the child has "the first draft" and only then needs artistic education to develop it. Most 6–7-year-olds, according to Gardner, do not have the understanding of "style" and cannot classify according to stylistic clues. They attend primarily to content and not to the mood or feeling expressed in art.

Observing our Israeli sample of gifted 3- and 4-year-olds, we have found that some of them have a keen understanding of style and have responded well to aesthetic education. Following a relatively brief introduction, they could, for example, easily classify paintings into those produced by Picasso, Van Gogh, and Breugel. They could also make aesthetic decisions regarding their own clothes and those of others and concerning placement of objects in a room.

It appears that what a young child fails to produce in art, as in other domains, is related to limitations in past experience. It would be more constructive to avoid overgeneralizations based on developmental stage theories, inasmuch as doing so may lead to closing off exposure to stimulating objects and events. The young gifted child should be provided with art and aesthetic education in order to open a major avenue of self-expression, differentiation, and sensitivity to the environment. Content analysis of children's talk or artistic expression about art and design can provide a penetrating assessment of the way they look at, and respond to, art and design forms. For example, a naive response to, say, a painting or television advertisement characteristically focuses on the *literal content or subject matter* (i.e., on *what* is being represented) rather than on *how* it is represented.

A more sophisticated and educated response would refer additionally to the diverse perceptual properties, such as the colors, tones, textures, organization, and composition. It would also refer to the affective properties, with reasons being given for preferences and dislikes, as well as the inferred or explicit intentions and moods of the artist and the child looking at it. Likewise accessible to the educated, insightful young child is an appreciation of the artist's preferred style, materials, and techniques, and perhaps even something about the period and culture in which the painting was produced. A child, even a gifted one, looking at a painting, for example, can hardly be expected to pass beyond the basic level of reference to the representational content of a work of art (i.e., beyond what his or her eyes see) unless he or she is in the presence of an adult who is ready to mediate its meaning to him or her. Mediation should not be limited just by knowledge of the child's age, but by knowing the particular potentialities of the child in question. John Wilson (1986) highlights several points that one should not be satisfied with in aesthetic education:

1. We should not be satisfied with children who merely knew certain facts or could make certain correct judgments about works of art without enjoying them.

2. We should not be satisfied if s/he thoroughly enjoyed art, but for the wrong reasons (as we think).

3. Nor should we be satisfied even by a combination of 1 and 2. For s/he might still not actually be enjoying them for the reasons that truly make it a work of art.

One may repeat what a good critic has said about Eroica and yet we would not know whether that was his reason for liking it.

Being moved by works of art is more often like being in love than like valuing a trusted friend; more like what one may feel about one's native land than like one's rational preferences for Ruritania as a place for a touring holiday. Most of the crucial operations (as also in religious belief) are unconscious—if available to consciousness, available only with difficulty. (Wilson, 1986, p. 96)

We cannot show the appropriateness of our feelings even in relation to works·of art that fail to move us deeply or passionately. "It is no good saying 'strip it of its associations and look on it purely as a work of art.' For works of art would not affect us at all, if it was not for some associations, however deeply buried: the symbols have to be symbols of something" (Wilson, 1986, p. 96).

Most deliberate brands of "aesthetic education" try to meet only the demand for intellectual initiation; and much of this is in a way just a device, almost a cheat. When the person is already in love with a work to some degree, then the critic who knows it more and loves it better can say helpful things: things more closely relevant to what moves us or may move us when we connect what he or she says with what we know of the work already. As Wilson (1986) points out: "Perhaps what we need to know is what makes pupils really like any kind of good music (plays, books, poems, pictures, etc.) for almost any reason. Given some degree of commitment or love, we have some basis for teaching: not before then" (p. 106).

The identified developmental sequence of aesthetic appreciation suggested by Wilson (1986) may serve as the basis for educational planning of sequences designed to enhance it. In the case of the gifted child, accepting a stage-based developmental approach may be limiting. The young gifted child, looking at a painting, may be able to see its content and even derive the emotional message conveyed by the artist at an earlier age than expected. Quality mediation by the adult to this child may involve sharing one's experiences with art and presenting the reasons for liking or disliking it, the emotions it evokes, and some facts about the artist; but all of the above should be presented only if matched with the child's interest and only if considered genuinely of interest to the mediator. Thus, educators of the young and gifted must be knowledgeable about educational sequences and flexible in using them.

Quality mediation provided to young children incorporates focusing, arousing, and expanding. Focusing the child's attention on detail or stimulating his or her senses does not suffice in creating true aesthetic experiences that may build an appetite for further aesthetic experiences. Arousing the child involves sharing one's own reasons for excitement and expanding beyond the present, beyond what one sees or feels at the moment, into what the artist could have felt and into the realm of his or her times. Aesthetics can be introduced to children's awareness by pointing out and discussing with them interesting designs of buildings, products, and furniture, while sharing decisions as to where to place a beautiful object, how to arrange flowers, which jewelry to choose, and where to place it.

When the Center staff suggested to the parents of our Israeli sample of gifted 3–4-year-olds to visit an art museum with their children, they were surprised. During the interview held with the parents at the end of the program year, many of them noted taking their children to share an artistic experience they themselves loved, such as going to a concert, to the theater, to a ballet, or to a dance performance. They could also clearly describe what experiences they wished to share with their children, how much they all enjoyed it, and how this feeling was expressed by and to the children.

A small taste of many subjects, or the "smorgasbord" approach found in elementary education, may not be the best tactic in educating every young gifted child. These youngsters may benefit from bits of information or fragmented episodes of learning, but in terms of long-lasting effects, they require a balance between consistency and novelty presented by a mediator who shows great interest in the child himself or herself and a passion for the area he or she wishes to mediate to the child. One can hardly expect a toddler to remember the contents he or she has learned; however, these experiences may be more effective if they arouse the appetite for more.

One of the 4-year-olds seen at the Center, Danny, was a gifted artist. His drawings were considerably beyond expectation for his age and had a strong and fresh expressive message. Looking into Danny's history and background, it became apparent that, since infancy, he had spent hours every day with his grandfather, who is an artist and lives with the family. A grandfather who loved his own art and his grandson, and who had the time and patience to be a good mediator, apparently provided fertile ground for the development of the special artistic talents and "artistic appetites" of his grandson.

Every parent has the right to his or her own objectives in his or her child's development. Most parents, regardless of their cultural background or SES level, want their children to develop into well adjusted individuals. They may thus be concerned if their child does not do or like to do what other children of his or her age prefer doing. Danny's mother, for example, was concerned whether she was doing the right thing by allowing him to draw so much. She claimed that he does not wish to engage in any other activity, like playing with building blocks or watching TV. In fact, Danny's parents did not consider him to be a gifted child (probably because his language development did not exceed the norm for his age). They did, however, realize that he draws exceptionally well. They therefore collected and numbered his drawings, prepared albums, and showed them to all visitors to their home.

At an early stage of development, any content area can be used as a vehicle for educational enrichment, as long as the interaction with the child in relation to the content is meaningful and stimulating. Young artists may learn at least as much about the world around them through art as through play with building blocks, puzzles, or music. Development in language and thinking can be enhanced through experiences related to children's interest in art. Even social interactions with age peers may be related, directly or indirectly, to art (e.g., drawing a cooperative mural, sharing materials, preparing greeting cards for others, or visiting a museum).

The dangers in pushing young children to reach the same level of achievement across a number of subject areas brings to mind Rabinovich's (1977) story:

> Once upon a time, the animals decided they must do something heroic to meet the problems of a 'new world.' So, they organized a school. They adopted an activity curriculum consisting of running, climbing, swimming, and flying. To make it easier to administer the curriculum, all the animals took all subjects. The duck was excellent in swimming, in fact better than his instructor; but he made only passing grades in fishing and was poor in running. Since he was slow in running he had to stay after school and drop swimming in order to practice running. This was kept up until his webbed feet were badly worn and he was only average in swimming . . . . The rabbit started at the top of his class in running, but had a nervous breakdown because he had to make up so much in swimming. (p. 19)

The case of Jasmin further illustrates that specific interests and what may have appeared as an obsession in a young gifted child actually contributed to her development. Jasmin was 3 years, 4 months when I first met her. She was highly verbal and self-confident. She walked over to me and immediately started describing my clothes in terms of style, color, and where she thought they were bought. She then proceeded to tell me about her own clothes, demonstrating in the process an unusual memory for types of materials, styles, designers, and shops. It was quite an astonishing experience to hear all this information offered almost spontaneously from a 3-year-old child.

Jasmin was the first born of a 33-year-old mother who had been a career woman, a buyer in one of the big department stores. She gave up her career in order to raise Jasmin, but she did not give up her love for color and style. From early in life Jasmin accompanied her mother while she was shopping. Her mother, aware of the importance of talking with her child, engaged her in conversation about clothes as she was pointing out, touching, matching, and choosing them. Jasmin was caught up by her mother's enthusiasm and demanded further mediation in relation to clothing. It appears that her acute differentiation of color and shape, her memory, both visual and verbal, as well as her sensitivity and social skills, mostly acquired through shopping, served as a good basis for motivation to learn from new experiences in other content areas. It should be noted that, at the age of 6, Jasmin was enrolled in her school in a special program for the gifted and her IQ was above 140.

The relationship between academic achievement in particular subjects and positive affect towards these areas of study has been repeatedly demonstrated in the professional literature. Steinkamp and Maeher (1983) concluded, following a summary of 66 studies of the subject, that one should like what one does and do well what one likes. A child's likes and dislikes are based, to a large extent, on his or her previous experiences and on the interpretation of these experiences by the adults mediating to him or her. In order to do well what one likes, one needs practice time and opportunities to practice. Elkind (1970) speaks of periods in children's cognitive development in which they are preoccupied with the cultivation of a specific skill and show a specialized "cognitive appetite" or need to repeat the behaviors that are part of the newly acquired skill. The young and gifted may develop a stronger appetite for some areas of performance than for others and should be given the opportunity to satisfy such a taste.

The joy of learning, the eagerness to acquire new skills, knowledge, and understanding, is partially intrinsic as suggested, for example, by Piaget's notion of the need to operate the schemas of thought as the basis for development of higher thinking processes. There is, however, no doubt that the need for novelty, the quest for knowledge, is largely acquired through the process of interaction between the child and his or her environment. This is true for all children and perhaps more so for children who are more active, demanding, and verbal as toddlers. The toddler years can be a sensitive period for a generalized curbing or encouragement of the appetite for learning. The growing mobility, the newly developed language skills and experimentation of self-hood, bring the young children into many situations which allow them to learn whether it is worthwhile to exert effort, and whether there is something beyond what is seen or sensed momentarily.

FINALLY, THE MESSAGE OF UNIQUENESS

One of the most important social objectives of Western education is to convey to all children the message of equality—everyone is equal. Young children also need the opportunity to feel unique, to sense that their family is the most loving, their parents the best, their community the most beautiful, etc. One cannot expect to create a sense of belonging in young children without endowing this rootedness with positive affect. A toddler must establish first that he or she is special before learning that others are special, too. He or she cannot be expected to learn the significance of the objects, people, or relations around him or her if they are not interpreted by someone who really loves or deeply feels for each of them.

One can take a trip through a desert area, see, smell, and feel it and still return untouched by the experience. Taking the same trip with a guide who loves the desert, and has the need to share his or her knowledge and love for it with others, makes the desert come alive. The guide shares his or her excitement if he or she can convince people how vital it is for survival in the desert to be able to identify footprints and the qualities of various species of wildlife or vegetation. It becomes exciting because what appeared at first as sand and emptiness turns into a differentiated, well-focused kaleidoscope of visions, sounds, and movements bearing a direct effect on visitors' lives, and thus making the experience informative and perhaps inspirational as well.

For the adult on a first trip to the desert, the quality of that experience may determine whether he or she will choose to return to it or to learn more about it on other occasions. Similarly, for a toddler or young child, a positive, exciting learning experience may determine his or her appetite for exploring and learning from new experiences in the future. It may also enhance the general learning processes needed for making the most of first encounters with people, places, ideas, and the world of beauty.

REFERENCES

Abroms, K., & J. B. Gollin (1980). Developmental study of gifted preschool children and measures of psychological giftedness. *Exceptional Children, 46*, 334–343.

Allison, B. (1986). Some aspects of assessment in art and design education. In M. Ross (Ed.), *Assessment in education* (pp. 113–135). New York, Pergamon Press.

Bamberger, J. (1986). Cognitive issues in the development of musically gifted children. In R. J. Sternberg & J. E. Davidson (Eds.), *Conceptions of giftedness* (pp. 338–413). Cambridge: Cambridge University Press.

Beckwith, L. (1971). Relationships between attributes of mothers and their infants' I.Q. scores. *Child Development, 42*, 1083–1097.

Belsky, J., Good, M. K., & Most, R. K. (1980). Maternal stimulation and infant exploratory competence: Cross-sectional, correlational, and experimental analysis. *Child Development, 51*, 1163–1178.

Berg, L. (1985). *Bringing out head start talents (BOHST). General programming: defective inventor and judge activities.* Campaign, IL: Disabled Citizens Foundation, 1304 W. Bradely.

Birns, B., & Golden, M. (1972). Prediction of intellectual performance at three years from infant tests and personality measures. *Merrill-Palmer Quarterly, 18*, 53–58.

Brainin, S. S. (1984). Mediating learning: Pedagogic issues in the improvement of cognitive functions. *Review of Research in Education, 12*, 121–149.

Brown, J. L. (1964) States in newborn infants. *Merrill-Palmer Quarterly, 10*, 313–327.

Brown, J. L. (1970). Precursors of intelligence and creativity: A longitudinal study of one child's development. *Merrill-Palmer Quarterly, 16*, 117–137.

Caldwell, B. M. (1967). Social class level and stimulation: Potential of the home. *Exceptional Infant, 1*, 455–466.

Clarke-Stewart, K. A. (1973). Interactions between mothers and their young children: Characteristics and consequences. *Monographs of the Society for Research in Child Development, 38*(6–7, Serial No. 153).

Edwards, C. P. (1986). Another style of competence: the caregiving child. In A. Fogel & G. D. Melson (Eds.), *Origins of nurturance.* Hillsdale, NJ: Erlbaum.

Elkind, D. (1970). *Children and adolescents, interpretative essays of Jean Piaget.* New York: Oxford University Press.

Elkind, D. (1987). *Miseducation.* New York: Knopf.

Feldman, R. D. (1982). *Whatever happened to the quiz kids.* Chicago: Chicago Review Press.

Feuerstein, R. (1979). *The dynamic assessment of retarded performers.* New York: University Park Press.

Feuerstein, R. (1980). *Instrumental enrichment: Redevelopment of cognitive functions of retarded performers* (pp. 361–372). New York: University Park Press.

Freeman, J. (1985). A pedagogy for the gifted. In J. Freeman (Ed.), *The psychology of gifted children* (pp. 1–20). New York: John Wiley & Sons.

Gardner, H. (1982). *Art mind and brain, a cognitive approach to creativity.* New York: Basic Books, Inc.

Guilford, A. M., Scheuerle, J., & Shonburn, S. (1981). Aspects of language development in the gifted. *Gifted Child Quarterly, 25*, 159–163.

Hanson, I. (1984). A comparison between parent identification of young bright children and subsequent testing. *Roeper Review, 7*(1), 44–45.

Hofstaetter, P. R. (1954). The changing composition of 'Intelligence': A study of technique. *Journal of Genetic Psychology, 85*, 159–164.

Hunkins, F. P. (1987). Sharing our instructional secrets. *Educational Leadership, 45*(3), 65–67.

Jacobs, J. C. (1971). Rorschach studies reveal possible misinterpretations of personality traits of the gifted. *Gifted Child Quarterly, 6*, 195–200.

Karnes, M. B., & Johnson, L. J. (1987). Head start expands services to gifted children. *Children today, 16*(6), 27–31.

Kellog, R. (1970). Understanding children's art. In P. Cramer (Ed.), *Readings in developmental psychology today*. Del Mar, CA: CRM Books.

Klein, P. S. (1984). *Criteria for observation of mediated learning experience*. Unpublished manuscript, Bar-Ilan University, Ramat Gan, Israel.

Klein, P. S. (1985). *More intelligent child* [in Hebrew]. Ramat Gan: Bar Ilan Press.

Klein, P. S. (1988). Stability and change in interaction of Israeli mothers and infants. *Infant Behavior and Development, 11*, 55–70.

Klein, P. S., & Alony, S. (1991). *Immediate and sustained effects of maternal mediating behaviors in infancy*. Manuscript submitted for publication.

Klein, P. S., & Feuerstein, R. (1984). Environmental variables and cognitive development: Identification of potent factors in adult-child interaction. In S. Harel & W. N. Anastasio (Eds.), *The at-risk infant: Psycho-socio-medical aspects* (pp. 369–377). Baltimore: Paul H. Brookes.

Klein, P. S., & Hundeide, K. (1989). *The more intelligent, sensitive child (MISC) program: A training manual*. Blindern, Norway: University of Oslo, Institute of Psychology.

Klein, P. S., Raziel, P., Brish, M., & Birenbaum, (1986). Cognitive performance of 3-year-olds born at very low birth weight. *Journal of Psychosomatic Obstetrics and Gynaecology, 7*, 117–129.

Klein, P. S., Weider, S., & Greenspan, S. J. (1987). A theoretical overview and empirical study of mediated learning experience: prediction of preschool performance from mother-infant interaction patterns. *Infant Mental Health Journal, 8*, 2.

Koopman-Dayton, J. D., & Feldhusen, J. F. (1987). A resource guide for parents of gifted preschoolers. *Gifted Children Today, 10*(6), 207.

Lehman, E. B., & Erdwins, C. J. (1981). The social and emotional adjustment of young intellectually-gifted children. *Gifted Child Quarterly, 25*, 134–137.

Leonard, J. E., & Causler, D. P. (1980). Serving gifted/handicapped preschoolers and their families: A demonstration project. *Roeper Review, 2*(3), 39–41.

Lerner, R. (1982). Children and adolescents as producers of their own development. *Developmental Review, 2*, 342–370.

Lewis, M., & Michalson, L. (1985). The gifted infant. In J. Freeman (Ed.), *The psychology of gifted children* (pp. 35–57). New York: John Wiley & Sons.

Oden, M. H. (1968). The fulfillment of promise: 40-year follow-up of the Terman gifted group. *Genetic Psychology Monographs, 77*, 3–93.

Rabinovitch (1975). "Animal farm," personal reference cited by Pihl, R. D. Learning disabilities. In H. Myklebust (Ed.), *Progress in learning disabilities* (Vol. 3). New York: Grune & Stratton.

Reid, L. A. (1986). "Art" and the arts. In M. Ross (Ed.), *Assessment in education* (pp. 3–23). New York: Pergamon Press.

Renzulli, J. S. (1978). What makes giftedness? Reexamining a definition. *Phi Delta Kappan, 60*, 18–24.

Rimm, S., & Loew, B. (1988). Family environments of underachieving gifted students. *Gifted Child Quarterly, 32*(4), 353–358.

Roedell, W. C. (1985). Developing social competence in gifted preschool children. *Remedial and Special Education, 6*(4), 6–11.

Shweder, R. A. (1982). Beyond self-constructed knowledge: The study of culture and morality. *Merrill-Palmer Quarterly, 28*, 41–69.

Spock, B. (1986, October 27). Don't push your kids too hard. In *U.S. News & World Report*, p. 64.

Steinkamp, M. W., & Maeher, M. L. (1983). Affect, ability, and science achievement: A quantitative synthesis of correlational research. *Review of Educational Research, 53*(3), 369–396.

Tannenbaum, A. J. (1983). *Gifted children, psychological and educational perspectives.* New York: Macmillan.

Tannenbaum, A. J. (1989). *The social psychology of giftedness.*

Thomas, A., & Chess, S. (1977). *Temperament and development.* New York: Brunner/Mazel.

Torrance, E. P. (1962). *Guiding creative talent.* Englewood Cliffs, NJ: Prentice-Hall.

U.S. News & World Report. (1986, October 27). Children under stress; are we pushing our kids too hard? pp. 58–63.

White, B. S., Kaban, B. T., & Attanucci, J. S. (1979). *The origins of human competence.* Toronto: Lexington Books.

Willard, A., Hartwell, L. K., & Marson, R. A. (1985). Early identification of the preschool child: A study of parent and teacher effectiveness. *Gifted Education International, 3*(2), 127–129.

Willerman, L., & Fiedler, M. F. (1974). Infant performance and intellectual precocity. *Child Development, 45*, 483–486.

Wilson, J. (1986). Assessing aesthetic appreciation: A review. In M. Ross (Ed.), *Assessment in education* (pp. 95–111). New York: Pergamon Press.

Yarrow, L. J., Rubenstein, J. L., & Pedersen, F. A. (1975). *Infant and environment.* New York: Wiley.

chapter 10

Early Interactions and Metacognitive Development of Gifted Preschoolers*

Ellen Moss

University of Quebec at Montreal
Montreal, Canada

Metacognitive competence has consistently been associated with the performance of gifted children on a variety of cognitive tasks. Jackson and Butterfield (1986) have identified the superordinate processes involved in the regulation of task analysis and the self-management of problem-solving behavior as important components differentiating the performance of gifted and average children. Peck and Borokowski (1983) describe how use of planning, monitoring,

* This chapter is based on a doctoral dissertation presented by Ellen Moss at McGill University and subsequent analyses published by the first author in collaboration with Dr. Fred Strayer in the *International Journal of Behavioral Development*. The author thanks Dr. Bruce Shore for inspiring and supporting the original research project and Michelle Dumont for her comments on this manuscript. Financial support was provided by doctoral, postdoctoral, and a 5-year National Research Fellowship awarded to Dr. Ellen Moss by the Social Sciences and Humanities Research Council of Canada and the Quebec Ministry of Education. Requests for reprints should be sent to: Ellen Moss, Department of Psychology, University of Quebec at Montreal, C.P. 8888, Succ. "A", Montreal, Quebec H3C 3P8.

and evaluative strategies accounts for performance discrepancies between gifted and nongifted 7-year-olds on problem-solving tasks. Shore and Dover (1987) and Sternberg (1986) have all demonstrated how various cognitive executive functions mediate the superior performance of gifted individuals throughout the lifespan.

Although these studies indicate that considerable progress has been made in studying individual differences in older children's metacognitive skills, the developmental pathway leading to such knowledge remains virtually unexplored. This is somewhat surprising considering that almost every chapter or article dealing with metacognitive development includes at least one or two lines referring to its hypothetical origins in early parent–child interactive contexts. For example, John Flavell (1987) writes: "Parents may unintentionally model metacognitive activity for their young children. They may also deliberately demonstrate and teach it, helping the child to regulate and monitor his or her actions" (p. 26). Borokowski and Peck (1986) speculate that parents of gifted children lay the groundwork for metacognitive competence by providing greater intellectual stimulation in the form of challenging tasks that elicit more planful and strategic problem-solving behavior.

Speculative interest in social roots of metacognitive competence is not limited to researchers interested in cognitive development. Willard Hartup (1987), a well-known researcher in the field of social development, states: "I would like to suggest that the cognitive functions most closely linked to social relationships are the executive regulators—the planning, monitoring and outcome-checking skills involved in problem-solving" (p. 76). Supportive of Hartup's idea are recent studies that link the affective quality of the primary attachment relationship with the development of cognitive executive functions—specifically those related to socially coordinated task engagement between mother and child (Bretherton & Waters, 1985; Main, Kaplan, & Cassidy, 1985; Matas, Arend, & Sroufe, 1978). The mediating factor in these patterns is presumed to be the effective self-direction of behavior through selecting, accessing, and otherwise organizing components of intrapsychic working models. Internal working models, or mental representations constructed by the individual, reflect the history of interactional patterns experienced by the infant with the attachment figure. Babies who can depend on the availability of a caregiver who will provide assistance in dealing with obstacles encountered in the course of exploration are freer to take risks in attempting to solve more difficult problems. The infant who lacks this "secure base" (Bowlby, 1969) will show poorer mastery motivation in engaging objects or collaborators in play. As discussed by Klein (this volume), it is highly likely that the persistence shown by young gifted children is, in part, a derivative of the quality of mediated learning they have become accustomed to.

THE RELATION BETWEEN SOCIAL
AND METACOGNITIVE PROCESSES

Although there are virtually no longitudinal studies that have directly traced the early development of different metacognitive skills, several studies suggest that the interactive context of early parent–child relations may influence different metacognitive skills that emerge in later childhood. Flavell (1976) has identified three dimensions of metacognitive knowledge observed by later childhood: Briefly, *person* variables refer to cognitions about what human beings (oneself and others) are like as cognitive agents. *Task* variables concern awareness of different task environments and how task demands influence actions and decisions related to performance. *Strategy* variables are related to monitoring progress towards cognitive goals including knowledge of planning and checking operations.

Concerning social precursors of metacognitive knowledge related to person variables, Bandura's research (1977, 1983) indicates that the internal standards people use to influence their own motivation and actions are acquired through modelling and evaluative actions by significant others. Heckhausen (1987) suggests that positive self-attribution patterns emphasizing competence in learning situations will be facilitated by parental learning expectations that are developmentally appropriate and encourage child participation. Shure (1987) has shown that preschoolers' knowledge of interpersonal problem-solving skills is positively related to maternal efforts to guide and encourage the child to consider alternative solutions to problems and negatively related to maternal avoidance of communication, solution-giving, and belittling of the child's partial efforts.

With respect to metacognitive understanding of task environments, families of children later identified as musically or mathematically talented are known to have introduced their young children to these knowledge domains during informal play sessions (Bloom, 1985; Robinson, 1987). Walters and Gardner (1986) consider that these early contacts between persons with unusual talent or potential, and pertinent materials of the field, may be initial crystallizing experiences which motivate the desire to continually reconstruct these occasions.

In the area of strategy learning, Wertsch (1985) has described the child's transition from other-regulation to self-regulation. His observational studies of mother–child interaction illustrate the gradual emergence of responsibility for co-directing joint problem solving in the preschool-aged child (Wertsch, McNamee, McLane, & Budwig, 1980). The child thus becomes more capable of generating a particular cognitive strategy such as using a model in a copying task, while the mother assumes a more indirect role allowing maximal opportunities for the child to test and practice emerging skills. Gauvain and Rogoff (1988), in a study of 5-year-old children's planning in both adult–child and peer contexts, also found that experiences in shared decision making during collaborative tasks was related to greater planning efficiency by the child on later individual trials. These authors discuss how sharing responsibility for progress during a task requires that the metacognitive processes involved in problem definition, strategy organization, and evaluations of efficiency are made explicit. Experiences in jointly using these initial planning skills may support the emergence and organization of higher level strategies.

But how does early experience in interactive contexts influence the development of metacognitive knowledge about strategies, tasks and personal competencies? Is the pathway primarily an indirect one, as suggested by Shatz (1984) and Matas et al. (1978), whereby the sensitive and contingently responsive parent indirectly nurtures skill development? Alternatively, are we to adopt the more direct pedagogical paradigms of the instructional literature that conceptualize adults as modellers and shapers of specific skills (Brown, Palinscar, & Armbruster, 1986)? Since research to date has primarily adopted a correlational approach in analyzing the effects of parental behavior on the development of child cognitive competence, it has been difficult to distinguish between competing explanations. For example, it is empirically well established that mother–child object-oriented communication during play is a significant predictor of preschool IQ scores (Farran & Ramey, 1980; Olson, Bates, & Bayles, 1984; Wachs & Gruen, 1982). These studies support the idea that dyadic exchanges are fundamental to the development of individual cognitive processes; yet they do not help clarify the underlying psychological processes that link parent and child measures (Moss & Blicharski, 1986). In other words, is toy demonstration important to cognitive development primarily as a reinforcer to the child's own explorations, as a model of possible uses of the object, or simply because the emotional involvement of parent and child affects child motivation in a general sense?

In fact, the real picture is probably far more ambiguous than that suggested by either simple socialization or individual difference models of human development. The bidirectional influences involved in parent–child interaction can more appropriately be thought of as dynamics of interpersonal communication involving mutual mother and child adjustments that facilitate the co-construction of representational abilities (Moss & Strayer, 1990). The work of Gauvain and Rogoff (1988) and Wertsch et al. (1980) described above provide empirical models for exploring developmental changes in metacognition within co-constructive contexts. However, neither has emphasized the relationship of individual differences in child intelligence to shared problem solving. The objective of this chapter is to systematically study the early development of gifted children's metacognitive skills in the context of parent–child interactions.

SOME THEORETICAL TOOLS: INTERNALIZATION AND THE ZONE OF PROXIMAL DEVELOPMENT

In developmental theory, the psychologist who is perhaps best known for his conceptualization of the early establishment of a collaborative cognitive context is Lev Vygotsky. Vygotsky's concept of the social origins of cognitive functions involves the gradual transfer of cognitive executive functions from the interpersonal to the intrapersonal plane. Vygotsky (1978) emphasized that patterns of coregulation established in the context of early social relations are *internalized* as individual metacognitive functions. According to his theory, children first experience active problem-solving activities in the presence of others, gradually acquiring the ability to perform these functions for themselves. As part of this process, the child must learn to share in executing and eventually directing joint activity, although the adult is initially responsible for overall coordination and regulation.

By the preschool period, parental directives which have been internalized by the young child are becoming manifest in social and self-directed speech. Note that, in Vygotsky's (1986) model, this egocentric speech is not evidence of the child's conceptual immaturity in a Piagetian sense, but indicative of the birth of metacognitive processes. As Wood (1989) discusses, the young child's speech serves both a regulatory and communicative function. The preschool child's verbal commentaries on (his own) experiences are evidence of the emergence of self-regulated control over (his own) nonverbal activities. At the same time, the child is learning (that he can) control over the actions of others through speech. As the child develops greater expertise in language skills, he or she both increases (his) executive abilities and heightens (his) access to sociocultural sources of information, hence becoming a more active player in the co-constructive context.

The notion of the *zone of proximal development* (ZPD) was introduced by Vygotsky to describe a dialectical relation between two states of mental organization—actual and potential—mediated by the child's transactions with the sociocultural environment (Moss, in press; Kanevsky, this volume; Valsiner & Van der Veer, 1991). The child's level of cognitive functioning under adult guidance is the proper context for observing emerging psychological functions that will subsequently come under the more independent control of the child. According to Vygotsky's multidimensional model, independent cognitive activity is an index of already developed functions or past accomplishments. Bruner's (1983, 1986) studies of adult mediation or *scaffolding* of infant learning represent an empirical model of how the zone of proximal development construct can be used to study environmental facilitation of the development of cognitive skills such as labeling (e.g., Ninio & Bruner, 1978). In early labeling exchanges, caregivers assign meanings to infant behaviors that qualify their function in routine interactive formats (Bruner, 1986). For example, while reading picture books, mothers will point at pictures asking questions such as "What's this?" At first, with young infants, she will accept any infant babbling as a response and then will provide the correct label herself. Through repetition of these maternal prompts, the infant learns to express the correct word in the right sequence. At this point, the mother can raise the level of exchange requesting a more elaborate response. For example, once the infant can answer "Doggie" to mother's "What's this?" question, she will change to "What's the doggie doing?"

In addition to leading the child towards more complex language acquisitions, caregivers also provide opportunities for the expression of mastery of acquired skills. Infants will display mastery in both their greater independent use and social control of a skill. For example, 2-year-olds will pick up a book, point at pictures, and name objects in a sequence that replicates former adult–child joint reading contexts. They will also show their internalization of the social roles involved in collaborative contexts by attempting to show a book to a younger child or by initiating a joint reading activity with the adult.

My collaborators and I recently completed a series of studies showing how mothers developmentally adjust their scaffolding styles during the first 3 years of life (Moss, 1983, 1990 in press; Moss & Strayer, 1990; Strayer & Moss, 1989; Strayer, Moss, & Blicharski, 1988). We observed three zones of development (acquisition, consolidation, and inhibition), each requiring a different scaffolding style with respect to the degree of child dependency on adult regulation. Our studies showed that, in general, mothers supported child *acquisition* of new skills, which were just emerging in the child's cognitive repertoire by frequent modeling and repetitions. They likewise allowed greater opportunities for child self-regulation of skills acquired in earlier developmental periods, thus assisting their *consolidation*. They also actively encouraged the *inhibition* of consolidated problem-solving strategies and their replacement with newly emerging skills.

Young children are most dependent on adults to orient them towards new skills and away from more facile solutions to a problem. They express greater autonomy in the application of more familiar tactics during joint enterprises. It is important to understand that adult support of children's learning consists, not only of providing the appropriate cognitive resources, but also of being able to modify flexibly the socioaffective context in keeping with the phase of learning the child is passing through. For example, when the child is acquiring a new skill under adult tutelage, it is important that instructors model the skill, evaluate the correctness of the child's attempts at learning, and coach pupils to complete the process. However, it is vital that the affective attitudes that will motivate and maintain the learning process are also modeled as an integral part of the acquisition process. For example, as suggested by Meichenbaum and Biemiller (1990), instructors should make explicit the positive self-attributions that underpin task persistence, such as "Look how well this is going!" or "I'm going to get this answer after all." When skills are consolidating, the child who has experienced tutoring that is facilitative in both a cognitive and affective sense shows mastery of the cognitive tactics involved in the skill as well as a positive sense of ownership of the outcome of the activity.

The high self-direction of gifted students can be attributed, not only to greater metacognitive understanding of task process, but also to their ability to maintain positive affect even when encountering obstacles to the realization of their objectives. At the point where the child discovers that an acquired procedure is no longer useful in solving a problem, it is necessary to inhibit these activities, replacing them with a more adapted strategy. As I have discussed elsewhere (Moss, in press) the ability to reorganize one's cognitive resources effectively may be related to earlier experiences in joint adult–child learning contexts. Taking the risk of letting go of habitual patterns may be facilitated by a history of cognitively and affectively supportive experiences in interactive learning situations. In reorganizing cognitive processes, the child needs to mobilize positively affective self-attributions which support more effortful and reflective cognitive activity. On the other hand, the child's internalization of reactions by parents or teachers that have focused on personal incompetence may cause him or her to emphasize negative affects linked to failure. Such anxious, avoidant or angry emotions interfere with the activation of more cognitively reflective activity. This model may have implications for understanding the development of some gifted underachievers. As suggested by Gross (this volume) in cases where a child of exceptional ability is not performing at a high-level, exceptional cognitive abilities may not be supported by healthy levels of self-concept.

In considering how adult interventions influence young children's progress, it is also necessary to consider the various developmental challenges associated with the infancy and preschool periods. These studies also permitted us to describe how the zone of proximal development changes with age during the infancy period. Results of our studies have shown that basic dyadic social skills such as orienting the partner to one's activity or providing simple affective feedback must be in place before any kind of meaningful cognitive collaboration can occur. This is the essential focus of the zone of proximal development during the first year of life. These established nonverbal affiliative and communicative functions are extended and differentiated with the emergence of infant language. By the second year of life, mutual goal-directed communication is extended into imitative labeling exchanges where infants learn to link signs and representational symbols (Ninio & Bruner, 1978; Bruner, 1986). By the third year, we observed that these consolidated labeling skills become the building blocks for the co-construction of verbal perceptual and functional associations. The mastery of labelling skills involves flexibly incorporating object names in diverse strategies adapted to particular social and affective situations (Moss, in press). For example, the infant learns that calling "Mommy!" with a smile and outstretched hands results in getting picked up. The same word will probably function very differently when accompanied by an angry expression. The consistency of adult responses to these infant strategies plays a vital role in the construction of infant representations. For example, if the infants' affiliative "Mommy!" action sequence is as likely to elicit rejection as the angry one, then the meaning and sociocultural value of such acts remains ambiguous to the child. The young child is dependent on adult expressions of affect in order to assimilate the meaning of acts in particular contexts (Klein, this volume; Rogoff, Malkin, & Mc Bride, 1984).

In summary, by the preschool period, the competent child has consolidated the basic representational tools needed to construct higher level strategies. On a socioaffective level, the sense of self has evolved to permit the active initiation and manipulation of these representations in socially coordinated goal-directed activity. The stage is set for the development of metacognitive strategies that involve, not only the use of more complex thinking strategies, but also the ability to further one's own conceptual development.

JOINT COGNITIVE ACTIVITY DURING THE PRESCHOOL PERIOD

With the preschool period, the zone of proximal development shifts to the co-ordination of representations within problem definitions, plans, and subsequent evaluations. However, development of these metacognitive operations depends, not only on learning specific planning, monitoring, and evaluative strategies, but also on providing opportunities for the child to actively participate in the problem-solving process (Gauvain & Rogoff, 1988; Moss & Strayer, 1990; Wertsch et al., 1980). To concretize these ideas, consider the range of diverse representational components involved in completing a puzzle or a matching game with a 4-year-old child. Perceptual cues are involved in comparing the size, shape, or color of pieces. Discussions about functional or contextual cues relate individual pieces to their locations on the puzzleboard. Similarly, in a matching task, prior identification or labeling of the elements to be associated is prerequisite to the application of more sophisticated strategies involving new combinations of these elements.

The application of each of these cognitive tactics presents a different level of cognitive challenge to the child and consequently necessitates a different scaffolding style on the part of the adult. Metacognitive competence involves, not only the acquisition of organizational strategies like planning and evaluation, but also more autonomous selection and application of simpler tactics like subgoal sequencing and labeling. Although these simpler cognitive tactics may have been acquired during the infancy period, it is not until the preschool period that the child becomes conscious of these representations as potential components of self-initiated strategies (Vygotsky, 1986).

Before embarking on empirical study of the role of maternal scaffolding in metacognitive development, we attempted to situate the relative developmental challenge of various problem-solving strategies to the preschool-age child. In order to predict how maternal teaching strategies might facilitate preschool children's progress through the zone of proximal development, we conducted an extensive search of the experimental and information-processing literature concerned with instructional effects on young children's problem-solving behavior as well as of studies related to maternal teaching strategies. We regrouped the instructional components that were repeatedly associated with preschoolers' performance into three general classes: structuring, elaborative, and regulatory strategies. These classes served as the basis for specifying the multiple informational components involved in parent–child exchanges during the preschool period.

Problem Structuring—Goals, Subgoals, and Rules

At the simplest structural level, tasks can be procedurally analyzed in terms of subgoals. In order to realize the overall goal by means of intermediate subgoals, the child must organize his or her available knowledge and also apply it in an appropriate sequence. Subgoal sequencing itself may not be expected to present a major problem to 3- to 4-year-old children on a puzzle or matching task where subgoals are perceptually evident (e.g., pieces or squares on the formboard). However, keeping sight of a still-unsatisfied supergoal while carrying out these subgoals presents a cognitive task of considerable difficulty to the young child (Case, 1978; Klahr, 1978). Thus, by frequently reminding the child of the overall goal or rules, the adult may help mediate the young child's memory deficiencies and at the same time model an effective strategy for problem solution. As Wertsch (1985) explains, although many children are capable of executing the steps of a task, they do not often organize and structure their efforts in a task-appropriate manner.

Problem Elaboration—Labeling and Perceptual and Functional Cue Highlighting

Rohwer (1973) has defined *elaboration* as "the generation of an event that jointly implicates two or more items that are initially disparate" (p. 276). Campione and Brown (1978) have explained the goal of elaborative strategies as the creation of a meaningful context in which to imbed items. These relational contexts serve as multiple access routes to memory through the particular modality of cues that they represent (e.g., verbal, sensory, context of occurrence) (Paris & Lindauer, 1978). During the second year of life, mothers actively encourage infants to develop networks of object and event labels as described by Ninio and Bruner (1978). Once the infant shows evidence of having consolidated labelling skills during the third year, mothers decrease their demands for child labelling (e.g., "What's this?" questions), replacing them with questions about object function that encourage the development of representations based on subordinate categories. An important function of instruction during the preschool period is the explicit description of object features that the child may not spontaneously attend to. This teaching strategy is closely linked to cue highlighting (Case, 1978) and encoding training (Siegler, 1978) and is dealt with extensively in research relating to attentional and perceptual pretraining in young children (Nelson, 1977; Gibson, 1969). Hence, a prime function of instruction for this age group is the highlighting of perceptual and functional cues that can be stored in relational networks and used as access routes to memory. There is a notable parallel between these "elaborative" adult–child exchanges and the "focusing" behaviors described as part of the *mediated learning experience* (Feuerstein, 1979; Klein & Feuerstein, 1984). As discussed by Klein (this volume), adult selection, exaggeration, and accentuation of objects and events focuses the young child's perception and selective attention. As the child internalizes these adult-structured exchanges, he or she also becomes capable of selectively focusing the partner's attention, thus creating the reciprocity basic to true collaboration.

Behavioral Regulation—Approval, Disapproval, and Behavioral Monitoring

As mentioned above, during the preschool period the child experiences a transition from dependency on external sources of regulation to more internalized self-regulatory mechanisms. During the infancy period, basic dyadic skills of social regulation are consolidated that enable both parent and child to keep one another on task, and to evaluate one another's contributions to the problem-solving process (Moss, in press; Strayer & Moss, 1989). Adult positive reinforcement has long been considered to be an important regulatory strategy in the experimental literature (Baer & Wolfe, 1968; Bruner, 1966) as well as by researchers who have explored the effects of maternal style on cognitive development (Farran & Ramey, 1980;

Hess & Shipman, 1964; Olson et al., 1984; Sigel, 1982). Performance-contingent approval provides specific feedback as to goal attainment as well as general recognition of the child's competence. Thus rewarding activity has been identified by Feuerstein (1979) and Klein and Feuerstein (1984) as a prime mediator of the young child's developing sense of self-competence.

A developmental model of the role of various forms of adult regulation has been put forth by Deci and Ryan (1985). They suggest that the relative amount of approval, disapproval, and behavioral monitoring experienced in parent–child interactions during the infancy and early preschool years influences the child's mastery orientation. Their model describes the child's passage from an extrinsic or externally regulated motivational set to a more autonomous, intrinsically regulated one. Performance during the stage of extrinsic regulation is controlled solely on the basis of expected external contingencies. At the second level, the child regulates himself or herself with self-administered approval or disapproval applied contingently. By the third stage, early experiences in other-affirming, informationally adequate contexts are internalized as facilitative internal working models that permit organization of behavior according to value orientations. Conversely, intrusive or unstructured contexts result in internal working models dominated by superordinate, self-critical functions that interfere with the consolidation of strategies for achieving valued objectives.

Our comparison of the interaction patterns of securely and insecurely attached children and their mothers during joint problem solving (Moss, in press; Strayer & Moss, 1989) demonstrated the interdependency of social regulative and cognitive developmental processes. During socially coordinated task engagement, we noted overconcentration on monitoring the partner's behavior and greater expression of disapproval in the insecure dyads. By 30 months, these relational dysfunctions were interfering with mother and child joint investment in more challenging cognitive activity. As discussed earlier, in a healthy collaborative context, partners must maintain a positive affective climate even when encountering obstacles to the realization of their objectives. An inability to do so may result in restriction of communication to less challenging levels of information exchange.

Metacognitive Abilities of the Preschool Period

According to Flavell, Speer, Green, and August (1981), between the ages of 3 and 5, the child shows a readiness to operate on his or her own mental representations—this age span may thus be seen as the beginning of the sensitive period for metacognitive development. Researchers interested in the development of self-regulation have also identified the beginning of the third year as a turning point in the acquisition of autonomous control strategies (Kopp, 1982; Vaughn, Kopp, & Krakow, 1984). As we have discussed elsewhere (Moss & Strayer, 1990), cognitive psychologists associate emerging self-regulatory ability during the third year with enhanced skills in memory, problem solving, and representation that permit redirection of attention in the service of an overall goal. Other researchers with a co-constructionist focus emphasize the importance of adult verbal modeling of the planning, monitoring, and evaluative functions they are structuring for the child during joint problem solving (Collins, Brown, & Larkin, 1982; Gauvain & Rogoff, 1988; Wertsch et al., 1980).

Brown and Deloache (1978) have identified four basic metacognitive activities that enter into the zone of proximal development during this period: (a) predicting the consequences of actions or events, (b) checking the results of one's own actions, (c) monitoring one's ongoing activity, and (d) reality testing or comparing subjective impressions with more objective criteria. In our studies with younger children, we noted that, by 30 months, children begin to verbally participate in reality testing exchanges with their mothers that involved comparisons between different social contexts that the child is familiar with. For example, mothers of day care children frequently asked: "Is our dollhouse like the one at your school?" Reality testing is remarkably similar to what Sternberg (1986) refers to as *selective comparison*—one of the processes involved in insightfully dealing with novel tasks and situations. As defined by Sternberg, selective comparison entails realizing the similarities and dissimilarities between new information and information acquired in the past, and using these relations to better understand a current object or event. Given that Sternberg has identified such insight skills as being of primary importance in differentiating the intellectually gifted from others, it is of considerable interest to see if these abilities are being practiced on an interpersonal plane by young gifted preschoolers and their parents.

Summary

Theoretically speaking, the zone of proximal development implies that parental support be assessed in terms of individual child capacities to comprehend and incorporate information made available during joint problem solving. Empirically, we know little about how the zone of proximal development changes with age (Paris & Cross, 1988) and even less about how parents modulate their scaffolding styles to children of the same age who may differ in intellectual abilities (Moss & Strayer, 1990). The information categories described above provide the basis for an observational system describing the age-appropriate strategies used by mothers and preschool children in joint problem-solving situations. However, in order to identify differences in gifted and nongifted children's zones of proximal development, it is necessary to reorganize various tactics in terms of their relative developmental challenge to the preschool child. We have adopted Sigel's (1982) concept of cognitive distancing to represent the degree to which various representational activities focus away from more concrete aspects of single objects and events, towards their more abstract interrelations.

With reference to problem *structuring*, the ability continually to adapt performance to an external set of rules and to an overall goal presents the greatest challenge to the preschool child. Sequencing a series of moves is a relatively simple task once the relation between these subgoals and the overall goal and rule structure has been determined. With respect to *elaborative* strategies, perceptual and contextual cue highlighting should be considered normative tactics that assist preschoolers' developing categorization skills. By comparison, object labeling at this developmental period is a relatively low-level distancing strategy of limited use in achieving success on problem-solving tasks adapted to the preschool period. Although labelling exchanges between adult and child are important in identifying elements of the problem space, further progress in joint problem-solving activities is dependent on isolating and recombining actions and object attributes. Problem *regulation* can be assumed to be in a transitory phase between dependence on adult affective and cognitive monitoring, and emerging self-regulatory strategies. The greatest developmental challenge is the acquisition of simple *metacognitive* skills such as predicting consequences, checking results, activity monitoring, and reality testing.

GIFTED CHILDREN AND THE ZONE OF PROXIMAL DEVELOPMENT

The Vygotskian model of learning suggests that children first experience a particular set of problem-solving activities in the presence of an adult and gradually come to perform these functions themselves. One way of conceptualizing the influence of early experience on the development of giftedness is that it provides a highly developmentally challenging mediated learning context (Klein, this volume). We can operationalize this context as one which encourages more complex levels of information exchange and at the same time allows the child to achieve mastery of more normative skills. The comparison of the informational context of verbal exchanges between mothers and gifted preschoolers with that of mothers and preschoolers of normal ability is a way of empirically identifying individual differences in children's zones of proximal development. For example, what proportion of verbal activity is concentrated in the elaboration of more developmentally challenging strategies as compared with more normative ones? What are the respective mother and child contributions to these exchanges in normal dyads and dyads where children have been identified as gifted?

Equally important is an examination of the social processes that, through internalization, come to structure and direct cognitive functions. As Wood (1989) has described, children who have experienced cognitively as well as socially engaging instruction are far more likely to subsequently take a more active role in facilitating their own learning than are children who have been exposed to teaching which is less attuned to compensating for their difficulties and allowing expression of areas of competency. Borokowski and Peck (1986) have suggested that gifted children gain their metacognitive advantages from an enriched environmental context prompted by parental reactions to signs of perceptual efficiency. This implies that parenting young gifted children involves somehow raising their consciousness about their memory, attention, and other skills. Klein (this volume) has described what this might entail on a practical level: "creating in the child a greater urge to focus clearly on stimuli, to search for meaning, to associate, to relate, compare, and contrast perceptions, to seek explanations, relations, and general information beyond what is perceived through the senses."

On a research level, we are faced with a number of intriguing questions: Are preschool high-IQ children more active in using normative cognitive skills during problem solving, and how is their expression of these competencies coordinated with the learning of more difficult metacognitive skills? If, as the work of Sigel (1982) suggests, parents of intellectually precocious children model metacognitive strategies to a grater extent than do parents of normal-ability children, how is such modelling related to child behavior? Is the greater metacognitive content of parental speech primarily a response to evidence of emerging metacognitive awareness in preschool high-IQ children which is not shown by normal-ability children? Do parents somehow assist the child in transforming other information-processing components into metacognitive strategies? The analysis of the interaction of mothers and their above-average and average-ability preschoolers during joint problem-solving provides a means for exploring these bidirectional influences between children's cognitive abilities and qualitative aspects of parental tuition during the preschool period (Moss & Strayer, 1990).

Mother—Child Interactions of High-IQ and Average-IQ Preschoolers

Our subjects for this study were 28 preschool children between the ages of 3 and 4 years of age. These children were selected from an initial pool of 150 middle-class nursery school students who had completed the Stanford-Binet Intelligence Test (Terman & Merrill, 1973). From this group, 20 children who had obtained overall IQ scores which exceeded 130 (and who are referred to here as "gifted"), and 20 who had obtained average scores, were selected for further testing. These 40 subjects completed the following battery of tests to provide additional data on cognitive and academic skills: The Block Design and Mazes subtests of the Wechsler Preschool and Primary Scale of Intelligence (Wechsler, 1974) assessing spatial-perceptual skills; the Numerical memory subtest of the McCarthy Scales of Children's Abilities (McCarthy, 1972) testing memory for short-term auditory stimuli; and the Reading and Math subtests of the Peabody Intellectual Achievement Test (Dunn & Markwardt, 1970) assessing preacademic skills. We combined these identification components to provide a valid, comprehensive index of intellectual precocity (Roedell, Jackson, & Robinson, 1980).

The final sample designated as "gifted" included 14 preschoolers who had obtained exceptionally high scores (at least two standard deviations above the mean) on at least one of the five tests in addition to the 130+ Binet score. The selection of a control group of 14 nongifted children who had average scores on all tests completed the final sample. Comparison of the two samples on demographic variables showed no difference with respect to family income, maternal mean age, number of hours of employment or level of education, child birth order, and number of siblings. Fathers' educational level was significantly higher in the gifted group.

Each mother and child pair completed three problem-solving activities during a filmed visit to a private apartment which served as our observation laboratory. The tasks (puzzles, a peg game, and free-block play) were designed to be informal and attractive to preschool children and to encourage adult participation. Tasks were pretested for difficulty level in order to ensure that they encouraged some form of teaching behavior from mothers and that comparable data could be obtained for all children. Mothers were instructed to do the tasks with their children, helping them as much or as little as they felt necessary. Each task was available for at least 10 minutes, with order constant for all subjects.

On arriving at the lab, mothers were shown a series of eight wooden puzzles graded according to difficulty. The puzzles, containing from 8 to 20 pieces, were colorful and attractive to young children. The mothers were asked to select one they thought their child would require some assistance to complete. When the mother–child pair had completed the first puzzle, the experimenter offered a second one. If the child's performance on the first puzzle revealed that the task had been too easy or too difficult, then a puzzle more suited to the child's ability level was presented. In order to assure comparable performance indices for all subjects, measures of interaction were derived only from the second and subsequent puzzles.

The second task was a modified version of the "Animal House" subtest of the WPPSI (Wechsler, 1974). The mother and child were given a white peg board divided into 24 squares, and a box of colored pegs. In each square there was a hole above which was a picture of one of four animals. The top row of the form board was already fitted with appropriate animal pictures and colored pegs, constituting a model for completing the rest of the board. The child's task was to associate the demonstrated animal–color pair and to place appropriate pegs under all animals to finish the game. The experimenter first explained the task to each mother and then directed her to help the child complete the board proceeding row by row from left to right.

The third task differed from the other two in that there was no specific solution. The experimenter presented a set of multicolored blocks and asked the mother–child pair to make something together. The blocks were quite attractive, and all children readily began to play with them.

Verbal behavior of each mother and child was coded from video segments using a coding system designed to specify in a means–end analysis the ongoing contribution of each partner's behaviors to arriving at the final goal. Information about coding rules, descriptive validity and interobserver reliability data are reported in Moss and Blicharski (1986) and Moss and Strayer (1990). Verbal categories were arranged in five content classes graded according to the level of cognitive distancing demands (Sigel, 1982). The following (as reported in Moss & Strayer, 1990) are brief class and category definitions:

The simplest level of information included statements or questions which did not highlight specific representational components of the problem space. This class, called *Maternal Low-level Distancing Demands* included: (a) Gives Solution—telling child to do a specific action leading to the solution of a particular subgoal; (b) Negative Feedback—indicating that the child made a wrong move, without providing an alternative strategy; (c) Disapproval—verbalizing displeasure noncontingent on task performance; and (d) Conduct Management—focusing the child's attention on nontask behavior (e.g., "Sit up straight"). *Child Low-level Distancing Demands* included: (a) Request Help—asking for aid, and (b) Reject Help—refusing mother's offer of assistance. The class of *Approval* included instances of positive reinforcement by mother contingent upon task performance. This class of activity was not scored for children.

Elaborative Tactics included: (a) Perceptual Cuing—describing size, shape, or color features of objects, or soliciting such information; (b) Functional Cuing—highlighting less perceptually salient contextual or logical associations (e.g., "Does a head go at the bottom of the puzzle?"); and (c) Labeling—naming an object or person.

The class of *Structuring Tactics* included: (a) Goal Stating—identifying the overall aim or goal of the activity (e.g., "I'm going to make a house"), or asking the other to do so (e.g., "What do you want to make with these blocks?"); (b) Identifying Subgoal—determining an intermediate stage of problem solution (e.g., "Let's put a roof on the house") or asking the other to do so (e.g., "where does this peg go?"); and (c) Rule Stating—indicating procedural boundaries for the ongoing activity (e.g., "You have to go from left to right") or asking for such information (e.g., "Which way do you have to go?").

Metacognitive Regulatory Tactics included: (a) Predicting Consequences—referring to the impact of future actions (e.g., "Will this piece fit in that space?"), (b) Checking Results—verifying already accomplished actions (e.g., "Is that right?"), (c) Monitoring Activity—judging the appropriateness of moves in terms of available resources such as time and materials (e.g., "I'm going too fast"), and (d) Reality Testing—matching subjective discriminations of events against more objective criteria (e.g., "Should you use such small blocks for the foundation?").

Teaching Strategies of Mothers of Gifted and Nongifted Children

Since we had chosen to observe interactive problem solving adapted to a wide range of problems, we chose three tasks (described above) differing with respect to both difficulty level and structure. Our first analyses were carried out to test whether groups differed significantly with respect to the type of strategies used on each task and whether mother or child strategies differed as a function of child sex. The answer to both of these questions was negative. In order to increase the power of any further analyses, we therefore combined data across the three tasks and across sex focusing only on child giftedness as the criterion group variable.

Tables 10.1 and 10.2 show the mean rate of mother and child use of different informational categories during the joint problem-solving sessions.[1]

Table 10.1. Mean Hourly Rate of Mother Strategies*

Class: Category	Gifted		Nongifted		
	Mean	SD	Mean	SD	p level
Nonfacilitative:	*15.4*	*8.6*	*45.7*	*19.9*	.001
Give Solution	8.4	7.1	30.0	15.0	.001
Negative Feedback	1.7	2.6	5.1	6.1	.06
Disapproval	0.4	0.9	1.6	2.2	.09
Conduct Management	4.9	5.4	9.0	9.0	.05
Approval:	*18.7*	*7.9*	*10.9*	*9.5*	.05
Elaboration:	*46.4*	*14.7*	*32.1*	*24.5*	.07
Perceptual Cueing	13.9	4.8	9.0	7.4	.05
Functional Cueing	18.3	10.1	7.1	7.1	.01
Labeling	14.3	7.8	16.0	12.9	—
Structuring:	*44.7*	*18.2*	*38.6*	*26.9*	—
Goal	7.0	3.2	3.4	4.5	.05
Subgoal	24.7	12.6	25.6	18.4	—
Rule	13.0	11.1	9.6	9.1	—
Metacognition:	*31.7*	*15.3*	*12.1*	*11.7*	.001
Predict Conseq.	5.7	4.8	0.6	1.7	.001
Check Results	5.1	3.9	4.7	5.8	—
Monitor Activity	11.6	8.6	3.0	3.1	.01
Reality Test	9.3	6.5	3.9	4.0	.05
Total	152.1	41.0	130.4	70.2	—

*Reprinted from "Interactive Problem-Solving of Mothers and Gifted and Nongifted Pre-schoolers," by Moss & Strayer, *International Journal of Behavioral Development*, 13(2), 1990. Reprinted by permission of Erlbaum.

---

[1] F values for all significant effects discussed in this section will not be reported here but are available in Moss and Strayer (1990) or upon request from the author.

Table 10.2. Mean Hourly Rate of Child Tactics*

Class: Category	Gifted		Nongifted		
	Mean	SD	Mean	SD	p level
Nondistancing:	*4.1*	*3.5*	*7.3*	*7.8*	ns
Requests Help	2.6	2.9	5.0	5.4	ns
Rejects Help	1.6	2.0	2.3	3.8	ns
Elaboration:	*19.9*	*13.0*	*14.6*	*8.5*	ns
Perceptual Cueing	8.7	4.5	7.0	6.6	ns
Functional Cueing	5.3	4.8	2.6	4.0	ns
Labeling	5.9	8.1	5.0	5.7	ns
Structuring:	*15.6*	*11.6*	*8.9*	*5.8*	.07
Goal	4.4	3.7	2.1	1.5	.05
Subgoal	6.6	7.6	5.9	4.9	ns
Rule	4.6	5.4	0.9	1.3	.05
Metacognition:	*13.0*	*9.0*	*3.1*	*2.9*	.001
Predict Conseq.	1.4	1.8	0.4	0.8	.08
Check Results	1.2	2.3	0.3	0.7	ns
Monitor Activity	4.3	5.3	0.7	0.9	.05
Reality Test	5.9	4.2	1.7	2.1	.01
Total	52.6	20.0	33.9	12.5	.01

*Reprinted from "Interactive Problem-Solving of Mothers and Gifted and Nongifted Pre-schoolers," by Moss & Strayer, *International Journal of Behavioral Development*, 13(2), 1990. Reprinted by permission of Erlbaum.

Comparisons on a global category level using t-tests showed that the greatest differences between mothers of gifted and nongifted children were in the highest and lowest distancing category levels. Mothers of gifted children were far more likely to use metacognitive strategies, while mothers of nongifted children were more likely to verbalize low-level distancing strategies. Mother groups did not differ significantly with respect to the two categories that represented their use of normative information levels, that is, statements and questions related to problem structuring and elaboration. If we look more closely within categories, the same pattern is evident. Mothers of the gifted group are more likely to converse at the upper limits of the zone of proximal development, while the comparison group is more likely to situate conversation in the middle range of information complexity. Results for the low-level distancing category clearly show that mothers of the nongifted group provide solutions far more often than do the other mothers, who seem to structure a context in which the child is sensitively manipulated into finding his or her own solution. For example, asking the child to predict what an anticipated series of moves will lead to (predict consequences), or to judge how a projected plan conforms to the goal and rule structure (reality testing), will help the child more autonomously restrict the set of possible solutions. Particularly in the case of young children the effective and emotionally satisfying application of strategies is dependent on such adult restrictions in problem definition (Moss, 1990). Valsiner (1984) and Klein (this volume) have also emphasized the positive function of adult mediation in reducing the complexity of the set of possible events and thus empowering the child to transcend the immediate present.

It is also apparent from the pattern of within-category results, that mothers of the nongifted group are spending more time managing the behavior of their children (conduct management) while the gifted mothers more actively encourage their children to monitor their own activity. *Conduct management* refers to comments aimed primarily at getting the child back on task, whereas the metacognitive skill of activity monitoring refers to adult comments that help children judge how they are proceeding while they are on task. It is likely that individual differences in children's self-controllability are affecting these maternal differences. In support of this explanation, Moss, Strayer, Cournoyer, and Trudel (1987) showed that 33-month-old toddlers of higher intellectual ability required significantly less maternal intervention during a delay of gratification task than did mothers of normal-ability children.

It is important to point out the similarities in the results of both groups. Both groups infrequently use negative feedback and disapproval, which are present in disproportionate amounts in the interactions of mother–child dyads with affective dysfunctions (Strayer & Moss, 1989). Rather, their extrinsic regulation of their children's behavior is more focused on providing positive evaluations, with mothers of gifted children being more approving or "rewarding" (Klein, this volume) in mediating their children's feelings of competence. In addition, the mothers do not differ overall in the proportion of their activity, which is concentrated on teaching normative structuring and elaborative skills, even though the gifted group is higher on some individual categories. Both mother groups also talk about subgoals and labels, tactics their children acquired at earlier ages, to a similar extent. This indicates that both mother groups are not only encouraging the learning of relatively new strategies like contextual and perceptual cue highlighting but are providing opportunities for their children to consolidate earlier acquisitions. The teaching styles of both groups can thus be considered to be informationally adequate and affectively affirmative. Contrary to certain myths, mothers of gifted children do not overcontrol the learning environment by exclusively concentrating on teaching developmentally challenging strategies. Their focus is not on restricting commu nication to cognitively enriching activities, but on also allowing the child to feel a sense of effectiveness and mastery with respect to the use of easier, more familiar tactics. As Renshaw and Gardner (1989) and Wood (1989) have emphasized, children who have experienced reciprocal and cognitively engaging instruction are far more likely to subsequently take a more active role in facilitating their own learning than are children who have been exposed to teaching methods which do not allow the child to express competence. As discussed above and elsewhere (Moss, in press), children need opportunities to consolidate learned skills as well as to acquire new ones.

Comparison of Gifted and Nongifted Children's Strategy Use

One of the questions posed at the beginning of this chapter concerned the extent to which differences in mother's verbal behavior was associated with individual child differences. It is possible that mothers of gifted children are more verbally active on a metacognitive level because their children precociously initiate planning, monitoring, and verification strategies. They are thus reacting to evidence of emerging metacognitive awareness that is not shown by nongifted preschoolers. In Table 10.2, the strategies used by gifted and nongifted preschoolers during joint problem solving with their mothers are compared. The far fewer number of statistically significant effects present here, as compared with Table 10.1, shows that the child groups are overall much less distinct than the mother groups. Both gifted and nongifted preschoolers are similar overall in focusing most of their exchanges with mother in the developmentally normative elaborative and structural categories. With respect to their use of various elaborative strategies, both gifted and nongifted children focus mostly on perceptual cues that highlight object attributes such as shape, size, and color. Both child groups request or reject help relatively infrequently.

The primary difference is in the metacognitive category. Gifted children more frequently reality test and monitor their activity. Besides these striking differences in metacognitive expression, gifted preschoolers also talk about problem rules and define goals to a greater extent than do their average-ability peers. As discussed above, these two structuring tactics present a greater developmental challenge to children of this age than does simple subgoal sequencing, since they require viewing the problem more abstractly.

These apparent differences in the rate of metacognitive strategies used by gifted and nongifted preschoolers could indicate that individual differences in metacognitive abilities are already present. Maternal differences could then simply be a reflection of differing child competence levels. However, when mean rates of all tactics used by gifted children are compared with those of the nongifted group, it is evident that gifted children are higher in use of all strategies except for those involving low-level distancing demands. This is reflected in their total rate of verbal behavior which is significantly higher than that of the nongifted group.

In order to test the hypothesis that gifted children's use of metacognitive tactics represented a distinctive strategy, we reanalyzed our data controlling for these overall differences in verbal ability by using proportional rather than rate measures. These results showed that, whereas the differences evident in maternal use of different tactics were upheld, gifted children's greater use of reality testing and activity monitoring was no longer evident when their higher verbal rates were controlled. These results suggest that, unlike mothers who showed clearer stylistic differences within and across-categories, the child differences are at least, in part, a reflection of gifted children's greater language fluency.

ANALYZING THE SEQUENCE OF INTERACTION

Although these first analyses had established contrasting patterns in mothers' use of high-level (metacognitive) and low-level (primarily solution-giving) distancing strategies, they did not clearly indicate the contribution of individual child differences to these effects. The comparison of rate and proportional measures had indicated that gifted children did not yet have a distinct metacognitive profile although their mothers certainly did. The young gifted children's emerging metacognitive competence seemed somehow connected to their superior language abilities and to their immediate social context. The link between these findings and Vygotsky's (1986) theoretical ideas about the gradual transformation of the role of language from a tool of communication to one of structuring higher level thinking was fascinating. Yet further empirical navigation of the "murky embryonic waters" of metacognition required a methodology that permitted us to explore how individual contributions to ongoing activity are combined into dyadic patterns.

The examination of correlations between mother and child individual measures was rejected as a solution to this problem, since this method is not adapted to capturing the mutual adjustments which characterize the dynamics of joint participation. As a more interesting alternative, we chose to further analyze mother–child interaction within a sequential framework. In essence, sequential analysis allows one to see if particular behaviors of one partner will regularly lead to a particular response from another partner. This technique can be useful in operationalizing certain Vygotskian concepts discussed above, such as the zone of proximal development, the transition from other-regulation to self-regulation, and internalization of higher cognitive functions (Vygotsky, 1978, 1986).

We can trace developmental changes in the zone of proximal development by examining how particular sequences of mother–child behaviors change as a function of age. Whereas some patterns are more probable at later ages, others that may have dominated the interactive repertoire at an earlier age become extremely rare events. For example, whereas mothers and toddlers engage in frequent imitative labelling sequences, this kind of interaction is quite infrequent during the preschool period. Changes in the zone of proximal development can thus be traced in terms of the stability of particular combinations of social and cognitive tactics at different ages.

Assessing whether one partner "other-regulates" the behavior of the other to a greater extent, or whether interaction is more reciprocal, involves looking at each interactant's contribution to the exchange. If one partner's probability of using a particular cognitive tactic alters in response to a behavior performed by the other, then the first act can be interpreted as dependent on the second act. For example, if mothers of gifted children primarily use metacognitive strategies contingent to their children's statements at the same high-distancing level, then it is reasonable to conclude that the child act is directing the maternal response. Alternatively, if gifted children's metacognitive tactics are expressed contingent to maternal metacognitive initiations then the former's behavior can be considered to be largely under maternal control. If children can demonstrate their metacognitive competence freely regardless of what maternal act precedes, then they are showing considerable self-regulation in its use.

The developmental examination of changing initiation and response tendencies of partners engaged in joint cognitive activities also gives empirical meaning to the Vygotskian concept of internalization. For example, one indication of a child's increasing autonomous control over a particular strategy is decrease in the extent to which the child's use is dependent on external elicitation. Certain planning or evaluative tactics may, at first, only be used following direct maternal elicitation. An example of a metacognitive exchange directly controlled by one partner is a mother asking her young

3-year-old child, who has placed a large block over two smaller ones, "What will happen to your tower if you put that big one on top?" and the child answering, "It'll fall down." Several months later, the child's prediction of consequences may be elicited as a response to a less direct maternal initiative, such as "There's something funny about your tower." When the child has fully consolidated a tactic, he or she should not only use it more frequently but be able to initiate it independently, combine it with other tactics and thus play a greater role in integrating the skill in newly created strategies.

Sequential Dependency in Gifted and Nongifted Mother-Child Exchanges

In order to see if the pattern of interactive dependencies was similar for the two groups, tactics used by both mothers and children in the gifted group were combined into two contingency tables. One table represented child responses to maternal initiations, while the second regrouped maternal responses to child initiations. The same procedure was followed for the nongifted group resulting in a total of four contingency tables.

Our first sequential analyses were aimed at determining if there was an overall pattern of dependency of maternal acts on child acts. In other words, is there a general tendency for particular maternal responses to follow particular child initiations? If, for example, it was found that maternal responses were largely controlled by the quality of preceding child activity, then this finding would support the hypothesis that individual child differences are largely responsible for the qualitative differences in the verbal behavior of mothers. Chi-square goodness of fit tests of the contingency tables representing maternal responses to child initiations were used to test this hypothesis.[2] The results of these sequential analyses were nonsignificant for both gifted and nongifted dyads. This indicated that mothers did not modulate the complexity of their verbal behavior as a function of specific child verbal initiations.

To test the alternative hypothesis that the quality of children's strategy verbalization was largely dependent on mothers' cues, this series of analyses was repeated on the two remaining tables, which showed gifted and nongifted child responses to maternal initiations (Table 10.3). This time the results of the chi square tests were highly significant for both groups. Both gifted and nongifted preschoolers

---

[2] Further methodological details concerning the sequential analyses are available in Moss and Strayer (1990).

Table 10.3. First-Order Transitions in Mother-Initiated Exchange*

A) Gifted Dyads

| Maternal Act | Child Response | | | | Maternal Initiation Probability |
	Non-Dist.	Elab.	Stru.	Meta-Cogn.	
Nondistancing	.02[b]	.02	.01	.01	.05
Approval	.01	.00	.02	.04[b]	.07
Elaboration	.01	.23[b]	.05	.05	.35
Structuring	.02	.09	.18[b]	.03[a]	.32
Metacognition	.02	.06	.05	.08[b]	.21
Child Response Probabilty	.08	.40	.31	.21	1.00

B) Nongifted Dyads

| Maternal Act | Child Response | | | | Maternal Initiation Probability |
	Non-Dist.	Elab.	Stru.	Meta-Cogn.	
Nondistancing	.12[b]	.12[b]	.06	.02	.32
Approval	.02	.01	.02	.01	.06
Elaboration	.03	.24[b]	.04	.02	.33
Structuring	.04	.10	.11[b]	.02	.27
Metacognition	.00	.01	.00	.01[b]	.02
Child Response Probabilty	.21	.48	.23	.08	1.00

Note: Chi-Square Tests for Transition Probabilities. Number of exchanges is 238 for gifted and 187 for nongifted.
[a]$p < .05$
[b]$p < .01$
*Reprinted from "Interactive Problem-Solving of Mothers and Gifted and Nongifted Pre-schoolers," by Moss & Strayer, *International Journal of Behavioral Development*, 13(2), 1990. Reprinted by permission of Erlbaum.

use of particular strategies was highly dependent on the type of strategy initiated in the directly preceding maternal utterance. Thus, mothers appear to control the level of verbal information exchange irrespective of individual child differences. It was clearly not the case that the metacognitive teaching style of mothers of gifted children was a response to gifted children's autonomous expression of self-regulatory tactics like reality testing and activity monitoring. Similarly, the solution-giving style of mothers of nongifted children could not be considered to be directly dependent on any particular child verbal activity.

Our finding of dependence of child verbal acts on preceding maternal statements prompted us to undertake further analysis of the two child-response matrices using chi square tests (Table 10.3). This time the focus was on the particular tactics rather than on global patterns. What patterns were evident within each group, and did these exchange patterns differ between groups? For example, what was the probability of gifted children using metacognitive tactics in conversational sequences initiated by mothers, compared with that of nongifted children? These results indicate striking similarity in the communicative context of both groups during joint problem-solving activity. Preschool children are most likely to verbalize a particular tactic just consequent to maternal utterance of the same strategy. This pattern of child matching of maternal strategy level simultaneously facilitates the development of cognitive, communicative, and affective processes (Strayer & Moss, 1989). On a cognitive level, such mutual comparison of subjective representations of objects and actions during joint activity extends the child's understanding of the conceptual group of which a particular object is an exemplar. On a communicative level, child matching of maternal tactics becomes a mechanism for the child to play a role in the coconstruction of joint activity (Trevarthen, 1979). On an affective level, reciprocal, repetitive acts with familiar partners both convey a sense of shared intimacy and constitute a vehicle through which the child actively differentiates self from other (Nadel, 1986). In this sense, gifted and nongifted children's verbal expression of strategies is largely dependent on the other-regulation provided by the mother.

The comparisons of gifted and nongifted children's response tendencies during unmatched exchanges with their mothers also shows emerging differences in more independent application of skills. Consolidating the acquisition of a skill involves knowing how to apply it in a new context (in this case, a pattern other than matching) as well as restricting it in inappropriate contexts. It is interesting that the two nonmatched transitions in the gifted dyads' contingency table both involve metacognitive responses, while the one other effect for the nongifted group involves elaboration. These results suggest that these preschoolers may be at a developmental crossroad between dependency on other-regulation by the adult and more independent control of strategies.

Gifted children use metacognitive strategies, not only in a modelling context, but also in a more generalized response style. Table 10.3 shows that gifted children also plan, monitor, and evaluate following maternal structuring cues such as goals, rules and subgoals, and after receiving mother's approval. For example, Mother might say, "Let's make a house together" and the child replies with an idea for a plan such as, "I want our house to look like a king's palace." Gifted children are also significantly more likely to express their emerging metacognitive competence following their mothers' positive remarks about their child's competence. For example, after mother says, "You did that item very well!" the child replies, "I hope the next one is just as easy." The last finding supports the idea discussed at the beginning of the chapter of a dependency between gifted children's emerging metacognitive competence and parents' modelling of the positive self-attributions that underpin task persistence. Parental emphasis on these positive affective attitudes which will motivate and maintain the learning process are modelled as an integral part of the acquisition process. When metacognitive skills are consolidating, the child who has interactive experiences that are both cognitive and affectively facilitative shows mastery of the procedures involved in the skill as well as a sense of ownership of the outcome of the activity.

Whereas these consolidating metacognitive patterns are not evident in the responses of nongifted children, these children are displaying control of elaborative tactics. Normal-ability preschoolers show that they can generalize a perceptual or functional elaborative response also following more indirect maternal elicitation. For example, when mothers say, "This piece belongs here," the child will elaborate in saying, "Blue and blue belong together." We interpret these patterns as an empirical illustration of the Vygotskian model that suggests that problem-solving strategies are first used as responses in adult-controlled contexts, and subsequently used as responses to more indirect elicitation before the child becomes capable of independently generating these strategies. Further evidence to support this interpretation is afforded by comparing the overall probability of gifted and nongifted children's responses for each different category. Twenty-one percent of gifted children's responses are at a metacognitive level, compared to only 8% of those of the nongifted group. Forty-eight percent of all nongifted children's responses involved elaboration, compared to 40% of gifted children's. These figures indicate distinctive response profiles even though, as our first analyses showed, the children's initiation profiles are not clearly differentiated. We suspect that these profile differences will continue to widen with development, showing much clearer differences in gifted children's independent initiation of metacognitive tactics by the early school-age period, as shown by Borokowski and Peck (1986).

THE ROLE OF CHILD LANGUAGE AND ATTENTION IN ELICITING MATERNAL RESPONSE

Although these results clearly demonstrated the role of mothers in influencing the development of problem-solving strategies, we were somewhat uncomfortable with the picture they presented of the child's contribution. Firstly, where were the bidirectional effects which Schaffer (1984) has nicely summarized as follows: "The recent picture of parent–child relationships which has emerged is that of parents taking great care to fit their behavior to the child's, sensitively taking account of his particular state and condition at the time, adjusting their behavior accordingly, and all along ensuring that their stimulus input is properly adapted to the child's abilities to meaningfully absorb it" (p. 169)? Secondly, what was the contribution of gifted children's greater verbal fluency which was related, as shown by the comparison of the rate and proportional analyses, to their use of metacognitive tactics like reality testing and activity monitoring?

These issues prompted us to undertake yet another series of sequential analyses focused not only on direct exchange of information but also on children's individual expression of tactics. One indication of verbal fluency is the child's ability to talk about a series of object or event representations. For example, "This is a house with a three-car garage and it is located in Westchester," is a combination of three tactics in our coding scheme—labelling, perceptual cue, and contextual cue. It is easy to imagine an adult replying to this child's statement with the question "Do you think it costs a lot of money?" which would be coded according to our taxonomy as a metacognitive cue encouraging the child to reality test. It is a lot more difficult to move the exchange to this more complex, integrative level in response to a more simple child description involving only one descriptive element, for example, "This is a house." We therefore compared the children in relation to the number of different tactics they were able to verbalize sequentially before eliciting a maternal response.

We found that gifted preschoolers regularly combined several informational components before a maternal intervention whereas nongifted children were more likely to note single object attributes or problem subgoals. On a communicative level, the verbal fluency of the gifted preschoolers results in their being more likely to engage their partners in more prolonged and higher level conversations. These overt signs of readiness to engage in task-oriented dialogues may be considered to be important social and cognitive cues of the child's emerging ability to combine and manipulate his or her own mental representations. The adult can build on the child's self-regulatory competence by combining it with the learning of specific procedures for reorganizing representational components in means–end analysis.

Since the contribution of maternal interventions and child independent abilities are necessarily confounded in a joint play situation, it was difficult to identify further components of gifted children's self-regulatory competence that might exist independently of maternal structuring. Furthermore, in deciding to choose difficult cognitive tasks for this study, we placed the children in a situation of greater dependency on adult verbal directives. A separate study of preschoolers co-ordination of self-control tactics during a delay of gratification task (Moss et al., 1987) enabled us and our collaborators to take a closer look at the relation between IQ and more independent child self-regulatory competence.

In this second study, in order to identify associations between intellectual ability, competence in self-control, and differential use of self-regulatory tactics, 48 toddlers aged 33 months were observed during two delay-of-gratification tasks with mother present (Moss, Strayer, Cournoyer, & Trudel, 1987). Since task demands were relatively easier than those of the study discussed above and the tasks were not predefined in a collaborative framework, these tasks elicited far more child than maternal activity. More than 80% of children's activity during the delay period consisted of nonverbal as compared with verbal behaviors. Previous research has shown the importance of looking away from forbidden materials in maintaining delay behavior (Vaughn, Kopp, Krakow, Johnson, & Schwartz, 1986). Our results showed that the child's ability to shift attention away from the task material covaried significantly with child IQ scores as assessed by the Stanford-Binet (Terman & Merrill, 1972). Interestingly, this delay tactic was not associated with any kind of maternal assistance of a verbal or nonverbal nature. In fact, the mothers of the highest controllers intervened significantly less than did those of the average group. Intellectually advanced children's ability to shift attention to and from objects as a function of task objectives can thus be considered to be an autonomously generated and executed cognitive operation by the third year of life.

The presence of this nonverbal self-regulatory mechanism can also be seen as a cue to mothers of the child's readiness to move to a more metacognitive level of problem solving. In combination with indices of verbal fluency, these child contributions to interactive situations help parents assess the child's individual zone of proximal development and modulate the complexity of information exchange accordingly. We noted also that the ability to shift attention was not associated with any other child behaviors which were shown to facilitate success on the delay task suggesting that our subjects could not yet coordinate this cognitive operation as a component in an overall strategy. As Vaughn et al. (1986) and Yates and

Mischel (1979) have noted, very young children do not seem to be conscious of specific plans which will facilitate delay but rather engage in tacit, unconscious strategies which later come under direct cognitive control.

In summary, two cognitive characteristics which distinguish young gifted children from those of average ability are the ability to verbalize a series of problem-solving tactics and to control attention to objects and events more flexibly and appropriately. In performing these operations, gifted children show considerable self-regulation by the age of 3 years. These qualitative differences in gifted children's information processing prepare them for a level of interaction which extends these existing competencies to a greater range of situations and problems. These conclusions are supported by other research, as summarized by Kanevsky (1990), which has identified gifted children's greater ability to solve problems, to quickly access and flexibly use stored knowledge and to benefit from feedback and information. It is likely that parents of gifted children are encouraged to focus interactions on a metacognitive level by these cues evident in their children's task performance and conversational style (Moss, 1990). In summary, the emergence of metacognitive functions in gifted children seems to depend on how social interaction helps to mediate and organize the young child's representational processes.

SUMMARY AND CONCLUSIONS

At the beginning of this chapter we posed several questions about the contributions of instructional contexts and individual child differences to the emergence of metacognitive competence in gifted children. In essence, we found that the level of metacognitive ability manifested by gifted and nongifted children during joint problem solving is a function of (a) the quality of instruction the child receives, (b) the extent to which the child is able to benefit from adult assistance, and (c) a relational context which permits flexible and reciprocal negotiation of roles as a function of ongoing task demands. Mothers of gifted children seem to direct development toward the metacognitive level globally in advance of the emergence of autonomous metacognitive strategies in their children's problem solving. However, the way in which the child demonstrates his or her ability to self-regulate acquisitions of earlier periods is an important clue to the adult about how quickly to progress within this zone of proximal development. Thus, the achievement of metacognitive levels of exchange also depends on the gifted child's greater cognitive flexibility in combining verbal representations and redirecting attention.

In what ways are the teaching strategies of mothers of gifted and nongifted children similar and how do they differ? Our results suggest that the interactive styles of both groups of mothers could be labelled as generally facilitative and comprehension-fostering. Both groups are generally approving of their children and do not overly criticize child behavior. It is expected that both groups of children will develop motivational styles that lead to the general feeling of being a competent learner. We base this conclusion on the fact that there were relatively few differences related to the acquisition of basic developmentally appropriate cognitive skills. Our analyses showed similar patterns for the gifted and nongifted groups in the matching of structuring and elaborative tactics. Few differences exist in how both groups assist their preschoolers in making functional and perceptual connections between objects and actions and foster vocabulary extension related to the acquisition of verbal labels. These normative teaching strategies are so salient to preschool development that they can be expected to be fostered in the parent–child interactions of normal populations.

However, the results obtained in this study can certainly not be simply described as different child responses to similar maternal teaching styles. This study suggested that mothers of gifted and nongifted young children differ most in terms of their mediation of skills that were clearly at the upper limits of the preschool child's zone of proximal development. It would be easy to say that mothers' stylistic differences were simply a result of gifted children's greater responsiveness to maternal metacognitive initiations. However, our results do not support this conclusion. With respect to nondistancing and metacognitive tactics, it is important to point out that both gifted and nongifted preschoolers followed their mothers' lead in the use of both of these categories. Nongifted children had established a significant response pattern for using metacognitive tactics following maternal initiation just as the gifted children did. However, the former were exposed to such initiations far *less* frequently than were the latter group. At the same time, the nongifted children participated more often in exchanges in which the adult provided solutions.

The interactive climate of parent–child play is as important in determining learning outcomes as the cognitive level of instruction. Mothers and their gifted children were significantly more likely to exchange metacognitive information about the problem-solving task than were the comparison group. Gifted children at first only used metacognitive tactics as responses to direct maternal elicitation. In order to appropriately scaffold their preschoolers' metacognitive development, it was critical that their mothers sought to raise the level of cognitive exchange with their preschoolers beyond the normative level. It was equally critical that the children complied with maternal initiations of these more advanced tactics by accepting the challenge to operate on their own mental representations—the essential operation involved in metacognitive thinking. The interactional pattern of mothers and gifted preschoolers shows both children's acceptance of mother's guiding role in facilitating their acquisition of difficult metacognitive strategies, and mothers' sensitivity to ceding control to their children in the application of more familiar problem-solving strategies.

Gifted and nongifted children's early joint cognitive experiences may leave the children with different internal working models of the kinds of adult help they can expect in learning situations. These models may subsequently influence the development of their different learning styles in the school context. Cullen (1985) has identified types of learning styles in 8-year-olds that are associated with different responses to perceived failure in individual learning situations. This author reports that strategy-oriented children showed effective high-level coping responses such as using study skills or renewing effort by checking or monitoring strategies. Action-oriented children also showed active and constructive, but less strategic attempts to deal with failure usually involving requests for help or general effort renewal. Corno and Rohrkemper (1985) have described such self-regulated learners as those who can intentionally "deepen and manipulate the associative network in a particular content area and monitor and improve that deepening process" (p. 69). An essential component of these transformational processes is learning to conceptualize the forms of influence in learning situations and use the social resources available to accomplish objectives. The joint experiences in activity monitoring and reality testing engaged in by gifted children and their mothers involves the early practice of these skills on an interpersonal plane. Through these experiences, gifted children may come to attribute greater efficiency to themselves as self-regulated learners.

Before concluding, I would like to point out certain limitations of this study. This microlevel investigation has attempted to clarify further how the dyadic context might facilitate the young child's strategy expression. We have been very cautious about making any connections between children's actual performance of the task and parental verbalization of different strategies since our data do not include nonverbal behavioral indices. It is likely that mothers are responding to child differences that have not been measured in this study, such as task performance and other child characteristics not situationally evident. However, we reject the idea that performance differences alone explain maternal differences in strategy use. In other words, mothers are not solely guided by their children's evident success or difficulty with the task in choosing their strategy level. If this was the case, then clear differences in mothers' strategy level should have been apparent on at least two of our three tasks. As described earlier, our puzzle task was individually adjusted so as to be above each child's ability level, whereas the matching task was the same for all subjects. Presumably then, even if the gifted children performed better on the common task than did their nongifted peers and subsequently influenced their mothers to adopt a higher metacognitive level, this was not the case for the puzzle task, which was equally difficult for all subjects. However, as we discussed earlier, mothers did not change their overall styles as a function of the difficulty level presented by the task. In studies we are currently conducting of differences between gifted and nongifted dyads, which include detailed measures of nonverbal behavior, we will have the opportunity to more directly test the relationship between child performance and maternal strategy level.

In this chapter, our primary focus has been on how early patterns of mother–child co-regulation affects the emergence of metacognitive abilities during the preschool period. Given the significance of the preschool period for the emergence of self-regulatory cognitive skills and the hypothesized importance of social experience in the development of such skills, comparison of joint problem solving of gifted and nongifted preschoolers with their mothers has both theoretical and practical significance for the wider fields of developmental and educational psychology. There are currently two prevailing viewpoints among researchers in cognitive development. Those primarily concerned with age-stage commonalities in development focus almost exclusively on the measurement of individual cognitive attainments related to logical structures or information-processing abilities. More recently, there has been extensive preoccupation with the examination of social and cultural processes which scaffold or guide cognitive development (e.g., Rogoff, 1984). To date, there has been little specification of how the sociocultural context of cognitive development both contributes to and is itself molded by individual differences in child ability levels.

As we have discussed elsewhere (Moss & Strayer, 1990), a great deal of research supports the idea that, during the infancy period, contingent responsiveness facilitates child learning of basic cognitive skills. The child may thus come to expect that the difficulties likely to arise when new skills are practiced will be corrected by more expert social partners. However, by the preschool period, such solution giving may inhibit the activation of more cognitively reflective activity. In contrast to earlier periods of development, optimal scaffolding during the preschool period may involve less contingent responsiveness. This provides the preschooler with opportunities to coordinate already-acquired tactics such as labels and subgoals and exercise emerging self-regulation. For example, allowing the child to verbalize a series of functional and perceptual representations before proposing a restructuring metacognitive strategy facilitates the child's mental separation in space and time from the ongoing observable field (Moss & Strayer, 1990). The child may be learning the essential metacognitive skill noted by Flavell (1976), that comprehension will improve with time and effort rather than only by asking for adult help. This kind of response is structured enough to provide the consistency of response to the results of the child's actions with which to develop evaluative structures. At the same time, it affords enough autonomy to the child as initiator and regulator of future occurrences of the action.

The way in which the child demonstrates his or her ability to self-regulate acquisitions of earlier periods may be an important clue to the adult about how quickly to progress within the zone of proximal development. Children who are more advanced in the acquisition of basic language skills by the preschool period are more suitable as partners for metacognitive verbal exchanges in which verbal skills are the tools for creating new combinations of strategies. The development of more complex representational abilities is thus directly related to language in two ways: both by allowing the child to direct his or her own cognitive activities through self-regulating speech, and to benefit from other's language that structures and directs thinking and concept formation processes. Moreover, gifted children's ability to attend spontaneously to several object features without explicit instruction means that mothers can more easily shift the dialogue to a more superordinate level. This finding supports Borokowski and Peck's (1986) speculation that gifted children gain their metacognitive advantages from an enriched environmental context prompted by parental reactions to signs of perceptual efficiency. Similarly, the ability to shift attention in the service of an overall goal indicates gifted children's greater readiness to participate in joint planning and monitoring operations with an adult. Finally, the general enthusiasm for joint cognitive enterprises evidenced by gifted children's maintenance of longer interaction sequences shows children's acceptance of mother's guiding role in facilitating their acquisition of difficult metacognitive strategies.

Gifted preschoolers are not more likely independently to initiate planning, coordination, and verification strategies than are nongifted preschoolers. They are, however, far more likely to do so in a matching context and also show emerging ability to respond with metacognitive tactics following more indirect maternal prompts. Although at preschool age, gifted children's metacognitive competence remains bounded within the other-regulation provided by the adult, they appear to be at a developmental crossroad. The fact that gifted children's response style already reflects maternal problem-solving style suggests a widening profile difference that, at a higher developmental level, will show stronger differences in the children's independent use of metacognitive strategies.

From a Vygotskian point of view, interactive contexts serve as a primary channel for the child's active learning of sociocultural information. Internalization of early patterns of mother–child co-regulation influences the developmental organization of cognitive procedures for engaging in socially mediated learning and problem solving. However, along with the internalization of operations and procedures in early social learning contexts, the child has also internalized self-concepts and social representations associated with domains of knowledge. Knowledge of how to analyze problems is acquired along with models of how to engage social resources in facilitating one's cognitive efforts and expectations about the outcomes of such collaborative endeavors. Thus, the metacognitive knowledge and abilities emerging by school-age are, in part, transformations of components of established social, affective, and cognitive schemas formed in the context of early relationships. As stated by Albert and Runco (1986), "We have assumed all along that the attainment of eminence involves the gifted child's family in a number of ways—as product, as experience, as canalization and as the outcome of the family values and emphases involved in its expression" (p. 332). We hope that this chapter has contributed to the clarification of some of these processes. Further research should focus on how differences in the early interactive context continue to influence metacognitive performance in both individualized and collaborative situations.

REFERENCES

Albert, R. S., & Runco, M. A. (1986). The achievement of eminence: A model based on a longitudinal study of exceptionally-gifted boys and their families. In R. Sternberg & J. Davidson (Eds.), *Conceptions of giftedness*. New York: Cambridge University Press.

Baer, D., & Wolfe, M. (1968). The reinforcement contingency in preschool and remedial education. In R. Hess & D. Baer (Eds.), *Early education: Current theory, research and action*. Chicago: Aldine.

Bandura, A. (1977). Self-efficacy: Toward a unifying theory of behavioral change. *Psychological Review, 84*, 191–215.

Bandura, A. (1983). The self and mechanisms of agency. In J. Suls (Ed.), *Social psychological perspectives on the self*. Hillsdale, NJ: Erlbaum.

Bowlby, J. (1969). *Attachment and loss: Vol. 1. Attachment*. New York: Basic Books.

Bloom, B. (1985). *Developing talent in young people*. New York: Ballantine.

Borokowski, J. G., & Peck, V. A. (1986). Causes and consequences of metamemory in gifted children. In R. Sternberg & J. Davidson (Eds.), *Conceptions of giftedness* (pp. 182–201). New York: Cambridge University Press.

Bretherton, I., & Waters, E. (1985). Growing points of attachment theory and research. *Monographs of the Society for Research in Child Development, 50*.

Brown, A. L., & Deloache, J. S. (1978). Skills, plans and self-regulation. In R. S. Siegler (Ed.), *Children's thinking: What develops?* Hillsdale, NJ: Erlbaum.

Brown, A. L., Palincsar, A., & Armbruster, B. B. (1986). Instructing comprehension-fostering activities in interactive learning situations. In H. Mandl, N. Stein, & T. Trabasso (Eds.), *Learning and comprehension of texts*. Hillsdale, NJ: Erlbaum.

Bruner, J. (1966). *Towards a theory of instruction*. Boston: Belknap.

Bruner, J. (1983). *Child's talk*. New York: Norton.

Bruner, J. (1986). *Actual minds, possible worlds*. Cambridge, MA: Harvard Press.

Campione, J. C., & Brown, A. L. (1978). Memory, and metamemory development in educable retarded children. In I. Kail & J. Hagen (Eds.), *Perspectives on the development of memory and cognition*. Hillsdale, NJ: Erlbaum.

Case, R. (1978). Intellectual development from birth to adulthood: A neo-piagetian interpretation. In R. S. Siegler (Ed.), *Children's thinking: What develops?* Hillsdale, NJ: Erlbaum.

Collins, A., Brown, J., & Larkin, K. (1982). Interference in text understanding. In R. Spiro, B. Bruce, & W. Brewer (Eds.), *Theoretical issues in reading comprehension*. Hillsdale, NJ: Erlbaum.

Corno, L., & Rohrkemper, M. (1985). The intrinsic motivation to learn. In C. Ames & R. Ames (Eds.), *Research on motivation in education (Vol. 2). The classroom milieu* (pp. 53–85). New York: Academic Press.

Cullen, J. (1985). Children's ability to cope with failure: Implications of a metacognitive approach for the classroom. In D. Forrest-Pressley, G. Mckinnon, & T. Waller (Eds.), *Metacognition, cognition and human performance* (Vol. 2). New York: Academic.

Deci, E. L., & Ryan, R. M. (1985). *Intrinsic motivation and self-determination in human behavior.* New York: Plenum.

Dunn, L. M., & Markwardt, F. C. (1970). *Manual for the Peabody Individual Achievement Test.* Circle Pines, MN: American Guidance Service.

Farran, D. C., & Ramey, C. T. (1980). Social class differences in dyadic involvement during infancy. *Child Development, 51,* 254–257.

Feuerstein, R. (1979). *The dynamic assessment of retarded performers.* New York: University Park Press.

Flavell, J. H. (1976). Metacognitive aspects of problem-solving. In L. B. Resnick (Ed.), *The nature of intelligence.* Hillsdale, NJ: Erlbaum.

Flavell, J. H. (1987). Speculations about the nature and development of metacognition. In F. Weinert & R. Kluwe (Eds.), *Metacognition, motivation and understanding* (pp. 1–30). Hillsdale, NJ: Erlbaum.

Flavell, H., Speer, J. R., Green, F. L., & August, D. L. (1981). The development of comprehension monitoring and knowledge about communication. *Monographs of the Society for Research in Child Development, 46.*

Gauvain, M., & Rogoff, B. (1988). Collaborative problem-solving and children's planning skills. *Developmental Psychology, 25*(1), 139–151.

Gibson, E. J. (1969). *Principals of perceptual learning and development.* New York: Appleton Century-Crofts.

Hartup, W. W. (1987). Relationships and their significance in cognitive development. In R. Hinde, A. Perret-Clermont, & J. Stevenson-Hinde (Eds.), *Social relationships and cognitive development.* Oxford: Clarendon Press.

Heckhausen, H. (1987). Causal attribution patterns for achievement outcomes: Individual differences, possible types and their origins. In F. Weinert & R. Kluwe (Eds.), *Metacognition, motivation and human understanding* (pp. 143–184). Hillsdale, NJ: Erlbaum.

Hess, R. D., & Shipman, V. C. (1964). Early experience and the socialization of cognitive modes in children. *Child Development, 36,* 869–886.

Jackson, N. E., & Butterfield, E. C. (1986). A conception of giftedness designed to promote research. In R. Sternberg & J. Davidson (Eds.), *Conceptions of giftedness* (pp. 151–182). New York: Cambridge University Press.

Kanevsky, L. (1990). Pursuing qualitative differences in the flexible use of problem-solving strategy by young children. *Journal for the Education of the Gifted, 13*(2), 115–140.

Klahr, D. (1978). Goal formation, planning and learning by preschool problem-solvers. In R. Siegler (Ed.), *Children's thinking: What develops?* (pp. 181–213). Hillsdale, NJ: Erlbaum.

Klein, P., & Feuerstein, R. (1984). Environmental variables and cognitive development: Identification of potent factors in adult-child interaction. In S. Harel & W. Anastasio (Eds.), *The at-risk infant: Psychosocio-medical aspects.* Baltimore: Paul H. Brookes.

Kopp, C. (1982). Antecedents of self-regulation: A developmental perspective. *Developmental Psychology, 18,* 199–214.

McCarthy, D. (1972). *The McCarthy scales of children's abilities.* New York: Psychological Corporation.

Main, M., Kaplan, N., & Cassidy, J. (1985). Security in infancy, childhood and adulthood: A move to the level of representation. In I. Bretherton & E. Waters (Eds.), *Growing points of attachment theory and research. Monographs of the Society for Research in Child Development, 50,* 41–65.

Matas, L., Arend, R. A., & Sroufe, L. (1978). Continuity of adaptation in the second year: The relationship between quality of attachment and later competence. *Child Development, 49,* 547–557.

Meichenbaum, D., & Biemiller, A.J. (1990, May). *In search of student expertise in the classroom: A metacognitive analysis.* Paper presented to the Conference on Cognitive Research for Instructional Innovation, Maryland.

Moss, E. (1983). *Maternal teaching strategies and information processing skills in gifted and nongifted preschoolers.* Unpublished doctoral dissertation, Department of Educational Psychology, McGill University.

Moss, E. (1990). Social interaction and metacognitive development in gifted preschools. *Gifted Child Quarterly, 34*(1), 16–20.

Moss, E. (in press). The socio-affective context of metacognitive development. In T. Winegar & J. Valsiner (Eds.), *Children's development within social contexts: Metatheoretical, theoretical and methodological issues.* Hillsdale, NJ: Erlbaum.

Moss, E., & Blicharski, T. (1986). The observation of teaching and learning strategies in parent-child and teacher-child interaction. *Canadian Journal of Research in Early Childhood Education, 1*(2), 21–36.

Moss, E., Strayer, F., Cournoyer, M., & Trudel, M. (1987). Social roots of metacognition and self-control. *Canadian Journal of Early Childhood Education, 2*(1), 4–12.

Moss, E. S., & Strayer, F. F. (1990). Interactive problem-solving of mothers and gifted and nongifted preschoolers. *International Journal of Behavioral Development, 13*(2), 177–197.

Nadel, J. (1986). *Imitation and communication between young children.* Paris: Presses Universitaires de France.

Nelson, K. (1977). Cognitive development and the acquisition of concepts. In R. Anderson & R. Spiro (Eds.), *Schooling and the acquisition of knowledge.* Hillsdale, NJ: Erlbaum.

Ninio, A., & Bruner, J. (1978). The achievements and antecedents of labelling. *Journal of Child Language, 5,* 1–15.

Olson, S., Bates, J., & Bayles, K. (1984). Mother-infant interaction and the development of individual differences in children's cognitive competence. *Developmental Psychology, 20*(1), 166–179.

Paris, S. G., & Cross, D. R. (1988). The zone of proximal development: Virtues and pitfalls of a metaphorical representation of children's learning. *The Genetic Epistemologist, 16,* 27–37.

Paris, S. G., & Lindauer, B. K. (1978). Constructive aspects of children's comprehension and memory. In I. Kail & J. Hagen (Eds.), *Perspectives on the development of memory and cognition*. Hillsdale, NJ: Erlbaum.

Peck, V. A., & Borokowski, J. (1983, April). *Emergence of strategic behavior in the gifted*. Paper presented to the Society for Research in Child Development, Detroit.

Renshaw, P., & Gardner, R. (1989, April). *Process vs. product task interpretation and parental teaching practice*. Paper presented to the Society for Research in Child Development, Baltimore.

Robinson, N. (1987). Early precocity. *Gifted Child Quarterly, 31*(4), 162–164.

Roedell, W., Jackson, N. E., & Robinson, H. (1980). *Gifted young children— perspectives on gifted and talented education*. New York: Teacher's College, Columbia University.

Rogoff, B. (1984). Adult assistance of children's learning. In T. Raphael & R. Reynolds (Eds.), *Contexts of literacy*. New York: Longman.

Rogoff, B., Malkin, C., & McBride, K. (1984). Interactions with babies as guidance in development. In B. Rogoff & J. Wertsch (Eds.), *Children's learning in the zone of proximal development*. San Francisco: Jossey Bass.

Rohwer, W. D., Jr. (1973). Elaboration and learning in childhood and adolescence. In H. W. Reese (Ed.), *Advances in child development and behavior* (Vol. 8). New York: Academic.

Schaffer, H. R. (1984). *The child's entry into a social world*. New York: Academic.

Shatz, M. (1984). Contributions of mother and mind to the development of communicative competence: A status report. In M. Perlmutter (Ed.), *Parent-child interaction and parent–child relations in child development* (pp. 33–60). Hillsdale, NJ: Erlbaum.

Shore, B., & Dover, A. (1987). Metacognition, intelligence and giftedness. *Gifted Child Quarterly, 31*(1), 37–39.

Shure, M. B. (1987). Interpersonal problem-solving: A cognitive approach to behavior. In F. Weinert & R. Kluwe (Eds.), *Metacognition, motivation and human understanding* (pp. 191–207). Hillsdale, NJ: Erlbaum.

Siegler, R. (1978). *Children's thinking: What develops?* Hillsdale, NJ: Erlbaum.

Sigel, I. E. (1982). The relationship between distancing strategies and the child's cognitive behavior. In L. Laosa & I. Sigel (Eds.), *Families as learning environments for children* (pp. 47–87). New York: Plenum.

Sternberg, R. J. (1986). A triarchic theory of intellectual giftedness. In R. Sternberg & J. Davidson (Eds.), *Conceptions of giftedness* (pp. 223–246). New York: Cambridge University Press.

Strayer, F. F., & Moss, E. S. (1989). The co-construction of representational activity during social interaction. In M. Bornstein & J. Bruner (Eds.), *Interaction in human development*. Hillsdale, NJ: Erlbaum.

Strayer, F. F., Moss, E. S., & Blicharski, T. (1988). Biosocial bases of representational activity during early childhood. In T. Winegar (Ed.),

Social interaction and the development of children's understanding.
Norwood, NJ: Ablex Publishing Corp.

Terman, L. M., & Merrill, M. A. (1973). *Stanford-Binet intelligence scale manual for the third revision form LM.* Boston: Houghton-Mifflin.

Trevarthen, C. (1979). Communication and cooperation in early infancy: a description of primary intersubjectivity. In M. Bullowa (Ed.), *Before speech: The beginning of interpersonal communication* (pp. 321–346). Cambridge, UK: Cambridge University Press.

Valsiner, J. (1984). Construction of the zone of proximal development in adult-child joint action: The socialization of mealtimes. In B. Rogoff & J. Wertsch (Eds.), *Children's learning in the "zone of proximal development".* San Francisco: Jossey Bass.

Valsiner, J., & van der Veer, R. (1991). The encoding of distance: The concept of the zone of proximal development and its interpretations. In R. Cocking & K. Renninger (Eds.), *The development and meaning of psychological distance.* Hillsdale: Erlbaum.

Vaughn, B., Kopp, C., & Krakow, J. (1984). The emergence and consolidation of self-control from 18 to 30 months of age: normative trends and individual differences. *Child Development, 55,* 990–1004.

Vaughn, B., Kopp, C., Krakow, J., Johnson, K., & Schwartz, S. (1986). Process analyses of the behavior of very young children in delay tasks. *Developmental Psychology, 22,* 752–759.

Vygotsky, L. S. (1978). *Mind in society: The development of higher psychological processes.* Cambridge, MA: Harvard University Press.

Vygotsky, L. S. (1986). *Thought and language.* Cambridge, MA: MIT Press.

Wachs, T. D., & Gruen, G. E. (1982). *Early experience and human development.* New York: Plenum.

Walters, J., & Gardner, H. (1986). The crystallizing experience: Discovering an intellectual gift. In R. Sternberg & J. Davidson (Eds.), *Conceptions of giftedness* (pp. 306–331). New York: Cambridge University Press.

Wechsler, D. (1974). *Manual for the preschool and primary scale of intelligence.* New York: Psychological Corporation.

Wertsch, J. V. (1985). *Vygotsky and the social formation of mind.* Cambridge, MA: Harvard University Press.

Wertsch, J. V., McNamee, G., McLane, J. B., & Budwig, N. A. (1980). The adult-child dyad as a problem-solving system. *Child Development, 51,* 1215–1221.

Wood, D. J. (1989). *How children think and learn.* Oxford: Basil Blackwell.

Yates, B., & Mischel, W. (1979). Young children's preferred attentional strategies for delaying gratification. *Journal of Personality and Social Psychology, 37,* 286–300.

part V

Early Giftedness in a Social Key

chapter 11

Moral Reasoning, Moral Behavior, and Moral Giftedness: A Developmental Perspective

Golda R. Rothman

*Formerly Teachers College
Columbia University
New York, NY*

Developmental psychologists such as Jean Piaget (1932/1965) and Lawrence Kohlberg (1969) have outlined stages in the development of the child's moral reasoning. These stages represent ways of thinking that define children's conceptions of right and wrong in moral conflict situations. They emerge as the child actively deals, on his or her own terms, with the social and moral world. Within this theoretical framework, the reasoning the child uses in responding to hypothetical conflict situations forms the basis of our understanding the child's conceptions of the sociomoral events that he or she encounters.

The foundation of this developmental process emerges quite early. Through the infant's interactions with others, whom he or she comes to recognize as distinct from himself or herself, there gradually emerges a moral awareness and concern in recognition of another's wants and needs in relation to one's own (cf. Gauthier, 1971). As the infant grows into early childhood, the earliest capacity for human interaction grows into a capacity for reflecting on that interaction, and for viewing the demands of others on oneself as reciprocal to one's own demands on others. As the young child begins to take others into account in social interactions (cf. Damon, 1977, 1980), responding to the environment not only in terms of his or her needs, but within the context of relations with others, moral reasoning begins to emerge. According to Damon (1977, 1980), our understanding of moral reasoning in early childhood may be promoted by examining the major concerns of 4-year-olds in their daily interactions with others, and their conceptualizations of such issues.

This approach to the development of the child's understanding of sociomoral events appears, not only within the realm of moral reasoning, but also with regard to such related domains as social-conventional thought, pertaining to the developmental concept of social rules and conventions implemented for pragmatic reasons, and which 4- and 5-year-olds can distinguish from moral rules (cf. Turiel, 1975, 1980, 1983), as well as prosocial thought (cf. Eisenberg, 1982; Eisenberg-Berg, 1979), a specific aspect of positive justice whose developmental course emerges in early childhood. Clear developmental patterns have been charted within these, as within the moral domain.

Among the weave of emerging developmental patterns, however, threads of individual differences begin to appear: Some children progress at a faster rate through the stages of moral reasoning, and while mutuality and sensitivity to others begin to emerge, not only in reasoning, but in actual behavior as well, some take others into account more readily in their behavior. Some of these children may be among those identified as gifted in cognitive or artistic domains, and some not. Nevertheless, as we view this differential moral advance and an emerging "moral giftedness," we might ask what contributes to such differential advance and how higher forms of moral thought may be encouraged. We also need to ask how such encouragement of the development of moral reasoning and decision making is related to ultimate behavior.

Insight into the developmental nature of this relationship between moral reasoning and moral behavior has emerged from such studies as those by Rothman (1976, 1980) and Turiel and Rothman (1972). A clearer understanding of this interrelationship is vital to our understanding of decision making in real-life situations, ranging from ordinary everyday events to those of extraordinary consequences to the social order. It is also vital to our conceptualization of a "moral giftedness" encompassing decision making and behavior guided by reasoning and by an awareness of one's responsibility in the decision-making process.

In arriving at such a conception of "moral giftedness," we will examine the ways in which the development of moral reasoning may be encouraged and its relation to ultimate behavior.

MORAL REASONING

When Piaget (1932/1965) first conceptualized and defined moral reasoning as a developmental process, he focused on young children's conceptions of rules and on their movement from a heteronomous toward an autonomous moral orientation. Whereas 4-year-olds initially perceive rules as sacred and unchangeable, within the context of a "morality of constraint," 8- to 10-year-olds begin to perceive these as a product of group agreement and an instrument of group purpose, subject to modification. Reciprocal relations among peers in middle childhood thus inspire a "morality of cooperation." The emergence of the 10-year-old's general, interiorized principles from the specific rules of the 4-year-old are attributed by Piaget to a self-constructive process as the child engages in an active, two-way interaction with the environment. Qualitative changes in the child's thought (which affect the way the environment is conceptualized), along with the process of adult constraint and peer cooperation, are said to play significant roles in this developmentally constructive process.

Using Piaget's approach as a theoretical base, Kohlberg (1969) formulated a sequence of stages in the development of the child's moral reasoning. Each stage is said to represent an organization of thought in terms of which the child adjudicates between conflicting claims in situations of right and wrong. Through a process of cognitive conflict and disequilibrium (cf. Turiel, 1966; Walker, 1983), the child comes to perceive his or her present stage as inadequate in dealing with the conflict at hand, and developmental change takes place. Moral reasoning is seen as changing in sequence from about the ages of 6 or 7 into adulthood as the child's thought moves toward an increasingly internal standard with the development of his or her understanding of justice and reciprocity.

Kohlberg's stages, encompassed within three developmental levels, include: a preconventional level of Stages 1 and 2 prevelant in children under age 9, in terms of which moral judgments are based on an orientation to punishment, with rules and expectations perceived as external to the self; a conventional level of Stages 3 and 4, usually achieved around adolescence, with an orientation toward maintaining rules and expectations of society and authority; and a postconventional, principled level attained by few adults, in terms of which autonomous moral judgments are based on universal principles of justice and on the formulation and acceptance of general principles underlying societal rules (cf. Kohlberg, 1976). Kohlberg's theoretical stages do not directly address the moral thinking of early childhood, since children as young as age 4, for example, have not yet differentiated the meaning of moral concepts from punishment, judging only in terms of good and bad consequences, nor do they distinguish the social perspectives of others from those of oneself in judging moral conflict situations (cf. Selman, 1976). Their justifications for moral choices usually involve primarily a reassertion of the choice.

Moral Reasoning in Early Childhood

William Damon's studies of moral reasoning, however, have focused on the development of conceptions of justice in children as young as age 4 (cf. Damon, 1977, 1980). By examining children's everyday concerns, such as sharing and fairness, Damon has delineated levels in the development of positive justice—levels that emerge within the context of social interaction with peers. These levels range from the practical, self-interest perspective of the 4-year-old, for whom fairness is one's own desires; to fairness based on equality, then merit, then need, from about 5 to 8 years of age; toward the distinction between the practical and the moral at age 8, a distinction which lacks a moral perspective outside the concrete situation.

Of significance in this process of emerging developmental conceptualizations, both in early and later childhood, are the opportunities for role taking the child encounters as he or she interacts with the environment through participation in the social world. Such participation in society exposes the child to a conflict among perspectives, the resolution of which parallels moral growth (Selman, 1971, 1976; Selman & Damon, 1975) in early childhood and beyond and becomes a prerequisite for certain moral stage transitions (Selman & Damon, 1975; Walker, 1980). Selman's (1976) and Selman and Damon's (1975) studies of children ages 4 and older clearly suggest that, as the developing child engages in active decision making regarding interpersonal claims, his or her understanding of social relations (as reflected in the ability to take the perspective of another) plays a significant and necessary, but insufficient, role in the way in which he or she resolves conflicts between people with disparate points of view.

Early prosocial concerns. Just as everyday problems of justice and early concerns with friendship and sharing, according to Damon (1977), form the basis for young children's moral reasoning, as do active interactions and social relations within Piaget's (1932/1965) and Kohlberg's (1969) theories, in ordinary everyday situations young children's capacity for moral thoughts and feelings may surpass our theoretical expectations.

Matthews (1980), in a study of philosophical thought in children as young as 3 and 4 years of age, suggests that they are quite capable of tackling classic problems of philosophy that come naturally to them, and that it is only later that they must conform their interests to the expectations of the adult world. So, too, in the realm of moral development we find, for example, early indications of moral reasoning and of prosocial concerns. Such indications may in essence suggest our need to delve further into these earliest processes and to encourage their emergence before conformity to alternative expectations becomes prevalent. For example, Hoffman (1975), in examining the development of a sense of the other, points to indications of the toddler's awareness of another's inner state and his or her ability to assess the needs of another which differ from his or her own. Even before age 2, the rudiments of role taking may be present in familiar, natural settings in which the child is spontaneously motivated prior to its emergence in more elaborate forms. Although the toddler may not necessarily be adept at effective forms of helping, rudimentary attempts may emerge as he or she engages in such behavior as sharing and comforting (e.g., cf. Dunn & Munn, 1986; Rheingold, Hay, & West, 1976). In preschool children, such spontaneous prosocial behavior has been further explored in relation to the child's reasoning about that behavior (Eisenberg, Pasternack, Cameron, & Tryon, 1984; Eisenberg-Berg & Hand, 1979; Eisenberg-Berg & Neal, 1979). An examination of the reasoning and motivation for young children's helping behavior has led Bar-Tal, Raviv, and Leiser (1980) to consider stages in the development of the quality of such behavior as sharing, as indicated by the child's differential expressed motivation within different sharing conditions.

Encouraging moral growth. By attempting to understand the child's earliest conceptions of the sociomoral world, which do not necessarily match those of adults, and by respecting these conceptions along with the child's concomitant attempts at prosocial behavior, we can provide a support system for moral growth. Providing social interaction opportunities for role taking and decision making as the child grows further encourages an emerging sense of responsibility and moral growth. Through social interaction and peer participation, the child's moral orientation becomes increasingly intrinsic, increasingly viewed in terms of ultimate consequences and the facilitation of the social order.

Encouraging Moral Reasoning: The Emergence of Individual Differences

In terms of the above developmental perspective, the process of peer interaction, with its concomitant opportunities for role taking and decision making, plays a crucial role in the development of moral reasoning and in attempts at encouraging and fostering moral growth. Studies of peer group participation and social roles have shown, for example, that leaders who are in positions of peer group centrality function at a higher level of moral reasoning than nonleaders (Harkness, Edwards, & Super, 1981; Keasey, 1971; Tietjen & Walker, 1985). Children's maturity of moral reasoning has, in fact, been found to be correlated with their concern for the welfare of others, with self-confidence, and with security in their social relations with peers (Harris, Mussen, & Rutherford, 1976), all of which are associated with leadership. Whether those functioning at a higher moral reasoning level more readily become leaders and develop those personal qualities associated with leadership, or leadership and its concomitant qualities foster higher reasoning, is not always clear. What does emerge clearly is the significance of the interactions involved in the process of leadership in relation to moral growth. Furthermore, when the social structure of society provides children with the opportunity for peer interaction, role taking, and decision making analogous to that which leadership provides, stage of moral reasoning is similarly accelerated. For example, children raised in Israel on a kibbutz, with its greater peer interaction (Levy-Schiff & Hoffman, 1985; Nahir & Yussen, 1977), autonomy (Lifshitz & Ramot, 1978), and cooperative organization (Avgar, Bronfenbrenner, & Henderson, 1977), show greater moral advance than those raised in the city (Snarey, Reimer, & Kohlberg, 1985).

The social context in which the child develops, with its varied opportunities for social interaction, thus plays a significant role in encouraging moral growth. Studies of the "moral atmosphere" of schools, for example, have suggested that young adolescent students in alternative programs that focus on participation and discussion within an atmosphere of trust, caring, and responsibility for others show greater moral gains than students in traditional schools (Crockenberg & Nicolayev, 1979; Higgins, Power, & Kohlberg, 1984; Power, 1979). What we learn from these studies is that a strong sense of group purpose, which emerges when group members participate openly in moral discussion and decision making within the context of concern and tolerance for others, is a condition conductive to moral growth.

Similarly, in the earlier years of education as well, individuals who create an atmosphere of trust, caring, and concern for others can foster moral growth. They respect the young child's decision-making capacities and encourage active participation in the moral issues that naturally arise within the context of daily social interactions, regardless of how simple or complex these may appear. Within the educational setting, Selman (1976) has suggested that the social and moral conflicts of the classroom be used as a "natural" basis for enhancing children's understanding of the moral aspects of social relations and for developing social thought (i.e., the perspectives and social reasoning of others in relation to one's own).

Within the home as well, such reciprocal "give and take" encourages the development of moral reasoning. Holstein (1972), for example, found that parents who reasoned at Kohlberg's highest principled level were more encouraging at their eighth-grade children's participation in family discussions of moral dilemmas than were lower level conventional parents; and Buck, Walsh, and Rothman (1981), studying 10- to 13-year-olds, concluded that such encouragement and consideration of the child's view were reflected in child-rearing methods. This also related to the children's higher moral reasoning levels and their inclusion in family decisions.

Such involvement of children in decision making may actually provide them with the resources that they need to exercise their own judgments in real-life situations of moral conflict. Parents' abilities to understand the child's viewpoint and a willingness to interact reciprocally with the child thus seem to be important in encouraging moral growth (cf. Leahy, 1981; Parikh, 1980). While this premise is based on studies of early adolescents, the parents' capacity to listen to and understand the young child's view, and take the role of the child, should also be vital in moral growth during early childhood. Such role taking on the part of the parents is quite challenging during the earlier years, when adults may overlook the implications and significance of early thoughts, concerns, and interactions. Perhaps those same parents in the early adolescent studies cited above set the groundwork for later advanced moral reasoning and decision making in their encouragement and reciprocity during early childhood as well.

Moral Discussion

Participation in moral discussion groups is the hallmark of many attempts at facilitating the "natural" progression in moral reasoning development by providing educational experiences that "stimulate" this growth. In a study of 11- to 12-year-olds that became the model for later moral education programs, Blatt and Kohlberg (1975) found that, through the active process of peer discussion of dilemmas, and with the encouragement of a leader who provided the students with reasoning that optimally "matched" their own (i.e., one stage above), stage acceleration took place. With younger children, Selman and Lieberman (1975) have used filmstrips which stimulate discussion to help second graders progress through the lower stages of moral reasoning. The active discussion process among peers, with teacher guidance, seems to stimulate moral thinking and growth. This process makes the children more aware of the ideas of others in integration with their own.

The results of such direct educational attempts have not necessarily been consistently dramatic (cf. Schlaefli, Rest, & Thoma, 1985), particularly since the lengthy developmental course provides for slow, gradually generalized, and consolidated stage change. It is also true that cognitive development, a necessary but insufficient condition for moral growth (Kuhn, Langer, Kohlberg, & Haan, 1977; Tomlinson-Keasey & Keasey, 1974), sets the limit for the effectiveness of such environmental influences (Faust & Arbuthnot, 1978; Walker, 1980; Walker & Richards, 1979). Nevertheless, studies have consistently suggested that the "give and take" involved in active problem solving with peers, which enhances cognitive problem-solving skills (Light & Glachan, 1985), is also significant in promoting moral reasoning. This is particularly true when the peer group discussion process involves social conflict, with an attempt toward achieving group consensus (Maitland & Goldman, 1974). In fact, moral discussion groups have been quite effective in dealing with such "deviant" groups as delinquent boys (Jennings & Kohlberg, 1983; Niles, 1986), encouraging them to resolve moral conflict at progressively higher stages of thought.

If moral discussion is a key influence on the growth of moral reasoning, we need to know more about the discussion process itself and, in turn, how to foster discussion skills most effectively so as to encourage the process of stage acceleration. In their study of moral discussion, Berkowitz and Gibbs (1983) analyzed its developmental features so as to establish the nature of developmentally effective discussion. They found that the justification of one's moral position by using reasoning that operates on the reasoning of another ("transactive discussion") was the single best predictor of stage change, the only other significant predictor being stage discrepancy between dyad partners. The extent to which "transactive discussion" is used by the participants thus appears to mediate the effectiveness of the discussion process. The success of moral education programs in promoting stage change would therefore be contingent upon fostering the participant's discussion skills.

MORAL REASONING AND INTELLECTUAL GIFTEDNESS

Longitudinal and cross-sectional studies of children and adults have suggested that age accounts for most of the variance in moral reasoning (Colby, Kohlberg, Gibbs, & Lieberman, 1983; Kohlberg, 1964; Rest, Davison, & Robbins, 1978; Walker, 1989), with variables such as IQ and socioeconomic status playing more moderate roles. That is, while level of moral thought is moderately related to IQ, for example, it is clearly distinct from general intellectual level (Kohlberg, 1964). Recent data additionally suggest the role of educational level in the relation between moral reasoning and intellectual level: The correlation between moral maturity score and IQ increases in adulthood, perhaps partly due to the differential educational experiences that are related to intellectual level and to maturity of moral thought (Colby et al., 1983).

Differential opportunities for moral growth via educational experiences into adulthood as well as peer participation and moral discussion within the earlier years, as described above, can potentially promote differential stage change. However, environmental influences converge on intraindividual factors, and there are age, stage, and cognitive differences in the susceptibility to such influences (Colby et al., 1983; Schlaefli et al., 1985). The impact of these influences is viewed within the realm of cognitive development (cf. Rutter, 1985), not only in terms of direct effects on cognition, but through indirect effects in altering one's self-concept, aspirations, attitudes, and styles of interaction. Similarly, influences on moral reasoning, such as opportunities for peer participation and moral discussion, may also be mediated by their indirect effects on one's self-esteem and interaction style.

The effect of environmental influences on moral growth is thus complex. Different children not only have differential opportunities for different kinds of environmental influences, but are also differentially affected by the same influence. Emerging from this complexity of social interaction are those whose interactions with the environment have optimized their stage of moral reasoning. Such children may appear "morally gifted" and differentially advanced within the moral realm. However, after examining the basis for their differential moral advance, we may then ask if such advance is similarly reflected in optimal behavior.

Differential moral advance may also be examined by studying the moral reasoning of those who have already been identified as intellectually gifted. While IQ explains but little of the variance in moral reasoning, Kohlberg (1969) suggests that the limited predictive power of IQ may be reflected in the association between more rapid cognitive development and social development. As such, the enhanced social interaction opportunities of children and adolescents identified as intellectually gifted may be reflected in accelerated moral reasoning. They, in fact, have been shown to be advanced in their level of moral reasoning (Falk, 1987; Henderson, Gold, & Clarke, 1984; Tan-Willman & Gutteridge, 1981), assuming multiple perspectives in approaching moral issues (Falk, 1987).

Intellectually gifted 4- through 10-year-old children have also been found to be advanced in their level of "prosocial" thought (Blumenthal, 1987; Simmons & Zumpf, 1986), in terms of the way they choose between the satisfaction of their own needs and those of others (cf. Eisenberg, 1982; Eisenberg-Berg, 1979). In addition, they tend to see themselves as more competent (Simmons & Zumpf, 1986), having a more positive self-concept in terms of overall self-esteem, particularly as regards their personal, physical, and sociomoral self (Milgram & Milgram, 1976). These qualities, along with these children's effectiveness as problem solvers (cf. Milgram & Milgram, 1976), would be associated with a greater potential for leadership, associated with higher level moral reasoning as noted above.

Intellectually gifted fourth- through eighth-grade children have also been shown to have a greater internal sense of control over the outcomes of their actions (Milgram & Milgram, 1976), a personal quality associated with generosity (Fincham & Barling, 1978) as well as autonomy. These qualities would also reflect and effect accelerated moral reasoning. It should be noted, however, that, although the enhanced social interaction opportunities and personal qualities of intellectually gifted children may provide them with greater potential for moral advance, classic studies by Hollingworth (1942) have suggested that, beyond a certain level of intellectual functioning, particularly as defined by an IQ exceeding 180, there may be obstacles to psychosocial development. Such children, for example, may find it difficult to relate socially to their peers and may become extremely sensitive to issues of right and wrong, so much so that social adjustment is further impaired.

On the whole, though, the earlier ethical sensitivity (Drews, 1972) and concern with questions of values and morals (Gowan & Bruch, 1971) displayed by intellectually gifted youth may well be reflected in differential moral advance. These youth are also more likely to intensely search for meaningfulness in the world around them (Malone, 1975), and they may have parents who themselves are more likely to formulate and stand by their own ideals (Fell, Dahlstrom, & Winter, 1984). As they are capable of formal operational thinking earlier (Piaget, 1973), showing an early developmental potential for abstract analytical reasoning in both the cognitive and moral domains (Vare, 1979), these children can more readily see the multiple possibilities and complexities in resolving moral conflict.

In spite of this earlier, more advanced functioning of those identified as intellectually gifted, their highly developed creative thinking may not necessarily be fully realized in their moral advance. In a study of the prosocial behavior of intellectually gifted 3-year-olds, for example, Abroms and Gollin (1980) conclude that their IQ and potentially greater capacity for role taking does not necessarily predict their behavior, and that such "psychosocial giftedness" may develop independently of IQ. A study of gifted adolescents (Tan-Willman & Gutteridge, 1981) has also suggested that, although their moral reasoning may be higher than average, in relation to their superior creative potential and academic capacity it is probably less developed than it could be. Although they achieved higher moral reasoning scores than their peers, their reasoning was still at their age group's conventional level. The link between creativity and morality thus needs to be further explored (cf. Tan-Willman & Gutteridge, 1981) and strengthened, as does that between intellect and conscience (cf. Tannenbaum, 1975) and giftedness and purposeful goals (cf. Gruber, 1985). The achievement of such linkage through the educational process and atmosphere, and through the heightened awareness of those who interact with intellectually gifted youth, would in turn heighten the youths' awareness of the "human consequences" (cf. Tannenbaum, 1975) of their moral reasoning and its implications for subsequent behavior.

Given that differential moral advance, however, is not necessarily limited to those identified as intellectually gifted, the relationship between higher level reasoning and its implications for behavior is an issue which needs to be addressed for all children. How does moral reasoning relate to moral behavior? An analysis of that issue

would be significant, not only for the overall study of moral development, but for the development of a perspective on "moral giftedness"
as well. The key to understanding the emergence of "moral giftedness" may lie in our understanding of how we can bridge the gap
between reasoning about moral issues and acting on those issues in
a way that reflects a responsible moral awareness and sensitivity. As
we strive to encourage moral reasoning in all children, then, we
must also strive for that reasoning to guide moral behavior effectively and responsibly.

MORAL BEHAVIOR

Studies that relate moral behavior to moral reasoning have illumi-
nated the meanings moral conflict situations have for an individual
and the relation of behavioral choice to that meaning (cf. Rothman,
1980). By examining behavior in terms of the developmental process
it reflects and by which people make their decisions, we can seek to
define the interrelationship between moral reasoning and moral
behavior. We may then better understand individual differences in
behavioral choices in particular situations of right and wrong.

Stage of Moral Reasoning and Behavioral Choice

When behavior is examined as springing from a moral decision,
different stages of reasoning may be used in arriving at a particular
choice and, conversely, the same stage may be used in arriving at
different decisions in particular situations of moral conflict. For
example, one person may keep a promise because he or she fears
retaliation from breaking that promise, whereas another may keep a
promise so as to maintain mutual trust. Conversely, a focus on
mutual trust could result in two different behavioral choices in two
different situations, depending upon the particular nature of each.

The multifaceted aspects of any particular real-life moral conflict
situation would thus imply that the relationship between stage of
moral reasoning and the behavioral choice that springs from a
moral decision is not necessarily straightforward or monotonic. Nevertheless, that relationship is most consistent at the higher stages
of moral reasoning. For example, principled subjects are less likely
to cheat, defining the situation, as they do, in terms of trust, inequality of opportunity, and justice (Grim, Kohlberg, & White, 1968;

Schwartz, Feldman, Brown, & Heingartner, 1969), and are less likely to shock a confederate victim (Kohlberg, 1969). They are also more likely to help the confederate victim of a drug reaction (McNamee, 1977) and to return questionnaires (Krebs & Rosenwald, 1977). Children functioning at higher levels of moral reasoning are more likely to resist temptation (LaVoie, 1974), and they are less likely to be among a group of delinquents (Campagna & Harter, 1975; Fodor, 1972; Hains & Miller, 1980; Hanson & Mullis, 1984) or among those with behavior problems (Bear & Richards, 1981).

Studies of kindergarten through elementary school age children's altruism have similarly found a relationship between particular measures of moral reasoning and generosity (Dlugokinski & Firestone, 1973; Dreman, 1976; Emler & Rushton, 1974; Grant, Weiner, & Rushton, 1976; Olejnik, 1975; Rothman & Sussman, 1976), and children's justifications for their generosity or selfishness in particular situations have been examined (Dreman, 1976; Dreman & Greenbaum, 1973; Rothman & Sussman, 1976) in an attempt at providing insight into the way children perceive and define those situations.

Hypothetical and real-life moral reasoning. While the above studies suggest that one's moral reasoning prompts the individual to define particular situations in particular ways, they do not necessarily imply that moral reasoning is directly related to moral behavior, or that we can directly predict behavior from knowing a person's level of moral reasoning. The complexity of the relationship between moral reasoning and moral behavior is further highlighted by the fact that moral reasoning in real life may not directly reflect stage of reasoning in response to hypothetical dilemmas. In everyday real-life situations, when the consequences of an act may impact on oneself as well as on another, prudential rules may guide behavior. Thus, even someone who is "advanced" in moral reasoning may not necessarily reason on that level consistently as we move from the realm of the hypothetical to the concrete.

Within the domain of critical thinking, a study by Dreyfus and Jungwirth (1980) similarly suggests that everyday situations may be less likely than logically equivalent situations to "prompt" critical thinking, since contextual factors may exert a "deflecting effect" from the logical task. It has been claimed that certain theoretical moral problems may be even further removed from practice than such intellectual problems (Kohlberg & Candee, 1984), when the real-life feature of immediacy may play a strong role (Straughan, 1975). Thus, in real-life moral conflict situations an individual may not necessarily use the highest level of reasoning of which he or she is capable, nor does higher level reasoning necessarily guarantee responsible moral behavior.

Although McNamee (1977) found that one's stage of reasoning regarding helping another paralleled one's level of hypothetical moral reasoning, and Walker, de Vries, and Trevethan (1987) have found consistency in reasoning between personally generated and hypothetical dilemmas for children of Grades 1 to 10, other studies have found that self-interest often prevails in concrete, real-life situations. For example, 4- to 10-year-olds are more likely to use lower levels of distributive justice reasoning (i.e., how to award resources fairly) in concrete than in hypothetical behavioral situations (Gerson & Damon, 1975; McNamee & Peterson, 1985), since the reward outcome directly affects themselves. Similarly, 5- to 7-year-olds are more likely to judge themselves than another based on intentionality (Keasey, 1977), again because the consequences of that judgment (in this case, potentially punitive) directly affect themselves. Similarly, higher level reasoning is more readily used by early and late adolescents for hypothetical, remote dilemmas involving others than for those which are "practical" and "familiar" or involve oneself (Freeman & Giebink, 1979; Leming, 1978; Rybash, Roodin, & Lonky, 1981), when "prudential" aspects may prevail.

The conflict that such studies have engendered between one's own spontaneous needs and moral norms, is one which 4- to 8-year-old children begin to encounter as they first come to develop moral understanding and awareness. While they may know and understand the "rules," their behavior reflects a more instrumental orientation geared toward fulfilling their individual needs (cf. Nunner-Winkler & Sodian, 1988). As the child grows into young adulthood, he or she must continue to come to terms with the discrepancy between prudential concerns when decisions affect oneself, and moral norms. The same personal involvement, though, that makes "lower" prudential forms of reasoning likely, may be the very involvement that is necessary in order to relate meaningfully one's own reasoning to one's real-life decision making. According to Weiss (1982), this ultimately results in an active search for considerations that are important for a "just" solution, and is reflected in progressive levels of moral understanding and awareness.

Moral Responsibility

The opportunities for active involvement that enhance one's moral understanding and awareness may also heighten one's sense of moral responsibility. In situations of moral conflict, this heightened moral responsibility among those children and adults whose social interaction opportunities have optimized their stage of moral reasoning may play a significant role in behavioral decisions and, ultimately, in "moral giftedness."

A hallmark of the highest stages is the increased consistency between judgments of what is right to do in a situation and judgments of the self's responsibility to carry this out. These judgments of responsibility may be viewed as mediating between judgments of rightness and ultimate action (Kohlberg & Candee, 1984). For example, in McNamee's (1977) study of helping behavior, there was greater consistency at the highest stages between such feelings of responsibility and actual helping. Whereas conventional stage subjects may have felt that it was right to help the confederate victim of a drug reaction, even though that help interfered with the task at hand, they did not feel that they had the responsibility to actually carry this out. They rather felt that the experimenter bore responsibility for the decision.

It is precisely this sense of responsibility to carry out one's moral decision that has been shown lacking in sociopaths (Saltzstein, 1983): While capable of the requisite role taking, they cannot or will not translate this into moral reactions like a sense of responsibility. At the other extreme are those individuals with a sense of responsibility to translate role taking into moral reactions which further justice (cf. Selman & Damon, 1975), for whom role taking, moral reasoning, and moral responsibility become intertwined.

The assumption of responsibility for acting in a way that is consistent with their judgments of rightness in a situation seems to be a hallmark of Principled Stage 5 individuals (Kohlberg, Levine, & Hewer, 1983). For example, in responding to the hypothetical dilemma of whether or not Heinz should steal a drug to save his wife's life, cross-cultural research has suggested that Stage 5 subjects agree with the "autonomous" choice that Heinz has the right to steal, in accordance with the principle of respect for life or personhood (Kohlberg et al., 1983). Whereas lower stage conventional subjects may also say that Heinz should steal, they say that he is not necessarily responsible if in fact the wife dies because he did not steal (Helkama, 1979, as cited in Kohlberg et al., 1983). That is, the same choice for the hypothetical Heinz may reflect different reasoning. That reasoning makes for a difference in consistency and in a sense of obligation and commitment to one's choice when confronting moral conflict.

This awareness of one's responsibility for the resolution of conflicting issues may be especially distinguishable among individuals who have been identified as intellectually gifted, who may apply their creativity in other domains to the moral realm (cf. Gruber, 1985). While their sense of moral responsibility may have certain uniquely creative dimensions, higher stage individuals in general, as noted above, see themselves as bearing the responsibility to act in a "morally right" manner. Their behavior may emerge as "moral giftedness" in situations demanding an inner resolve and commitment.

Generating and cultivating the foundation of this sense of responsibility in young children as we encourage the development of their moral reasoning, would thus hold great promise for the emergence of "moral giftedness." This ultimately would be reflected in behavioral decisions made within a wide range of moral conflict situations.

Additional Mediating Factors

Within most real-life moral conflict situations, a sense of moral obligation and responsibility must be successfully differentiated from those nonmoral aspects of a situation that may intervene in moral decision making. Affect is one such aspect. In a study of kindergarteners through sixth-graders, Arsenio (1988) examined the mediating role of affect in terms of children's conceptualizations of the emotional consequences of sociomoral events. The research found that these conceptualizations may in turn be further used as the basis for understanding such events and for planning behavior accordingly. However, age and cognitive development play a role in children's understanding of such feelings and of one another (Carroll & Steward, 1984; Eisenberg et al., 1987), and particular roles and behaviors further impact on affect during the course of prosocial development in early and middle childhood (Eisenberg et al., 1987; Lennon & Eisenberg, 1987). The extent to which *affective* reactions actually mediate behavior thus needs to further be explored.

With its complexities, however, the significance of affect in relation to moral decision making has been highlighted by Le Capitaine's (1987) studies of educational intervention techniques with third and fourth graders. These studies have coordinated feelings with dilemmas and conflict resolution, and have noted the interactive effect of those three dimensions in yielding gains in moral reasoning. The gains have been attributed to cognitive and affective dissonance aroused by such curricula and by the enhancement of the moral reasoning process when explicitly coupled with affect (cf. Le Capitaine, 1987).

Another factor which may intervene in moral decision making is *ego strength*. This includes such capacities as that of being able to delay gratification, control impulses, and be attentive to the situation at hand. These nonmoral "attentional-will" factors were examined in Grim, Kohlberg, and White's (1968) study of first and sixth graders' cheating behavior. In that study, distractibility, as measured by reaction time, correlated significantly with cheating, particularly for those at the conventional levels of moral reasoning (Krebs, 1967, as cited by Grim et al., 1968). That is, *stronger willed* conventional subjects cheated less than those who were *weak willed*. This relationship did not hold true as well for premoral or principled subjects. For the latter, ego strength factors were less important than their moral principles in affecting behavior. The impact of particular mediating factors on behavior may thus be affected by one's stage of reasoning. Kohlberg (1964) has furthermore suggested that the same social-experiential and cognitive factors that favor advance in moral reasoning may also favor such nonmoral factors as moral autonomy. Thus, the encouragement of children's moral reasoning would also reflect and affect the encouragement of moral autonomy.

Yet another factor mediating the way in which reasoning guides behavior is the *context* in which the individual finds himself or herself. In prisons, for example, inmates use lower levels of reasoning in response to prison dilemmas than they do to standard dilemmas (Kohlberg, Hickey, & Scharf, 1972). The shared expectations and group norms of the prison atmosphere may mediate an individual's behavior in accordance with that lower level of reasoning rather than with the higher level of which he or she is actually capable. The capacity for higher level reasoning thus does not necessarily guarantee responsible moral behavior, or even higher level reasoning in particular real-life situations. Conversely, an atmosphere that favors mutual respect and consideration of the views of another in autonomous, responsible decision making would ultimately encourage an active seeking of the considerations important for a "just" solution. As noted earlier, Weiss (1982) has suggested that such considerations are reflected in progressive levels of moral understanding and awareness.

"Moral Giftedness" and Behavior

Moral *understanding* and *awareness* may be important aspects of "moral giftedness," guiding and enhancing moral reasoning and a sense of responsibility within the decision-making process. Among those at higher stages of moral reasoning, whether they have been identified as intellectually gifted, or those whose enhanced opportunities for social interaction have optimized their moral reasoning, a heightened sense of responsibility and awareness may play a dynamic role in situations of moral conflict when decisions for concrete action must be made. The "morally gifted" may more readily use their heightened understanding as a basis for such action, as they take the initiative and assume responsibility for their moral decisions (cf. Gruber, 1985).

Such initiative in moral conflict situations would suggest that aspect of giftedness noted by Tannenbaum (1989) as the ability to be an "innovator." Furthermore, just as early accelerated development in intellectual or artistic domains does not necessarily guarantee later expressions of giftedness, which ultimately depend on the mutual reinforcement of such factors as ability, personal attributes, and enriching life experiences (cf. Tannenbaum, 1989), so too, ultimate "moral giftedness" would reflect the developmental convergence of personal and environmental mediating factors on moral reasoning. The way in which their moral reasoning ultimately guides individuals toward responsible behavior becomes a crucial dimension of the expression of "moral giftedness."

A developmental perspective on "moral giftedness," if it is to go beyond reasoning into the realm of behavior, thus must necessarily take into account the complex interrelationship between these two processes.

"Moral Giftedness" and the Coordination of Reasoning and Behavior

The developmental interrelationship between moral reasoning and moral behavior has been examined in studies by Rothman (1976, 1980) and Turiel and Rothman (1972). These studies have indicated that one's own reasoning, the reasoning of others, and behavioral choice interact differently at different stages, with a greater coordination of reasoning and behavior at higher than at lower stages of moral reasoning.

In the above research, early adolescents who reasoned primarily at Kohlberg's Stage 4 were more likely than those at Stage 3 to base their behavioral choices on higher stage reasoning presented to them for particular choices. Those at Stage 3, who did not integrate their choices with reasoning in reaching their behavioral decisions, indicated ambivalence in their decision making. This suggested a transitional phase between the separation and coordination of reasoning and behavior. The research thus further concluded that there may be developmental stages in the coordination of reasoning and behavior.

Such coordination of moral reasoning and moral behavior may actually represent a hallmark of "moral giftedness." If this coordination is more readily achieved at higher stages of moral reasoning, then the "morally gifted," who are advanced in their moral reasoning, would more readily integrate this reasoning with their subsequent behavior. It is this coordination which may play a role in the extent to which one's sense of responsibility effectively mediates between reasoning and behavior and in the extent to which one's moral understanding is effectively reflected in responsible decision making.

Just as there may be stages in the coordination of reasoning and behavior, as well as in one's understanding of moral thought, so, too, there may be parallel stages in the emergence of "moral giftedness." These stages would involve movement from a separation toward an integration of moral reasoning, decision making, and actual behavior, as guided by a process of moral deliberation and a sense of responsibility for one's own decisions. Such active integration might be a key dimension within the potential capacity of the "morally gifted," some of whom may be identified as intellectually gifted, for translating and channelling their creative achievements, their passion, and their initiative (cf. Gruber, 1985) toward creating a better world.

CONCLUSION

As we encourage within all children the developmental capacity for higher forms of moral thought and its translation into positive and responsible forms of moral behavior, a tremendous challenge confronts us as parents and as educators. As we take role of the child and respect his or her capabilities within the moral domain, we need to enable children to grow in an atmosphere that encourages and respects their active searching and personal involvement in moral decision making. In attempting to promote moral growth, we must provide our children, regardless of whether they have been identified as intellectually gifted, with opportunities for personally discovering, creatively using, and enhancing their capacities for responsible leadership, communication, and autonomous decision making while heightening their sensitivity to others.

As we encourage the development of moral reasoning within the context of optimal social interaction and autonomous, responsible decision making, we must cultivate an atmosphere of caring, of mutual respect, and of consideration of the other person's views. We must also encourage the child's developing reasoning processes to become a motivational force in guiding his or her behavior. The still greater challenge lies in building on this moral growth and encouraging the emergence of "moral giftedness," accompanied by a clear awareness of one's responsibility within the decision making process.

This challenge may be defined somewhat differently for those already identified as intellectually gifted, whose unique creative potential and cognitive capacities may readily lend themselves toward autonomous, principled moral growth. Such growth can only be achieved, however, if we respect and promote that potential for autonomous creative development and provide opportunities for leadership and responsibility.

As all children interact and grow with one another, we can strive to foster their moral undertanding and awareness within an atmosphere of respect and concern for others. As we view the world through their eyes, we may further ask ourselves how our own behavior and reasoning, in interaction with those of our children, affect their developing moral understanding and awareness, and its translation into decisions within everyday interactions.

With confidence in our children's capabilities and potential, we must appreciate the individual differences among them. With such appreciation, we can encourage all to confidently use their own resources of reasoning to guide their behavior, taking into account oneself, others, and society. In the process, the emergence of "moral giftedness," encompassing the active integration of moral reasoning and responsible decision making with actual behavior, would be reflected in the emergence of a stronger, caring world.

REFERENCES

Abroms, K. I., & Gollin, J. B. (1980). Developmental study of gifted preschool children and measures of psychosocial giftedness. *Exceptional Children, 46*, 334–343.

Arsenio, W. F. (1988). Children's conceptions of the situational affective consequences of sociomoral events. *Child Development, 59*, 1611–1622.

Avgar, A., Bronfenbrenner, U., & Henderson, C. R., Jr. (1977). Socialization practices of parents, teachers and peers in Israel: Kibbutz, moshav, and city. *Child Development, 48*, 1219–1227.

Bar-Tal, D., Raviv, A., & Leiser, T. (1980). The development of altruistic behavior: Empirical evidence. *Developmental Psychology, 16,* 516–524.

Bear, G. G., & Richards, H. C. (1981). Moral reasoning and conduct problems in the classroom. *Journal of Educational Psychology, 73,* 664–670.

Berkowitz, M. W., & Gibbs, J. C. (1983). Measuring the development of moral discussion. *Merrill-Palmer Quarterly, 29,* 399–410.

Blatt, M. M., & Kohlberg, L. (1975). The effects of classroom moral discussion upon children's level of moral judgment. *Journal of Moral Education, 4,* 129–161.

Blumenthal, G. (1987). *Prosocial moral reasoning of gifted and nongifted elementary school students.* Unpublished dissertation, Teachers College, Columbia University.

Buck, L. Z., Walsh, W. F., & Rothman, G. R. (1981). Relationship between parental moral judgment and socialization. *Youth and Society, 13,* 91–116.

Campagna, A. F., & Harter, S. (1975). Moral judgment in sociopathic and normal children. *Journal of Personality and Social Psychology, 31,* 199–205.

Carroll, J. J., & Steward, M. S. (1984). The role of cognitive development in children's understanding of their own feelings. *Child Development, 55,* 1486–1492.

Colby, A., Kohlberg, L., Gibbs, J., & Lieberman, M. (1983). A longitudinal study of moral judgment. *SRCD Monographs, 48* (Nos. 1–2).

Crockenberg, S. B., & Nicolayev, J. (1979). Stage transitions in moral reasoning as related to conflict experienced in naturalistic settings. *Merrill-Palmer Quarterly, 25,* 185–192.

Damon, W. (1977). *The social world of the child.* San Francisco: Josey-Bass.

Damon, W. (1980). Structural-developmental theory and the study of moral development. In M. Windmiller, N. Lambert, & E. Turiel (Eds.), *Moral development and socialization* (pp. 35–68). Boston: Allyn & Bacon.

Dlugokinski, E. L., & Firestone, I. J. (1973). Congruence among four methods of measuring other-centeredness. *Child Development, 44,* 304–308.

Dreman, S. B. (1976). Sharing behavior in Israeli schoolchildren: Cognitive and social learning factors. *Child Development, 47,* 186–194.

Dreman, S. B., & Greenbaum, C. W. (1973). Altruism or reciprocity: Sharing behavior in Israeli kindergarten children. *Child Development, 44,* 61–68.

Drews, E. M. (1972). *Learning together.* Englewood Cliffs, NJ: Prentice-Hall.

Dreyfus, A., & Jungwirth, E. (1980). A comparison of the "prompting effect" of out-of-school with that of in-school contexts on certain aspects of critical thinking. *European Journal of Science Education, 2,* 301–310.

Dunn, J., & Munn, P. (1986). Siblings and the development of prosocial behavior. *International Journal of Behavioral Development, 9,* 265–284.

Eisenberg, N. (1982). *The development of prosocial behavior.* New York: Academic Press.

Eisenberg, N., Pasternack, J. F., Cameron, E., & Tryon, K. (1984). The relationship of quantity and mode of prosocial behavior to moral cognitions and social style. *Child Development, 55,* 1479–1485.

Eisenberg, N., Shell, R., Pasternack, J., Lennon, R., Beller, R., & Mathy, R. M. (1987). Prosocial development in middle childhood: A longitudinal study. *Developmental Psychology, 23,* 712–718.

Eisenberg-Berg, N. (1979). Development of children's prosocial moral judgment. *Developmental Psychology, 15,* 128–137.

Eisenberg-Berg, N., & Hand, M. (1979). The relationship of preschoolers' reasoning about prosocial moral conflicts to prosocial behavior. *Child Development, 50,* 356–363.

Eisenberg-Berg, N., & Neal, C. (1979). Children's moral reasoning about their own spontaneous prosocial behavior. *Developmental Psychology, 15,* 228–229.

Emler, N. P., & Rushton, J. P. (1974). Cognitive-developmental factors in children's generosity. *British Journal of Social and Clinical Psychology, 13,* 277–281.

Falk, C. (1987). Gifted children's perception of divorce. *Journal for the Education of the Gifted, 11,* 29–43.

Faust, D., & Arbuthnot, J. (1978). Relationship between moral and Piagetian reasoning and the effectiveness of moral education. *Developmental Psychology, 14,* 435–436.

Fell, L., Dahlstrom, M., & Winter, D. C. (1984). Personality traits of parents of gifted children. *Psychological Reports, 54,* 383–387.

Fincham, F., & Barling, J. (1978). Locus of control and generosity in learning disabled, normal achieving, and gifted children. *Child Development, 49,* 530–533.

Fodor, E. M. (1972). Delinquency and susceptibility to social influence among adolescents as a function of level of moral development. *Journal of Social Psychology, 86,* 257–260.

Freeman, S. J. M., & Giebink, J. W. (1979). Moral judgment as a function of age, sex, and stimulus. *Journal of Psychology, 102,* 43–47.

Gauthier, D. P. (1971). Moral action and moral education. In C. M. Beck, B. S. Crittenden, & E. V. Sullivan (Eds.), *Moral education: Interdisciplinary approaches* (138–146). New York: Newman Press.

Gerson, R., & Damon, W. (1975, April). *Relations between moral behavior in a hypothetical-verbal context and in a practical, "real-life" setting.* Paper presented at EPA, New York.

Gowan, J. C., & Bruch, C. B. (1971). *The academically talented student and guidance.* Boston: Houghton Mifflin.

Grant, J. E., Weiner, A., & Rushton, J. P. (1976). Moral judgment and generosity in children. *Psychological Reports, 39,* 451–454.

Grim, P. F., Kohlberg, L., & White, S. H. (1968). Some relationships between conscience and attentional processes. *Journal of Personality and Social Psychology, 8,* 239–252.

Gruber, H. (1985). Giftedness and moral responsibility: Creative thinking and human survival. In F. D. Horowitz & M. O'Brien (Eds.), *The gifted and talented: Developmental perspectives* (pp. 301–330). Washington, DC: APA.

Hains, A. A., & Miller, D. J. (1980). Moral and cognitive development in delinquent and nondelinquent children and adolescents. *Journal of Genetic Psychology, 137,* 21–35.

Hanson, R. A., & Mullis, R. L. (1984). Moral reasoning in offender and nonoffender youth. *Journal of Genetic Psychology, 144,* 295–296.

Harkness, S., Edwards, C. P., & Super, C. M. (1981). Social roles and moral reasoning: A case study in a rural African community. *Developmental Psychology, 17,* 595–603.

Harris, S., Mussen, P., & Rutherford, E. (1976). Some cognitive, behavioral, and personality correlates of maturity of moral judgment. *Journal of Genetic Psychology, 128,* 123–135.

Henderson, B. B., Gold, S. R., & Clarke, K. (1984). Individual differences in IQ, daydreaming and moral reasoning in gifted and average adolescents. *International Journal of Behavioral Development, 7,* 215–230.

Higgins, A., Power, C., & Kohlberg, L. (1984). The relationship of moral atmosphere to judgments of responsibility. In W. M. Kurtines & J. L. Gewirtz (Eds.), *Mortality, moral behavior, and moral development* (pp. 74–106). New York: Wiley.

Hoffman, M. L. (1975). The development of altruistic motivation. In D. J. DePalma & J. M. Foley (Eds.), *Moral development: Current theory and research* (pp. 137–151). New York: Wiley.

Hollingworth, L. S. (1942). *Children above 180 IQ, Stanford-Binet: origin and development.* Yonkers-on-Hudson, NY: World Book Co.

Holstein, C. E. (1972). The relation of children's moral judgement level to that of their parents and to communication patterns in the family. In R. C. Smart & M. S. Smart (Eds.), *Readings in child development and relationships* (pp. 484–494). New York: Macmillan.

Jennings, W. S., & Kohlberg, L. (1983). Effects of a just community programme on the moral development of youthful offenders. *Journal of Moral Education, 12,* 33–50.

Keasey, C. B. (1971). Social participation as a factor in the moral development of preadolescents. *Developmental Psychology, 5,* 216–220.

Keasey, C. B. (1977). Young children's attributions of intentionality to themselves and others. *Child Development, 48,* 261–264.

Kohlberg, L. (1964). Development of moral character and moral ideology. In M. L. Hoffman & L. W. Hoffman (Eds.), *Review of child development research* (pp. 383–431). New York: Russell Sage Foundation.

Kohlberg, L. (1969). Stage and sequence: The cognitive-developmental approach to socialization. In D. A. Goslin (Ed.), *Handbook of socialization theory and research* (pp. 347–480). Chicago: Rand McNally.

Kohlberg, L. (1976). Moral stages and moralization: The cognitive-developmental approach. In T. Lickona (Ed.), *Moral development and behavior: Theory, research, and social issues* (pp. 31–53). New York: Holt, Rinehart and Winston.

Kohlberg, L., & Candee, D. (1984). The relationship of moral judgment to moral action. In W. M. Kurtines & J. L. Gewirtz (Eds.), *Morality, moral behavior, and moral development* (pp. 52–73). New York: Wiley.

Kohlberg, L., Hickey, J., & Scharf, P. (1972). The justice structure of the prison: A theory and intervention. *Prison Journal, 51,* 3–14.

Kohlberg, L., Levine, C., & Hewer, A. (1983). *Moral stages: A current formulation and a response to critics.* New York: Karger.

Krebs, D., & Rosenwald, A. (1977). Moral reasoning and moral behavior in conventional adults. *Merrill-Palmer Quarterly, 23,* 77–87.

Kuhn, D., Langer, J., Kohlberg, L., & Haan, N. (1977). The development of formal operations in logical and moral judgment. *Genetic Psychology Monographs, 95,* 97–188.

LaVoie, J. C. (1974). Cognitive determinants of resistance to deviation in seven-, nine-, and eleven-year-old children of low and high maturity of moral judgment. *Developmental Psychology, 10,* 393–403.

LeCapitaine, J. E. (1987). The relationship between emotional development and moral development and the differential impact of three psychological interventions on children. *Psychology in the Schools, 24,* 372–378.

Leahy, R. L. (1981). Parental practices and the development of moral judgment and self-image disparity during adolescence. *Developmental Psychology, 17,* 580–594.

Leming, J. S. (1978). Intrapersonal variation in stage of moral reasoning among adolescents as a function of situational context. *Journal of Youth and Adolescence, 7,* 405–416.

Lennon, R., & Eisenberg, N. (1987). Emotional displays associated with preschoolers' prosocial behavior. *Child Development, 58,* 992–1000.

Levy-Schiff, R., & Hoffman, M. A. (1985). Social behavior of urban and kibbutz preschool children in Israel. *Developmental Psychology, 21,* 1204–1205.

Lifshitz, M., & Ramot, L. (1978). Toward a framework for developing children's locus-of-control orientations: Implications from the kibbutz system. *Child Development, 49,* 85–95.

Light, P., & Glachan, M. (1985). Facilitation of individual problem-solving through peer interaction. *Educational Psychology, 5,* 217–225.

Maitland, K. A., & Goldman, J. R. (1974). Moral judgment as a function of peer group interaction. *Journal of Personality and Social Psychology, 30,* 699–704.

Malone, C. (1975). Implementing a differential school program for the gifted. *Gifted Child Quarterly, 19,* 316–327.

Matthews, G. B. (1980). *Philosophy and the young child.* Cambridge, MA: Harvard University Press.

McNamee, S. (1977). Moral behaviour, moral development and motivation. *Journal of Moral Education, 7,* 27–31.

McNamee, S., & Peterson, J. (1985). Young children's distributive justice reasoning, behavior, and role-taking: Their consistency and relationship. *Journal of Genetic Psychology, 146*, 399–404.

Milgram, R. M., & Milgram, N. A. (1976). Personality characteristics of gifted Israeli children. *Journal of Genetic Psychology, 129*, 185–194.

Nahir, H. T., & Yussen, S. R. (1977). The performance of kibbutz- and city-reared Israeli children on two role-taking tasks. *Developmental Psychology, 13*, 450–455.

Niles, W. J. (1986). Effects of a moral development discussion group on delinquent and predelinquent boys. *Journal of Counseling Psychology, 33*, 45–51.

Nunner-Winkler, G., & Sodian, B. (1988). Children's understanding of moral emotions. *Child Development, 59*, 1323–1338.

Olejnik, A. B. (1975, April). *Developmental changes and interrelationships among role-taking, moral judgments and children's sharing.* Paper presented at the Society for Research in Child Development, Denver.

Parikh, B. (1980). Development of moral judgment and its relation to family environmental factors in Indian and American families. *Child Development, 51*, 1030–1039.

Piaget, J. (1965). *The moral judgment of the child.* New York: Free Press, (Original work published 1932)

Piaget, J. (1973). *The child and reality.* New York: Grossman.

Power, C. (1979). *The moral atmosphere of a just community high school: A four-year longitudinal study.* Unpublished dissertation, Harvard University.

Rest, J. R., Davison, M. L., & Robbins, S. (1978). Age trends in judging moral issues: A review of cross-sectional, longitudinal, and sequential studies of the DIT. *Child Development, 49*, 263–279.

Rheingold, H. L., Hay, D. F., & West, M. J. (1976). Sharing in the second year of life. *Child Development, 47*, 1148–1158.

Rothman, G. R. (1976). The influence of moral reasoning on behavioral choices. *Child Development, 47*, 397–406.

Rothman, G. R. (1980). The relationship between moral judgment and moral behavior. In M. Windmiller, N. Lambert, & E. Turiel (Eds.), *Moral development and socialization* (pp. 107–127). Boston: Allyn & Bacon.

Rothman, G. R., & Sussman, R. (1976). *The influence of moral reasoning on children's charitable behavior.* Unpublished manuscript, Teachers College, Columbia University.

Rutter, M. (1985). Family and school influences on cognitive development. *Journal of Child Psychology and Psychiatry, 26*, 683–704.

Rybash, J. M., Roodin, P. A., & Lonky, E. (1981). Young adults' scores on the DIT as a function of a "self" vs. "other" presentation mode. *Journal of Youth and Adolescence, 10*, 25–31.

Saltzstein, H. D. (1983). Critical issues in Kohlberg's theory of moral reasoning. In Colby et al., A longitudinal study of moral judgment. *SRCD Monographs, 48* (Nos. 1–2), 108–119.

Schlaefli, A., Rest, J. R., & Thoma, S. J. (1985). Does moral education improve moral judgment? A meta-analysis of intervention studies using the Defining Issues Test. *Review of Educational Research, 55*, 319–352.

Schwartz, S. H., Feldman, K. A., Brown, M. E., & Heingartner, A. (1969). Some personality correlates of conduct in two situations of moral conflict. *Journal of Personality, 37*, 41–57.

Selman, R. L. (1971). The relation of role-taking to the development of moral judgment in children. *Child Development, 42*, 79–91.

Selman, R. L. (1976). Social-cognitive understanding: A guide to educational and clinical practice. In T. Lickona (Ed.), *Moral development and behavior: Theory, research, and social issues* (pp. 299–316). New York: Holt, Rinehart and Winston.

Selman, R., & Damon, W. (1975). The necessity (but insufficiency) of social perspective taking for conceptions of justice at three early levels. In D. J. DePalma & J. M. Foley (Eds.), *Moral development: Current theory and research* (pp. 57–73). New York: Wiley.

Selman, R. L., & Lieberman, M. (1975). Moral education in the primary grades: An evaluation of a developmental curriculum. *Journal of Educational Psychology, 67*, 712–716.

Simmons, C. H., & Zumpf, C. (1986). The gifted child: Perceived competence, prosocial moral reasoning, and charitable donations. *Journal of Genetic Psychology, 147*, 97–105.

Snarey, J., Reimer, J., & Kohlberg, L. (1985). The kibbutz as a model for moral education: A longitudinal cross-sectional study. *Journal of Applied Developmental Psychology, 6*, 151–172.

Straughan, R. R. (1975). Hypothetical moral situations. *Journal of Moral Education, 4*, 183–189.

Tannenbaum, A. J. (1975). A backward and forward glance at the gifted. In W. B. Barbe & J. S. Renzulli (Eds.), *Psychology and education of the gifted* (pp. 21–31). New York: Irvington Publishers.

Tannenbaum, A. J. (1989). *The social psychology of giftedness.* Unpublished manuscript, Teachers College, Columbia University.

Tan-Willman, C., & Gutteridge, D. (1981). Creative thinking and moral reasoning of academically gifted secondary school adolescents. *Gifted Child Quarterly, 25*, 149–153.

Tietjen, A. M., & Walker, L. J. (1985). Moral reasoning and leadership among men in a Papua New Guinea society. *Developmental Psychology, 21*, 982–992.

Tomlinson-Keasey, C., & Keasey, C. B. (1974). The mediating role of cognitive development in moral judgment. *Child Development, 45*, 291–298.

Turiel, E. (1966). An experimental test of the sequentiality of developmental stages in the child's moral judgments. *Journal of Personality and Social Psychology, 3*, 611–618.

Turiel, E. (1975). The development of social concepts: Mores, customs, and conventions. In D. J. DePalma & J. M. Foley (Eds.), *Moral development: Current theory and research* (pp. 7–37). New York: Wiley.

Turiel, E. (1980). The development of social-conventional and moral concepts. In M. Windmiller, N. Lambert, & E. Turiel (Eds.), *Moral development and socialization* (pp. 69–106). Boston: Allyn & Bacon.

Turiel, E. (1983). *The development of social knowledge: Morality and convention.* Cambridge, UK: Cambridge University Press.

Turiel, E., & Rothman, G. R. (1972). The influence of reasoning on behavioral choices at different stages of moral development. *Child Development, 43,* 741–756.

Vare, J. V. (1979). Moral education for the gifted: A confluent model. *Gifted Child Quarterly, 23,* 487–499.

Walker, L. J. (1980). Cognitive and perspective-taking prerequisites for moral development. *Child Development, 51,* 131–139.

Walker, L. J. (1983). Sources of cognitive conflict for stage transition in moral development. *Developmental Psychology, 19,* 103–110.

Walker, L. J. (1989). A longitudinal study of moral reasoning. *Child Development, 60,* 157–166.

Walker, L. J., de Vries, B., & Trevethan, S. D. (1987). Moral stages and moral orientations in real-life and hypothetical dilemmas. *Child Development, 58,* 842–858.

Walker, L. J., & Richards, B. S. (1979). Stimulating transitions in moral reasoning as a function of stage of cognitive development. *Developmental Psychology, 15,* 95–103.

Weiss, R. J. (1982). Understanding moral thought: Effects on moral reasoning and decision making. *Developmental Psychology, 18,* 852–861.

chapter 12

Meeting the Educational Needs of All Students in the Heterogeneous Class

Rachel Ben Ari   Yisrael Rich

School of Education
Bar-Ilan University
Israel

In recent years we have witnessed a worldwide trend towards increased diversity in the characteristics of student populations in schools at all levels of education (Blass & Amir, 1984; McPherson & Willms, 1987; Welch, 1987). This diversity or heterogeneity is reflected in the disparate cultural, social, and economic home environments of these students as well as in their widely varying levels of measured academic ability and in their school achievements.

Greater student heterogeneity is related to certain "natural" phenomena, including migration and social mobility, and to the widespread implementation of several important and controversial educational programs, such as comprehensive schooling, desegregation, and mainstreaming. These programs have become part of the educational scene in many countries in the last 30 years due to the increased endorsement by the general public of the belief that all children should have the opportunity to benefit from a quality education. As a result, over the years educational authorities have been pressured to register a greater number of students once considered inappropriate for the regular school program. At first, many of these children were assigned to special classes and had little contact with their educationally mainstream peers. More recently, heterogeneity has taken hold in the classroom, where, side by side, we find a jumble of children from different ethnic, cultural or racial groups, socioeconomic backgrounds, and ability levels.

Increased heterogeneity of student populations in the classroom creates special problems and challenges from the perspective of the educational system's mandate to provide a quality education to all children. As more attention has been focused, at all levels of education, on low-achieving and culturally different students, children who have demonstrated outstanding potential may not receive the best educational conditions to realize that potential. It is not unreasonable to argue that, with increased ability and talent differentials in the class, curriculum developers, principals, and teachers find it increasingly difficult to provide a high-quality educational experience for all students. As in any other class, the teacher in a heterogeneous setting has a multitude of important objectives to reach in the academic, social, and personal domains. And, as in any other class, the teacher must contend with a variety of omnipresent classroom conditions that hinder the accomplishment of these objectives. Heterogeneity serves to exacerbate these difficulties. For example, research indicates that extreme differences in student achievement levels tend to limit teachers' ability to adapt instruction to meet the academic and affective needs of students (Evertson, Sanford, & Emmer, 1981). In many cases, the provision of quality education in the heterogeneous class results in a zero-sum game where teachers juggle the different needs of various groups of students.

Certainly the task of creating a positive social climate is more demanding in the heterogeneous class, partly because people have a natural inclination to establish warm social relations with similar others while avoiding meaningful interaction with those who are dissimiliar. Furthermore, cultural and economic differences among children in the heterogeneous class often mirror differences in their achievement levels and in social acceptance. When this occurs, we have what Brewer and Miller (1984) call "convergent boundaries." Convergence of several relevant differences between groups gives rise to the tendency to perceive and to categorize students into in-

and out-groups which, in turn, plants the seed of intergroup tension. Thus, the heterogeneous class presents educational practitioners and theorists with a formidable social challenge as well as with an especially demanding pedagogical task.

Despite the difficulties accompanying instruction and learning in the heterogeneous class, we contend that this setting is the most appropriate educational framework for a society that strives for equality of educational opportunity among its various cultural, social, and economic groups. The heterogeneous class provides a symbolic promise of equality of opportunity. It suggests that every student, regardless of background characteristics, should receive an educational program that aims to maximize his or her potential.

We believe that the realization of this promise requires that all possible opportunities for the pursuit of excellence remain open to all students in the early years of formal education. As Tannenbaum (1983, 1986) has noted, predictions regarding children's future giftedness or talent fulfillment is a very precarious enterprise. They are especially unreliable when considering young children at the earliest stages of formal education. We also know that giftedness is characterized by multiple properties, that excellence in one area is not necessarily correlated with excellence in others, and that "schoolhouse giftedness" may not overlap with "creative-productive giftedness" (Renzulli, 1986; Siegler & Kotovsky, 1986; Tannenbaum, 1983). When educators are involved with young children, they simply may not have had adequate exposure to the many intellectual facets of the child, so that reasonable assessments of ability are not really possible. Accordingly, an educational policy that avoids premature labelling and that seeks to provide a stimulating experience for all children is most likely one that will foster the realization of the promise of the heterogeneous class for all young children (Mcleod & Cropley, 1989).

Unfortunately, as we shall discuss in detail, many schools act in ways that contradict this message, so the promise inherent in heterogeneity is rarely fully realized. However, this need not be the case. In some heterogeneous classes low- and high-status students, and exceptionally bright as well as very dull children, demonstrate significant academic, social, and personal progress. The key to this success seems to be related to the school's ability to create conditions where meaningful learning activities are accessible to all children. In the following pages we will consider some of the main issues related to developing meaningful access to learning and the realization of learning potential for all groups of children in heterogeneous settings.

MEANINGFUL ACCESS TO LEARNING

A necessary condition for sustained achievement in any area is the student's active participation in learning activities relevant to that area. Consequently, to ensure the intellectual and social progress of all pupils, one must guarantee that they all actively participate in the academic and social tasks in class. In heterogeneous settings this requirement is especially difficult to meet, due to the fact that participation in learning is related to pupils' status. Generally, high-status pupils participate in the process of learning more than do their low-status classmates (Cohen, 1982; Dembo & McAuliffe, 1988). Since prior achievement is a primary determinant of status (Cohen, 1986), in the absence of treatment a cycle is created as depicted in Figure 12.1, whereby over time the "strong" become stronger and the "weak" become weaker.

The influence of status on student participation in learning is mediated by prevailing expectations regarding pupils with different status levels. For example, during the early school years pupils' reading proficiency is a major determinant of student status (Cohen, 1986). Consequently, reading proficiency is a critical element in the formation of general expectations regarding competence in all tasks encountered in the classroom. As a result, when children are presented with a group task that does not demand reading skills at all, those who are perceived as better readers are usually more active and influential than their classmates who are perceived as poor readers (Rosenholtz, 1985; Stulac, 1975).

This phenomenon, termed by sociologists *status generalization* (Berger, Cohen, & Zelditch, 1972), is of central importance in heterogenous classes, which are characterized by pronounced status differences among pupils. In these classes, there is a danger that objective differences in present academic *performance* (e.g., reading proficiency in the early school years) are translated into a status order reflecting perceived differences in general academic *ability.* In other words, young pupils who demonstrate poor reading proficiency in the heterogeneous class are expected by teachers and students alike to demonstrate less general competence and lower ability on a

Figure 12.1.   Relation between status, participation and achievement

broad array of specific classroom tasks. Consequently, they will participate less in the learning process than will their more adequately performing classmates.

When this process occurs during the early years of schooling, it can seriously hamper efforts to expose potential areas of talent or giftedness among students whose reading proficiency is not up to par. Certainly there are many possible reasons why a child with extraordinary potential in some socially valued domain does not achieve academically at an adequate level during the early years of schooling (see Butler-Por, 1987; Tannenbaum, 1983). Whatever the reason may be, status generalization is likely to bring the talented low-achieving child, and his classmates and teachers, to doubt the quality of that potential. A likely outcome of this skepticism is the provision of less than satisfactory nurturance for the development of one's potential.

It follows that, in addition to a stimulating curriculum, one aspect of a comprehensive effort to foster meaningful participation of all pupils in learning is the weakening of the status–participation relationship so that participation is relatively independent of pupil status. Existing evidence from educational and psychosocial research points to two central factors that affect this relationship: the structure of the learning situation and teachers' perceptions and beliefs regarding the learner and the nature of learning. These factors separately and in interaction with one another affect the degree of participation in learning as mediated by the pupil's self-

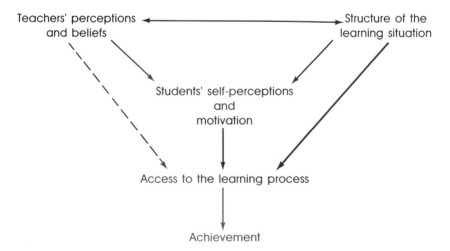

Figure 12.2. Some factors affecting academic success in the classroom

perceptions and motivation to learn. This participation, as we have noted, is essential for promoting achievement in both the social and the intellectual domains. The relationships among these factors are presented in Figure 12.2.

In the following sections we shall discuss the influence of the structure of the learning situation, and of teachers' beliefs on childrens' access to learning in heterogenous classes, with particular attention to exceptional students, both the gifted and low-achievers. Where relevant, special emphasis will be placed on the early years of schooling. In the final section, we shall consider the implications of this discussion for a technology of instruction and learning in heterogeneous classes.

THE STRUCTURE OF THE LEARNING SITUATION

Teacher-Directed vs. Child-Initiated Instructional Programs

The complexity associated with a heterogenous population of learners demands appropriate adjustments in our thinking about instruction and class management to ensure effective learning for all children. Research results indicate that conventional whole-class instruction that is primarily teacher directed and presents to all class members uniform academic tasks and uniform ways of performing them is inappropriate as the primary mode of instruction in heterogenous classes, since it fails to cope with differences among pupils, be they in achievement level, needs, or abilities (Ben Ari & Shafir, 1988; Karweit, 1987; Klein & Eshel, 1980). Many teachers in this kind of class fail to adapt the level and pace of instruction to suit the wide achievement differences among the pupils. Typically, the level of instruction is adjusted to meet the needs of high- or average-ability children (Oakes, 1985), while the pacing of instruction is based on feedback received from low-achieving pupils (Dahloff, 1971). As a result, the entire student body suffers. On the one hand, gifted children and fast-paced achievers may not be sufficiently stimulated intellectually. On the other hand, the low-achieving pupil who cannot successfully cope with classroom demands must face conditions that are likely to result in increased withdrawal from learning. Situations like this often lead to a clamor for homogeneous groupings of pupils, a form of coping that, at best, substitutes one set of problems for another.

Despite the difficulties of instruction in heterogeneous classes, there is good reason to believe that proper modifications of the learning situation can lead to enhanced academic, social, and personal outcomes for high-status and low-status children alike. This seems to be particularly true if the modifications are implemented from the earliest stages of schooling. Schweinhart and Weikart (1988) present evidence that high-quality educational programs implemented during the early school years can effectively cope with the schooling problems characteristic of disadvantaged social groups, and they may be equally beneficial for high-level performers. One of the key dimensions that defines the effectiveness of such programs is the use of a pedagogical approach that emphasizes child-initiated rather than teacher-directed learning. In the words of Schweinhart and Weikart,

> child-initiated learning activities in any curriculum take place within a framework created by the teacher. It is through this framework that the teacher maintains the purposefulness and direction of the programs. However, children may carry out self-initiated activities as they see fit, unconstrained by the teacher's definition of the "correct" answer or the "correct" use of materials. Child-initiated activity is distinguished from random activity by its purposefulness; it is distinguished from teacher-directed activity by the fact that the child controls what happens. (p. 216)

Relevant research indicates that teacher-directed programs during the early school years are not less effective and may sometimes be even more effective than child-initiated programs in enhancing short-term academic performance. But in the long run, they result in inferior academic performance (Schweinhart & Weikart, 1988; Stallings, 1975; Stallings & Stipek, 1986) and retard the development of metacognitive skills that evolve from social interactions (Azmitia, 1986; Gauvain & Rogoff, 1989; Stallings, 1980; Vygotsky, 1978). The social-based development of metacognitive skills is of course very important for all students, but it is especially critical for young children who have demonstrated outstanding intellectual promise. As Renzulli (1986) argues, giftedness is a condition that can be developed in some people if the environment provided is suitable. One aspect of such an environment involves exposure to and acquisition of a variety of ways of thinking and learning that enable the individual to apply flexibly different modes of problem solving to a broad array of novel situations. This skill will more likely arise in an educational system that encourages the student in the heterogeneous class to seek knowledge in a variety of ways from classmates, personal experience, and teachers, rather than to focus exclusively on the transfer of knowledge from teacher to student.

In addition, programs based on the teacher-directed approach are less effective in promoting social skills which are highly important for children's development (Stallings, 1975). In contrast, programs based on child-initiated learning approaches were found to be more effective in averting negative social consequences such as school dropout, adolescent delinquency, and social welfare dependence in adulthood (Stallings, 1975). It is clear that, in the early school years, the child forms attitudes and skills that contribute to subsequent success in coping with challenges in the personal and social realms and in refraining from antisocial behaviors (e.g., delinquency). Therefore, if the social domain is not adequately addressed during the early school years, there is reason to fear that the relevant attitudes and skills will not be acquired.

Teacher-directed instruction does not expose children to situations that facilitate the acquisition of social coping skills. Furthermore, it is reasonable to expect that compared to students in child-directed environments, pupils taught by teacher-directed methods will develop causal perceptions that focus on the teacher rather than on themselves, and will view the teacher as the primary agent responsible for what happens in the classroom. As a result, these children are less likely to develop a sense of personal responsibility or of self-efficacy regarding events at school. Nor is it likely that they will attain optimal levels of initiative or of self-monitoring skills necessary to excel in both academic and social endeavors. These are especially important characteristics for the realization of potential giftedness (Mcleod & Cropley, 1989). For example, Renzulli (1978) and Tannenbaum (1983) note the critical role of task commitment or motivation in giftedness. We would like to see educational programs couple the fostering of a personal desire to excell and "stick-with-it-ness" among students to the encouragement of considerations of personal and social responsibility. Child-initiated programs bear greater promise to accomplish this goal.

Another aspect of social learning is of particular significance in heterogeneous classes. Positive interpersonal relations in such classes are difficult to achieve, and positive intergroup relations are even a greater challenge. Extensive research indicates that positive intergroup relations require the existence of several conditions, such as equal status among individuals, opportunities for extended and meaningful contacts, cooperative activities, and institutional support for good relations (Allport, 1954; Amir, 1969; Cook, 1963). Usually these conditions are difficult to establish in heterogenous classes, especially in those with teacher-directed instruction (Ben Ari, 1989). Students from varied status groups outside of school (e.g., ethnic groups, SES levels) do not maintain equal status relations in class. And in teacher-directed settings there is little opportunity for meaningful contact or for cooperative activities among children from different status groups. Thus, it is virtually impossible to realize these social goals in such classes. In fact, there is a distinct possibility of deterioration in this domain. This line of argument is relevant to classes of young children as well as older pupils, although the problem is probably more acute in the latter. Research clearly indicates that preschool children are already aware of racial differences. Among many, stereotypes have begun to take root, and preference for within-race interaction is evident (Hartup, 1985). These inclinations are very likely better established among older pupils, but apparently they do exist and are meaningful for young children as well. Moreover, Katz (1976) reminds us of the central socializing role the school and its agents play in developing stereotyped perceptions and within-race preferences among young children.

Creating Differential Access to Learning via Homogeneous Grouping

Schools often attempt to cope with the vast difference in basic skills proficiency and other intellectual gaps among students in heterogenous classes by establishing homogenous groupings. In practical terms, the school creates relatively homogenous settings to which pupils are assigned according to their level of ability or achievement. These include within-class ability (or achievement) groups employed primarily in the early school years, between-class ability (or achievement) groups in higher grades, tracks, and homogenous classes of different kinds (curricular, ability, etc) in secondary schools.

Due to the relatively large degree of overlap between academic achievement and ethnic origin or socioeconomic status (e.g., Dar & Resh, in press; Yando, Seitz, & Zigler, 1979), high-achieving groups frequently consist primarily of pupils from the ethnic majority or from well-established SES levels, while low-achieving groups are composed disproportionately of low-SES or ethnic minority children (McKenzie, 1986). Thus, these homogeneous settings accentuate the overlap among socioeconomic status, ethnic group, and achievement level and thereby make the differences between the various social groups especially salient. Furthermore, pupils in high-achieving groups generally enjoy significantly higher social status in the school as compared to children in low-level groups (e.g., Hallinan & Sorenson, 1985; Schwarzwald & Cohen, 1982). At times, discriminating social labels, whether spoken or thought, become part of school life. As a result, children's attitudes towards one another develop, not only based on the personal qualities of the individuals involved, but largely determined by the stereotypes attributed to the individual's membership group. This situation tends to generate depersonalized relations, which provide fertile ground for the development of negative intergroup attitudes and stereotypes (Brewer & Miller, 1984; Miller & Brewer, 1986).

Grouping of pupils according to achievement or ability levels also yields differential access to learning (Hallinan, 1984, 1987; Karweit, 1987; Murphy & Hallinger, 1989; Sorensen, 1987). Recently, Murphy and Hallinger (1989) discussed three classes of factors by means of which homogeneous grouping of pupils contributes to differential access to learning. The classes of factors included instructional, curriculum, and learning environment variables. Research results convincingly demonstrate differences for all three classes of factors favoring members of high-level groups over pupils in low-level groups. One example from each class of factors should suffice to provide a sense of the potential impact of homogeneous grouping on access to learning. Regarding instructional factors, there is clear evidence that children in high-ability groups generally receive better quality instruction than do pupils in low-ability groups (Eder, 1981; Hallinan, 1987; Karweit, 1987; Oakes, 1985; Rosenbaum, 1976; Sorenson, 1987). Common sense and data from several studies indicate that pupils in low-achieving groups as compared to their peers in high-achieving groups are exposed to a restricted and lower quality curriculum (Oakes, 1985; Rosenbaum, 1980, 1984). Finally, in regard to the learning environment factor, researchers report that the learning atmosphere in high-ability groups is more task oriented than in low-ability groups (Evertson, 1982; Webb, 1989; Webb & Kenderski, 1984).

Since all of the factors discussed above play a central role in access to learning and in learning outcomes (Dreeben & Barr, 1984; Good & Marshall, 1984), it is not surprising that pupils' achievement varies as a function of their placement in ability groups. In summary, grouping of pupils into homogeneous ability or achievement groups does not allow equal access to learning. Consequently, the existing gaps among pupils from different status groups are not reduced and may even increase (see Slavin, 1987, 1988; Willms & Chen, 1989).

It logically follows from this discussion that the homogeneous grouping of especially high achievers in a single class may yield the most impressive achievement outcomes. Indeed, Slavin's (1987) metaanalysis suggests that this is the case. However, there are a number of methodological problems that frequently accompany assessments of gifted students in gifted versus regular programs: for example, teachers may be selected especially for the gifted classes, the curriculum may be enriched, the number of children may be smaller in the homogeneous gifted class, the gifted label may enhance motivation, and others. But even if it were clearly the case that homogeneous grouping of gifted children provides them with significant academic benefits, we contend that an arrangement of this sort for the whole school day would be inappropriate. This is because the separation of high achievers directly and indirectly causes educational damage to low and average achievers, as we noted earlier (also see Dar & Resh, 1986). Furthermore, the creation of special classes that totally separate gifted or high-achieving students from their "average" peers encourages the exaggeration of perceived status differentials. In the final analysis, students' special needs should be met primarily in the heterogeneous class, whenever possible. This does not deny the legitimate and essential role of special provisions for particular children; rather, we argue that educators should first ask if these special needs can be satisfied in the heterogeneous class. Only if the answer is negative after careful consideration should separate solutions be countenanced.

Why, then, do schools continue the practice of grouping pupils homogeneously? Why is homogeneous grouping such a ubiquitous phenomenon in education? Part of the answer is related to the fact that ability grouping constitutes an integral component of the accepted culture in many schools, and that there is little serious questioning whether this policy serves to advance student goals or to hinder their realization. In addition, many teachers and other staff members believe that grouping is an effective way to cope with heterogeneous pupil populations (Chen, Lewy, & Adler, 1978; Minkovich, Davis, & Bashi, 1980; Wilson & Schmits, 1978). Reasons presented to support this belief vary widely and are frequently contradictory. Over the years we have heard and read many arguments, including the following: disadvantaged children cannot develop positive self-perceptions when they are in constant contact with more advanced pupils; assignment to ability or achievement groups is part of a meritocratic system that encourages students to strive for enhanced achievement; it is easier to develop high-quality instruction in homogeneous groups (with high and low groups); high-quality classroom instruction is not possible when low-achievers are in the class.

Empirical evidence fails to support any of the above reasons. Except perhaps for gifted and very high-achieving students as discussed earlier, pupils in homogenous groups do not achieve at a high level as compared to children of similar ability in heterogenous groups, and this is particularly true for low-status homogenous groups (Oakes, 1985). Research shows that, in heterogenous classes, the presence of low-achieving pupils does not meaningfully lower the level of achievement of high-ability students, whereas the presence of high-achieving pupils significantly enhances the level of achievement of low-ability pupils (Dar & Resh, 1986). Furthermore, we know that the quality of available educational resources, both physical and human, is higher in heterogeneous than in low-achieving settings and is more similar to the norm in higher status classes and schools (Minkovich et al., 1980; Oakes, 1985). Also, contrary to assumptions regarding meritocratic systems, assignment to ability groups is not always based primarily on the individual pupil's measured ability, but is often determined to a great extent, by school-level variables such as the distribution of achievement in a given school, the number of available classrooms, teacher inclinations, and so on (Hallinan, 1987; Oakes, 1985). Moreover, in most schools, there is very little mobility among groups, particularly from the low-level groups upward, even when this is clearly warranted by the pupil's demonstrated academic ability (Hallinan & Sorensen, 1983). Reasons for this include a variety of technical, pedagogical, and administrative factors. The ultimate effect of this policy for many low-status children is to create a system that is perceived as inequitable and that depresses their motivation.

What remains is the issue of self-perceptions among gifted and low-achieving pupils who are in the same class as other children who function at very different academic levels. Although there is evidence that self-perceptions of low-status pupils tend to deteriorate in heterogeneous settings (Arzi & Amir, 1977; Stephan, 1978), this is apparently a result of the conventional, whole-class instructional method usually employed. When instructional approaches more appropriate to the heterogeneous class are also part of the pedagogical program, there is no impairment of the academic or social self-perceptions of low-status pupils (Rich, Ben Ari, Mevarech, Eitan, Ornan, Chanuka, & Amir, 1989). Among gifted and high-achieving children there is growing evidence that the degree of heterogeneity in the class has little effect on their self-perceptions (Kulik & Kulik, 1982; Schneider, Clegg, Byrne, Ledingham, & Crombie, 1989).

Cooperative Learning and Peer Interaction in the Heterogenous Class

It is clear, therefore, that homogenous settings do not provide an opportunity for redressing existing inequalities; instead they tend to perpetuate them. Thus, the search for appropriate pedagogical approaches in heterogenous classes should be directed towards instructional strategies that maintain the integrity of the heterogeneous setting and that, by and large, meet the needs of all groups of students. Cooperative learning is one alternative approach to instruction and learning which accomplishes this by creating a technology where pupils of varying achievement levels study together cooperatively in small groups within the heterogeneous class (Johnson & Johnson, 1989; Sharan & Rich, 1984; Sharan & Shachar, 1988; Slavin, 1983; Slavin et al., 1985). Most cooperative methods are designed to be implemented within the existing school curriculum and do not require any substantial change in curriculum content. They aim to enhance pupil motivation to learn by changing the structure of academic tasks and reward contingencies in the class. Their major goal is to promote achievement, but they also bear important implications for the nature of social relationships in the class.

Research conducted during the last two decades on cooperative learning in heterogenous classes demonstrates that this strategy is quite effective in advancing all groups of pupils in the class, high achievers as well as weak students, towards academic, social, and personal goals. This effectiveness is reflected in improved social relationships, enhanced academic achievement, positive change on various personality measures (e.g., self-esteem, locus of control), stronger attraction to the class, and greater willingness to collaborate among pupils (Johnson & Johnson, 1989; Sharan, 1990; Slavin, 1983; Slavin et al., 1985). This is not to imply that cooperative learning is a panacea for all educational ills, or that the scientific evidence overwhelmingly favors cooperative learning for all measures. There are a variety of drawbacks to the different cooperative learning methods and serious implementation difficulties (Rich, 1990). But, all in all, cooperative learning does provide an effective strategy of instruction that maintains the integrity of the heterogeneous class.

An outstanding feature common to all cooperative methods is the effort to increase academic interaction among pupils and to create conditions for more equal access to, and participation in, learning. There is abundant evidence that interaction among children can play a central role in promoting student achievement and cognitive development (Glaser & Bassok, 1989). Interaction in a group can broaden the individual's repertoire of metacognitive skills by providing external cognitive stimulation (Hartup, 1985; Vygotsky, 1978). Exposure to alternative ways of thinking challenges the individual's basic thought processes (Johnson & Johnson, 1989). Teamwork can improve the performance of complex tasks without reducing them to simplified forms or restricting the range of abilities required (Vygotsky, 1978).

The importance of interaction for young children has been demonstrated in several studies that examined their performance on planning and problem-solving tasks (Azmitia, 1986; Gauvain & Rogoff, 1989). These studies compared the performance of 5-year-old children who worked either individually or with a friend. Better performance was obtained in the latter condition, provided that the task demanded shared responsibility between the children. This finding demonstrates that, among young children, the superiority of working with others is due to the collaboration between the partners rather than to the mere presence of others. An additional important aspect of these studies relates to the developmental aspect of the capacity to collaborate in social interaction. Gauvain and Rogoff (1989) reported that 9-year-olds collaborated more than 5-year-olds did. This outcome is apparently related to the fact that 5-year-old children are still at a self-centered stage of development, whereas 9-year-olds are more capable of being considerate of and sharing with others.

It is important not to overlook certain benefits of cooperative study in small groups that may accrue to gifted children. Our experience with this instructional strategy teaches us that, when a child is known to have superior ability, members of the group naturally turn to him or her for guidance and leadership in executing the academic tasks. Thus the gifted child is thrust into a role that requires learning a variety of new skills, such as planning and management. Furthermore, collaborative efforts within a small group may help teach the gifted child important personal lessons, such as humility, when it is discovered that, in some important areas, the ability of the gifted individual is inferior to that of the other group members. Finally, the assistance provided by the high achiever in the small group yields especially important cognitive benefits for the tutor (e.g., Webb, 1989).

In summary, it is apparent that there is a significant relationship between the structure of the learning situation, pupils' access to learning, the quality of their participation, and their ultimate achievement. Structures involving conventional, whole-class teacher-directed instruction and grouping of pupils into homogenous settings do not allow equal access to learning for all pupils. High achievers are afforded greater access to more meaningful learning processes and content as compared to low-achievers. Despite this, there is evidence that high-achievers in these settings are frequently exposed to accelerated programs, or much more of the same, rather than to educational conditions that generate unique intellectual stimulation.

This discussion has focused on the direct influence of the structure of the learning situation on access to learning by means of differential educational inputs available to disparate groups of children. In addition, the structure of the learning situation has indirect influence on access to learning as mediated by students' self-perceptions. Differentiation of inputs is understood by the pupils as a message regarding systematically varying expectations of the school system from them. This message stimulates the development of parallel differentiation in pupils' self-expectations. As a result, pupils who receive more positive inputs, for example, those in high-level groups, have greater self-esteem, more positive academic and social self-image, higher academic aspirations, and stronger motivation to participate in the learning process as compared to children exposed to less positive learning conditions (Alexander, Cook, & McDill, 1978; Murphy & Hallinger, 1989; Oakes, 1985). Furthermore, students exposed to child-initiated instruction that encourages the development of personal responsibility, sustained motivation, and flexibility of problem solving will more likely realize their potential as compared to their peers in teacher-directed classes. In contrast, learning structures that give rise to uniformly high expectations regarding participation in learning for all pupils, such as cooperative learning groups, are more likely to enhance positive self-perceptions for all pupils and thus to foster greater participation in learning and maximum accomplishments.

TEACHERS' PERCEPTIONS AND BELIEFS

We have suggested above that one major factor affecting the relationship between pupils' status and participation in learning is structural aspects of the learning situation. The second factor that exerts a major influence on this relationship is teachers' perceptions of and attitudes towards the learner and learning. In recent years, educational research has directed attention to processes by which teachers' beliefs or implicit theories affect educational processes in the class. This research is based on the assumption that teachers' beliefs regarding the nature of learning and the nature of the learner help determine the class learning environment and ultimately affect student outcomes (Bussis, Chittenden, & Amarel, 1976; Clark & Peterson, 1986; Lynott & Woolfolk, 1989; Palinscar, Stevens, & Gavelek, 1989; Shavelson & Stern, 1981).

Intelligence as "Entity" or Incremental

Teachers' beliefs regarding the nature of learning are shaped by their beliefs regarding the nature of intelligence as a stable and largely unchanging entity or as incremental, dynamic, and open to improvement under appropriate conditions (Dweck & Bempechat, 1983). Teachers' differential beliefs regarding intelligence lead to differences in the perception of the teacher role and in a host of educational practices such as the choice of objectives for disparate student groups, teaching methods, and student evaluation procedures (Swann & Snyder, 1980). Dweck and Bempechat (1983) contended that teachers who treat intelligence as an entity generally set performance goals for their students; that is, they emphasize tasks in which pupils are requested to demonstrate the quality of their performance or the level of their ability. In addition, teachers with an entity orientation often view their role as an evaluator or as a judge of knowledge acquired, rather than as a developer or a stimulator of the search for knowledge. They tend to divide pupils dichotomously into the "capable" and the "incapable." Curricular content rather than the pupil often appears at the core of their lessons, with major emphasis placed on breadth of coverage. Their teaching strategies are dictated by the apparent static characteristics of the class membership. Such teachers tend to react to perceived class reality rather than to initiate strategies of changing this reality. In general, their expectations from and behavior towards pupils are directly related to pupils' characteristics (Dusek, 1985; Feldman & Saletsky, 1986; Graham, 1986; Harris & Rosenthal, 1986).

In contrast, teachers who view intelligence as incremental usually set learning goals aimed at gradually advancing pupils' learning mastery and at developing their learning capacity. Moreover, they tend to place the student and the process of learning at the heart of schooling. Also, teachers with an incremental orientation seem to be characterized by less stereotyped perceptions of pupils, and are more aware of differences among them. Since they assume that pupil ability is open to environmental influences, these teachers will not attribute the poor achievement of low-status pupils merely to children's unchanging group characteristics. Rather, they see *themselves* as responsible for student outcomes and for actively shaping the learning environment so that all children can succeed. Accordingly, if pupils' status covaries with degree of participation in learning (Cohen, 1982; Dembo & McAuliffe, 1988), these teachers will see themselves as the agent responsible to change the situation and to sever the status–participation connection.

An incremental view of intelligence has two unique advantages when considering the development of giftedness. First, children with extraordinary ability are not gifted or talented in all areas. Indeed, there may be a tendency among parents and teachers to ignore or play down the significance of nonexceptional areas because they are not outstanding. Teachers or parents maintaining an incremental approach to intelligence will actively seek ways to improve functioning even in those areas that have not demonstrated unusual excellence (see Taylor, 1973). Second, the incremental orientation encourages educators to constantly search for ways to enhance potential excellence among those students who have not yet displayed unique abilities. Thus, we would expect that, among those children educated for several years by teachers with an incremental approach to intelligence, more students will fulfill their potential for giftedness and in a greater number of areas.

Characteristics of these two types of teachers may also influence the classroom situation by means of their impact on pupils' self-perceptions and learning motivation. Dweck and Legett (1988) and Dweck (1986) note that pupils differ according to their pattern of responses to academic and social tasks ranging from those characterized by a helpless response pattern to those characterized by a mastery-oriented response pattern. These differences are reflected in pupils' strategies of coping with task-performance difficulties and other challenges arising in the course of classroom life. Mastery-oriented responses are adaptive, characterized by the search for reasonably difficult tasks and by high persistence in the face of obstacles. In contrast, the helpless response is maladaptive; it is characterized by the avoidance of even moderate challenges and is accompanied by low persistence in the face of difficulties. When teachers of heterogeneous classes view intelligence as incremental and act accordingly, they send powerful optimistic messages to their students. One message is, "No matter how poorly you are doing in school now, you have the capability of improving and of achieving at an adequate level. Don't give up. Your situation is not hopeless. You can do well." And another is, "You may be very good at math right now. But if you stick with it you can be *outstanding.* Strive for the best."

Differences in student response patterns derive from contrasting perceptions of self as a cluster of permanent characteristics or as a system of traits and qualities that develop over time as a consequence of a variety of factors, especially the effort invested by the individual. Diverse configurations of self-perception give rise to distinct patterns of motivation for achieving self-esteem. These motivation patterns are reflected in different goals set by the individual. Pupils with an entity orientation seek to achieve self-esteem by setting performance-oriented goals, high grades, for example, because their attainment indicates the adequacy of one's attributes, and thus increases self-esteem. In contrast, for pupils with an incremental orientation, self-esteem is attained by means of meeting learning goals. Progress toward the mastery of challenging and valued tasks raises self-esteem or maintains it at adequate levels. Maximum student realization of potential requires the adoption of a mastery orientation. Performance-oriented goals, on the other hand, almost always hamper creative efforts.

Dweck and Legett (1988) found that, when the teacher presents classroom goals as performance or learning oriented, pupils generally accept that definition. This implies that the teacher has the capacity to shape pupils' understandings of and attitudes towards learning processes and outcomes. This finding is consistent with the self-fulfilling prophecy phenomenon (Brophy & Good, 1986; Dusek, 1985) and with expectancy theory (Berger et al., 1972), which describe and explain the processes whereby teachers' expectations and behavior affect their pupils' self-perceptions and behaviors.

The influence of the teacher on children's self-perceptions is especially critical for young children. There is evidence that the self-perceptions and self-evaluations of young children tend to be positive and unrelated to their measured achievements or the other appraisals they receive from teachers and peers (Dweck, 1986; Harter, 1988; Klein & Eshel, 1980; Nicholls, 1979; Stipek, 1981). During the early years of school they become increasingly realistic. In the second and third grades, a relationship is already evident between pupils' self-evaluations and those received from teachers. Thus, at this early stage, the teacher provides a vital source of feedback that shapes pupils' self-perceptions.

Unidimensionality vs. Multidimensionality of Learning and the Learner

Teachers' perceptions of the learning situation as unidimensional or multidimensional, and of the learner as uniability or multiability, is another central factor that affects the nature of the learning environment. These differential perceptions are related to contrasting orientations regarding the nature of intelligence as uni- or multidimensional.

In recent years, there has been a growing trend to view intelligence as multidimensional (e.g., Gardner, 1985; Gardner & Hatch, 1989; Neisser, 1979; Sternberg, 1985). In contrast to the traditional approach, which identified intelligence primarily with verbal ability, today we tend to identify several kinds of intelligence, such as musical, mathematical, spatial, interpersonal, and others. According to this approach, there are individual differences regarding each of the various kinds of intelligence, so that a person can simultaneously exhibit strength in one type of intelligence and weakness in another. It follows that, as the multidimensionality of a learning situation increases, the probability that such a situation will be meaningful to a variety of pupils will also increase, because it bears promise to promote feelings of competence among a larger percentage of children. Gardner (1985) hopes that we shall eventually succeed in identifying a "specific intellectual profile" for each individual, which will allow the creation of learning situations that provide maximum possibilities and options to suit the particular individual. This may sound like an educational utopia, but even today it is reasonable to anticipate that the educational system would acknowledge the complexity of human cognition and design a variety of educational alternatives that may be appropriate for a broad array of student profiles. Sternberg (1985) expressed this orientation when he recommended that

> Programs that train intellectual skills should acknowledge and actively encourage individuals to manifest their differences in strategies and styles. In particular, the programs should help students learn their strengths and weaknesses, and they should help them learn to capitalize upon their strengths at the same time that they compensate in whatever ways are available for their weaknesses.

However, many schools have adopted a unidimensional approach. They stress one kind of intelligence for all pupils and do not make serious efforts to encourage the development of a variety of abilities. In a study which assessed teachers' perceptions of intel-

ligence, Fry (1984) found that teachers in primary schools emphasized verbal and social domains, whereas teachers in secondary
schools emphasized cognitive domains. A conspicuous result regarding all teachers was their narrow and unidimensional perception of intelligence. This kind of approach seriously limits the intellectual development of all students, gifted, dull, or average, by
actively depressing proven areas of excellence and by preventing any
serious educational enrichment of domains considered unimpor-
tant.

This finding has important implications for heterogenous classes
where pupils reflect a multitude of abilities, as well as limitations, in
various domains of intelligence. A unidimensional learning situation that emphasizes skills for which some pupils may have deficits,
such as reading proficiency, is likely to give rise to the process of
status generalization (Berger et al., 1972) whereby these pupils'
perceived deficiency in one specific area is generalized to all other
areas. Status generalization is, in part, an outcome of the unidimensional class reality in which task demands are in those few
achievement domains already characterized by deficits, and where
students do not have opportunities to express their abilities in other
domains where they are more accomplished. Consequently, they are
repeatedly exposed to failure and are not afforded meaningful opportunities to experience success. Thus, it is not surprising that these
pupils' perceptions of their global ability is a function of the specific
abilities they are allowed to exhibit in the class. Likewise, it is
reasonable to expect that, under such conditions, the motivation of
the "weak" pupils to actively participate in learning will decline, in
order to avoid the feeling of frustration associated with repeated
experiences of failure. In contrast, as the learning environment
becomes increasingly multidimensional, pupils' perceptions of their
own abilities and their classmates become more varied and complex,
and status generalization is minimized.

Multidimensionality and Motivation to Learn

A recent alternative conceptualization of pupil motivation provides
another powerful argument for adopting a multidimensional approach to the learner and to learning. Maehr (Baden & Maehr, 1986;
Maehr, 1984; Maehr & Braskemp, 1986) suggests that we view
motivation in terms of personal investment. He contends that individual differences in motivation are reflected in the fact that different pupils choose to invest their time, effort, skills, and other
resources in different enterprises, and not necessarily in those ex-

pected of them by the educational system. Thus, when a pupil does not actively participate in the learning process, it is inappropriate to attribute the lack of participation to either lack of motivation or lack of ability. Rather, the pupil simply may not be investing energy and resources in a manner and direction expected by the school. In other words, the problem of insufficient participation in the learning process is related, not only to the pupil, but also to the learning situation, which, for some reason, impedes potential investment.

This description may be especially characteristic of very bright students who do not take an active role in class activities because they are not adequately stimulated by classroom events. It is paradoxical that, because of their outstanding ability, some gifted children participate very little in class life, and thus both they and their classmates are deprived of important educational resources.

It follows that the personal meaning of the situation for the pupil will partially determine the extent to which he or she chooses to invest energy or resources. Among the major factors researchers found that contribute to meaningfulness of the learning situation for the pupil were the following: availability of different academic options for students, self-perceptions as pupils capable of performing tasks with competence, and the provision of personally meaningful incentives for performance (Baden & Maehr, 1986; Maehr, 1984; Maehr & Braskemp, 1986).

Although disparate pupils have different repertoires of meaning which they bring with them into the learning situation, and these are especially varied among young children in the heterogeneous class, it is clear that we cannot ignore the crucial role played by the specific conditions of the learning situation in determining its meaning for the pupil. The more the situation is multidimensional, and the more the pupil is viewed as having multiple abilities, the more likely it is that the factors creating meaning for the pupil will be present. This increases the probability that, in one or more areas of educational significance, each pupil will be able to perform with competence and to receive positive reactions from teachers and peers. Furthermore, greater numbers of children will realize their potential of giftedness.

SUMMARY AND A LOOK FORWARD

We have argued that a necessary condition for attaining the academic and social goals set by the school is to guarantee all pupils meaningful access to learning. Increased heterogeneity of pupil

characteristics confronts the school with unique pedagogical difficulties in achieving these goals. One major difficulty stems from the
fact that meaningful participation in learning is generally linked to
pupil status, so that the participation of high-status pupils in learning is quantitatively and qualitatively superior to that of low-status
pupils. This dynamic contributes to the markedly greater academic
progress among high-status pupils than among their low-status
classmates and has a negative effect on perceptions of equity. One
solution to this problem lies in designing pedagogical strategies that
weaken the status–participation relationship while maintaining a
high-quality educational program for all students. Educational and
psychological research points to two central factors at the core of
this relationship: the structure of the learning situation, and teachers' perceptions and beliefs regarding the learner and the learning
situation. These two factors can either maintain (or strengthen) the
status–participation relationship or can contribute to its attenua-
tion, depending on their particular characteristics.

There is abundant evidence regarding the structure of the learning situation that certain conventional pedagogical practices, such
as teacher-directed whole-class instruction and homogeneous grouping of pupils, are inappropriate means to attain meaningful access
to learning when considering the needs of all pupils in a heterogenous class. Therefore, there is a need to resort to other learning
structures. An important principle that should guide the design of
alternative structures is the maximization of meaningful task-related
interaction among pupils. High-quality peer interaction increases
the probability that all pupils will have access to the learning process
and will have significant opportunities to advance their intellectual
development as well as their social well-being.

Evidence brought here regarding the teacher underlines the significance of teachers' beliefs about the nature of the learner and the
learning situation. These beliefs are related to teachers' implicit
theories regarding the nature of intelligence along the two dimensions presented in Figure 12.3.

Research indicates that teachers who view intelligence as unidimensional and stable tend to reinforce the status–participation
link by means of their influence on the structure of the learning
situation and on pupils' self-perceptions. In contrast, teachers who
treat intelligence as multidimensional and incremental tend to
weaken this relationship. Since teachers with the multidimensional
incremental approach are less likely to attribute differential participation of pupils in learning merely to their personal characteristics,
they will be more open to consider adopting alternative methods of

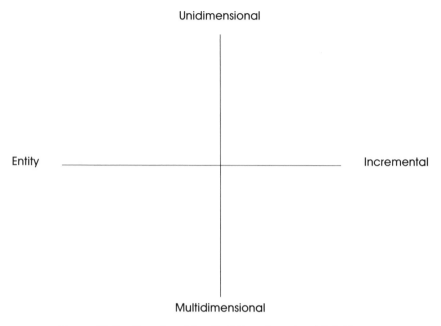

Figure 12.3.   Teachers' implicit theories about intelligence

instruction and class management which have the potential of promoting access to learning and enhanced development of potential for all pupils in the class.

Putting It All (or Most of It) Together: Complex Instruction

A leading example of such an alternative method is provided by the "complex instruction" strategy that was originally developed by Elizabeth Cohen (e.g., 1986) at Stanford University, and has since been expanded at the Institute for the Advancement of Social Integration in the School at Bar-Ilan University. The central purpose of this strategy is to ensure meaningful access of all pupils to the learning process in the undivided heterogeneous class. Complex instruction attempts to accomplish this by altering the structure of the learning situation and teachers' beliefs, so that pupils' task-related behavior and self-perceptions become more academically functional and facilitative of learning.

Learning takes place in small heterogeneous work groups of approximately four pupils. Tasks are designed in a manner that requires significant cooperative interaction among the members of the group and that builds on the multidimensional nature of both learning and the learner. For example, when second-grade pupils study a poem by L. Goldberg ("On Three Things"), they are asked to cooperatively conduct a variety of activities, including reading it aloud, drawing a group portrait of the characters in the poem, discussing how each character understands his or her world, preparing a brief skit or dance representing the ideas in the poem, and relating the content of the poem to material learned in another academic subject. The principle of multidimensionality guides the training of teachers, the design of the learning tasks, and the shaping of pupils' self-perceptions. Within this orientation, class heterogeneity ceases to constitute a serious obstacle and, instead, becomes a resource which can be utilized productively to yield benefits for pupils.

The principle of multidimensionality shapes teachers' expectations for pupils as well as pupils' self-expectations. Tasks that demand a variety of abilities for successful performance make it likely that no single child possesses all the skills necessary and that each pupil is capable of excelling in something related to the task. Consequently, the initial stereotyped expectations from pupils at different status levels are thwarted, and each new task provides an opportunity for more equal levels of participation as well as qualitatively new growth.

Learning goals within this strategy derive from the perception of intelligence as incremental rather than as a static entity. Accordingly, the teacher is unlikely to attribute pupils' differential participation rates to enduring personal characteristics. The guiding belief is that it is possible, by means of structuring the learning situation and teachers' behavior, to alter the degree of meaningful participation of pupils in the learning process. Thus, with the passage of time we expect that most pupils, including gifted children, will increase their active participation in learning activities, and that their attainments will show corresponding development.

Finally, the multidimensional approach enhances pupil motivation. Ways for each child to express his or her unique skills in the learning task are expanded. Tasks seem more personally meaningful for each pupil because an opportunity is provided to demonstrate competence or even excellence in those domains in which one's strengths lie. The child is spared the frustration associated with repeated failure in learning tasks, or boredom, that often leads to reduced motivation to participate in the learning process. At the core of complex instruction is an educational belief that all students have socially valued potential that deserves to be developed, and that it is the responsibility of the teacher to identify that potential and to provide a stimulating and enriching environment. Thus, at the early stages of schooling, a cardinal guiding principle is to leave open all socially valued endeavors as options for children to pursue (see Renzulli, 1986).

Complex instruction is being implemented in Grades 1–6 of 22 Israeli elementary schools (during the 1991–1992 academic year) and so far has received enthusiastic responses from teachers, pupils, and parents. At this stage we are collecting data regarding a variety of process and outcome measures among students and teachers, and are relating them to individual and school characteristics. In the U.S.A., some research has been conducted on complex instruction and points to improvement in the academic achievement of all pupils and enhanced social acceptance of low-status pupils. Most importantly, results suggest that this strategy weakens the link between status and participation in learning as well as the corresponding connection between status and academic achievement (Cohen, Lotan, & Catanzarite, 1988; Cohen, Lotan, & Leechor, 1989). Thus, there are initial indications that this pedagogical strategy does fulfill its promise by enhancing achievement while stimulating positive social relations.

REFERENCES

Alexander, K., Cook, M., & McDill, E. (1978). Curriculum tracking and educational stratification: Some further evidence. *American Sociological Review, 43,* 47–66.

Allport, G. (1954). *The nature of prejudice.* Reading, MA: Addison-Wesley.

Amir, Y. (1969). Contact hypothesis in ethnic relations. *Psychological Bulletin, 71,* 319–342.

Arzi, Y., & Amir, Y. (1977). Intellectual and academic achievements and adjustment of underprivileged children in homogeneous and heterogeneous classrooms. *Child Development, 48,* 726–729.

Azmitia, M. (1986). *Interactive problem solving in preschool children: When are two heads better than one?* Unpublished doctoral dissertation, University of Minnesota.

Baden, B., Maehr, M. (1986). Confronting culture with culture: A perspective for designing schools for children of diverse sociocultural backgrounds. In R. Feldman (Ed.), *The social psychology of education.* Cambridge, UK: Cambridge University Press.

Ben Ari, R. (1989). Improving social relations in heterogenous schools. In R. Ben Ari, Y. Rich, T. Agmon, & Y. Amir (Eds.), *I, you, we: Promoting social relations in integrated schools* [In Hebrew]. Tel-Aviv: Am Oved.

Ben Ari, R., & Shafir, D. (1988). *Social integration in elementary school* [In Hebrew]. Ramat-Gan, Israel: Institute for the Advancement of Social Integration in the Schools, Bar-Ilan University.

Berger, J., Cohen, B., & Zelditch, M. (1972). Status conceptions and social interactions. *American Sociological Review, 37*, 241–255.

Blass, N., & Amir, B. (1984). Integration in education: The development of a policy. In Y. Amir, S. Sharan, & R. Ben Ari (Eds.), *School desegregation*. Hillsdale, NJ: Erlbaum.

Brewer, M., & Miller, N. (1984). Beyond the contact hypothesis: Theoretical perspectives on desegregation. In N. Miller & M. Brewer (Eds.), *Groups in contact*. Orlando, FL: Academic Press.

Brophy, J., & Good, T. (1986). Teacher behavior and student achievement. In M. Wittrock (Ed.), *Handbook of research on teaching*. New York: Macmillan Publishing.

Bussis, A., Chittenden, E., & Amarel, M. (1976). *Beyond surface curriculum*. Boulder, CO: Westview Press.

Butler-Pur, N. (1987). *Underachievers in school: Issues and intervention*. New York: Wiley.

Chen, M., Lewy, A., & Adler, C. (1978). *Process and outcome in education: Evaluating the contribution of the middle school to the educational system* [In Hebrew]. Tel Aviv, Israel: Tel Aviv University and Hebrew University.

Clark, C., & Peterson, P. (1986). Teachers' thought processes. In M. Wittrock (Ed.), *Handbook of research on teaching*. New York: Macmillan.

Cohen, E. (1982). Expectation states and interracial interaction in school settings. *Annual Review of Sociology, 8*, 209–235.

Cohen, E. (1986). *Designing group work*. New York: Teachers College Press.

Cohen, E., Lotan, R., & Catanzarite, L. (1988). Can expectations for competence be altered in the classroom? In M. Webster, Jr. & M. Foschi (Eds.), *Status generalization*. Palo Alto, CA: Stanford University Press.

Cohen, E., Lotan, R., & Leechor, C. (1989). Can classrooms learn? *Sociology of Education, 62*, 75–94.

Cook, S. W. (1963). Desegregation: A psychological analysis. In W. Charters, Jr. & N. L. Gage (Eds.), *Readings in the social psychology of education*. Boston: Allyn & Bacon.

Dahloff, M. (1971). *Ability grouping, content validity, and curriculum process analysis*. New York: Teachers College Press.

Dar, Y., & Resh, N. (1986). *Classroom composition and pupil achievement: A study of the effects of ability-based classes*. New York: Gordon and Breach.

Dar, Y., & Resh, N. (in press). Socioeconomic and ethnic gaps in academic achievement in Israeli junior high schools. *Megamot, 33*, 164-186, [In Hebrew].

Dembo, M., & McAuliffe, T. (1988). Effects of perceived ability and grade status on social interaction and influence in cooperative groups. *Journal of Educational Psychology, 79*, 415–423.

Dreeben, R., & Barr, R. (1987). An organizational analysis of curriculum and instruction. In M. Hallinan (Ed.), *The social organization of schools*. New York: Plenum Press.

Dusek, J. (1985). *Teacher expectancies*. Hillsdale, NJ: Erlbaum.

Dweck, C. (1986). Motivational processes affecting learning. *American Psychologist, 41,* 1040–1048.

Dweck, C., & Bempechat, J. (1983). Children's theories of intelligence: Consequences for learning. In S. Paris & G. Olson (Eds.), *Learning and motivation in the classroom.* New York: Wiley.

Dweck, C., & Legett, E. (1988). A social-cognitive approach to motivation and personality. *Psychological Review, 95,* 256–273.

Eder, D. (1981). Ability grouping as a self-fulfilling prophecy: A microanalysis of teacher-student interaction. *Sociology of Education, 54,* 151–161.

Evertson, C. (1982). Differences in instructional activities in higher- and lower-achieving junior high English and Math classes. *Elementary School Journal, 82,* 329–350.

Evertson, C., Sanford, J., & Emmer, E. (1981). Effects of class heterogeneity in junior high schools. *American Educational Research Journal, 18,* 219–232.

Feldman, R., & Saletsky, R. (1986). Nonverbal communication in interracial teacher-student interaction. In R. Feldman (Ed.), *The social psychology of education.* Cambridge, UK: Cambridge University Press.

Fry, P. (1984). Teachers' conceptions of students' intelligence and intelligent functioning: A cross-sectional study of elementary, secondary and tertiary level teachers. *International Journal of Psychology, 19,* 457–474.

Gardner, H. (1985). *Frames of mind. The theory of multiple intelligences.* New York: Basic Books.

Gardner, H., & Hatch, T. (1989). Multiple intellgences go to school: Educational implications of the theory of multiple intelligences. *Educational Researcher, 18,* 4–10.

Gauvain, M., & Rogoff, B. (1989). Collaborative problem solving and children's planning skills. *Developmental Psychology, 25,* 139–151.

Glaser, R., Bassok, M. (1989). Learning theory and the study of instruction. *Annual Review of Psychology, 40,* 631–666.

Good, T., & Marshall, S. (1984). Do students learn more in heterogeneous or homogeneous groups? In P. Peterson, L. Wilkinson, & M. Hallinan (Eds.), *The social context of instruction.* Orlando, FL: Academic Press.

Graham, S. (1986). An attributional perspective on achievement motivation and black children. In R. Feldman (Ed.), *The social psychology of education.* Cambridge, UK: Cambridge University Press.

Hallinan, M. (1984). Summary and implications. In P. Peterson, L. Wilkinson, & M. Hallinan (Eds.), *The social context of instruction.* Orlando, FL: Academic Press.

Hallinan, M. (1987). Ability grouping and student learning. In M. Hallinan (Ed.), *The social organization of schools.* New York: Plenum Press.

Hallinan, M., & Sorensen, A. (1983). The formation and stability of instructional groups. *American Sociological Review, 48,* 838–851.

Hallinan, M., & Sorensen, A. (1985). Class size, ability group size, and student achievement. *American Journal of Education, 94,* 71–89.

Harris, M., & Rosenthal, R. (1986). Four factors in the mediation of teacher expectancy effects. In R. Feldman (Ed.), *The social psychology of education*. Cambridge, UK: Cambridge University Press.

Harter, S. (1988). Developmental processes in the construction of the self. In T. Yawkey & J. Johnson (Eds.), *Integrative processes and socialization: Early to middle childhood* (pp. 45–78). Hillsdale, NJ: Erlbaum.

Hartup, W. (1985). Relationships and their significance in cognitive development. In R. Hinde & A. Perret-Clemont (Eds.), *Relationships and cognitive development*. Oxford: Oxford University Press.

Johnson, D., & Johnson, R. (1989). *Cooperation and competition*. Edina, MN: Interaction Book Company.

Karweit, N. (1987). Diversity, equity and classroom processes. In M. Hallinan (Ed.), *The social organization of schools*. New York: Plenum Press.

Katz, P. (Ed.) (1976). *Towards the elimination of racism*. New York: Pergamon Press.

Klein, Z., & Eshel, Y. (1980). *Integrating Jerusalem schools*. New York: Academic Press.

Kulik, C., & Kulik, J. (1982). Effects of ability grouping on secondary school students: A meta-analysis of evaluation findings. *American Educational Research Journal, 19*, 415–428.

Lynott, D., & Woolfolk, A. (1989, March). *Teachers' educational goals and their implicit theories of intelligence*. Paper presented at the annual meeting of the American Educational Research Association, San Francisco.

Maehr, M. (1984). Meaning and motivation. In R. Ames & C. Ames (Eds.), *Research on motivation in education: Student motivation*. New York: Academic Press.

Maehr, M., & Breskamp, L. (1986). *The motivation factor: A theory of personal investment*. Lexington, MA: Lexington Press.

McKenzie, J. (1986). The influence of identification practices, race, and SES on the identification of gifted students. *Gifted Child Quarterly, 30*, 93–95.

Mcleod, J., & Cropley, A. (1989). *Fostering academic excellence*. Oxford: Pergamon Press.

McPherson, A., & Willms, J. (1987). Equalisation and improvement: Some effects of comprehensive reorganization in Scotland. *Sociology, 21*, 509–539.

Miller, N., & Brewer, M. (1986). Social categorization theory and team learning procedures. In R. Feldman (Eds.), *The social psychology of education*. Cambridge, UK: Cambridge University Press.

Minkovich, A., Davis, D., & Bashi, Y. (1980). *Success and failure in Israeli elementary education*. New Brunswick, NJ: Transaction Books.

Murphy, J., & Hallinger, P. (1989). Equity as access to learning: Curricular and instructional treatment differences. *Journal of Curriculum Studies, 21*, 129–149.

Neisser, V. (1979). The concept of intelligence. In R. Sternberg & D. Detterman (Eds.), *Human intelligence.* Norwood, NJ: Ablex Publishing Corp.

Nicholls, J. (1979). Development of perception of own attainment and causal attributions for success and failure in reading. *Journal of Educational Psychology, 71*, 94–99.

Oakes, J. (1985). *Keeping track: How schools structure inequality.* New Haven, CT: Yale University Press.

Palincsar, A., Stevens, D., & Gavelek, J. (1989). Collaborating with teachers in the interest of student collaboration. *International Journal of Educational Research, 13,* 41–53.

Renzulli, J. (1978). What makes giftedness? Reexamining a definition. *Phi Delta Kappan, 60,* 180–183.

Renzulli, J. (1986). The three-ring conception of giftedness: A developmental model for creative productivity. In R. Sternberg & J. Davidson (Eds.), *Conceptions of intelligence.* Cambridge, UK: Cambridge University Press.

Rich, Y. (1990). Ideological impediments to instructional innovation: The case of cooperative learning. *Teaching and Teacher Education, 6,* 81–91.

Rich, Y., Ben Ari, R., Mevarech, Z., Eitan, T., Ornan, E., Chanuka, L., & Amir, Y. (1989). Cooperative approaches to instruction in the heterogeneous class and their influence on student self concept and perception of climate [In Hebrew]. *Iyunim B'Chinuch, 51/52,* 207–222.

Rosenbaum, J. (1976). *Making inequality: The hidden curriculum of high school tracking.* New York: Wiley.

Rosenbaum, J. (1980). Social implications of educational grouping. *Review of Research in Education, 8,* 361–401.

Rosenbaum, J. (1984). The social organization of instructional grouping. In P. Peterson, L. Wilkinson, & M. Hallinan (Eds.), *The social context of instruction.* Orlando, FL: Academic Press.

Rosenholtz, S. (1985). Treating problems of academic status. In J. Berger & M. Zelditch, Jr. (Eds.), *Status, attribution and justice.* New York: Elsevier.

Schneider, B., Clegg, M., Byrne, B., Ledingham, J., & Crombie, G. (1989). Social relations of gifted children as a function of age and school program. *Journal of Educational Psychology, 81,* 48–56.

Schwarzwald, J., & Cohen, S. (1982). Relationship between academic tracking and degree of interethnic acceptance. *Journal of Educational Psychology, 74,* 588–597.

Schweinhart, L., & Weikart, D. (1988). Education for young children living in poverty: Child-initiated learning or teacher-directed instruction? *The Elementary School Journal, 89,* 212–225.

Sharan, S. (1990). *Cooperative learning: Theory and research.* New York: Praeger.

Sharan, S., & Rich, Y. (1984). Field experiments on ethnic integration in

Israeli Schools. In Y. Amir, S. Sharan, & R. Ben Ari (Eds.), *School desegregation.* Hillsdale, NJ: Erlbaum.

Sharan, S., & Shachar, H. (1988). *Language and learning in the coopera-tive classroom.* New York: Springer.

Shavelson, R., & Stern, P. (1981). Research on teachers' pedagogical thoughts, judgments, decisions and behavior. *Review of Educational Research, 51,* 455–498.

Siegler, R., & Kotovsky, K. (1986). Two levels of giftedness: Shall ever the twain meet? In R. Sternberg & J. Davidson (Eds.), *Conception of giftedness.* Cambridge, UK: Cambridge University Press.

Slavin, R. (1983). *Cooperative learning.* New York: Longman.

Slavin, R. (1987). Ability grouping and student achievement in elementary schools: The best evidence synthesis. *Review of Educational Re-search, 57,* 293–336.

Slavin, R. (1988). Synthesis of research on grouping in elementary and secondary schools. *Educational Leadership, 46,* 67–77.

Slavin, R., Sharan, S., Kagan, S., Hertz-Lazarowitz, R., Webb, C., & Schmuck, R. (Eds.), (1985). *Learning to cooperate, cooperating to learn.* New York: Plenum Press.

Sorenson, A. (1987). The organizational differentiation of students in schools as an opportunity structure. In M. Hallinan (Ed.), *The social organization of schools.* New York: Plenum Press.

Stallings, J. (1975). Implementation and child effects of teaching practices in follow through classrooms. *Monographs of the Society for Research in Child Development, 40*(7-8, serial no. 163).

Stallings, J. (1980). Allocated academic learning time revisited, or beyond time on task. *Educational Researcher, 9,* 11–16.

Stallings, J., & Stipek, D. (1986). Research on early childhood and elemen-tary school teaching programs. In M. Wittrock (Ed.), *Handbook of research on teaching.* New York: Macmillan.

Stephan, W. (1978). School desegregation: An evaluation of predictions made in Brown vs. Board of Education. *Psychological Bulletin, 85,* 217–238.

Sternberg, J. (1985). *Beyond IQ: A triarchic theory of human intelligence.* Cambridge, UK: Cambridge University Press.

Stipek, D. (1981). Children's perceptions of their own and their classmates' ability. *Journal of Educational Psychology, 73,* 404–410.

Stulac, J. (1975). *The self-fulfilling prophecy: Modifying the effects of a unidimensional perception of academic competence in task-oriented groups.* Unpublished doctoral dissertation, Stanford University.

Swann, W., & Snyder, M. (1980). On translating beliefs into action: Theo-ries of ability and their application in an instructional setting. *Jour-nal of Personality and Social Psychology, 38,* 879–888.

Tannenbaum, A. (1983). *Gifted children: Psychological and educational perspectives.* New York: Macmillan.

Tannenbaum, A. (1986). Giftedness: A psychosocial approach. In R. Sternberg & J. Davidson (Eds.), *Conceptions of giftedness.* Cambridge, UK: Cambridge University Press.

Taylor, C. (1973). Developing effectively functioning people. *Education, 94,* 99–110.

Vygotsky, L. (1978). *Mind in society: The development of higher psychological processes.* Cambridge, MA: Harvard University Press.

Webb, N. (1989). Peer interaction and learning in small groups. *International Journal of Educational Research, 13,* 21–40.

Webb, N., & Kenderski, C. (1984). Student interaction and learning in small-group and whole-group settings. In P. Peterson, L. Wilkinson, & M. Hallinan (Eds.), *The social context of instruction.* Orlando, FL: Academic Press.

Welch, F. (1987). A reconsideration of the impact of school desegregation programs on public school enrollment of white students, 1968–76. *Sociology of Education, 60,* 215–221.

Willms, J., & Chen, M. (1989). The effects of ability grouping on the ethnic achievement gap in Israeli elementary schools. *American Journal of Education, 97,* 237–257.

Wilson, B., & Schmits, D. (1978). What's new in ability grouping? *Phi Delta Kappan, 59,* 535–576.

Yando, R., Seitz, V., & Zigler, E. (1979). *Intellectual and personality characteristics of children: Social-class and ethnic group differences.* Hillsdale, NJ: Erlbaum.

Author Index

Subject Index